RESSOURCEMENT AFTER VATICAN II

ESSAYS IN HONOR OF JOSEPH FESSIO, S.J.

Ressourcement after Vatican II

Essays in Honor of Joseph Fessio, S.J.

Edited by
Nicholas J. Healy, Jr., and Matthew Levering

IGNATIUS PRESS   SAN FRANCISCO

Unless otherwise indicated, all English translations of papal and council documents have been taken from the Vatican website.

Cover photo:
Fontana Piazza San Pietro
© iStock/Muttley572

Cover design by Roxanne Mei Lum

CONTENTS

INTRODUCTION

Nicholas J. Healy, Jr., and Matthew Levering

Joseph Fessio founded Ignatius Press forty years ago, in 1978, the same year that Karol Wojtyła became pope and after a decade of crisis and confusion in the Church and world. In 1978, the works of the great theologians of the *Ressourcement* movement were generally still unavailable in English translation. The leading American doctoral programs in theology functioned on a steady diet of translated works by Karl Rahner, Edward Schillebeeckx, and Jürgen Moltmann. The Catholic seminaries made do with Karl Rahner and more Karl Rahner—an odd situation since in his 1972 *The Shape of the Church to Come*, Rahner had taught that priests were not strictly necessary for celebrating the Eucharist. Robert Barron, now auxiliary bishop of Los Angeles, has recalled that during his seminary studies in the 1980s, he was constantly assigned Rahner's works, so much so that when he became a professor at the seminary, the natural thing for him to do first was to teach an S.T.L. course on Rahner's theology.

The editors of this volume were born around 1970. In 1994, one of the editors (Matthew Levering), while attempting to become a novelist, asked himself whether there was a God and what would it mean if there were no God. For three days, he experienced the world as a place of shells and phantoms on the verge of eternal annihilation. On the third day, he went to Duke University Divinity School on the chance that there would be some books in their library that could teach him why people believed in God and in Jesus Christ and whether such belief was plausible today. Fortunately, the Duke Divinity School library was just then in the process of acquiring a number of books from Ignatius Press. Despite the old adage that one should not judge a book by its cover, their beautiful binding and design stood out on the Divinity School library's "New Books" shelf. Picking up books by von Balthasar, de Lubac, Ratzinger, and so on, Levering sat down to read and was profoundly moved, inspired, and changed by what he read.

The other editor, Nicholas Healy, also found himself gifted by Father Fessio and Ignatius Press at a crucial moment of his life. Raised Catholic, he was working at a corporate law firm in Pittsburgh, with plans to apply to law school. Following a recommendation from a professor of English literature, he subscribed to the journal *Communio* and borrowed a friend's copy of von Balthasar's *Heart of the World*. Within a few months, Healy's plan to enter law school was replaced with an application to the graduate program in philosophy at Franciscan University of Steubenville. Through the mediation of another friend, Father Fessio encouraged Healy's studies by sending an enormous box with volumes by von Balthasar, de Lubac, Pieper, and Ratzinger.

Such stories are legion; so many young Catholics and converts have gained access to the breadth and depth of the Catholic tradition by reading the books of Ignatius Press. Charles Péguy coined the term *ressourcement* to describe a movement "from a less perfect tradition to a more perfect tradition, a call from a shallower tradition to a deeper tradition, a backing up of tradition, an overtaking of depth, an investigation into deeper sources; in the literal sense of the word, a 're-source.'"[1] For the authors translated and published by Father Fessio and Ignatius Press—de Lubac, Ratzinger, von Balthasar, Daniélou, von Speyr, Bouyer, and many others—the deepest source of theology is the Word of God interpreted within the Church. In a secondary sense, the Fathers and Doctors of the Church represent an abiding source for theological renewal. Like his mentor Henri de Lubac, Father Fessio has sought to make the Catholic tradition better known and loved. In the spirit of Saint Ignatius, his life has been characterized by obedience and service to the incarnate Word, whose humility reaches down to the written word that mediates the living tradition of the Church.

Thanks to the efforts of Ignatius Press in publishing the writings of *Ressourcement* theologians, young Catholics in seminaries and doctoral programs have received an attractive alternative to the theological

---

[1] As quoted in Marcellino D'Ambrosio, "Ressourcement Theology, Aggiornamento, and the Hermeneutics of Tradition", *Communio* 18 (Winter, 1991):5.

liberalism that has severed its roots in the Catholic tradition. Classical theological liberalism began with Friedrich Schleiermacher as a Protestant enterprise but soon moved to the Catholic Church. Theological liberalism begins with the assumption that the biblical and dogmatic core of the Christian faith is unreliable and cannot be trusted as a witness to the truth of Christ and of God. Instead, therefore, the early (Protestant) liberal theologians proposed that Christian faith is actually simply about personal experience of the ineffable, of the ground of being. Liberal theology of all stripes argues that this experience cannot really be translated into propositional judgments, since personal experience of the ineffable is inextricably embedded within the specific historical contexts and world views of particular eras. Each era, then, should express its own God-consciousness in new formulations and new moral norms that are authentic to its own historical context and world view.

For liberal Christianity, the role of Christ in all this is to stand as an enduring model of human liberative praxis, of human commitment to the liberation of the poor and human freedom to manifest the presence of God in the world by not being bound by narrow legalisms or doctrinal systems. Christ, as the supreme manifestation of what it means to be human (and thus, on this view, as the supreme human manifestation of the divine), serves liberal theology as the basis for a constantly renewed thinking about liberative practices that will build an authentic human community of peace, justice, openness to the outcast, freedom from repressive systems, and love for all.

As the great *Ressourcement* theologians help us to see, however, theological liberalism unfortunately is built upon partial truths as well as upon the neglect of the more central truths of divine revelation. Theological liberalism's fundamental mistake is not recognizing that God has indeed spoken an enduring, intelligible word that commands the obedience of faith and that includes doctrinal and moral content for our salvation. By failing to allow for human knowledge of the transcendent God, by failing to perceive the depths of sin and death from which we must be rescued, and by failing to see the biblical story of the living Creator God (himself a Triune Communion) who comes forth in wondrous mercy and humble love to unite us to the life of the Trinity in an intimacy so supreme as to be marital, theological liberalism has failed to see the true source of peace and love-filled human community. The fruit of theological liberalism, as has been shown over and over again, is the death of living Christianity and the parallel emergence of a culturally approved standpoint of hedonistic statism mingled with existential despair.

Young Father Fessio experienced theological liberalism firsthand, but he did not simply bemoan it or collapse into negativity. Instead, in planning his doctoral studies, he sought out mentors in Christ— and found them in Henri de Lubac, Hans Urs von Balthasar, Louis Bouyer, and Joseph Ratzinger. For his doctoral dissertation, Father Fessio produced a significant study of von Balthasar's ecclesiology. When he returned to the United States, he wanted to share what he had received. However, the books by his great mentors were not available in English. Inspired by the Holy Spirit to fill a tremendous need in the postconciliar English-speaking Church, Father Fessio founded Ignatius Press. We speak for the contributors to this Festschrift in thanking God for what Father Fessio and Ignatius Press have done to enable us to receive, and to share with others, the writings of his mentors.

After the council, Henri de Lubac warned sharply against currents of classical liberal theology, rooted in Friedrich Schleiermacher and Ernst Troeltsch, among others, that were spreading in the Church. If one is seeking to grasp what distinguishes the Neoscholastics and the *Ressourcement* theologians, on the one hand, from Catholic liberal theology, on the other hand, one might compare four books published by Ignatius Press—Charles Journet's *The Theology of the Church* and *What Is Dogma?* and Henri de Lubac's *The Motherhood of the Church* and *The Splendor of the Church*—with two books published by Crossroad Press, Rahner's *The Shape of the Church to Come* and Schillebeeckx' *Church: The Human Story of God*. The richness of Journet's and de Lubac's explorations of the Christ-centered illuminative and transformative power of divine revelation contrasts strikingly with the dismay about the Church's doctrinal and moral patrimony that one finds in Rahner and Schillebeeckx.

In a recent conversation, a good friend described a major shift in his theological outlook that occurred when he was around thirty, now about fifteen years ago. He had been taught that Joseph Ratzinger was a polemicist—a narrow mind with a negative spirit. One day, however, he actually read a book by Ratzinger in translation by

Ignatius Press. What he discovered was a Christian open in all directions to dialogue, a Christian who was rooted in divine revelation as communicated uniquely and for our salvation by Scripture within the living tradition, a Christian who knew the entirety of the Catholic theological tradition and who also drew positively from Orthodox and Protestant sources. He discovered, in other words, the transformative power of theological wisdom, and this changed his life and filled him with joy.

Ignatius Press has devoted itself to awakening such joy in its readers by giving them the works of Father Fessio's mentors (de Lubac, Ratzinger, von Balthasar, Bouyer) as well as books by Newman, Chesterton, Pieper, and so many others. The Christian faith can only be spread by witnesses who have themselves touched and been touched by the realities of faith, preeminently the living Jesus Christ. We wish to thank Father Fessio for being a witness to Christ and for devoting his entire life, joined by the staff of Ignatius Press, to the task of sharing the beauty, goodness, and truth of Catholic faith and life.

Let us now briefly set forth the contributions made by the essays in this volume. In tribute to Father Fessio and Ignatius Press, we asked contributors to focus on works by authors whom Ignatius Press has published.

The first essay in the volume is more personal than the others, as befits a tribute to Father Fessio from a longtime friend. David L. Schindler describes his friendship with Father Fessio, which began in 1965. This friendship involved most notably the founding of the American edition of *Communio* and their shared connections to de Lubac, von Balthasar, and Ratzinger (Pope Emeritus Benedict XVI).

David Vincent Meconi, S.J., reflects upon the Mystical Body ecclesiology of the great *Ressourcement* theologians—also known as the *nouvelle théologie*—represented in his essay by Hans Urs von Balthasar, Louis Bouyer, Henri de Lubac, and Joseph Ratzinger. These theologians show that to be a Christian does not mean a mere formal adherence but rather means deification: being united to Jesus Christ by sharing in his radical self-surrender, nourished by the Eucharist.

Aaron Riches explores tradition and the liturgy. Numerous books on the liturgy have appeared from Ignatius Press, not only from Joseph Ratzinger but also from English-speaking scholars such as Uwe Michael Lang. Riches perceives a crisis in the postconciliar liturgy, a crisis that he notes was also perceived by de Lubac and has been well written about by Father Fessio. Riches argues that for overcoming the crisis, a crucial task will be to recover a proper sense of liturgical tradition and of the sacrificial character of the Mass, determined by the Person and work of Christ.

Michael Dauphinais writes about Ratzinger's *Introduction to Christianity*. Ratzinger published this commentary on the Apostles' Creed in 1968, a time during which the Church in Germany was experiencing a massive defection from the faith, especially among young people. Dauphinais shows how Ratzinger emphasizes the intelligibility or profound rationality of faith, without undermining its character as divine mystery. The "Ratzinger Option" for evangelization involves removing intellectual obstacles to believing the gospel, but doing so without watering down the challenging call to conversion that the gospel brings in every age. Central to this task is responding, in the light of the *Logos*, to reductionary understandings of human reason (*logos*).

Peter Casarella treats von Balthasar's effort to lead all disciplines back to God's wisdom, namely, Christ. In engaging von Balthasar's theology of culture, Casarella responds to the charge that it is elitist, abstracted from concrete history, and insufficiently attentive to political and economic liberation. As a key resource for responding to this charge, Casarella identifies von Balthasar's largely neglected engagement with the German writer and critic Reinhold Schneider. He also attends to von Balthasar's research into the Fathers and dialogue with Erich Przywara.

Stephen M. Fields, S.J., compares von Balthasar and Rahner on the analogy of being and the analogy of faith. In this regard, he tracks von Balthasar's creative readings of Plato, Plotinus, and Dionysius (Denys) the Areopagite. In correlating the analogies of being and of faith, Fields shows that Rahner's *The Trinity* also makes a contribution, in distinguishing "ontic" and "logic". Fields adds his own reading of pro-Nicene theology to exemplify his points, and he concludes by reflecting upon how philosophical reasoning is fulfilled, not simply in Platonic myth, but in Christian "myth".

Joseph S. Flipper probes the influence of Ignatius Loyola on the approach that de Lubac takes to biblical interpretation. He shows that de Lubac is interested, not primarily in challenging modern methods, but in insisting upon the importance of (Ignatian) Christian spirituality. To read Scripture rightly is to read it in a manner informed by the traditional practice of spiritual interpretation and discernment. Scripture, mysticism, and theology come together when history itself is recognized to be marked interiorly by spiritual realities and spiritual warfare.

Matthew Levering reflects upon the question of whether marriage is the image of God. He shows the persuasiveness of von Balthasar's position that marriage images the Trinity. For von Balthasar, this image consists in fruitful self-surrendering love. The Divine Persons are characterized by fruitful self-surrender, and so should be the married couple. Levering compares von Balthasar's position to that of Scheeben and others. Whereas Scheeben seeks to find an image of the Trinitarian processions in the generation of Eve and Seth from Adam, von Balthasar helpfully places the emphasis on fruitful self-surrender.

Francesca Aran Murphy addresses recent critiques of von Balthasar's theology. She argues against the notion that a theo-dramatics should be minimalist in its teaching about the figure of the Triune God; after all, it is the Triune God who truly reveals himself in the drama—which, of course, is "drama" in an analogous sense rather than in a sense that requires it to be fitted to the limited genres of the stage. She draws upon the literary theorist Mikhail Bakhtin for insight into von Balthasar's efforts to present human life as truly historically contextualized and dialogical. She argues that von Balthasar's use of vivid cataphatic language in his depiction of the intra-Trinitarian life pertains to his strategy of insisting that the Trinity has actually revealed itself so as no longer to be merely an aloof spectator about whose life we cannot really speak. Here she makes a fruitful parallel with Maurice Blondel's reflections upon the figure of Jesus in the Oberammergau Passion Play.

Matthew J. Ramage explores Pope Benedict XVI's use of his General Audiences to acquaint believers with the history of the Church's greatest saints and teachers through the centuries, as well as with the power of beauty to instruct faith. Although Ignatius Press has published these General Audiences in seven volumes, they have yet to receive much scholarly attention. Ramage shows how Benedict XVI finds, in the figures of the apostles, models for the virtues that pertain to our pilgrim faith (or new exodus in faith), such as humility, docility, willingness to ask challenging questions, and patient endurance of trials—all in relation to the Truth who is Christ. Such exemplars are found through the centuries in the diversity of the Church's canonized saints and, in our own lives, also in ordinary persons who exemplify the beauty of Christ's Truth.

D. C. Schindler reflects upon Josef Pieper's philosophy of tradition. Tradition involves a particular kind of giving, namely, a giving that bonds two generations. Whatever belongs to tradition must bridge generations while also transcending them; whatever belongs to tradition must also be something that requires the mediation of the transmitter for it to be known, so that the transmitter is not simply discarded once one possesses what has been handed down. Furthermore, whatever belongs to tradition must itself demand to be handed down: the one who receives tradition must carry it forward and pass it on. For Pieper, these elements of tradition show that it must have its origin in divine revelation; and Pieper therefore distinguishes between an "original revelation" in creation and the "special revelation" in Christ. In its unity of thought and practice, tradition hands on the most important truths about the origin and goal of the world, the providence of God, the requirement to do good, the fact that the human being is not solely material, and so on.

Anne M. Carpenter explores theological aesthetics as grounding the coherent unity of the transcendentals. She argues for von Balthasar's understanding of beauty as an integrative principle that opens up otherwise closed theological vistas. She points to the "constellations" of voices that von Balthasar gathers in developing a theological argument and to his ability to perceive a "whole" within fragments. She calls this a "patterned multiplicity" that finds unity in the real plurality of tradition. Von Balthasar offers a polyphonic vision, but not a formlessly postmodern one: given his commitment to certain principles, polyphony enables him instead to illumine a specific form, that of Christ's self-surrendering love. In this regard, Carpenter shows von Balthasar's debt to the field of Germanistics in which he did his doctorate. She demonstrates that his trilogy functions by gesturing to the glory of the form of Christ—which is beautiful in its uniting of truth and goodness—as manifested in the incarnate Son and through tradition's polyphonic variety of texts and in the *justesse* of the words and deeds of Christians.

Nicholas J. Healy, Jr., presents Henri de Lubac's understanding of the development of doctrine. Drawing on the work of John Henry Newman, de Lubac brings to light the concrete and personal form of the *depostium fidei*, which is summed up in the Person of Christ. For de Lubac, the mystery of Christ's Eucharist is the innermost heart of doctrinal development. It is here that the Church receives a share in the Lord's "traditioning", whose unity of completeness and newness, in turn, enables the development of doctrine while distinguishing it from arbitrary innovation. Healy suggests that the common teaching of Newman and de Lubac is a promising resource for resolving the disputed question of how to interpret *Amoris laetitia*. De Lubac reminds us that what is most deeply at stake in the current discussion is the Church's fidelity to the form of truth embodied in her divine Spouse, the form of truth exhibited in the "traditioning" of his own flesh and blood in the Holy Spirit.

Among the very first books published by Father Fessio and Ignatius Press was Hans Urs von Balthasar's *Heart of the World*, originally published in German in 1954. Its opening line reads as follows: "The very form of the Cross, extending out into the four winds, always told the ancient Church that the Cross means solidarity: its outstretched arms would gladly embrace the universe."[2] This sentence, so rich in Catholic substance and so evocative of the central message of the Second Vatican Council, encapsulates the vision that has animated the life's work of Father Fessio. Devoting his life to Christ, he has sought through Ignatius Press to spread the gospel to the whole world, out of love for the whole world.

---

[2] Hans Urs von Balthasar, *Heart of the World*, trans. Erasmo S. Leiva (San Francisco: Ignatius Press, 1979), 13.

Father Joseph Fessio, S.J.: A Personal Memoir

David L. Schindler

I first met Father Joseph Fessio in the fall of 1965, when we both studied philosophy at Mount Saint Michael's, a Jesuit house of studies affiliated with Gonzaga University and situated on a beautiful hill overlooking the city of Spokane, Washington. We were at the time both Jesuit seminarians, I in the Oregon province and he from the California province. The practice then was that the California Jesuits would join the Oregon Jesuits for the study of philosophy. Father Fessio and I arrived at "the Mount" (as we called it) in 1965 and spent two years together there. Of course, 1965–1967 were important years immediately following the Second Vatican Council, and, along with our philosophical discussions, we spent much time reflecting on and debating the changes that were being made at the council and the new documents that were being issued.

My purpose in this personal reflection is to speak about him in light of his course of studies as well as in regard to the work he has done in this past half-century that I have known him—insofar as I was familiar with his undertakings and sometimes involved in them. But let me first provide some historical markers. Father Fessio was born in 1941 and was trained in high school by the Jesuits at Bellarmine Prep in San Jose, California, graduating in 1958. He then studied civil engineering at the University of Santa Clara, before entering the Jesuit novitiate in 1961, followed by the normal course of classical languages (Greek and Latin) and culture. After studying in Spokane for two years, he taught philosophy at Santa Clara for three years.

In the early 1970s, Fessio studied theology under Henri de Lubac in Fourvière-Lyon, France, serving as Father de Lubac's assistant while completing his master's degree. De Lubac recommended that he go to Regensburg for further work in theology, suggesting that he study with a certain young theologian who had made a mark at the Second Vatican Council: Joseph Ratzinger. De Lubac recommended specifically that Fessio write his doctoral dissertation under Ratzinger on the ecclesiology of Hans Urs von Balthasar. Fessio followed de Lubac's advice and received his doctorate from the University of Regensburg in 1975. When I visited Fessio on one occasion during his time in Regensburg, we spent half a day at the home of a young philosophy professor by the name of Ferdinand Ulrich, whose *magnum opus, Homo Abyssus,* a fundamental study in metaphysics, was published in English in 2018.[1] Fessio had gotten to know Ulrich well, and the latter was a great help to him in the writing of his dissertation on von Balthasar.

Such, in sum, was Father Fessio's educational formation: to have had as his main teachers for his master's and doctoral degrees in theology four of the truly great Catholic thinkers of the twentieth century: de Lubac, Ratzinger, von Balthasar, and Ulrich![2]

The founding of the international periodical *Communio* took place in the early seventies, and Fessio was the central figure involved in beginning the American edition; but more on that later. In 1975–1976, he along with others started the Saint Ignatius Institute at the University of San Francisco. The Institute, which flourished for some thirty years, was a showcase development of an integrated Catholic undergraduate education centered in the "great books" of the Western and Catholic tradition and continues now, some three generations later, to bear fruit in its graduates. In 1978, Father Fessio founded what most people today know him for, Ignatius Press (about which we will also say more below). In 1991, he started *Catholic*

---

[1] Ferdinand Ulrich, *Homo Abyssus: The Drama of the Question of Being*, trans. D. C. Schindler (Washington, D.C.: Humanum Academic Press / John Paul II Institute; Baltimore, Md.: Catholic University of America Press, 2018).

[2] During his years in Regensburg, Fessio was invited on occasion to spend time (with von Balthasar and de Lubac) at von Balthasar's modest chalet overlooking Lake Lucerne on the Rigi in the Swiss Alps. He recounted to me stories about his experiences there, for example, regarding de Lubac's playful, sometimes mischievous, sense of humor.

World Report, which still continues today. These examples represent an incomplete listing of the important initiatives in which Father Fessio has played a leading role, but they suffice to suggest the breadth and depth of his contribution to American Catholic life and thought. Let us now comment more extensively on Fessio's time studying philosophy as a Jesuit scholastic; his role in founding the American *Communio* and Ignatius Press; and the character of his priestly work.

Mount Saint Michael's

As mentioned, Fessio and I studied philosophy on the hill at the Mount, where the philosophy professors and scholastics lived together. My recollection is that he and I were not on the same academic schedule and that we had few classes together. But we were in constant dialogue with each other. We went for walks during the period available in the afternoon several times a week, and we often played basketball together. I visited Spokane this past summer and took a trip back up to the Mount, now owned by a Catholic community that runs a school there. The Mount of course has changed in many ways, but there is still the remnant of a basketball court in the back of the building, and I recall the times that Fessio and I, as an alternative to walking, played one-on-one basketball there. In this, as well as in everything else, he was a fierce competitor. We probably have different recollections of who most often won these games; but my lasting memory of them is Fessio's left-hand hook shot, which I would say without hesitation is the ugliest shot I have ever witnessed. He would loft the ball aimlessly high in the sky; and it would then bounce several times on the rim before (seemingly) always circling down through the net.

Regarding our conversations in connection with the council, there were questions about revelation and Scripture; the nature of the Church; Christology and fundamental-"apologetic" theology. Fessio was already at that time keenly interested in issues of the liturgy and the use of the vernacular. It is remarkable in retrospect that, a few years later, Fessio was to go on to study with people who were so directly involved in the conciliar debates regarding these questions— for example, de Lubac with respect to *Dei Verbum* and *Ad gentes* and

Ratzinger with respect to *Gaudium et spes*. Finally, there was Fessio's achievement in the study of languages. He anticipated that he would eventually go to study in Europe, and so he began teaching himself privately with tapes (these were the days before electronics!). He taught himself by listening to tapes at a set time every day. Of course, he had already studied Latin and Greek as part of his earlier Jesuit formation, but during his time at the Mount he learned to speak at least two modern languages (my recollection is French and German—to which he later added Italian). He may also have been studying Hebrew. When he eventually went to Europe, he went already with an adequate ability to speak and write the languages.

The American Communio *and* Ignatius Press

It was during the time of Fessio's study with de Lubac in the early 1970s that the first meeting regarding the beginning of *Communio* was held, in Rome. What was his involvement? Fessio, working for de Lubac, was in the latter's room when de Lubac received a call from Rome. De Lubac was on the International Theological Commission, and someone—I am uncertain who—telephoned him, inviting him to a dinner meeting to be held in Rome coincident with the ITC meeting. Expected at the meeting (as I recall) were Ratzinger, Louis Bouyer, von Balthasar, Marie-Joseph Le Guillou, and de Lubac (among others), all theologians serving on the ITC. When the call came, Fessio asked if he should leave the room, and de Lubac said he should remain there; and then he overheard de Lubac turn down the invitation to the meeting, since it was difficult for him to travel. (De Lubac had been wounded in the war and had some shrapnel still lodged in his skull and would get dizzy and have headaches, and so he traveled little.) When de Lubac hung up, Fessio apologized for listening to the conversation, but then immediately offered his services, saying that he would be happy to handle everything and accompany de Lubac to Rome. De Lubac thought that was a good idea, called back whoever it was that had called him from Rome, and announced that he would be coming. So Fessio went with him, and that turned out to be the first organizational meeting for what in the early 1970s would become the International *Communio*.

The first German issue came out in 1972. The purpose of *Communio*, as von Balthasar originally conceived it, was to articulate the meaning of Vatican II for people who were confused and overwhelmed in the face of developments in the Church and Catholic theology in the wake of the council. The purpose was not to counter any other theological-religious publications, but simply to address this (positive) need that von Balthasar thought it urgent to address: to clarify the sense in which these conciliar developments expressed—and should be read in the light of—the authentic ecclesial tradition.

The people gathered at the Rome meeting were theologians whom von Balthasar expected to write, but the intention of the original project was simply to publish a book or two. Nevertheless, in the discussions, the nature of the project quickly changed: it would take the form of a theological journal to be published simultaneously in different countries and languages. Since von Balthasar had taken initiative in calling this group together, those involved at the outset handed over to him the responsibility to oversee the ecclesial-theological direction of the various editions. Von Balthasar and Ratzinger remained on the board of the German edition. De Lubac declined any administrative leadership or duties but remained active as an author. Three young students and collaborators of de Lubac—Jean Duchesne, Rémi Brague, and Jean-Luc Marion (among others)—assumed responsibility for the French edition, and Angelo Scola served as one of the original board members for the Italian edition. Karol Wojtyła, who was familiar with the work of de Lubac already at the time of the council, was interested in the *Communio* project and as archbishop of Kraków supported its publication in Poland. (One of the means whereby he was able to do that—at a time when Poland was still under Communist control—was through his distribution of the paper allotment for Catholic publications in Poland: he re-allotted the available pages to make possible the emergence of a Polish *Communio*.)

Coincident with the above developments, Fessio sought and received permission from Father von Balthasar and the other founders to explore the possibility of starting an edition of *Communio* in America. I was then writing my doctoral dissertation in Southern California. Since Fessio was studying in Europe and would continue writing his own dissertation there, he asked me to help him contact some established Catholic philosophers and theologians to serve on the initial editorial board. Catholic historian James Hitchcock became the first editor of the journal, and theologian Father Gerald van Ackeren, S.J., of Saint Louis University, the first chair of the board. I myself attended my first *Communio* meeting, at which I met von Balthasar for the first time, in May 1972 in Munich, and I served for the first several years as the assistant editor of the American edition, until becoming editor in 1982.

Fessio was thus the person responsible for the founding of the American *Communio*. When he returned from Europe (about 1975), he became involved in establishing the Saint Ignatius Institute and, shortly after that, Ignatius Press, and so he left me my responsibility with *Communio*.

It was at one of the earliest planning meetings of the American *Communio*, which took place in the mid-1970s at the home of a secular religious institute overlooking the city of Los Angeles and involved just a few of the eventual board members, that we first learned of Father Fessio's intentions regarding the founding of Ignatius Press. He announced that he was going to start a publishing house, a main purpose of which would be to translate into English all the works of von Balthasar, de Lubac, and Adrienne von Speyr. I remember us laughing because we immediately tallied up the count—somewhere close to 300 books! But he insisted that he would publish at least one book a year by each of these authors (eventually including the works of Joseph Ratzinger in the lineup as well). I remember that conversation well, because I had already long had the sense that when Fessio makes such a commitment, it should not be set aside as unrealistic. The first two books published by the Press—Louis Bouyer's *Woman in the Church* and von Balthasar's *Heart of the World*—appeared in 1980; and since that time, over 32 million copies of books by hundreds of different authors have been sold, including a vast proportion of the books by the four authors named above!

Father Fessio's Lifework

Father Fessio undertook the above initiatives first and last as a priest. His endeavors have never been about securing public position or extending personal influence. He has been drawn into controversy on some occasions, and if a principle was involved, one could expect a very vigorous and, I would say, courageous and intelligent argument, but an argument intended to avoid polemics or *ad hominem* criticisms. His main principle has been fidelity to the truth of his priesthood, with all that that implies in terms of administering the sacraments and service to the Church. I will conclude with three brief stories that testify to Father Fessio's character as a priest.

First, Jesuits historically conclude their period of formation after ordination to the priesthood by spending a year devoted mostly to prayer and final formation, a period referred to as tertianship (that is, "the third stage of probation"). This occurs some years after ordination and involves "an apostolic placement of teaching or service". One day in the early 1990s, I received a call from Father Fessio saying that arrangements had finally been approved for him to do tertianship in Siberia, for which he had sought permission. I could hear him laughing, and I laughed heartily myself! "Siberia!?" I said. "Yes," he continued, still laughing, "I've always wanted to go to Siberia." Ignatius Press had a connection with a mission in the Far East of Russia, which it supported by sending supplies. Of course, at the time, he was running Ignatius Press, and this was when the electronic communication revolution was only just beginning, so I asked him how he was going to manage the Press from such a remote place. But he brushed this aside. He immediately began to learn the language so that he could communicate with parishioners in their own tongue, in at least some rudimentary way. He was able to communicate with the Press through an internet connection at the university in Vladivostok, relying also on faxes. He stayed there for several months, Ignatius Press went on, and he came back. He told me that the time had been difficult, that the parishioners there had not wanted him to leave, and that after he left some of them had remained in contact with him for years. They had so appreciated that this priest would come to such a distant place to help out with an emerging Catholic presence over a very large area—and had been able to live, despite very unfamiliar physical conditions, a simple existence as a parish priest.

Second, though I do not recall the precise issues raised in the controversy, Father Fessio had taken public positions on questions of gender in the Church (as these bore implications regarding priestly ordination and the translation of scriptural and liturgical texts). In response to these positions, a well-known reporter who publicly identified himself as gay wrote very critical articles regarding Fessio in the Catholic press. At least one major criticism appeared on the front page of a leading Catholic newspaper, calling attention to Father Fessio's relation to Rome and in particular to then Cardinal Ratzinger. I do not recall the details of the exchange(s) between Father Fessio and this reporter. I know only that in the course of the controversy, Father Fessio apparently communicated with this man in a manner that projected the genuineness of Father Fessio's priesthood, assuring him that there was no personal animus on his part, that he had been concerned simply with the issue and not this man's person. Sometime after the controversy, this reporter had contracted AIDS and was dying. He had gone for care in his last months to a home run by the Missionary Sisters of Charity. He called Father Fessio when he was near death and asked Fessio if he would come and administer to him the last rites and hear his last confession so that he could die in peace, in the Church. Father Fessio went to him, and that is how the controversy ended. Fessio had communicated to this man no personal animosity throughout the course of the controversy. On the contrary, he was able to communicate the reality of a priest as a sacramental minister of the love of Christ and the Church.

Finally, I remember two conversations with Cardinal Ratzinger/ Pope Emeritus Benedict XVI in which the name of Father Fessio came up. The first, which was very brief, was at Casa del Clero. Walking from a meeting room with Cardinal Ratzinger, I mentioned Father Fessio in connection with the topic of our conversation, *Communio*. Ratzinger immediately responded to the name of Fessio by saying that he was a "good and obedient priest". It has always impressed me that this was the phrase that first occurred to him to describe Fessio. One could see the respect and affection that Cardinal Ratzinger had for his former student. Several years later, in 2013, I had the privilege of meeting with Pope Emeritus Benedict XVI at Mater Ecclesiae Monastery, where he lives in retirement. Toward the end of our conversation, I recalled Father Fessio's name as the person responsible for translating into English the two theologians whose reception in America we were discussing, von Balthasar and de Lubac. Benedict asked emphatically, "How *is* Father Fessio?" I laughed because I had just heard from Fessio that he had begun recently to grow several small vineyards and make wine at the Ignatius Press retreat house, which is located near the Russian River in Sonoma County, California. Father Fessio had described the new endeavor as a matter of "channeling his inner Italian and making wine". I didn't use that exact phrase to Benedict, but rather said something to the effect that Fessio was recovering his Italian roots and making wine. Pope Benedict leaned back and laughed, saying: "Is that so? Is that so?" I then assured him that Fessio had not abandoned his work as a priest publishing Catholic books and that wine-making was an additional undertaking, and he smiled. The memories of Father Fessio and the respect and affection the pope still had for him were evident.

It is impossible to envision Catholic life and thought in North America without the massive contribution of Ignatius Press. The present collection of essays on some of the most significant authors published by the Press testifies to an astonishing achievement in service to the Church in America, all of it inspired by the integrity of a man faithful to his vocation as a Jesuit priest.

The Mystical Body in the *Nouvelle Théologie*

David Vincent Meconi, S.J.

When Ignatius Press broke into the world of publishing, its arrival was announced by bringing forward two books—Louis Bouyer's *Woman in the Church* and Hans Urs von Balthasar's *Heart of the World*. This was 1978, and Father Fessio and his fledgling editorial staff aimed to help the Catholic world wake from its catechetical slumber by introducing the English-speaking world to two major figures of the *nouvelle théologie*, a "new" way of doing theology seeking to unite the vibrancy of the Church Fathers and the systematic clarity of Aquinas with the demands of modernity. In 1978, it became more and more clear to many that the sporadic experimentations of the sixties were failing to take any permanent hold; the dissenting voices of the seventies were clearly aging; and Christians everywhere were realizing the intelligence and the élan, the power and the poetry, of Saint John Paul II. Here was a world leader whose mere presence assured us, "Do not to be afraid" (those first papal words, *Non abbiate paura!*). Here was a true *vir ecclesiasticus* who represented a personalism and eclectic theological approach that would open many important doors hitherto closed or at least untried. Here was a man who would expose the sterility of secularism and the barrenness of bad theology. But John Paul was never alone. He seemed to ride onto the world stage with a cohort of other trustworthy thinkers, bringing along with him the likes of Joseph Ratzinger, Henri de Lubac, von Balthasar and Adrienne von Speyr, Louis Bouyer, Jean Daniélou, and others. This constellation of faithful thinkers helped to right Peter's Barque and set the Church back on a course able to give the mysteries of the faith the creative intelligence the Bride of Christ deserves.

One theme running throughout all of these thinkers was the centrality of the Mystical Body of Christ. The Mystical Body is an ecclesiology committed to the view that the Church is an extension of the divine Incarnation: Christ as the Head organically and intrinsically united to the baptized in a mystical union that empowers the faithful to live divinely informed lives of supernatural mercy and charity. The Mystical Body in the *nouvelle théologie* emerges as a key component of the way in which this new generation of theologians both defended and advanced the faith beyond what they found to be a rather ossified and ever-increasingly infertile Scholasticism. In fact, the appellation *nouvelle théologie* stems from an essay by the diehard Dominican Garrigou-Lagrange, O.P., who saw in these thinkers a deviance and a danger that could be avoided by staying more explicitly committed to the tenets of strict Thomism.[1] However, history has clearly vindicated the scholars we shall here treat as faithful and orthodox Catholic thinkers and leaders.

Men like de Lubac, Ratzinger, von Balthasar, and Bouyer were early in their intellectual and pastoral vocations when, in 1943, Pope Pius XII issued *Mystici Corporis*, in which he called the whole world of humanity back to its intended unity and to its ultimate call to reflect Christ. No doubt the combination of the world's ferocity throughout the twentieth century and the Church's call for greater concord, not only between Christians but between the Christ and all human persons, influenced the way in which these four embraced and invigorated a theology able to elucidate a real and transformative union between Christ and the Christian. This essay will accordingly treat the use of the Mystical Body as it appears in the works of these four major figures of the twentieth-century renewal of the Church. We shall in turn treat (in chronological fashion) the Mystical Body as it appears in the works of Hans Urs von Balthasar, Louis Bouyer, Henri de Lubac, and Joseph Ratzinger, Pope Emeritus Benedict XVI. The reason for treating only these four theologians is that they are truly

---

[1] As far as I can tell, the common name *nouvelle théologie* in reference to the men we are treating here first appeared in Reginald Garrigou-Lagrange, O.P., "La Nouvelle théologie où va-t-elle?", *Angelicum* 23 (1946): 126–45.

representative of a rich and robust theology of the Mystical Body and that their major works on this central Christian doctrine are readily available in English today.

The *Catechism of the Catholic Church* (*CCC*) treats the Mystical Body fittingly enough under the Nicene-Constantinopolitan declaration that we "believe in the holy catholic Church" (*CCC* §§781–810). It falls under a larger heading, "The Church—People of God, Body of Christ, Temple of the Holy Spirit", thus situating any theology of the Mystical Body in a more amplified framework. As "the Church" is simultaneously the triptych of (1) People of God, (2) Body of Christ, and (3) Temple of the Holy Spirit, we thus learn that whatever the Mystical Body is, it is never detached from lives of real, living men and women, the People of God. Neither is the Mystical Body ever detached from its Head, thus being the "Body of Christ", nor is it active apart from the mutual indwelling of the Holy Spirit and is thus his "Temple" on earth. In this way, the Church wants to maintain that our own individual lives are really graced extensions of Christ's own humanity as we become more and more fully ourselves in him and as he continues to take on human flesh so as to be present on earth for all generations.

In perhaps what proves to be the pivotal passage in this entire section, the Church introduces the Mystical Body by way of Saint Augustine's rich concept of the *Christus totus* and ends with an evocative claim by Joan of Arc. Section §795 of the *CCC* thus teaches that:

> Christ and his Church thus together make up the "whole Christ" (*Christus totus*). The Church is one with Christ. The saints are acutely aware of this unity: "Let us rejoice then and give thanks that we have become not only Christians, but Christ himself. Do you understand and grasp, brethren, God's grace toward us? Marvel and rejoice: we have become Christ. For if he is the head, we are the members; he and we together are the whole man.... The fullness of Christ then is the head and the members. But what does 'head and members' mean? Christ and the Church" [St. Augustine, *Tractates on the Gospel of John*, 21.8]. "Our redeemer has shown himself to be one person with the holy Church whom he has taken to himself" [Pope St. Gregory the Great, Preface to the *Moralia on Job*, 14]. "Head and members form as it were one and the same mystical person" [St. Thomas Aquinas, *Summa Theologiae* III, 48, 2]. "A reply of St. Joan of Arc to her judges sums

up the faith of the holy doctors and the good sense of the believer: 'About Jesus Christ and the Church, I simply know they're just one thing, and we shouldn't complicate the matter' " [*Acta* of Saint Joan of Arc's Trial].

As we meet these figures from late antiquity to the high Middle Ages in order, we read in the *CCC* how all of these saints attest to the unity of Christ and Christian, of Head and Body. Here there is not just Christ and Christians; there is the Christ as created continuations through grace of his enfleshed presence in the world. For this reason there is an organic and inseparable bond between the Church's Founder and her followers.

Let us now turn to the twentieth-century theologians who were so pivotal in helping the Church think this way and make such bold and beautiful statements about the Christic centrality of the People of God. Hans Urs von Balthasar is arguably the most influential intellectual of the twentieth century; Henri de Lubac produced an ecclesiology that is at once both ancient and contemporary, while Louis Bouyer's central contributions lie in the areas of liturgy and spirituality; and we conclude with one of the most fertile minds of our (or any) age, Joseph Ratzinger, Pope Emeritus Benedict XVI. These four minds are conveniently brought together here because it is these four who provide the most Catholic and comprehensive vision of what it means to belong to the Mystical Body of Christ. Thanks to Ignatius Press, the major works of these theologians are now available to an English-speaking world, advancing a theology of the Mystical Body. Each of these Churchmen argues in his own way that what it means to be a Christian is not merely to follow the rules or to fulfill one's ecclesial duties, but to become another Christ as one is ever more firmly grafted onto the life of Jesus through personal prayer and surrender, through and in the Eucharist, and as a living instantiation of the Lord's ongoing Incarnation.

Hans Urs von Balthasar (1905–1988)

Born into a wealthy aristocratic family in Lucerne, Switzerland, in 1905, von Balthasar was first trained as a boy by the Benedictines before being sent to study during his high-school years with the Jesuits in Austria. From the famed *gymnasium* at Feldkirch on the Swiss-Austrian border, this very successful student moved almost automatically into the doctoral program in philosophy and German literature at the University of Zurich. After completing his doctorate in 1928, he entered the Society of Jesus and was almost instantly immersed in the writings of Erich Przywara (d. 1972) and Henri de Lubac (d. 1991). After priestly ordination in 1936, von Balthasar served as an editor of the Bavarian Jesuit journal *Stimmen der Zeit*, before being missioned back to Switzerland with the rise of the Third Reich in 1940 in order to serve as a chaplain at the University of Basel. For ten years, his soul was fed by his intellectual work, his care of his students, and his friendship with Adrienne von Speyr, whose visions and mystical experiences left forever a mark on von Balthasar's writings. In 1950, he was forced to choose between staying in the Society of Jesus or incardinating into the diocesan life so as to further his and von Speyr's work in their newly founded community, the Community of Saint John (*Johannes-gemeinschaft*), on which von Balthasar's superiors were not altogether keen. Despite these bumpy years and his eventual departure from the Society, von Balthasar's brilliance and fidelity were recognized by Saint John Paul II, who invited him into the College of Cardinals. Von Balthasar, however, died on June 26, 1988, only two days before he would have received the red hat.

Wary of what he perceived to be an ossified Neo-Thomism, von Balthasar returned to the Church Fathers in order to recover that unique convergence between theological doctrine and Catholic spirituality. To do this, he had to return squarely to the merits of the Incarnation as evidenced in the great tradition of the Church. Not to do so would be to fall back into a self-fueled Pelagianism in which the Christian and the Christ act as two separate agents or into some Neoplatonic absorption wherein the Christian has absolutely no individuated graces to enjoy or unique contributions to offer God's saving plan. That is why the merits of Christ are understood as his unceasing enfleshment, which continues to create one mystic person through grace, and why von Balthasar draws from Aquinas' question on the dual operations of the Incarnation. What is surprising in this *quaestio* is not that the Christ acts as both divine and human (something already defined at the Council of Chalcedon in 451), but that Christ never works apart from drawing creatures into his own life mystically. This is the life of grace and the only vivacity of the Church, the desire of God to unite all into himself: "Grace was in Christ not simply as in an individual man, but as in the Head of the whole Church, to whom all are united as members to the head, forming a single mystic person. In consequence, the merit of Christ extends to others insofar as they are his members. In somewhat similar fashion in an individual man the action of the head belongs in some measure to all his bodily members."[2] By selecting this passage from the Angelic Doctor, von Balthasar intends to highlight how the Church's ability to preach and administer the sacraments, to heal and to prophesy, to love neighbor and forgive enemy are all actions that find their source and sustainment in the person of Jesus Christ. Consequently, no one Christian can claim any one salvific action for only himself; all meritorious deeds (and, obviously, thoughts and words) are of Christ in cooperation with those graced enough to surrender to their true Head.

From this selection from Aquinas, von Balthasar finds what he needs to note that the personal merit of Christ himself is offered to the entire human race, as the Head offers its supereminence to all members of the body. A responsible twentieth-century theologian can see that what is labeled here as the "old patristic Head/Body concept"

is understood as a *presupposition* of the possibility of him acting on our behalf. It is necessary to go beyond this and say that it is the personal, freewill acceptance of the guilt of the "members" on part of the "Head" that is the presupposition of his effective representative action; it is essential if the Head/Body relationship is to come about in the first place. On the one hand, the Redeemer takes the entirety of human nature upon himself, which links him organically with all who are to be redeemed; on the other hand, there is his personal constitution, which makes him uniquely meritorious, for the benefit of all;

[2] Thomas Aquinas, *Summa theologica*, III, q. 19, a. 4: "*In Christo non solum fuit gratia sicut in quodam homine singulari, sed sicut in capite totius Ecclesiae cui omnes uniuntur sicut capiti membra, ex quibur constituitur mystice una persona. Et exinde est quod meritum Christi se extendit ad alios in quantum sunt membra eius.*" As quoted in Hans Urs von Balthasar, *Theo-Drama: Theological Dramatic Theory*, vol. 3, *The Dramatis Personae: The Person in Christ*, trans. Graham Harrison (San Francisco: Ignatius Press, 1988), 242.

between these two there is an element that, lacking in the "classical" doctrine, is clearly indicated in the Fathers (though not specifically discussed), at least in what they say about the Eucharist.[3]

Von Balthasar's Eucharistic theology thus enables him to stress how the Mystical Body of Christ ensures real membership, as every day the communicant consciously chooses to join this Body and not that one in which he plans the day, chooses to live, explicitly seeks grace, and so on. The second effect of the Eucharist here is, in von Balthasar's own words, the awareness at each Mass that "the One who gives us his body and blood does so in a '*commercium*': he gives back to us what he has taken from us and transformed into himself."[4]

    This metaphor of deification is at the heart of the *nouvelle théologie*'s Mystical Body: in the Son's *kenosis* is our *theosis*, and these two movements are constituted of the one and same mystical person. Yet, while the deifying Christ and the deified Church are mutually dependent, the instrumentality and role of each are ever distinct. Von Balthasar never tires of assuring us that speaking of Christ and the Church as in fact constituting "one person" is never wrong, as long as the roles are never confused. This (what he calls a) diastasis is found most readily and rightly in Saint Augustine, for whom the Mystical Body concept is so strong that he coins multiple phrases to make this organic unity memorable: "we too are Christ", "he too is us", allowing von Balthasar to continue:

> Accordingly, Augustine can say, "*Christus sumus*", particularly when thinking of the way the Eucharist mediates Christ to us. In Thomas Aquinas, the realism of the Head-Body relationship between Christ and his members in the Church is shown to have a significant effect on soteriology: because of the concrete unity between the two, forming *quasi unam personam*, the Head (who possesses the *gratia capitis* for the whole Body) can "merit" for the members. As a counterblast to Luther's theology of justification, Cajetan and several theologians of his school (especially Bellarmine, Lessius, R. Tapper, J. P. Nazarius, J. Nacchiante), basing themselves on Augustine and Thomas, develop the idea that Christ is also the Church's final *suppositum* or *hypostasis*;

[3] Ibid., 242–43.
[4] Ibid., 243.

thus he merits our salvation in virtue of two titles: *without* merit on our part insofar as he merits personally as Head of the Church; and (as it were) *with* merit on our part insofar as he works in and through us as our Head. In this way it was possible to speak (with Nazarius) of "two aspects of the subsistence" of Christ, "one in him himself as the Head and one in the faithful who share in his grace and love".[5]

The erudition of von Balthasar often shines through in this manner; his grasp of the intellectual history of the West is quickly evident in any of his works. Describing Christ as the Church's hypostasis, he is drawing from an ancient tradition, finding its roots in the middle of the fifth century (the Councils of Ephesus and Chalcedon most notably), using the Greek word for "person" to maintain that the ultimate identity of the Church is Christ-and-Christian. In this view, the divine and the human as perfectly united in the Christ can no longer be separated or divided, and, consequently, neither can the baptized human person ever be separated from his divine source and telos. Together, both Christ and Christian form one mystical person. This is the Church. In other words, just as the divine Son has hypostatically united himself to a nature foreign to his godliness, humans can now similarly partake of a divinity itself that is not intrinsically their own. The difference of course lies in the matter of union: where the Son's assumption of humanity is hypostatic and thus eternally personal, our union with the divine is always participatory and thus never wholly of our own person. This is how all merit and all goodness are communicated to the elect, and in this two-becoming-one, von Balthasar sees the perfect marriage.

He accordingly tends to rely on nuptial imagery to show the greatest of unions. The prime analogate is not the human marriage but the union of the Second Adam and the Second Eve, in whose love all our loves are made possible. That is why, for von Balthasar, the Bridegroom/Bride image is always in need of that of the Head/Body, so that within the act of deifying transformation, the initiative and power are always Christ's and never ours:

The Christ/Church relationship is expressed both in terms of Bridegroom/Bride (n.b. as "one flesh") and of Head/Body; no aspect

[5] Ibid., 342–43.

should be obscured, since each throws light on the others. This in itself should warn us against rationalistic oversimplification. Incorporated into Christ's obedience, we become obedient with him; but, incorporated into his freedom, we also become truly free. As members of his Body, "which is the Church", we are equipped by the Holy Spirit with our most personal mission—and this is, as we have shown, the very core of our personal being—but this mission can be nothing other than a participation in the once-and-for-all, all-embracing mission of Christ. In this sense, grace perfects nature: if by "nature" we mean that man is free to make his own decisions and action, this freedom is perfected by the grace of a sublime participation in the absolute, divine freedom. This comes about through our being incorporated into the Eucharist that, in the Spirit, Christ makes to the Father. And it is precisely in participating in Christ's mission that our elevated freedom is placed at the service of the communion of the saints.[6]

To anyone familiar with the Jesuit spirituality out of which von Balthasar writes, Saint Ignatius' *Suscipe* (the Latin imperative for "take") is the impulse behind such a beautiful passage: "Take, Lord, and receive all my liberty, my memory, my understanding, and my entire will, all that I have and possess. Thou hast given all to me. To Thee, O Lord, I return it. All is Thine, dispose of it wholly according to Thy will. Give me only Thy love and Thy grace, for this is enough for me." Allow me a personal anecdote.

Early one morning in the Jesuit chapel at the University of Innsbruck in Austria where I had been sent for my seminary studies, I had Father Ignatius' prayer poised on the pew in front of me. Another Jesuit passed by me, looked down to notice Ignatius' words, and said to me: "You can pray that only because Jesus prayed it to you first." I wondered what he meant, and, knowing him to be a good and solid Jesuit, I turned those words around and imagined Jesus speaking them to me: "Take my liberty, my memory, my understanding, and my entire will, O creature, all that I have and possess." It worked: all we have, we have because Jesus gives it to us first. Pelagianism is that particular heresy of imagining any good within us that God did not first

---

[6] Hans Urs von Balthasar, *Theo-Drama: Theological Dramatic Theory*, vol. 4, *The Action*, trans. Graham Harrison (San Francisco: Ignatius Press, 1994), 406.

place there. But we can only offer God ourselves, our souls, because he first has given himself to us in Christ, in the Eucharist. Here at this altar is where God himself says, "Take, and become like me ... give me only your love and your grace, my child, for this is enough for me." This is where true freedom lies, this is how the divine nature is opened up to sinners (2 Pet 1:4), enabling us to achieve superhuman acts and to become eternal children of the perfect Father.

For this his only begotten Son entered our state. He is the divine hypostasis, now uniting that which all people have longed to see in his visible humanity; the Word becomes flesh. But this flesh is not an arcane museum piece of our past; he is still as present now in his Eucharist, in his Scriptures, in his people. This communion provides the Church with her ultimate mission: to become evermore the Body of Christ on earth, prolonging his union of heaven and earth:

> Having spoken of the transposition of vision into faith, and of Christ's time into our time, we have already said some fundamental things about the way the Church issues from, and is set on her way by, him who is the Mediator between heaven and earth. The Church is the prolongation of Christ's mediatorial nature and work and possesses a knowledge that comes by faith; she lives objectively (in her institution and her sacraments) and subjectively (in her saints and, fundamentally, in all of her members) in the interchange between heaven and earth. Her life comes from heaven and extends to earth, and extends from earth to heaven.
>
> If, in God, the idea of the world exists as an organism to which he has given its own freedom, this idea now becomes concrete in the risen Mediator. "He has made himself the exponent of our nature as heaven designed it, and we have this nature in him", insofar as he has borne our personal sin and put us in concrete touch with God's idea of us. "In this sense we are in him before he is in us", and by being "in him" we are given a participation in his being begotten of the Father.[7]

Bearing our lives this way cost God his life, of course, and on that Cross we see the ultimate gift. "Take, and receive." Like her founder, the Church, too, is divine and human, the "prolongation of Christ's

---

[7] Hans Urs von Balthasar, *Theo-Drama: Theological Dramatic Theory*, vol. 5, *The Last Act*, trans. Graham Harrison (San Francisco: Ignatius Press, 1998), 131.

mediatorial nature and work". The Church must therefore aim to bring all persons everywhere and at all times to her enfleshed God. This is what von Balthasar means by being "in him", in the sense of that ancient phraseology, *in Filio, filii*—in the Son we, too, are made sons and daughters, graced participants in the very life of God.

Such access to the Father's eternal embrace has been made possible through the Cross, and von Balthasar more than any other twentieth-century theologian argues for the beauty of Calvary: "Through the bloody Sacrifice of the Cross and the form it takes in the Church as baptism and Eucharist ('sharing in the blood of Christ' [1 Cor 10:16]) we are actually incorporated into the holiness of Christ. The entire doctrine of the Body of Christ, of which we are 'individually members' (1 Cor 12:27), issues directly from the event of the Cross."[8] The Lord's crucified flesh on the Cross, as his body and soul part, is what paradoxically unites the scattered children of the first Adam. The Mystical Body is brought together through the defeat of the one reality that alone can dispense the intended unity the Father wills for his children, the death that stems from disobedience.[9] Having united even this to his sacred humanity, the only begotten Son of God renders all humans capable now of the same filiality through grace.

As with all the other thinkers included here, manuscripts and monographs could be multiplied (and in fact are) trying to cover fully von Balthasar's range and influence. But let us now turn to a very influential mentor of his. The year was 1932, and von Balthasar's Jesuit provincial sent him to Fourvière, the theologate in Lyon run by the Society of Jesus. For the next four years, von Balthasar would be freed from active teaching and many daily duties to immerse himself in theological texts and the requisite preparation for priesthood. Here he would meet one of the (other) great minds of the twentieth-century revival, the *nouvelle théologie*, Henri de Lubac, S.J.

---

[8] Hans Urs von Balthasar, *Paul Struggles with His Congregation: The Pastoral Message of the Letters to the Corinthians*, trans. Brigitte L. Bojarska (San Francisco: Ignatius Press, 1992), 14–15.

[9] This is how von Balthasar argues that " 'persons,' in the Christian sense, are just such as, in imitation of the divine-human Person Jesus, 'no longer live for themselves' and also no longer die for themselves. It is here that the catholic and missionary task of the Catholica first becomes visible in its ultimate essence; in every instance, she anticipates, in prayer, devotion, sacrifice, and death for her brethren, that which she brings them through her outward missionary work. The proof: 'little' Thérèse, as the patron of all missions"; *Credo: Meditations on the Apostles' Creed*, trans. David Kipp (San Francisco: Ignatius Press, 2005), 86.

Henri de Lubac (1896–1991)

Whereas von Balthasar lifted our minds toward the beauty of God's *kenosis*, de Lubac stretches our minds back through the unbroken trajectory that is the Church's life streaming forth from the Savior's own will. In many ways, de Lubac's life mirrors von Balthasar's: both joined the Society of Jesus to offer the Church their minds and intellectual gifts, both fell out with their Jesuit superiors and consequently endured years of personal turmoil, but both were thereafter recognized as true Churchmen and invited into the College of Cardinals for their scholarly and spiritual contributions to the Church's mission (de Lubac refused this invitation under Pope Paul VI because all cardinals then [1969] had to become bishops; but John Paul II dispensed de Lubac from this requisite and made him a cardinal in 1983).

Consistent with millennia of sacred tradition, de Lubac stressed the Church as *the mediating sacrament* that makes possible the transmission of the Christ-life and the lives of individual believers. It was in this Church that de Lubac would pour out his life: entering the Jesuits at the age of only seventeen, drafted after only a year of novitiate to serve in World War I in Northeast France before being sent home after suffering a head wound. Ordained in 1927, de Lubac completed his Jesuit training and was thereafter missioned to teach theology at the University of Lyon in 1929. During these fertile years before World War II, de Lubac taught, wrote, and, along with Father Jean Daniélou, S.J., founded *Sources chrétiennes*, a rather novel publishing of ancient Christian texts with Greek or Latin on one side of the page and a modern French translation on the other.

In June of 1950, the Vatican called for de Lubac's censure, and these (what he called) "Dark Years" lasted until 1958, when Father de Lubac was allowed to return full time to his university posts. What was the issue? Those like de Lubac and Daniélou who wanted to return to the Christian sources and not simply repeat what Neoscholasticism had been saying the past few decades were under suspicion by many leading Thomists, like Father Garrigou-Lagrange, O.P., who accused those associated with the *nouvelle théologie* of Modernism. Two works of de Lubac were particularly toxic during these years: his 1946 classic, *Surnaturel*, which traced how an order of supernatural grace became disassociated from a purely natural order of reality, a problem that de Lubac does not see until Cajetan (d. 1534) but that he argues cannot be found in Thomas himself; and then came the 1950 publication of *Histoire et Esprit*, which is a defense of the condemned but misunderstood third-century Origen. Both these speculative works were unjustly pilloried by de Lubac's detractors, and pressure was put on the relatively recently elected Father General of the Jesuits, Jean-Baptiste Janssens, to silence de Lubac until he could clarify what seemed to be dangerously heretical positions.

During this time, de Lubac turned his ever-active mind to less controversial topics, publishing important works on the nature of Buddhism, the history of biblical exegesis, and the nature of the Church. For ten years, de Lubac found himself on the margins of university as well as ecclesiastical life. His three main works, *Surnaturel, Corpus Mysticum*, and *De la Connaissance de Dieu*, were removed from all Jesuit houses, and all his writings and interactions with students, especially seminarians, were closely monitored during these years. In 1950, Pope Pius XII released his encyclical *Humani generis*, which, in part, argues that faithful theologians should not aim to overturn major tenets of the Church's intellectual patrimony. One cannot help but think of the members of the *nouvelle théologie*, de Lubac in particular, when *Humani generis* avers that some modern thinkers "cherish the hope that when dogma is stripped of the elements which they hold to be extrinsic to divine revelation, it will compare advantageously with the dogmatic opinions of those who are separated from the unity of the Church and that in this way they will gradually arrive at a mutual assimilation of Catholic dogma with the tenets of the dissidents."[10] As dissenting as de Lubac may have appeared during the 1950s, his fidelity to the tradition (especially Augustine), to a tradition much larger than what the Neoscholastics of his day wanted to make it, was eventually recognized. By the time the groundwork for the Second Vatican Council had begun to be envisioned, Pope John XXIII appointed de Lubac as one of the first lead consultants to the preparatory commissions; Pope Paul VI made him a member of the International Theological Commission; and John Paul II welcomed him into the College of Cardinals.

[10] Pius XII, Encyclical *Humani generis* (August 12, 1950), no. 14.

When it comes to a theology of the Mystical Body, de Lubac clearly shines as a star within the great constellation of two thousand years of Catholic reflection. His work really is a return to the ancient sources (*ressourcement*) in order to make these perennial verities intelligible and attractive to a modern seeker (*aggiornamento*). His work with Daniélou and the many bilingual volumes of *Sources chrétiennes* attest to this most clearly, but also do de Lubac's works on the Church, where both his heightened sense of historical context as well as his mysticism come out beautifully at times. For he appreciates deeply how the Church is the work of sinful mortals while simultaneously being the unblemished Bride of Christ; she is not an association bound together by human will or mutual agreement. The Church is infinitely more than a conglomerate, however concordious. The Church is a unified body caused, not by human merit or intelligence, but by the Father's gratuitous call:

> The Church is not a result; at least she is not a mere result, the simple fruit of confluence. She has not been formed by individuals who, having believed in Jesus Christ each on his own part and each in his own way, decided to join together in order to organize their belief and their life in common. The Church, composed of men, was not made by the hands of men. She is not an organization. She is a living organism, what Saint Irenaeus called "the ancient organism of the Church".[11]

Here de Lubac quotes Irenaeus, whose point is that the Gnostic heretics have cut themselves off from the living community of Truth. By revising the Church's Sacred Scriptures to fit their own philosophical notions, the Gnostics have reduced the Church from a divinely decreed body to a human association based on like-mindedness. Seeing the Church as consisting of humans but never made by humans, de Lubac rejects the label "organization" in order to uphold the Christic centrality of the Church's nature.

This is also how de Lubac is able to enter more deeply, mystically, into the Church's nature as the Body of Christ espoused to the perfect Bridegroom, who thereby incorporates creatures into his own

---

[11] Henri de Lubac, *The Motherhood of the Church*, trans. Sr. Sergia Englund, O.C.D. (San Francisco: Ignatius Press, 1982), 15.

divine life. He tends to read the New Testament metaphors for the Christian people through the primal lens of the Church as the sacramental continuation of Christ's own theandric presence. Whether it be the biblical imagery of Vine/branches, Head/body, Bridegroom/bride, or Builder/temple, Christ and Christian form only one person:

> The Church is the sacrament of Christ. This means, to put it another way, that there is between her and him a certain relation of mystical identity. Here again we encounter the Pauline metaphors and the rest of the biblical images, which the Christian tradition has continually explored. One and the same intuition of faith is expressed throughout. Head and members make one single body, one single Christ; the Bridegroom and the Bride are one flesh. Although he is the Head of his Church, Christ does not rule her from without; there is, certainly, subjection and dependence between her and him, but at the same time she is his fulfilment and "fullness". She is the tabernacle of his presence, the building of which he is both Architect and Cornerstone. She is the temple in which he teaches and into which he draws with him the whole Divinity.[12]

For de Lubac makes quite clear that the visible Church on earth should be seen and treated as "the vestibule of the Church in heaven", as he writes elsewhere.[13] Here is the true gate of eternal life, as she is the sign as well as the securer of heavenly joys.

This can be true only because of the connaturality between the Son and the Father eternally and between the Son and the Church in time. Just as the Son is the face of the otherwise invisible Father, the Church gathered in worship around the Eucharist is a manifestation of the otherwise ascended Lord: "If Christ is the sacrament of God, the Church is for us the sacrament of Christ; she represents him, in the full and ancient meaning of the term; she really makes him present. She not only carries on his work, but she is his very continuation, in a sense far more real than that in which it can be said that any human institution is its founder's continuation."[14]

---

[12] Henri de Lubac, *The Splendor of the Church*, trans. Michael Mason (1986; San Francisco: Ignatius Press, 1999), 209.

[13] Henri de Lubac, *Catholicism: Christ and the Common Destiny of Man*, trans. Lancelot C. Sheppard and Sr. Elizabeth Englund, O.C.D. (San Francisco: Ignatius Press, 1988), 72.

[14] Ibid., 76.

But does this mean we can simply equate the visible Church with the Mystical Body? History will show us how the theologians we have selected in this essay each had a role to play in the development of Vatican II's *Lumen gentium*, the Dogmatic Constitution on the Church, which most people see as the natural blossom of Pope Pius XII's *Mystici Corporis*. At the oft-quoted section 8, we learn that the Church Christ founded subsists (*subsistit in Ecclesia catholica*) in the visible Catholic Church but can never be limited or facilely equated with that Church without qualification.

> The Church, without being exactly co-extensive with the Mystical Body, is not adequately distinct from it. For this reason it is natural that between her and it—as within the Mystical Body itself between the head and the members—there should arise a kind of exchange of idioms: *Corpus Christi quod est ecclesia*. "I am Jesus whom thou persecutest." "He who beholds the Church", says Gregory of Nyssa, "really beholds Christ." And just as the term "supernatural" is applied equally to the means that shape man on his course toward his end and to that end itself, so the Church is properly called Catholic, and it is right to see in it in truth the Body of Christ, both in its actual and visible reality and in its invisible and final achievement.... In the likeness of Christ who is her founder and her head, she is at the same time both the way and the goal; at the same time visible and invisible; in time and in eternity; she is at once the bride and the widow, the sinner and the saint.[15]

Here an important aspect of any theology of the Mystical Body comes to the fore: the recapitulation and subsequent incorporation of the entire human family back into the New Adam. The body intended by the Head is reserved, not for the virtuous or any select group, but for all humans ever conceived. For this reason, the unity of the Mystical Body of Christ demands a fragile but essential unity, the organic commonality of the entire human race.

For any theology of the Mystical Body to be effective, a literal understanding of a first Adam and Eve is required, so as to make sense of the Second Eve and Second Adam. Why so? As we all sinned and thus incurred our radically innate need for grace, we all, too, have

[15] Ibid., 72–74.

been recapitulated and renewed in Christ and in his Blessed Mother, who offered him the fullness of humanity at her *fiat*. This is the whole point and purpose of the Incarnation: to regather all humans into a perfect state now free from division and decay. This is what the Christ achieves in assuming the fullness of the human condition himself, an ancient teaching as described by de Lubac:

> So the Fathers of the Church, in their treatment of grace and salvation, kept constantly before them this Body of Christ, and in dealing with the creation were not content only to mention the formation of individuals, the first man and the first woman, but delighted to contemplate God creating humanity as a whole. "God", says Saint Irenaeus, for example, "in the beginning of time plants the vine of the human race; he loved this human race and purposed to pour out his Spirit upon it and to give it the adoption of sons." For Irenaeus again, as indeed for Origen, Gregory Nazianzen, Gregory of Nyssa, for Cyril of Alexandria, Maximus, Hilary and others, the lost sheep of the Gospel that the Good Shepherd brings back to the fold is no other than the whole of human nature; its sorry state so moves the Word of God that he leaves the great flock of the angels, as it were, to their own devices, in order to go to its help. The Fathers designated this nature by a series of equivalent expressions, all of a concrete nature, thus demonstrating that it was in their view a genuine reality.[16]

Whereas death effects division, true life achieves unity. This is the intent and aim of the Incarnation, as the New Adam regathers and thus bears all of humanity in himself: "For the Word did not merely take a human body; his Incarnation was not a simple *corporatio*, but, as Saint Hilary says, a *concorporatio*. He incorporated himself in our humanity, and incorporated it in himself. *Universitatis nostrae caro est factus*. In making a human nature, it is *human nature* that he united to himself, that he enclosed in himself, and it is the latter, the whole and entire, that in some sort he uses as a body."[17] In this view, the Incarnation is still underway, and all humans are "enclosed" in Christ and thus able to partake of his perfections. This is the aim of ecclesial

[16] Ibid., 25–26.
[17] Ibid., 37–39.

unity, to regather the hostilely divided and inevitably mortal sinner and regather him into an eternally deified body of praise.

To make this real, de Lubac often ventures a spirituality of ecclesial belonging. While never avoiding the reality of the Church's hierarchical and political structure, he moves beyond these structures to what is truly life-giving; de Lubac knows all too well that Christ's Church is more than her visible leaders (but more, not less). In his view, "the Church, the only real Church, the Church which is the Body of Christ, is not merely that strongly hierarchical and disciplined society whose divine origin has to be maintained, whose organization has to be upheld against all denial and revolt." But like Thomas himself (*Summa theologiae* I, 1, art. 8), de Lubac realizes that while authority is at play in most cognitive functioning, bare authority is the weakest of all arguments. That is why he continues to help his readers see that authority must give way to what he calls "effective union". So surrendering to the teachings and traditions of the Church can be only "a partial cure for the separatist, individualist tendency",

> a partial cure because it works only from without by way of authority, instead of effective union. . . . The highly developed exterior organization that wins our admiration is but an expression, in accordance with the needs of this present life, of the interior unity of a living entity, so that the Catholic is not only subject to a power but is a member of a body as well, and his legal dependence on this power is to the end that he may have part in the life of that body. His submission in consequence is not an abdication, his orthodoxy is not mere conformity, but fidelity. It is his duty not merely to obey her orders or show deference to her counsels, but to share in a life, to enjoy a spiritual union. *Turpis est omnis pars universo suo non congruens.*[18]

Here de Lubac shows also his Augustinian mind, paraphrasing the Doctor of Grace (*Conf.* 3, 8) in saying that it is truly vile for every part to disagree with its own whole, showing that members of the Mystical Body of Christ are invited to be of one mind and one heart, not out of a slave mentality, but because what the Church shows forth is true and virtuous, the very one for whom all are created. There

---

[18] Ibid., 76.

is no division between Christ and Christian teaching, knowing full well that fidelity to the Church is an expression of one's own love for Christ: "To describe this Church of Christ—which is the holy, catholic, apostolic, Roman Church—there is no name more noble, none more excellent, none more divine, than 'the Mystical Body of Jesus Christ'!"[19]

Louis Bouyer (1913–2004)

A friend of Hans Urs von Balthasar, Joseph Ratzinger, and J.R.R. Tolkien, as well as a co-founder of the international review *Communio*, Bouyer was a former Lutheran minister who entered the Catholic Church in 1939. Known mainly for his work in the history and nature of liturgy as well as his writings on prayer and spirituality, Bouyer was drawn to the charism of the Oratory in France, which allowed him to consecrate the love of liturgy he developed as a "high church" Protestant but also to be immersed in the daily blessings and burdens of a Catholic parish community. One important aspect of his intellectual influence was his deep friendship while in Paris with two of the greatest Russian Orthodox theologians ever, Sergei Bulgakov (d. 1944) and Vladimir Lossky (d. 1958). A mind as keen as von Balthasar's knew of this influence and so dedicated his great work on the patristic thinker dearest to Bulgakov and Lossky, Maximus the Confessor, to Bouyer himself.[20]

Bouyer published a collection of late-life memoirs, recalling the amazing life to which God's providence faithfully led him.[21] Born in Paris during the early rumblings of what would be World War I, Bouyer was quickly recognized as an excellent student and studied divinity at the Sorbonne and was ordained a Lutheran minister in 1936. By his own accounting, he wandered too close to the Church Fathers, Athanasius in particular, and eventually sought reception into that same ancient Body. Drawn to the regularity as well as the interiority of the cloister, Bouyer was regularly seeking extended days

---

[19] De Lubac, *Splendor of the Church*, 125, quoting Pius XII, Encyclical *Mystici Corporis Christi* (June 29, 1943).

[20] See the dedication page in Hans Urs von Balthasar, *Cosmic Liturgy: The Universe according to Maximus the Confessor*, trans. Brian Daley, S.J. (San Francisco: Ignatius Press, 2003).

[21] Louis Bouyer, *Memoirs*, trans. Anne Englund Nash (San Francisco: Ignatius Press, 2015).

of silence and prayer at a Benedictine monastery in Normandy and was eventually received into the Church there, the Abbey of Saint Wandrille, in 1939. Only five years later, he sought permission to enter and was accepted into the Oratory in Paris, teaching at the Institut Catholique for the next few decades.

Bouyer's main contribution to the theology of the Mystical Body is found primarily in his major ecclesiological work, *The Church of God: Body of Christ and Temple of the Holy Spirit*. Published first in 1970, the book was critical of the liturgical liberties taken after the Second Vatican Council (first laid out, quite severely, in his 1969 *Decomposition of Catholicism*). *The Church of God* is therefore an examination of what the Church was meant to be, what she has come to be, and what she must become to reflect Christ most fully. The pivotal chapter, 4 of part 2, is entitled "The Church: The Body of Christ" and synthesizes how members of Christ's Body are never deprived of their own personal characteristics and personal gifts, but are in fact made eternally perfect as their truest selves.

To describe this incorporation and consequent divinization, Bouyer prefers the image of fullness: of being filled with God, what the Oxford Divines referred to as being engodded, what the Greeks knew as *entheos* and the Latins as *plenus Deo*. He writes:

With St. Paul, "fullness" is closely connected with the developments of the mystery in relation to the Church. He uses three complementary and accepted meanings of the word. The first is the "fullness of time". The mystery was revealed at *that* time because it was then that the People of God were ready to attain their fullness in Christ. But Christ, as the Epistle to the Colossians says, is himself the "fullness of God". This means that God is fully revealed and communicated in him. And since the Church—that is, the People of God, who have become his Body—is filled with his divine fullness, he finds in her, in return, his own fulfillment; he reaches in her the fullness of his perfect stature. It is here, then, through the transition of this threefold fullness—of time, of God's own fullness to his People in Christ, and finally of Christ in his People—that the changing of the People of God into the Church/Body of Christ takes place through the revelation of the mystery.[22]

---

[22] Louis Bouyer, *The Church of God: Body of Christ and Temple of the Holy Spirit*, trans. Charles Underhill Quinn (San Francisco: Ignatius Press, 2011), 166.

As a liturgical theologian, Bouyer knew how the Church is to mediate the divine to the human. This is the entire goal of the Church's rites: to transmit sacramentally what Christ himself performed historically, so as to make these otherwise inaccessible truths real in the lives of those who appropriate them mystically.

This is really the heart of Bouyer's classic, *The Church of God*: all saving actions of Christ in first-century Jerusalem must be available to more than those limited number of persons who lived there and then. For this Christ founded his Church, which makes those saving actions realities for those born after Christ's glorious Ascension. In turn, these sacramental actions are executed with only one goal in mind, to let them become appropriated mystically in the lives of God's faithful. Historical-Sacramental-Mystical describes well the synergy between Christ the Head and his Body the Church. This happens most centrally in the Eucharist, as Bouyer attests:

> But it is also from the fact that the Church is the Body of Christ, formed and nourished in the Eucharist, that her permanent historical dependence with respect to Christ, as Head, results—that is, as the source and master of this way in her. This dependence, which is also "mystical" (though its "mystique", like the mystery, remains basically historical), is the object of the ecclesiological developments of the Captivity Epistles. The "body" theme unfolds there in discovery of the "head" theme. And this discovery is made from consideration of the "ministries" that Christ established in the Church and that appear there as a permanent representation of his character and function as Head.[23]

Bouyer follows an ancient pattern in seeing a multiplex Body of Christ: his historical Body, which he received in the womb of Mother Mary, the Eucharistic Body he himself instituted, and the Mystical Body that makes real the Incarnation in every time and place. This is the ultimate "ministry" Christ granted his Church, to continue his enfleshment as one enters ever more sincerely into Christ's own Body.

Like the other writers associated with the *nouvelle théologie*, Bouyer, too, sees that this mystic appropriation is done only because of the Eucharist. This is how the Christ-life is transmitted to all of posterity.

---

[23] Ibid., 167.

Here is where the bodies of salvation history all coalesce: the Lord, his sacraments, his Church: "... a mysterious participation of the whole Church in the Eucharist, in the true body of Christ, but a participation so real that it makes this whole Church one 'body' in a sense that is no less mysterious or real".[24] As a human, we can know Christ's Spirit only by entering his Body; the two are one, and we and he are meant to become one in an analogous manner, diverse members unified by the Holy Spirit thereby making up one Body.

Once again we see how unity and charity are really synonymous in Catholic taxonomy. Think of root words for this phenomenon: as "holy" is derived from the same word as "whole", so are "sane" and "saint" from the same word in Latin, *sanus* or *sanctus*. To be a saint is to be about one thing, Love. This, according to Bouyer, is the "sense and the content of the eucharistic celebration", not only the unification of an individual's divided heart, but the unity of the entire human family bound up together by the Holy Spirit. This is the Church:

> The unity, the communion of the *agape*—of the very love that makes the eternal life of the Father—is the communication of the Spirit of the Father, who is also the Spirit of the Son, because it is the communion in the Body (i.e., in the concrete, total human existence, definitively glorified through the Cross, the Son of God made man), the communion in his Blood (i.e., in his life, which from now on is transfigured, "divinized"). Simultaneously, this vision of faith gives inexhaustible realism and depth to the affirmation that the Church is "the body of Christ". It signifies and certifies that the life of the Church, her concrete life, when she is gathered together especially for celebrating the Eucharist—but also all the activities, collective and individual, which flow from it, within the Christian community itself or in the midst of the hostile world—is the life "with Christ" and "in Christ" about which the Apostle constantly speaks.[25]

The apostolic faith demands this consistency: that the individual lives of the faithful are to be spent both "with Christ" and "in Christ" as they become Christ! This is how the Church is one body, distinct

[24] Ibid., 318.
[25] Ibid., 319–20.

from the Head but never separate. In fact, this is the only true way of keeping diversity within unity.

That is, Bouyer sees the perfect distinctiveness of the Trinity as a consummated unity as the pattern of the Church's life as well. Here he is unique in talking about the Church's having a distinct personality that, like that of each of the Divine Persons, is made to be wholly other-centered. While Father, Son, and Holy Spirit are of course perfect in se, created persons become perfect-ed (or reach "super-existence", as Bouyer holds) through imitation of the divine gift, of pouring oneself out in truth and charity. This is possible, Bouyer suggests, only in the Church, where the example of the saints and the grace of Christ are available.

> But at present, we must underline that this personality, so often attributed by Scripture to the Church, exists only in human persons who have arrived at their perfection, just as the personality of God himself does not exist except in the three Divine Persons. What we are told about that personality of the Church helps us to understand that in entering into the Church—far from melting into one another, all together in Christ—our persons prepare to find in their union with him and their unity in him, brought about by the Holy Spirit, a supernatural superexistence which, as such, is eternal, not only in the sense of perpetual duration but of participation in the very life of the Divine Persons.
>
> This, in turn, brings that reciprocity that we will not be truly ourselves, completely ourselves, as God foresees and wills us from all eternity, *except in the eschatological Church. In her alone* will be revealed that ultimate human personality of the divine-human Being of Christ, the Head and the body—of the Head completing himself in the fullness of the consummated union with his body, the total Christ, Christ everything in all.[26]

We again see how theologians of the *nouvelle théologie* rely on the Augustinian *totus Christus* to explain how perfect diversity can be realized only within absolute unity: constituted for other-centeredness, persons, divine and human, are made to find themselves in the other. This is what the Church can offer that the world cannot.

[26] Ibid., 529–30; my emphasis.

In these ways, Father Bouyer's *The Church of God* still stands as a necessary text in understanding how the Mystical Body informed the best of twentieth-century Catholic theology. The Body of Christ is presented as necessarily hierarchical in structure but is always also positioned evangelically outward for the sanctification of souls, as all humans are called to surrender to the only love that can perfect but not possess, consummate and not control. This is how Bouyer distinguishes the world from the Church, in that only in a community of true love can lovers know their true selves and receive grace to become such. The courage to love is seen throughout all the authors we have chosen to examine in this essay, but one still remains.

Joseph Ratzinger/Pope Emeritus Benedict XVI (b. 1927)

In 1981, Pope John Paul II selected a relatively shy and reserved German theologian to head up the Congregation for the Doctrine of the Faith, but what he was really doing was showing the world the face of Catholic theology for decades to come. Joseph Ratzinger has influenced generations of theologians, biblical scholars, and preachers in countless ways. What was seen as a perhaps rather reserved and overly academic demeanor melted when he preached the funeral Mass for John Paul II in 2005, just weeks before his own pontificate commenced. He took the name Benedict so as to remind the world that we are all in need of the stillness of the monastic way and that *ora et labora* are indispensable tools in our pursuit of holiness. The Mystical Body was not only a common theme through the many messages and teachings of Pope Benedict XVI but also a true thread found in the earliest of Ratzinger's writings.

Joseph Ratzinger was born on Holy Saturday in 1927 in Bavaria to a devout Catholic couple. His only brother, Georg, would also become a diocesan priest (they also had a sister, Maria). Influenced in his early studies by the writings of Romano Guardini (d. 1968, whose popular phrase "The Church is awakening within souls" resonated particularly with Ratzinger), he was selected for an academic apostolate. After his ordination in 1951, he completed his doctorate in theology only two years later, writing on Augustine's understanding of the Church. After his *Habilitation* (the required "second doctorate" in German-speaking universities), he went on to teach in the Catholic Faculties of the universities in Bonn (1959–1963), Münster (1963–1966), and Tübingen (1966–1969). With an internationally recognized acumen, he was next made the vice president of the University of Regensburg, and, in 1972, he, de Lubac, and von Balthasar founded the theological journal *Communio*.

Pope Emeritus Benedict's writings over the years show how the Church grows organically and without rupture. She continues "from within", as he prefers to imagine it: the Body of Christ is formed by integrating freely surrendered persons who know their call to become their truest selves in Christ. Christ without Christian would soon become a sort of historical nostalgia that has nothing to do with the real lives of people today, and Christian without Christ would be just one more form of ideology that inevitably pits persons against one another. The truth is that in forming a body for himself, God has humbly chosen to rely on mortal men and women to complete the intention of his Incarnation. He chooses to need us, to undergo a new *kenosis* in relying on sinners to extend his presence in the world. Without Christ, no group of persons could actualize true community or avoid eventual collapse; without this body, Christ would not be able to reach ever more fully into the human condition and would thus remain a generalization, a perfect and immaculate ideal, but an abstraction all the same. On the Feast of the Annunciation in 1977, Ratzinger was made archbishop of Munich and Freising.

These are the two extremes between which Ratzinger theologizes. As an Augustinian, Ratzinger has always worked from a deep appreciation of the Church as a *corpus permixtum*, a Body that is made up of both saints and sinners. This is a divide that is not facilely discerned between "Church" and "world" or between the "baptized" and the "non-baptized"; it is a break within every divided heart. Despite sin, the Church is the inbreaking of the Kingdom now and, through God's power, will be the eschatological realization of his Kingdom. This is why the Church becomes the locus where God makes himself present, where he invites and calls, and where he is willing to sanctify the sinful but only if they allow him. "He does not simply dispose things as he wishes through his own power. In this creature, man, he has created a free being to stand over and against him, and he now has need of the freedom of this creature, that his Kingdom may truly come to be, that Kingdom which is based, not upon external power, but upon freedom."[27] Like the great bishop of Hippo, Ratzinger, too, stresses the collaboration (in fact, when made bishop, Ratzinger picked as his episcopal motto, "Co-Workers of the Truth" from 3 John 8) between God's sovereign will and our fickle wills. The Divine Persons of the Trinity are other-centered in a loving humility so as to show how we must offer our wills to them; perfect Love never powers or extorts, but is always patient and enticing.

When it comes to the Mystical Body, Ratzinger translates this divided desire for holiness into explicit language of the body. This is why his ecclesiology is so Eucharist-centered, since here the mystery of love is visible and poured out for anyone willing to approach:

> The Eucharist effects our participation in the Paschal Mystery and thus constitutes the Church, the body of Christ. Hence the necessity of the Eucharist for salvation. The Eucharist is necessary in exactly the sense that the Church is necessary, and vice versa. It is in this sense that the saying of the Lord is to be understood: "Unless you eat the flesh of the Son of man and drink his blood, you have no life in you" (Jn 6:53). Yet thereby appears the necessity of a visible Church and of visible, concrete (one might say, "institutional") unity. The inmost mystery of communion between God and man is accessible in the sacrament of the Body of the Risen One; and the mystery, on the other hand, thereby demands our body and draws it in and makes itself a reality in one *Body*. The Church, which is built up on the basis of the Sacrament of the Body of Christ, must for her part likewise be one body and, in fact, be a single body so as to correspond to the uniqueness of Jesus Christ, and the way she corresponds to this is seen, again, in her unity and in remaining in the teaching of the apostles.[28]

Always a pastor of souls, here Ratzinger likens the hylomorphic unity of Jesus Christ, body and soul, to the ecclesial unity of those who bear his name. The reality of the Eucharist must be manifest in the unity of the Christian people. Who will believe, say, the Church's

[27]Joseph Cardinal Ratzinger, *God Is Near Us: The Eucharist, the Heart of Life*, trans. Henry Taylor (San Francisco: Ignatius Press, 2003), 19.

[28]Joseph Ratzinger, "Communion: Eucharist—Fellowship—Mission", in *Pilgrim Fellowship of Faith: The Church as Communion*, trans. Henry Taylor (San Francisco: Ignatius Press, 2002), 82–83.

teaching on Transubstantiation if those who purportedly receive this very Body and Blood of Christ fail to love and be of one mind and heart, as many grains of wheat constitute one host and many grapes come together in one chalice?

Eucharist and ecclesiology are obviously interlocked in Ratzinger's theological macrostructure. This is how he keeps the gathering of Christians from being a merely horizontal or merely human association. While the Ancients (for example, Aesop, *Fable* no. 66; Livy, *Ab Urbe Condita* 2.16.33) used the metaphor of the body to describe political and social harmony, the Christian sense of the Body is different, elevated, divine. It is here the Incarnation has changed how all of mankind is to think of the created order, of the possibility of matter conveying divinity, and of the intended goodness of all visible realities. That is why Ratzinger stresses that the Mystical Body of Christ

> is more than just some term that might be taken from the social pattern of the ancient world to compare a concrete body with a body consisting of many people. This expression takes as its starting point the Sacrament of the Body and Blood of Christ and is therefore more than just an image: it is the expression of the true nature of the Church. In the Eucharist we receive the Body of the Lord and, thus, become one body with him; we all receive the same Body and, thus, ourselves become "all one in Christ Jesus" (Gal 3:28). The Eucharist takes us out of ourselves and into him, so that we can say, with Paul, "It is no longer I who live, but Christ who lives in me" (Gal 2:20). I, yet no longer I—a new and greater self is growing, which is called the one body of the Lord, the Church. The Church is built up in the Eucharist; indeed, the Church *is* the Eucharist. To receive Communion means becoming the Church, because it means becoming one body with him. Of course, this "being one body" has to be thought of along the lines of husband and wife being one: one flesh, and yet two; two, and yet one. The difference is not abolished but is swallowed up in a greater unity.[29]

As we have seen throughout our reflection here, language of the Mystical Body swiftly becomes language of bride and bridegroom. For the truly Catholic mind, the union of two into one is not only

---

[29]Joseph Ratzinger, "Eucharist and Mission", in *Pilgrim Fellowship of Faith*, 102–3.

transformative and covenantal, it is nuptial. From here, reflections on Mary can be expected, she who is the face of the Bridal Church.

The Theotókos, the Spouse of the Holy Spirit, the perfect daughter of the Father, our Lady is the living person and pattern of what the Mystical Body is to be. According to Ratzinger, she is both the Woman appearing in heaven at the end of time (Rev 12:1–6) and the Bride who even now makes the flesh of Christ real (Eph 5:31–32), referring here to the "corporate personality model". Such a model he finds thoroughly biblical and patristic: "recognizing in the Woman, on the one hand, Mary herself and, on the other hand, transcending time, the Church, bride and mother, in which the mystery of Mary spreads out into history".[30] Because God relies on Mary for his humanity, he saves her from all stain of sin. This immaculateness does not remove Mary from who we are, creating an unreachable distance. Rather, in her perfection she provides us sinners with the hope that we too can become who we are truly meant to be as well. She is who we are to become, and that is why her love is not only maternal but ecclesial. For in the Church we continue Mary's Yes insofar as we are freely allowing the Lord to make us more and more into who we were meant to be. The Church is a person, a collection of persons, on her pilgrim way to the Father as she more and more allows herself to become a more befitting temple, an adopted people, and so "the more we become one, the more we are the Church, and the more the Church is herself."[31]

What amazes when one reads Ratzinger on the Church is his optimism. The gift of hope, the power of the pilgrim, is truly his and his pontificate's. No pope had to deal more with the fallout of the filth of the clergy abuse scandals, but Pope Emeritus Benedict never abandoned his theology of the Church as both human and divine. The scandals may sadden, but they do not surprise; they may be cause for alarm but never abandonment. The Church can sustain such lapses of virtue because her sustenance has never been and never will be creaturely. As a young theologian, as the head of the Congregation for the Doctrine of the Faith, and as the Church's beloved Holy

[30] Joseph Ratzinger / Pope Benedict XVI, *Jesus of Nazareth II. Holy Week: From the Entrance into Jerusalem to the Resurrection*, trans. Philip Whitmore (San Francisco: Ignatius Press, 2011), 222.

[31] Joseph Ratzinger / Pope Benedict XVI, *Credo for Today: What Christians Believe*, trans. Michael Miller et al. (San Francisco: Ignatius Press, 2009), 58.

Father, Pope Emeritus Benedict XVI has produced a fruitful theology of the Mystical Body wherein the baptized and the Messiah form one person, an organic unified whole. The entire purpose of the Christ's Incarnation is to recapitulate himself in all mankind; for those who open themselves to this new union of divinity and humanity, an unimaginable new reality takes hold of them: they can now love and rejoice; they can forgive enemies and show mercy to those who persecute them; they can live forever and spend eternity as a beloved child of God.

Pope Emeritus Benedict was very careful to make sure the Church understood that this transformation would not only affect every aspect of human living, but it would ameliorate all of creation. The Christ to whom we are called and for whom we have all been created is not simply "present", he is alive and active. The Mystical Body is apostolic and so on the move; the explosion of the advent of God into the human condition reverberates eternally, and Benedict therefore teaches that in the Church, in the Eucharist, we are invited to do more than receive some static Savior:

> "The Eucharist draws us into Jesus' act of self-oblation. More than just statically receiving the incarnate *Logos*, we enter into the very dynamic of his self-giving." Jesus "draws us into himself". The substantial conversion of bread and wine into his Body and Blood introduces within creation the principle of a radical change, a sort of "nuclear fission", to use an image familiar to us today, which penetrates to the heart of all being, a change meant to set off a process which transforms reality, a process leading ultimately to the transfiguration of the entire world, to the point where God will be all in all (cf. 1 Cor 15:28).[32]

This is the meaning of all of history, and here the conundrums of all ancient thought are reconciled: in Christ, greatness means to serve, to die means to live, and to become fully human means to enter the divine. All opposites are unified now in the Divine's becoming human, and that is how God desires "to construct the meaning of history in our service to one another and with one another.... God

---

[32] Benedict XVI, *Heart of the Christian Life: Thoughts on the Holy Mass* (San Francisco: Ignatius Press, 2008), 71–72, quoting his encyclical *Deus caritas est* (December 25, 2005), no. 13, and his homily at Marienfeld Esplanade (August 21, 2005).

wants to come to men only through other men."[33] The Eucharistic Body of Christ "overflows", enabling God to be "all in all", and not a miserly despot who demands all attention and allegiance.

The entire point of creation is accordingly God's encounter with all things, and this is why the Creator enters his good creation, so as to be able to come to men as a man, thereby injecting his divine presence by means of who we are. All of God's work *ad extra* is aimed at such a divinization of creatures, each in a way fitting its nature. The Eucharist for Benedict is thus the "social sacrament in the highest degree", as it transforms all strata of society and the world.[34]

Pope Emeritus Benedict's theology of the Mystical Body is thus at once a cultural and a cosmic call: he understands that God respects our humanity enough to assume it once and for all to himself in Christ, but also to rely on it to bring his divinity to others through and as each of us. Benedict realizes how the Church is necessarily structured hierarchically but is called to go not only "up" but "out". This was a major theme in his first post-synodal apostolic exhortation, *Sacramentum caritatis* (2007). In many ways, Benedict stands as a fitting summation of the other theologians we have introduced here: a truly expansive mind with a heart made for his flock, he never tires of encouraging sinners to trust that God is in fact at work in who they are and what they are experiencing.

Conclusion

Admittedly we have studied none of these four theologians in the depth each certainly deserves. We have only grazed the depths of what the *nouvelle théologie* still gives the Church today. Yet what this study has done is to introduce the major figures of this theological movement by examining how they all understood the Church as the Mystical Body of Christ, a continuation of his own theandric mission. For each of these theologians, creation has an integrity that is fully understood only by discerning the divine within; of course,

---

[33] Benedict XVI, *What It Means to Be a Christian*, trans. Henry Taylor (San Francisco: Ignatius Press, 2006), 57 and 56.

[34] Joseph Ratzinger, *On the Way to Jesus Christ*, trans. Michael Miller (San Francisco: Ignatius Press, 2004), 118.

some natural truths can be known but never fully without seeing how God is Creator, sustainer, and accomplisher of all that is. All creation therefore "groans" (Rom 8:22) for the wholeness that can come only from the Incarnation. At the center of this panoply of praise stands Adam, who was the *forma futuri* (Rom 5:14) of a New Adam in whom all diseased and disparate mankind would be regathered.

The bloodiest century on human record needed a call to communion perhaps more than any time before. Pope Pius XII's *Mystici Corporis* made this call magisterial, and von Balthasar, de Lubac, Bouyer, and Ratzinger, among others, made it a central point of their theological and pastoral work. The visible Church in which we all live and die is not a simple human institution but a divinely desired continuation of God's own break into human history. Here everything changes, here everything is made new, and the truth of human nature is finally revealed. We are made to become godly, like the One in whose image and likeness we have been made, and through the Mystical Body we are reborn and elevated to the fullest degree our natures can know. Of course none of this would be possible without the Eucharist, and that is why the Consecration and Communion of the liturgy play such an essential role in each of the theologians we examined.

As Christ dwells in the Eucharistic Body from the Last Supper on, he continues to dwell in his Church, his Mystical Body. This concretizes the Christ and now literally makes him my neighbor (Mt 25:31–46); it allows the Church to speak with the voice of Christ (Lk 10:16). The Mystical Body is what provides Church teaching with the magisterial consistency and universality that ever continue to speak to how Christ still guides his true shepherds (Mt 16:18). The Church now becomes the guarantor that the Lord is knowable and able to be encountered on earth; she provides the awesome ability to know the mind of God and to hear his voice. This is the Church, the extension of the Son's own Incarnation, and this is what our four major figures of the *nouvelle théologie* advanced so beautifully.

Mysterium Fidei: On Tradition, Liturgy, and Being at the Service of the Church

Aaron Riches

The year 1968 began, for Father Henri de Lubac, with the unhappy task of examining French translations of the soon-to-be-promulgated *Novus Ordo Missae*.[1] The septuagenarian Jesuit was not impressed. On February 14, he wrote to his friend, the sometime rector of l'Institut Catholique de Toulouse, Msgr. Bruno de Solages: "I have had to examine the proposed translation of the new 'canons' that will be recommended for the Mass: a first glance shows me the same old prejudices. I will oppose their use. This will make me some more firm enemies."[2] Ten days later, he wrote again to Solages, asking him to alert those with whom he had contact in the French episcopate in order to warn them of "the obstinacy with which our translators have sought to suppress every word that recalls the divine initiative of salvation, grace, sin, [or] the mercy of God".[3] Even as de Lubac did not place much hope in moving the bishops to action, he implored Solages to make every effort "before it is too late".[4]

---

[1] Georges Chantraine and Marie-Gabrielle Lemaire, *Henri de Lubac*, vol. 4, *Concile et après-Concile* (1960–1991), "Études Lubaciennes", vol. 9 (Paris: Cerf, 2013), 433–34.

[2] Letter from H. de Lubac to Bruno de Solages, February 14,1968; quoted in Chantraine, *Henri de Lubac*, 4:433–34.

[3] Letter from H. de Lubac to Bruno de Solages, February 24, 1968; quoted in Chantraine, *Henri de Lubac*, 4:434.

[4] It would seem de Lubac finally took his own initiative on the matter. In his *Memoirs*, Louis Bouyer tells of a letter de Lubac submitted to the French-speaking members of the *Consilium* (the commission of about fifty episcopal members and some 150 liturgical experts,

The ordeal was, for de Lubac, a disconcerting confirmation of what he had already perceived in the last year of the Second Vatican Council: a broad "abandonment of tradition"[5] within the Church and a "new ideology ... becoming established" in its place.[6] Confronted with this crisis, what he would later call an *apostasie immanente*,[7] de Lubac was moved after the council to take up what he took as the responsibility of the theologian who, "when the severity of the moment demands it", suspends his academic interests "in order to remember that his entire existence as a theologian, and all the authority his occupation is worth, is based first and foremost on the charge that he has received: to defend and expound the faith of the Church."[8] The decision put de Lubac at odds, not only with the theological culture of his day, but with the postconciliar direction of the Jesuits in France.

De Lubac had learned to suffer before the council under the cloud of suspicion that swirled around his *Surnaturel* (1946).[9] The controversy culminated with the publication of Pope Pius XII's 1950 encyclical, *Humani generis*, which many took as containing a censure aimed directly at him.[10] Until his death, de Lubac refuted this as well as the suggestion that there is a point of doctrinal discord between

---

tasked by the pope with implementing the liturgical reform mandated by the council), a letter addressed to Pope Paul VI. De Lubac's letter noted in detail the intentional inaccuracies of the French translation, which the secretary of the *Consilium*, Fr. Annibale Bugnini, had nevertheless declared in conformity with the Latin text. The scandal of this deliberate tampering, under the authority of Bugnini, led to the French members' decision to add their signatures to de Lubac's letter to the Paul VI. This, it would seem, may have been the catalyst behind Pope Paul's mysterious decision to fire Bugnini abruptly from the commission. See Louis Bouyer, *Memoirs*, trans. Anne Englund Nash (San Francisco: Ignatius Press, 2015), 264–65.

[5] Le Centre d'Archives et d'Études Cardinal Henri de Lubac, no. 58507; quoted in Chantraine, *Henri de Lubac*, 4:217.

[6] Henri de Lubac, *Vatican Council Notebooks*, vol. 2, trans. Anne Englund Nash (San Francisco: Ignatius Press, 2016), 423.

[7] Henri de Lubac, *La Prière du père Teilhard de Chardin, suivi de Teilhard missioniare et apologiste, Œuvres complètes*, vol. 24 (Paris: Cerf, 2007), 386.

[8] Henri de Lubac, "L'Église dans la crise actuelle", *Nouvelle Revue Theologique* 91 (1969): 580–96, at 596.

[9] Henri de Lubac, *Surnaturel: Études historiques* (Paris: Aubier, 1946).

[10] For de Lubac's account, see Henri de Lubac, *At the Service of the Church: Henri de Lubac Reflects on the Circumstances That Occasioned His Writings*, trans. Anne Elizabeth Englund (San Francisco: Ignatius, 1993), 67–74 and 289–300. Cf. Aidan Nichols, O.P., "Thomism and the nouvelle théologie", *The Thomist* 64 (2000): 1–19; Étienne Fouilloux, *Une Église en quête de liberté: La Pensée catholique française entre modernisme et Vatican II (1914–1962)* (Paris: Desclée de Brouwer, 1998), 149–244; and "H. de Lubac au moment de la publication de 'Surnaturel'", *Revue thomiste* 101 (2001): 13–30.

his *Surnaturel* and the encyclical of Pius XII.[11] Nevertheless, in the wake of the encyclical, the General Superior of the Jesuits notified de Lubac that his authorization to teach was withdrawn by the Society, while subsequently a number of his works were removed from Jesuit libraries and circulation. De Lubac suffered this humiliation as a son of Ignatius, that is, obediently and faithfully, and not as a rebel. Now, after the council that had fully rehabilitated him and called him to serve as a *peritus*, de Lubac would learn to suffer again, as an unfashionable defender of the Magisterium and the tradition against the "para-council" and the progressivist zeitgeist of the postconciliar era.

* * *

This little sketch of Henri de Lubac "at the service of the Church"[12] is the basis of the continuity he handed on to his disciple, Father Joseph Fessio, which the younger Jesuit has carried on especially through Ignatius Press. In 1986, under the title *The Splendor of the Church*, Ignatius Press republished Henri de Lubac's seminal 1953 book, *Méditation sur l'Église*.[13] The Ignatius edition bears a dedication written by Father

[11] Henri Cardinal de Lubac [interviewed by Angelo Scola], *Entretien autour de Vatican II: Souvenirs et réflexions* (Paris: Cerf, 1985), 13; and de Lubac, *At the Service of the Church*, 401–2. De Lubac's sense that he was never the pope's target would seem to be substantiated by personal gestures of Pope Pius toward him after the publication of the encyclical (cf. De Lubac, *At The Service of the Church*, 88–90). Significantly, on the point in question, a year before the publication of the pope's encyclical, de Lubac had already specified his theology precisely according to the terms the encyclical would later stipulate. In 1949, de Lubac wrote that, "if God had not so willed it, he need not have given us being, and this being that he has given us he need not have called to vision of himself.... God cannot be compelled to give me being, not from anything within or without. Nor can he be compelled by anything to imprint upon my being a supernatural finality" ("Le Mystère du surnaturel", *Recherches de science religieuse* 36 [1949]: 80–121, 104). Whatever one argues about the implication or interpretation of *Surnaturel*, de Lubac had already before Pius spoke affirmed his own understanding of the *Surnaturel* in terms convertible with the magisterial limit of 1950, against those who "destroy the gratuity of the supernatural order, since God, they say, cannot (*non posse*) create intellectual beings without ordering and calling them to the beatific vision" (*Humani generis*, 26 [Henrich Denzinger, *Compendium of Creeds, Definitions, and Declarations on Matters of Faith and Morals*, ed. Peter Hünermann; English ed. Robert Fastiggi and Anne Englund Nash, 43rd ed. (San Francisco: Ignatius Press, 2012; hereafter cited as *DH*), 3891]).
[12] The English title given by Ignatius Press to de Lubac's *Mémoire sur l'occasion de mes écrits*, *Œuvres complètes*, vol. 33 (Paris: Cerf, 2006).
[13] Published originally as *Méditation sur l'Église* (Paris: Éditions Montaigne, 1953), the English translation was first published as *The Splendour of the Church*, trans. Michael Mason (New York: Sheed and Ward, 1956), and republished in the same translation as *The Splendor of the Church* (San Francisco: Ignatius Press, 1986; repr. 1999). All citations are to the Ignatius Press edition.

Fessio: "to Cardinal de Lubac in the year of his ninetieth birthday". In the dedication, Father Fessio took occasion to register his "personal debt of gratitude" to a "loyal churchman" and "gracious and patient teacher", who "has received all from the Church" and "returned all to the Church".[14] Again in 2008, Father Fessio recapitulated his dedication in the foreword he wrote for Father Rudolf Voderholzer's *Meet Henri de Lubac*. Therein he explained further this debt of gratitude to Father de Lubac: "I count it as one of the great blessings of my life that as a young Jesuit I spent three years with him at the Jesuit theologate in Lyon, France, and acted as his assistant on the occasions when, because of illness, he needed help with his correspondence."[15]

But if the elder Jesuit was for the younger a flesh and blood incarnation of *homo ecclesiasticus*, and so a living example of what it means to be a son of Ignatius, the evidence of the encounter was its generative capacity for the Church. For this was, perhaps, for Father Fessio the key encounter from which flowed the decisive and apostolic mission that constituted Ignatius Press: "It was because of my getting to know Father de Lubac, and through him Fathers von Balthasar, Bouyer and Ratzinger, that ... I gathered together a group of collaborators to found Ignatius Press. The original vision was to make available to the English-speaking world the works of these great theologians."[16]

But if the founding of Ignatius Press was motivated to disseminate the works of these masters (along with their associates, such as Adrienne von Speyr, Jean Daniélou, Yves Congar, and Josef Pieper, among others), the urgency of the task was born of that "severity of the moment" to which de Lubac was moved: the conscious responsibility of the theologian "to defend and expound the faith of the Church". And so, Ignatius Press has been animated from its origin by a mission to propose the tradition and the faith in their splendor against the banality of the postconciliar *apostasie immanente*. A central concern in this regard has had to do with what Cardinal Ratzinger has called the "question of the liturgy",[17] the postconciliar reform of

---

[14] Joseph Fessio, dedication to de Lubac, *Splendor of the Church*, [5].

[15] Joseph Fessio, foreword to Rudolf Voderholzer, *Meet Henri de Lubac: His Life and Work*, trans. Michael J. Miller (San Francisco: Ignatius Press, 2008), 8.

[16] Fessio, foreword to Voderholzer, *Meet Henri de Lubac*, 8.

[17] See Alcuin Reid, O.S.B., ed., *Looking Again at the Question of the Liturgy with Cardinal Ratzinger: Proceedings of the July 2001 Fontgombault Liturgical Conference* (Farnborough: St. Michael's Abbey Press, 2003).

the liturgy de Lubac encountered at the beginning of 1968. Thus my purpose in this essay, which I have written to honor Father Joseph Fessio, is to offer some thoughts on the *traditio* that is the basis of authentic liturgy and so the mystagogical basis of the sacred encounter with the Savior. Additionally, I wish to show that much of the reform of the liturgy, as it has been realized in the life of the Church these last fifty years, is nothing if not an evidence of what de Lubac referred to at the end of the council as the occlusion of *fides christiana* by *conceptio christiana*,[18] that is, the reduction of the life of faith to a conceptual abstraction.

In doing so, I hope also (however obliquely) to gesture toward a spiritual path beyond the crisis. This path, for a layman, cannot be contingent on either a "restoration" of the traditional liturgy or a "reform of the reform" of the ordinary form of the Mass, but rather must rest on an internal disposition toward the liturgical self-gift of Jesus and the encounter with him in the sacred rites. I take as my point of departure not only the thought of Father de Lubac but also an occasional yet crucial writing of Father Fessio on the liturgy, along with other Ignatius Press authors, in particular, Cardinal Ratzinger, Father Uwe Michael Lang, and German novelist Martin Mosebach.

The essay is divided into six parts: (1) The Original *Traditio* and *Conceptio Christiana*; (2) Against the Postconciliar Caesura; (3) The Mass of Vatican II; (4) *Versus Deum per Iesum Christum*; (5) Christology and Liturgy; and (6) The Way of Beauty and the Cross.

1. The Original Traditio and Conceptio Christiana

In the opening pages of *Méditation sur l'Église*, de Lubac argues that in the most traditional periods of Church history "the monuments of Tradition were not things to be examined minutely with all the resources of scholarship and the critical method."[19] In such epochs, the tradition (and her liturgy, which is both her heart and conduit) was understood as it was lived, not as something to be looked upon with the categorical gaze of a modern academic, but as something to be received with childlike gratitude. There was nothing abstract

---

[18] De Lubac, *Vatican Council Notebooks*, 2:336.
[19] De Lubac, *Splendor of the Church*, 15.

about the tradition; it was a carnal fact of life and the means of living salvation. People of such epochs were so "possessed ... [by] the thing-in-itself, they were ... freed from the need for conceptualizing it."[20]

Neither the faithful nor clerics knew much about the circumstantial origins of the particular rites or rubrics of the liturgy. Devotions and prayers were not primarily sought in books, nor were they intentionally memorized; rather, they were unconsciously absorbed by the hearts of a people who were formed in a rhythm of constant repletion. This is not to say that the freedom of the individual human heart was not in dramatic play; always and in every epoch, to assent to apostolic faith is a labor of the freedom of the "I", who must make personal use of the tradition in a concrete human experience.[21] But the tradition as a factor of life, as *the* factor of life, was not a thing to be schematized or sorted; these "men were not in the habit of questioning themselves about Tradition."[22]

The tradition, in such epochs, was a fact like language, learned by a child on the lap of a parent or learned by a foreigner through the patient friendship of a native speaker. To receive the tradition was to receive it in its entirety, a texture of life received through a carnal and proximate other. There was no way of skipping over five or six generations to go back and get a "purer" version of the tradition, something closer to the "original". Rather, the ancient and mysterious "origin", the *principium*, was understood as a contemporary presence, held within the tension of the tradition's present and living texture, which embodied the memory of a cumulative and concrete history. And so to receive the tradition as it was, was to come into carnal contact with the Person of Jesus Christ now, who by his Incarnation had condescended to pass through the hands of the preceding generation (with all of its accretions, fumbles, and futilities). The tradition, thus, was more than a "transmission" of teachings, prayers, and liturgical rubrics: it was the handing on of the substance of the faith itself: the Mystery made flesh in our midst.

The basis of this experience of the tradition lay concretely in the original *traditio* Jesus himself made in the gift of handing himself over

[20] Ibid.
[21] Cf. Luigi Giussani, *The Religious Sense*, trans. John Zucchi (Montreal and Kingston: McGill-Queen's University Press, 1997), 37–40.
[22] De Lubac, *Splendor of the Church*, 15.

to the Father in the Spirit.[23] And so, the *sacra traditio* was bound both to the Person of Christ and to the generative means by which he had given himself on the night in which he was betrayed, thereby establishing his Paschal Mystery as the means by which his Incarnation would be handed down (and so continue) from generation to generation until the end of the world (cf. Mt 28:20). And so, as de Lubac put it, for the people of these epochs, all "the richness of Tradition was theirs; they brought it to flower and handed it on without very much conscious reflection on what they were doing."[24]

Long before Pope Paul VI commissioned the reform of the Roman Rite that ultimately produced the *Novus Ordo*, the unity of tradition and life had already been fissured. According to Martin Mosebach, this fissuring of life and tradition in the liturgy occurred long before the council, when a "unspiritual, legalistic, and scholastic [*sic*][25] way of looking at the things [of the liturgy]" came into

---

[23] Hans Urs von Balthasar and Luigi Giussani, *El Compromiso del Cristiano en el Mundo* (Madrid: Encuentro, 1978), 103.

[24] De Lubac, *Splendor of the Church*, 15. Of course this is a rather romantic description and raises the question of when and where the tradition was so organic to life. But the real point de Lubac is trying to make has to do not so much with a romantic ideal lost (which would be unhistorical) as with a premodern receptivity of authentic Christian life to tradition, that is, a relation not determined by the critical method of modern rationalism. Cf. Peter Kwasniewski, *Noble Beauty, Transcendent Holiness: Why the Modern Age Needs the Mass of the Ages* (Kettering, Ohio: Angelico Press, 2017), 37–50, esp. at 38–39: "The rejection of tradition and the cult of change embodies a peculiarly modern attitude of 'mastery over tradition,' which is the social equivalent of Baconian and Cartesian 'mastery over nature.' The combination of capitalism and technology has allowed us to abuse the natural world, treating it as raw material for exploitation, in pursuit of the satisfaction of our selfish desires. In a similar way, the influence of rationalism and individualism has tempted us to treat Catholic tradition as if it were a collection of isolated facts from which we, who are autonomous and superior, can make whatever selection pleases us. In adopting this arrogant stance, we fail to recognize, with creaturely humility, that our rationality is socially constituted and tradition-dependent. By failing to honor our *antecessores*, we fail to live according to our political nature and our Christian dignity as recipients of a concrete historical revelation that endures and develops organically over time and space. The psalm verse comes to mind: 'Know ye that the Lord, he is God: he made us, and not we ourselves' (Ps 99[100]:3). *Ipse fecit nos et non ipsi nos.* We do not make ourselves, nor do we make our religion or our liturgies; we *receive* our existence, we receive our faith, we receive our worship. Tradition comes to us from outside ourselves, before and beyond us. It unambiguously expresses our dependence on God—as creatures, as Christians, as coheirs with the saints. An heir is one who inherits, not the 'self-made man' of capitalism."

[25] I do not think this is the right use of word "scholastic". I think what Mosebach means is a particular variant of Neoscholastic or late-Scholastic rationalism, which is certainly not the mystical ethos of classical Scholasticism, as represented by Thomas Aquinas or Bonaventure.

dominance, eclipsing the centrality of the experience of the total *forma* of the liturgy.[26] Elsewhere Mosebach calls this reductive and fragmentary approach a "Roman-juristic" attitude, which he argues is "completely foreign to the first Christian millennium that formed the [Roman] rite".[27] Mosebach's judgment is more or less convertible with what Catherine Pickstock has elsewhere called the "evacuation of liturgy", the genesis of which she claims can be located in the thirteenth century, in shifts in our understanding of being.[28] What ultimately happened, according to both, is that the consistency of the wholeness of the liturgical action, the "complete consort dancing together",[29] was fragmented and then lost from view. And so, a new "reduction" and "formal minimalism"—we can say a *conceptualization* of the Mass—began to take hold, in which the ultimate liturgical question concerned now only "whether the minimal prerequisites for the validity of a certain Mass" have been met or not.[30] By contrast: "Ancient Christian belief [East and West] understood the entire liturgy in all its parts as 'consecrating.' The presence of Christ in the liturgy is not centered only on the words of

[26] Martin Mosebach, *The Heresy of Formlessness: The Roman Liturgy and Its Enemy*, trans. Graham Harrison (San Francisco: Ignatius Press, 2006), 37.

[27] Martin Mosebach, "For Pope Benedict XVI, on His Ninetieth Birthday", foreword to Kwasniewski, *Noble Beauty, Transcendent Holiness*, xi–xxvi, at xx–xxi.

[28] Catherine Pickstock, *After Writing: On the Liturgical Consummation of Philosophy* (Oxford: Blackwell, 1997), 121–66. Pickstock argues that these shifts in our conception of being began occurring already as early as the thirteenth century, with Duns Scotus' univocal conception of being. This, she claims, undermined the participatory vision of *analogia entis*, found in Thomas Aquinas. Clarifying the above-cited passage of *After Writing*, see also Pickstock's "Duns Scotus: His Historical and Contemporary Significance", *Modern Theology* 21 (2005): 543–74. It should be noted that Mosebach and Pickstock differ interestingly on their assessment here of the standardization of the traditional Latin by the Missal of Pope Pius V. According to Mosebach (*Heresy of Formlessness*, 194), "The Tridentine Missal no longer assumes that there is an all-pervading Catholic culture that supports the cult because it springs from it." Pickstock would agree. The event of the Missal is a sign for both of a cultural crisis that directly threatened the life of traditional liturgy (the impact of the Reformation, the scientific revolution, etc.). But whereas Mosebach tends to celebrate the event of the Missal as offering a "Noah's Ark" in which the Catholic cult can live in the crisis of a culture that no longer necessarily supports the cult, Pickstock tends to see the Missal as a further move toward the "spacialization" of modernity.

[29] T. S. Eliot, *Four Quartets*, "Little Gidding", V, 10, in *The Poems of T. S. Eliot: The Annotated Text*, 2 vols., ed. Christopher Ricks and Jim McCue (London: Faber & Faber, 2015), 1:208.

[30] Mosebach, "For Pope Benedict XVI", xxi.

consecration in the strict sense, but runs through the entire liturgy in different forms till it experiences its summit in the form of the sacrificial death made present in the consecration."[31]

The loss of the liturgical sense of the *forma* of the whole of the liturgy, what Mosebach terms a "Roman-juristic" attitude, is the "wrong path" against which Joseph Ratzinger warned.[32] According to Ratzinger, the crisis of the postconciliar liturgy is rooted in "a Neoscholastic sacramental theology that is disconnected from the living form of the Liturgy".[33] What was lost from view, long before the council, was the total encounter of the mystagogical event in the irreducibility of the liturgy's symphonic factors. Now the theology of the Mass became so dominated by "the categories of 'validity' and 'minimal requirements'"[34] that the *forma* received through the tradition became somehow secondary (even while it may have remained intact for some time to come). The vital texture of the rite became subordinated to a more or less ahistorical and acultural gaze on the sacrament as the essential "kernel", to which all else was either reducible, extrinsic, or decorative.[35] The liturgy as a complex gesture of beauty was occulted by a conceptualization of the sacramental life, now more or less divorced from human postures and gestures, architecture, images, music, and the tastes and smells that once constituted the organic link of the liturgy to history and the common culture of the Church. Reduced to "validity" and "minimal requirements", the greatest "monuments of Tradition" could now be "examined minutely with all the resources of scholarship and the critical method". With the postconciliar revision of the Mass, as de Lubac discovered to his great vexation in 1968, not only was the greatest monument of tradition, the Holy Mass, being laid upon the table of theoretical examination, it was being dissected, examined, and reconstructed.

[31] Ibid., xxii.

[32] Joseph Ratzinger, foreword to Alcuin Reid, O.S.B., *The Organic Development of the Liturgy: Principles of Liturgical Reform and Their Relation to the Twentieth-Century Liturgical Movement Prior to the Second Vatican Council*, 2nd ed. (San Francisco: Ignatius Press, 2005), 11.

[33] Ibid.

[34] Mosebach, *Heresy of Formlessness*, 37.

[35] See Tracey Rowland, *Ratzinger's Faith: The Theology of Pope Benedict XVI* (Oxford: Oxford University Press, 2009), 125–26.

The result was the *Novus Ordo* liturgy, which consists both of the *Missale Romanum* of Paul VI and its translation into the culture and life of postconciliar Catholicism. The experience of this new liturgy was overwhelmingly disjunctive, effectively breaking with the *forma* in which the original *traditio* of Jesus had been lived in the Roman Rite for more or less a millennium and a half. To be sure, this event of disjuncture consists of two rather distinct aspects: (1) the text of the new *Missale Romanum*, which is in Latin and has few rubrics; and (2) the cultural realization of this Missal as a liturgy, which includes the various vernacular translations and the new common norms of celebrating the rite, which are determined overwhelmingly by extra rubrical norms (because the rite itself contains so little in the way of rubrics). These two aspects, while experienced as a unity by lay-people, are not only distinguishable; but more, the former, the text of the Missal, does not necessarily entail the experience of the latter, the cultural norm according to which it is realized. Notwithstanding, what ultimately occurred, according to Ratzinger, was that "in the place of liturgy as the fruit of development came fabricated liturgy."[36] To borrow de Lubac's dichotomy, the liturgy of *fides christiana* was replaced by a liturgy of *conceptio christiana*. And so the texts de Lubac examined in 1968 were not so much the sacred things of *traditio*, received with childlike gratitude through the hands of the preceding generation, as they were the products of theological construction and discovery. To be sure, some theological insights of the reform were well founded and reasoned, and some legitimate pastoral concerns that motivated all of this were not unjustified. There were also acts of important *ressourcement*, rediscoveries of treasures of Christian antiquity long forgotten. But the ultimate product of the reform could not help but risk being (or becoming) less a fact of faith "traditioned" and more the result of human composition,[37] and so a "fabricated liturgy". Hence, the experience of the liturgical reform was often that of a caesura in the mystical life of the Church.

---

[36]Joseph Cardinal Ratzinger, preface to the French edition of Monsignor Klaus Gamber, *The Reform of the Roman Liturgy: Its Problems and Background*, trans. Klaus Grimm (Fort Collins, Col.: Roman Catholic Books, 2007), printed on the back cover of the English edition.

[37]Cf. Bouyer, *Memoirs*, 255–61.

2. Against the Postconciliar Caesura

The liturgy, for de Lubac, was the mystical nexus of the Church's life. As he insisted, the Church herself is constituted through the Mass she celebrates, "as cause to each other".[38] And so the Church gives the Eucharist, while she in turn is generated (and so constituted) by the sacrament.[39] The Church, in other words, lives from the heart of her liturgical life, which is her résumé, repetition, and participation in the original *traditio* of Jesus. The whole mission of the Church flows from and is contained within her celebration of the sacred liturgy. And so, as *Sacrosanctum concilium* would later put it, the liturgy is the Church's source and summit (*culmen et fons*).[40] If the Church truncates or fragments this gesture, then she begins to separate herself reflexively from her own life, from what has been "traditioned" to her. If she conceptualizes the source of her life as something separate from her, distances it so as to reinvent it, or acts to dominate what has been "traditioned" to her—then she risks no longer *receiving* the ultimate gift of her being, the gift that makes possible the basis of her very existence: her correspondence with the original *traditio*. Only a disposition of radical receptivity to the sacred action, as an event and form the Church herself cannot conceive or "make" but only receive and "give", is capable of safeguarding her from a hubris that would distort her at the center of her inmost being.

And yet this distancing is precisely what de Lubac seems to have encountered that February in 1968. In the French translations of the "new canons", he saw an "obstinacy" that would "suppress" the very essence of the original *traditio* of Jesus himself: in the negation of "every word that recalls the divine initiative of salvation, grace, sin,

---

[38] De Lubac, *Splendor of the Church*, 133.

[39] This thesis, that the Eucharist makes the Church (and vice versa), first appeared in 1938 in de Lubac's *Catholicisme*; see *Catholicism: Christ and the Common Destiny of Man*, trans. Lancelot Sheppard and Sister Elizabeth Englund, O.C.D. (San Francisco: Ignatius Press, 1988), 100n69. The thesis was developed in 1944 in *Corpus Mysticum* (*The Eucharist and the Church in the Middle Ages*, trans. Gemma Simmonds, C.J. [London: SCM, 2006]), before it was reiterated in 1953 in *Méditation sur l'église*. It informs certain passages of *Lumen gentium* (cf. 3, 11) and is crucial to Pope John Paul II's final encyclical, *Ecclesia de Eucharistia* (cf. 21–26).

[40] Second Vatican Council, Constitution on the Sacred Liturgy *Sacrosanctum concilium* (December 4, 1963; hereafter cited as *SC*), 10 (*DH* 4010).

[or] the mercy of God".[41] In his first encounter with the *Novus Ordo*, de Lubac did not see the evidence of the original *traditio* handed on through the ages; he saw a conceptualization of the tradition that threatened to put sociological concerns in the place of genuine theology, human activism in the place of authentic adoration, the gathered community in the place of the sacred encounter with the Savior. In short, he saw an accomplishment of *conceptio christiana* occulting the life of *mysterium fidei*: he saw an over-determination of that humble receptivity that allows the Church to live and be who she is.

The general triumph of *conceptio christiana* after the council was, in large measure, linked by de Lubac to the ascendancy of academic theology and the putative "freedom" from the Magisterium that academic theology sought to declare for itself in the name of scholarship.[42] When in 1968 the journal *Concilium* published the so-called "Nijmegen Declaration", the *Déclaration pour la liberté des théologiens*, de Lubac saw a spectacle "completely improper and demagogic".[43] A petition addressed ultimately to the pope, the *Déclaration* conceived the "freedom" of theological inquiry as "freedom from" the Magisterium. The office of pope and bishop, the *Déclaration* avowed, "cannot and must not supersede, hamper and impede the teaching task of theologians as scholars", while claiming that "the freedom of theologians, and theology in the service of the church, regained by Vatican II, must not be jeopardized again."[44] Composed by the editors of the journal, the document was signed by, among others, some of the most eminent *peritii* of the council, including Hans Küng, Yves Congar, Karl Rahner, Jean Daniélou, Joseph Ratzinger, and M.-D. Chenu. De Lubac's name was conspicuously absent from the *Déclaration*. Congar had approached him with an invitation to sign, but the Jesuit categorically refused to put his name on what he judged a piece of "propaganda".[45]

[41] Letter from H. de Lubac to Bruno de Solages, February 24, 1968; quoted in Chantraine, *Henri de Lubac*, 4:434.

[42] De Lubac, "L'Église dans la Crise Actuelle", 596.

[43] See de Lubac, *At the Service of the Church*, 366–68, at 366, and Chantraine, *Henri de Lubac*, 4:440–48. Cf. Hans Küng, *My Struggle for Freedom: Memoirs* (London: Continuum, 2002), 389–91; and John L. Allen, Jr., *Pope Benedict XVI: A Biography of Joseph Ratzinger* (London: Continuum, 2005), 67.

[44] As quoted in Allen, *Pope Benedict XVI*, 67.

[45] De Lubac, *At the Service of the Church*, 367.

What the authors and signatories of the *Concilium* petition had lost from view, according to de Lubac, was the essential ecclesial form of the theological vocation. That vocation, for him, could never consist in "demanding ... freedoms and guarantees ... in a unilateral way", because it is a vocation essentially rooted in a "duty to preach the Word, in season and out".[46] The true vocation of theology has nothing to do with the dichotomy between servile obedience and negative freedom: it consists, rather, in the freedom of readiness and receptivity at the service of the Church. The true theologian is one who recognizes that he has received "all" from the original *traditio*, handed down through the life of the Church, to which he is ready to give "all" in return.

What was the cause of the loss of this ecclesial disposition in theology? In part, the rise of rationalism, which in the realm of theology led to a more formalistic and legalistic approach, with a new aspiration to conceptual clarity and syllogistic logic, coupled with the rise of an academic "archaeologism"[47] as a substitute for tradition.

---

[46] Ibid.

[47] "Archaeologism" stands for what Pope Pius XII warned against in his encyclical *Mediator Dei* on the Sacred Liturgy (November 20, 1947; hereafter cited as *MD*). Therein he wrote: "it is a wise and most laudable thing to return in spirit and affection to the sources of the sacred liturgy [presumably here he means through scholarship]. For research in this field of study, by tracing it back to its origins, contributes valuable assistance towards a more thorough and careful investigation of the significance of feast-days, and of the meaning of the texts and sacred ceremonies employed on their occasion" (*MD* 62). Scholarship, in other words, according to Pius, can contribute something important to our understanding of the tradition; it ought not be simply set aside. Pius' argument here is basically convertible with the argument of Benedict/Ratzinger in *Jesus of Nazareth* concerning the use of the historical-critical method in Catholic study of the Bible: it is permissible and useful, and even indispensable, but it cannot be determinative. And so Pius concludes: "But it is neither wise nor laudable to reduce everything to antiquity by every possible device" (*MD* 62). Why is it unwise to reduce everything to antiquity? Why is "archaeologism" ultimately contrary to Christianity? Because, on the one hand, "archaeologism" suggests that access to the "origin" (the *principium* who is Jesus Christ) is reducible to temporal proximity, so that the closer a gesture or idea is to the historical origin of the Christian claim, the purer and more authentic it must be, so that ever since the beginning, the history of Christianity has been a process of declension. But also "archaeologism" elevates the archeological method of study and discovery *over* the method of *traditio*, which is the method elected by God himself in the Incarnation. The substance of the Christian claim and the Christian event is not a thing scholarship can achieve; it is a carnal fact that must be received. Hence Pius warns against "exaggerated zeal for antiquity in matters liturgical" (*MD* 203), which he understands to be tantamount to negating the method of tradition and so the truth of the faith. Cf. Louis Bouyer, *Liturgical Piety* (Notre Dame, Ill.: University of Notre Dame Press, 1955), 20.

This occurred at the expense of the more mystical disposition of the Fathers and early Scholastics, for whom the wisdom of theology was not so much its prowess to achieve conceptual clarity as its capacity to deepen the disposition of the heart in love, an openness to the sacred presence "traditioned".[48]

Already before the council de Lubac lamented how the "orthodoxy" of the Roman school tended to an arid and overly systematic "integrism",[49] in the sense of a closed system of theological reasoning impervious to the tensions of the paradoxes of faith.[50] He had complained further of the limited sense of tradition that held sway in the Roman school, which consisted, not in intimate dialogue with the Fathers and great masters of the Scholastic period, but rather in a series of reactive citations of modern papal documents.[51]

But if the old Roman school had tended to aridity and abstraction, he intuited clearly that the triumphant postconciliar progressivism, which he called an "inverse integrism",[52] was far more dangerous. Accordingly, de Lubac judged the postconciliar crisis "a spiritual crisis in the Church, such as she has hardly been shaken before".[53] The modernist crisis now seemed to him a mere foreshadowing of what was to come:

> More serious [than the modernist crisis] is the present [postconciliar] crisis. Without having anything to do with the council [that is, with the letter of her texts or the intention of the Council Fathers], [the present crisis] risks making an abortion of it. Already, here and there,

[48] Cf. Adrienne von Speyr, *John*, vol. 1, *The Word Becomes Flesh*, trans. Lucia Wiedenhover, O.C.D., and Alexander Dru (San Francisco: Ignatius Press, 2015), 61.

[49] This conceptual "integrism" can be understood as a theoretical expression of the politics of *Nacionalcatolicismo*, in the sense that an integral ideal comes to govern the whole in the place of the Person of Jesus and the encounter with him. In both cases, a scheme (an arrangement of Church-state relations or a conception) replaces the unequalizable event, which is the gaze of the Savior on the sinner. Cf. Hans Urs von Balthasar, *Who Is a Christian?* trans. Frank Davidson (San Francisco: Ignatius Press, 2014).

[50] See Chantraine, *Henri de Lubac*, 4:243–54.

[51] Henri de Lubac, *Vatican Council Notebooks*, vol. 1, trans. Andrew Stefanelli and Anne Englund Nash (San Francisco: Ignatius Press, 2015), 31.

[52] Cf. de Lubac, *Carnets*, 1:308–9. Here the *Nacionalcatolicismo* of the old "integrist" political settlement becomes secular liberal progressivism. In both cases, the role of the Church is that of a handmaid to the modern state and the political program determined by it.

[53] De Lubac, *La Prière du père Teilhard de Chardin*, 382.

under the name of the postconciliar Church or the "new Church", there is another Church, other than that of Jesus Christ, which sometimes seeks to establish itself.... [The situation] risks infusing infidelity into the very heart of the Church of Christ. The danger now is no longer merely that of an apostasy through immanence (*apostasie par immanentisme*), as was rightly diagnosed by Jacques Maritain, but of an immanent apostasy (*apostasie immanente*).[54]

So while de Lubac judged the old Roman "standard theology" (in its emphasis on textbook systematic clarity) as tending to reduce the mystery of faith to a *conceptio christiana*, the new progressivism represented not merely an abstraction from the fundamental basis of faith, but an agenda diametrically opposed to it: "under the ruse of merely changing the language, the very essence of the faith itself is evacuated."[55]

At its essence, the theological loss of the sense of *fides christiana* from which the progressivism of the postconciliar crisis issued could be seen nowhere more concretely than in the reduction of the sense of the mystical nature of the Church. The Church's mystical nature is the living reality in which the life of faith is sustained and fed. The loss of this was evidenced, for de Lubac, in the cavalier manner with which the council was being construed as a caesura, delineating discrete "Churches", one preconciliar the other postconciliar. For de Lubac, there could be no "Church of Vatican II", no "Church of Trent", nor one of "Pius X" or of "Paul VI"—there is "only one Church, the Church of all time, the Church of Jesus Christ".[56]

This conviction set de Lubac against, on the one hand, the "integrist" position of Archbishop Marcel Lefebvre, who characterized the council as the Church's "French Revolution".[57] While on the

---

[54] Ibid., 383–86.

[55] Henri de Lubac, *L'Église dans la crise actuelle*, in *Paradoxe et mystère de l'Église, suivi de L'Église dans la crise actuelle, Œuvres complètes*, vol. 9 (Paris: Cerf, 2010), 234.

[56] Henri de Lubac, *More Paradoxes*, trans. Anne Englund Nash (San Francisco: Ignatius Press, 2002), 38.

[57] See Archbishop Marcel Lefebvre, *An Open Letter to Confused Catholics*, trans. Father M. Crowdy (London: Fowler Wright Books, 1986); and *I Accuse the Council*, 2nd ed. (Kansas City, Mo.: Angelus Press, 1998). The relationship between Lefebvre and de Lubac is more interesting than most people know and breaks with schematic prejudices about them. At the council, they were opposed, in the sense that they represented two different "positions", Lefebvre linked to the *Coetus Internationalis Patrum*, de Lubac the leader of the so-called *nouvelle théologie*. Their theological differences came acutely into play around the question of

other hand, it also set him against the progressivism of the theology associated with the *Concilium* school, such as that of Karl Rahner and Hans Küng, who celebrated the council as a watershed in the life of the Church, bringing to an end the "Pian" order and ushering in a new epoch of Church history.[58]

De Lubac opposed these two conceptions of the council-as-rupture, insisting, rather, that the Church "is never renewed except in order to remain herself".[59] The only legitimate understanding of the council, thus, requires a hermeneutic of the unity of faith, according to which the authenticity of the council's teaching is determined by its continuity and authentic re-form of the tradition it receives. The council must take its place, therefore, in the tension of a simultaneous

---

religious freedom, but also regarding the meaning and distinction of "pastoral" as opposed to "dogmatic" theology, especially as it tended to repeat the old grace-nature debate (cf. de Lubac, *Carnets*, 1:435 and 2:198–99; *More Paradoxes*, 45–46; and Marcel Lefebvre, *Religious Liberty Questioned—The Dubia: My Doubts about the Vatican II Declaration of Religious Liberty* [Kansas City, Mo.: Angelus Press, 2001]). After the council, however, they were alike dismayed by the postconciliar crisis in France; and it seems they came mutually to recognize the authenticity of the man of Christian faith, the one in the other. While de Lubac criticized Lefebvre's tacit rejection of the council, he conceded that if the crisis that followed the council was in fact the direct result of the council, Lefebvre would be right to reject it. It seems de Lubac may have even visited at some point the Fraternity's seminary at Écône. In 1973, de Lubac wrote in a letter to Georges Chantraine that while he did not agree with the "integrist" spirit of Lefebvre, at the seminary he had founded at Écône he had found there "a moral sanity [*Nota bene!*], an apostolic élan, and a spirit of prayer that greatly mitigate the defects of the institution" (Chantraine, *Henri de Lubac*, 4:592). In 1976, as tension mounted around the "affaire d'Écône", de Lubac wrote to Cardinal Renard that if schism were to come, the blame for it would have to be put at the feet of the bishops of France, and not at the feet of Lefebvre and the Priestly Fraternity of St. Pius X (see Chantraine, *Henri de Lubac*, 4:593). Little known, perhaps, is the fact that de Lubac and Lefebvre did correspond after the council. In one letter, which cannot but have been written by a man of faith who recognized it in the other, Lefebvre begins to de Lubac: "Your amiable letter has touched me deeply, for your love for the holy Church is well known, and I do not doubt it in what you have written me" (see Chantraine, *Henri de Lubac*, 4:595). In 1968, Lefebvre wrote to de Lubac on the occasion of reading his *Athéisme et sens de l'homme: une double requête de Gaudium et spes* (1968): "I have read with great interest and much joy this precious little volume, which clarifies many of the dangerously controversial points of our day and resolves numerous ambiguities and misunderstandings. I will not fail to recommend it … to my priests…. [I]n this time of troubled spirits, for my part, I strongly hope that many works of this kind and in this vein might appear" (Chantraine, *Henri de Lubac*, 4:463).

[58] Cf. Karl Rahner, "Basic Theological Interpretation of the Second Vatican Council", in *Theological Investigations*, vol. 20, trans. Edward Quinn (London: Darton, Longman & Todd, 1981), 77–90; Hans Küng, "The Council: End or Beginning?" *Commonweal* 81 (1965): 631–37.

[59] De Lubac, *More Paradoxes*, 38.

order of the whole of the Magisterium, whose one aim is, not to invent or even "develop", but to serve and safeguard the space of the saving encounter with Christ.[60] In this way, de Lubac anticipated, in the 1980s, what Pope Benedict XVI would later clarify to the Roman Curia in December 2005: that the "hermeneutic of discontinuity and rupture" is a false and fallacious hermeneutic of the council; the only legitimate hermeneutic is that of "the 'hermeneutic of reform,' of renewal in the continuity of the one subject-Church".[61] For both Benedict and de Lubac, the unity of the Christian experience requires this, because, as de Lubac put it in 1985, "the development of doctrine is never a relative progress, since the faith that has come from the apostles was transmitted to the Church 'once and for all'."[62]

If the Church "is never renewed except in order to remain herself", then likewise the liturgy develops organically only to remain what it has always been—the privileged place of the encounter with Christ and the means of being united with the perfect sacrifice he renders to the Father in the Spirit. The unitive experience of the Catholic faith is the *mysterium fidei*, so that, regarding the liturgy, the hermeneutic of continuity must apply again, only now at an even higher pitch of intensity. This is the key to the logic of Pope Benedict XVI's *Summorum pontificum*, with the insistence that the *Usus Antiquior* was "never abrogated",[63] for two reasons: (1) because in "the history of the liturgy there is growth and progress, but no rupture"; and (2) what "earlier generations held as sacred, remains sacred and great for us too, and it cannot be all of a sudden entirely forbidden or even considered harmful."[64] And this means, according to Benedict, that

---

[60] Cf. Luigi Giussani, *Why the Church?* trans. Viviane Hewitt (Montreal & Kingston: McGill-Queen's University Press, 2006), 172–74.

[61] Benedict XVI, "What Has Been the Result of the Council?" in Norman Tanner, S.J., ed., *Vatican II: The Essential Texts* (New York: Image, 2012), 3–13, at 4; also present on the Vatican website under Benedict XVI, Address to the Roman Curia Offering Them His Christmas Greetings (December 22, 2005).

[62] De Lubac, *Entretien autour de Vatican II*, 44.

[63] Benedict XVI, Apostolic Letter Given Motu Proprio *Summorum pontificum* on the Use of the Roman Liturgy Prior to the Reform of 1970 (July 7, 2007; hereafter cited as *SP*), art. 1 (*DH* 5109).

[64] Benedict XVI, Letter of Benedict XVI to the Bishops on the Occasion of the Publication of the Apostolic Letter "Motu Proprio Data" *Summorum pontificum* on the Use of the Roman Liturgy Prior to the Reform of 1970 (July 7, 2007).

the *Usus Antiquior* and the *Novus Ordo* are not "two rites" (even if phenomenologically they may be experienced and even function as such),[65] but are "two usages of the one Roman rite".[66] This must be the case, since, if the *Novus Ordo* is a legitimate liturgy, this legitimacy does not arise *sui iuris*, but from within the *traditio* in which the *Novus Ordo* is rooted. The *traditio* originates from the self-gift of Jesus (cf. 1 Cor 11:23–24), from whom the Christian truth is "traditioned" into

---

[65] This is not really to disagree with what Robert Spaemann argues in what I take to be a decisive intervention: "'The Reform of the Reform' and the Old Roman Rite", in Reid, *Looking Again at the Question of the Liturgy*, 115–23. The essence of what Spaemann argues concerns the experience of the *Usus Antiquior* and the *Novus Order*, which very obviously differ much more than do the experiences of hearing or celebrating, for example, the Dominican Rite and the traditional Roman Rite. This is the kernel of the liturgical crisis of the Roman Rite: that the reform of the rite has introduced so much artificiality, novelty, archeology, and space for spontaneous improvisation that it gives the clear sense of being (practically and formally) wholly divested from the *forma* of its generative "root". The *Novus Ordo* does indeed function experientially like a "rite" unto itself (with no real parallel), but to the extent that it is ontologically authentic, it must not be an "invention" but must be the product of a "reception" from the *traditio* and so must have a particular genealogical root. In this light, at least it seems, the only hope for an authentic prolongation of the *Novus Ordo* is a "reform of the reform" that radically puts it in contact with the *Usus Antiquior*, so that the organic link between these two expressions of the one Roman Rite becomes experientially obvious. One thing that it seems to me cannot be done is some kind of "mutual enrichment" whereby a "synthesis" is made between the *Usus Antiquior* and the *Novus Ordo*. If the former is, for the time being, somewhat "frozen", this is the salvation of the latter, since it has frozen an authentic expression of organic life of the *traditio*, which has been handed down. And so the *Usus Antiquior* could be said to lie in wait, ready to be reactivated into the general organic life of the universal Church, but only after the *Novus Ordo* has been sufficiently conformed to the more original *forma* of the *Usus Antiquior*. The *Novus Ordo*, by contrast, is in radical flux— every priest, every parish, every national community can celebrate it according to its own "form", so that the experiential difference between the *Novus Ordo* celebrated in the Granada Cathedral, the London Oratory, and the chaplaincy at the University of San Francisco will each differ one from the other more than the Dominican Rite and the Roman Rite differed from each other seventy years ago. The trouble would seem to be that what is most in flux in the *Novus Ordo* concerns precisely what is most purely "invention" and so has nothing to do with organic development, much less with what has been handed on from one generation to the next though the *traditio*. It seems that if there may be some authentic organic development underpinning some of the postconciliar "reform" that produced the *Novus Ordo*, any "mutual enrichment" of the two expressions of the one rite would have to be, at least for some generations, not a "mutual enrichment", but a "unilateral enrichment" by the *Usus Antiquior* enriching and stabilizing the *Novus Ordo*. In any case, to elevate the *Novus Ordo* to the status of a "rite" of its own seems to me too much: to the extent that it is authentic, it is an expression of the Roman Rite, while to the extent that it is experienced as something wholly "other", it must be *re*-formed in order to be legitimately sustained.

[66] Benedict XVI, *SP*, art. 1 (*DH* 5109).

distinct histories, geographies, and cultures, and so branching into particular *traditii* within the great *traditio* that flows from the Cross of Jesus.

The integrity of the particular rites of the Church, whether Roman, Byzantine, Mozarabic, Antiochian, and so on, lies always in what they proximately receive, going back to the single trunk rooted in one soil, from which the whole tree grows to produce fruit under the rays of one and the same Sun. The *Novus Ordo*, to the extent that it has a place on this tree, must grow from a branch, a particular *traditio*, that is supported by the one trunk of the great *traditio*. The only branch from which the *Novus Ordo* could have grown and received its "organic being" (that is, a way of being that is neither an innovation nor an archeological discovery but is truly a "traditioned" fact of life) is the so-called "Tridentine Rite", that is, the Roman Rite according to *Missale Romanum* promulgated in 1570 by Pope Pius V in obedience to the Council of Trent.

The reform that produced what we call the Tridentine Mass was, in fact, rather limited in the sense of changes introduced. What the Tridentine Mass more nearly means is the universalization and standardization of the liturgy of the bishop of Rome through the Missal of 1570, the rite of which, in its essential form, reaches back at least to the time of Pope Gregory the Great (d. 604).[67] Specifically, in the name of the Council of Trent, as Uwe Michael Lang clarifies, the Mass was reformed according to the concrete standard of "the plenary missals of the Roman rite in the form used by the Roman curia".[68] The reform of the Mass, in this way, aimed not so much to reform the Roman Rite as to export synchronically the *forma* of the Mass celebrated by the pope to the universal Church, which could boast a patrimony stretching back through the Gregorian Reform of the eleventh century and essentially continuous with the early medieval papal stational Mass.[69]

---

[67] Joseph Jungmann, S.J., *The Mass of the Roman Rite: Its Origins and Development*, 2 vols., trans. Francis Brunner (New York: Benziger, 1951), 1:49–60. Cf. Adrian Fortescue, *The Mass of the Roman Liturgy* (London: Longmans, 1912), *passim*, at 173.

[68] Uwe Michael Lang, "The Tridentine Liturgical Reform in Historical Perspective", in Uwe Michael Lang, ed., *Authentic Liturgical Renewal in Contemporary Perspective* (London: Bloomsbury, 2017), 109–24, 123.

[69] Ibid., 123.

What the *Missale Romanum* of Pius V most basically achieved, therefore, was to make general throughout the churches of the Latin Rite what had been basically perennial to the popes and the curia for a millennium and a half previous. The meaning of "reform" in this context consisted of making normative for the Church the liturgical *forma* of the Supreme Pontiff, and not more. On one level, this is the basis of the postconciliar reform of 1969, in the sense of the juridical prerogative of the pontiff to universalize his missal throughout the Latin Church (even if what was being universalized in the post-Vatican II reform was not a perennial and ancient *forma*, at least in the sense of a *forma* being handed on from one generation to the next). Setting aside the question of the two "reforms" of the Missal, at the very least we can say that if the *Novus Ordo* and the *Usus Antiquior* do not belong to the same Roman Rite, then the whole legitimacy of the *Novus Ordo* must be called into question. If the Mass of 1969 has indeed been "valid" (as even Marcel Lefebvre conceded), then it must form part of the one Roman Rite. The liturgical authenticity of the *Novus Ordo* is accordingly sustained by the *Usus Antiquior*, as the life of a child is sustained by the life of the mother. They are "two usages of the one Roman rite",[70] as Pope Benedict insists, because they are two liturgical expressions of the Mass of the bishop of Rome. This cannot be to say that they are "equal", however.

The *Usus Antiquior* possesses an authenticity of Catholic experience of the Mystery that has been verified and refined over some 1,500 years. In this way, it cannot but remain the standard of the *forma* of the *Novus Ordo*, the experiment of which is not yet even a century old. What is more, the *Usus Antiquior* remains the sufficient support of every subsequent expression of the Roman Rite, and so of the *Novus Ordo* (and not otherwise). This means, I think, that the spiritual authenticity of the *Novus Ordo* must be judged in part by how it expresses and adheres to the essence of the *forma* of the *Usus Antiquior*. But just as there cannot be a Church of Pius X and another of Paul VI, so there cannot be a Mass of Pius V and another of Paul VI: there can be only the one Mass of the Roman Church.

---

[70] Benedict XVI, *SP*, art. 1 (*DH* 5109), in Bishop Marc Aillet, *The Old Mass and the New: Explaining the Motu Proprio* Summorum Pontificum *of Pope Benedict XVI*, trans. Henry Taylor (San Francisco: Ignatius Press, 2010), 100.

3. The Mass of Vatican II

De Lubac was always insistent that, whatever the postconciliar crisis, the council itself could not be held responsible.[71] He charged that after the council (and even during the council) a "para-council" had installed itself and disingenuously claimed for itself legitimacy in interpreting the council according to its "spirit". In fact, as de Lubac noted, this "para-council" largely contradicted the letter of the council's documents. For this reason, de Lubac always urged a return to the letter of the council as the necessary locus of an authentic response to the postconciliar crisis and the reestablishment of the council's truthful continuity with the magisterial tradition as a whole.

In the case of the liturgical crisis, this is precisely the approach Fessio takes in his essay "The Mass of Vatican II",[72] an account of the letter of *Sacrosanctum concilium* under the question of what kind of Mass the Council Fathers envisaged generating.[73]

It is significant that de Lubac, in the journal he kept at the council, hardly mentions the issuance of the Constitution on the Liturgy on December 4, 1963. The reason for this cannot be that de Lubac was indifferent to liturgical innovations—as early as 1965 he wrote to Georges Villepelet of his anxiety at the new "liturgical disorder" in the Church.[74] But in 1963, concerning the letter of *Sacrosanctum concilium*, de Lubac seems to have seen nothing controversial on which to comment.[75] That de Lubac saw nothing on which to comment is

---

[71] On de Lubac and the council, see my "Henri de Lubac and the Second Vatican Council", in Jordan Hillebert, *T&T Clark Companion to Henri de Lubac* (London: Bloomsbury, 2017), 121–56.

[72] Joseph Fessio, S.J., "The Mass of Vatican II", *Catholic Dossier* 6, no. 5 (2000): 12–20.

[73] Fessio's program in this regard is more or less convertible with that of Uwe Michael Lang, who proposes a rereading of *Sacrosanctum concilium* as the "Criteria for a Renewal of Sacred Art", which is a key element of the renewal of "beauty" as transcendental in the liturgy. See Lang's *Signs of the Holy One: Liturgy, Ritual, and Expression of the Sacred* (San Francisco: Ignatius Press, 2015), 105–14.

[74] Le Centre d'Archives et d'Études Cardinal Henri de Lubac, no. 58507; as quoted in Chantraine, *Henri de Lubac*, 4:217.

[75] The Council Fathers were in general consensus on the liturgy, viz., that some reform was welcome. For example, most were, it seems, at least in principle open to the Liturgy of the Word being celebrated in the vernacular, the lectionary being expanded, some elements of the ritual being simplified. But, overwhelmingly, they were opposed to a "revolution" in the liturgy. It is perhaps significant to remember that Archbishop Lefebvre was one of the

perhaps a hint to the meaning of Fessio's insistence that *Sacrosanctum concilium* is "one of the most important documents of the Council", which has nevertheless "wrought the most havoc".[76] The importance of the constitution, clearly for Fessio, lies in the continuity and unity it sought to mandate regarding the "reform" of the Roman Rite, while the "havoc" it wrought concerns the revolution carried out in its name, but against its letter.

As Fessio notes, the "central intent of the Council concerning the liturgy"[77] was not spontaneous innovation, but a provocation to *actuosa participatio* understood as it had already been clarified in 1903 by Pope Pius X in *Tra le sollecitudini*: "Special efforts are to be made to restore the use of Gregorian chant by the people, so that the faithful may again take a more active part in the ecclesiastical offices."[78] On the further question of the innovation of liturgical rites, the council was resolute: "There must be no innovations unless the good of the Church genuinely and certainly requires them."[79] And any innovation introduced ought to "grow organically from forms already existing".[80] According to Fessio, this means that the liturgical development the council sanctioned is like the growth of "a plant, a flower, a tree—not something constructed by an intellectual elite".[81] In other words, an authentic development of the liturgy cannot be the result of *conceptio christiana*, no matter how pious and well-intentioned. The liturgy is a thing that grows from the generative life of the Church herself, from *fides christiana*, from the life to which the

---

signatories of the Constitution. On this, see Alcuin Reid, "On the Council Floor: The Council Fathers' Debate of the Schema on the Sacred Liturgy", in Lang, ed., *Authentic Liturgical Renewal*, 125–44.

[76] Fessio, "Mass of Vatican II".

[77] Ibid.

[78] Pius X, *Tra le sollecitudini*, Instruction on Sacred Music (November 22, 1903), II, 3: "Cantus gregorianus, quem transmisit traditio, in sacris solemnibus omnino est instaurandus, et omnes pro certo habeant sacram liturgiam nihil solemnitatis amittere, quamvis hac una musica agatur. Praesertim apud populum cantus gregorianus est instaurandus, quo vehementius Christicolae, more maiorum, sacrae liturgiae sint rursus participes." As translated at https://adoremus.org/1903/11/22/tra-le-sollecitudini/ by *Adoremus*. Cf. Pius IX, *Divini cultus* on Divine Worship (December 20, 1928); and *MD* 191–92.

[79] *SC* 23 (*DH* 4023).

[80] Ibid.

[81] Fessio, "Mass of Vatican II".

Christian is docile because he cannot either synthesize it or capture it, dominate it or modify it.

Attendant to this is the special importance Fessio affords to the title given by *Sacrosanctum concilium* in the chapter dedicated to the Mass itself: "The Most Sacred Mystery of the Eucharist".[82] As Fessio notes, in the chapter title the great sense of the Mass' import is fixed: "mystery, sacredness, awe, the transcendence of God".[83] Here we approach the very heart of *fides christiana*. The Eucharist is the privileged place of encounter with the Lord. It is not a place of discourse or syllogism, it is not a scheme of social betterment or a learned synthesis of *dogmata*: it is the holy ground in which the human being encounters and recognizes Jesus as present.

> You are here to kneel
> Where prayer has been valid. And prayer is more
> Than an order of words, the conscious occupation
> Of the praying mind, or the sound of the voice praying....
> Here, the intersection of the timeless moment[.][84]

The heart of Christian prayer is this encounter with the Mystery made flesh, this entering into the saving sacrifice the Son made on Calvary when he gave himself for the life of the world.

To illustrate this, in his book on the liturgy, Martin Mosebach recalls a small detail in the rubrics of the traditional form of the Roman Rite, still prescribed in the 1962 Missal but usually unobserved, which highlights the centrality of the appearance of the resurrected Jesus to his disciples on the road to Emmaus. Prior to the Consecration, an additional candle is to be placed on the altar beside the tabernacle. The candle is ignited and not to be extinguished until after Communion when the tabernacle is closed. According to Mosebach, the candle "upsets the symmetry" for a very precise reason: the candle is "Christ, coming to join the disciples on the Emmaus road ... and then withdrawing from their sight".[85] This mysterious candle

---

[82] SC, II: "De Sacrosancto Eucharistiae Mysterio" (DH 4047).
[83] Fessio, "Mass of Vatican II".
[84] Eliot, *Four Quartets*, "Little Gidding", I, 45–52, in *Poems of T. S. Eliot*, 1:202.
[85] Mosebach, *Heresy of Formlessness*, 38.

clarifies a threefold fact of the encounter of the Mass: the presence of Christ, our recognition of him, and how our encounter with him leaves our hearts burning with wonder, confirming the mystery of *fides christiana*.

As we have said, the authenticity of this encounter handed down from Jesus to the apostles and then to the Fathers through the whole history of the Church is the heart of the *traditio*. This is what all of theology—whether exegetical, speculative, dogmatic, or magisterial—is meant (according to its particular function) to safeguard, affirm, and secure. Everything, in other words, is enacted, as Fessio puts it, "that they might enter more fully into the mysteries celebrated".[86]

This is the same justification *Sacrosanctum concilium* gives for the development of the liturgical rite, "that Christ's faithful, when present at this mystery of faith, should not be there as strangers or silent spectators ... [but] should take part in the sacred action conscious of what they are doing, with devotion and full collaboration."[87] The eyes of faith must be opened anew to the truth of his presence, that the hearts of the faithful might burn afresh with the mystery of Christ handed over through the fragile hands of his ministers.

As Fessio grants, as much as the essential accent of *Sacrosanctum concilium* lies on the side of continuity, it did recommend changes to the liturgy, including the amplification of the lectionary;[88] greater valuation of the homily "as part of the liturgy itself";[89] the institution of "the prayer of the faithful" in the Mass;[90] the urging of reception of Communion (when possible) from Hosts consecrated in the liturgy attended, as well as allowance for Communion under both species in limited circumstances;[91] recognition of the two "liturgies" of the Mass (the Word and the Eucharist), urging pastors to encourage the faithful to participate in both parts;[92] and the permission for concelebration and the urging of a new rite to be written for it.[93] In

---

[86] Fessio, "Mass of Vatican II".
[87] *SC* 48 (*DH* 4048).
[88] Ibid., 51.
[89] Ibid., 52.
[90] Ibid., 53.
[91] Ibid., 55.
[92] Ibid., 56.
[93] Ibid., 57–58.

addition to these eight suggestions, the council urged that the vernacular be suitably introduced into some Masses (for readings and prayers of the faithful), while yet insisting that "steps should be taken so that the faithful may also be able to say or to sing together in Latin those parts of the Ordinary of the Mass which pertain to them."[94]

Of these nine changes recommended by the council, the one with the greatest impact for the faithful was the introduction of the vernacular. But, as Fessio notes, when one looks at the letter of the Council Fathers, one is struck to read that their recommendation was strictly limited and that their intention certainly entailed the preservation of Latin in the Ordinary of Mass and in the musical patrimony of the Roman Rite.

For Fessio, the latter emphasis of the Council Fathers is highly significant. In the first place, *Sacrosanctum concilium* affirms that the Church's musical patrimony is "a treasure of inestimable value, greater even than that of any other art".[95] The Council Fathers understood themselves, moreover, in this regard, as doing nothing more than reaffirming the *actuosa participatio* recommended by Pope Pius X: the "Church acknowledges Gregorian chant as specially suited to the Roman liturgy: therefore, other things being equal, it should be given pride of place in liturgical services."[96] Even while they reaffirmed the normativity of Gregorian chant in the liturgy of the Roman Rite, they allowed that "other kinds of sacred music, especially polyphony, are by no means excluded from liturgical celebrations, so long as they accord with the spirit of the liturgical action."[97] All of this, moreover, was envisaged as in Latin according to the tradition. But according to *Sacrosanctum concilium*, as Fessio points out,

> The most appropriate use of music at Mass, as seen by Church tradition and reaffirmed by the Council, is singing the Mass itself: the *Kyrie, the Agnus Dei, the Sanctus, the Acclamations, the Alleluias* and so on.... this is what the Council actually says. Paragraph 112 [of *Sacrosanctum concilium*] adds, "Sacred music is to be considered the more

94 Ibid., 54.
95 Ibid., 112.
96 Ibid., 116.
97 Ibid.

holy in proportion as it is the more closely connected with the liturgical action itself."[98]

After reiterating what the council positively proposed, Fessio recapitulates what the council did not propose. The council "did not say that tabernacles should be moved from their central location to some other location".[99] Nor did it require that the priest should abandon the traditional posture *ad orientem* in order to say Mass "facing the people" (the council did not so much as mention liturgical posture). The council did not call for the removal of altar rails. Neither did it call for a multiplication of Eucharistic "canons". That these things nevertheless did transpire, and the unrestrained fashion with which they transpired, would seem to be, for Fessio, evidence of a "paracouncil", which betrayed not only the broad tradition of the Church's sacred rite but also the letter of the council itself.

But as soon as we have said the foregoing, we have to acknowledge that whatever else *Sacrosanctum concilium* affirmed, the fundamental principle of the constitution, espoused from the very beginning of the document, concerns "adaptation".[100] The first article of the constitution states: "This sacred Council has several aims in view", the first of which is: "it desires to impart an ever increasing vigor to the Christian life of the faithful"; and on this basis, it desires "to adapt more suitably to the needs of our own times those institutions which are subject to change".[101] Clearly the divine liturgy, as an "institution" of the Church's patrimony, was not understood by the Council Fathers as a reified artifact, impervious to some dynamic of living change and development. No one thought the apostle Paul had received and handed on the Roman Rite itself. The *forma* of the

---

[98] Fessio, "Mass of Vatican II".

[99] Ibid.

[100] In this paragraph, I am indebted to personal correspondence with Father Uwe Michael Lang.

[101] SC 1 (*DH* 4001). On the authentic interpretation of *Sacrosanctum concilium*, see Joseph Ratzinger, "Fortieth Anniversary of the Constitution of the Sacred Liturgy: A Look Back and a Look Forward", in Joseph Ratzinger, *Collected Works*, vol. 11, *Theology of the Liturgy: The Sacramental Foundation of Christian Existence*, ed. Michael J. Miller, trans. John Saward, Kenneth Baker, S.J., Henry Taylor, et al. (San Francisco: Ignatius Press, 2014), 574–88; and Robert Cardinal Sarah, "Towards an Authentic Implementation of *Sacrosanctum Concilium*", in Lang, *Authentic Liturgical Renewal*, 3–20.

liturgy was known to have grown and developed over history, in an organic fashion. The innovation of the council, here, was to mandate something within this organic and dynamic development of the living reality of the liturgy. Concretely, the Council Fathers authorized that the Roman Rite, the rite of the bishop of Rome, can and should now be "developed" under the authority of the pope to meet the exigencies of certain objective factors. And thus we see the word "adaptation", which in fact "runs through the document like a red thread".[102] This implies that the Fathers who signed the constitution (the overwhelming majority, 2,147 to 4, including Marcel Lefebvre) sanctioned that in the matter of the reform of the Roman Rite, at this juncture of history, something beyond "organic development" was required and that, indeed, "in some places and circumstances ... an even more radical adaptation of the liturgy is needed."[103] The basis of the innovation that resulted in the *Novus Ordo* is in this way justified by *Sacrosanctum concilium*, that is, by the solemn authority of an ecumenical council of the Church. Insofar as some "adaptation" was licensed by the council, however, the deeper question now has to do with the validity of those postconciliar reforms, with respect not only to how they nevertheless maintain continuity with the *forma* of the traditional Roman Rite (which seems to me the basis of their liturgical authenticity), but also to the extent to which they have met or failed to meet the two concrete objectives for which the council justifies "adaptation"—viz., (1) the impartation of new vigor to the life of the faithful and (2) a liturgy more suitably adapted to "the needs of our own times". It must be noted that, in the case of the latter, the idea cannot be the production of a liturgy "conformed to this world" (Rom 12:2). Rather, to the contrary: a liturgy more suitably adapted to "the needs of our own times" must be a liturgy sufficiently "transformed" by the renewing encounter with Christ so as to be able adequately to "prove what is the will of God, what is good and acceptable and perfect" (Rom 12:2) in a world in which everything now points against the life of faith. These two criteria must become part of how we judge the adequacy of the reform of the Roman Rite and its cultural translation. In any case, it must be said

---

[102] Uwe Michael Lang, from personal correspondence, January 6, 2018.
[103] SC 40 (4040).

that the fundamental principles set forth for the reform of the liturgy in *Sacrosanctum concilium*, which have to do with both continuity and adaptation, have to be accepted since they enjoy the highest authority.[104] This, however, is not to say that particular aspects of the liturgical reform and the work of the *Consilium*, or even particular points of *Sacrosanctum concilium*, are above criticism.

The sharpest and most serious critiques of the *Novus Ordo* and the status quo liturgical culture concern especially the latter point of the adaptation of the liturgy to "the needs of our own times". In particular, one thinks, here, of Pickstock's critique of the postconciliar reform, which concerns for her, not the fact that the Fathers licensed "adaptation", but that "the Vatican II revisions of the mediaeval Roman Rite ... were simply *not radical enough*."[105] The echo of *Sacrosanctum concilium* is here critical—"in some places and circumstances ... an even *more radical adaptation* of the liturgy is needed." What is intended by "radical", here, has nothing to do with the modern sense of a "disjunctive" or "rebellious" change, but rather "radical" in the sense of its Latin root, *radix*, that is, a reform more deeply rooted in the tradition, which in turn becomes generative of a more radical response to the root of the religious crisis of our epoch. The liturgy must be capable of generating a deconstruction of the logic of modernity and, so, cannot be a product of it. This is a salient argument of Peter Kwasniewski, who argues for a restoration of the *Usus Antiquior*, not out of rigid servility, but out of a conviction that the "adaptations" incarnated in the postconciliar liturgy have neither increased the vigor of Christian life nor furnished the modern Christian with a more authentic spiritual character with which to resist the "wisdom of this age" (cf. 1 Cor 2:6). To the contrary, Kwasniewski argues, the reform of the Roman Rite has reconfigured the liturgy more according to a pattern more or less convertible with a culture determined by the bureaucratic, capitalist, and liberal qualities that characterize modernity. The reform, in his view, has produced "a liturgy of the Enlightenment, ahistorical, social, accessible, efficient, unthreatening ... [and ultimately free] of that primitive or medieval *mysterium tremendum et fascinans*".[106] This, according to Kwasniewski, has been disastrous for

[104] Cf. Sarah, "Towards an Authentic Implementation", 13–19.
[105] Pickstock, *After Writing*, 170–76, at 171.
[106] Kwasniewski, *Noble Beauty*, 48.

the life of the Church because it has occurred at precisely the moment in history when the exigencies of the crisis of modernity required of the Catholic imagination a new and more total adherence to something "*outside* of modernity, transmitting a wisdom which originated *before* its rebellion and which aims at goals *not* of this world—this political age of great violence and failed originality".[107] Fessio would be perhaps sympathetic with Kwasniewski's critique of the current state of the liturgy, even if Fessio is convinced that the road forward is not a normative and universal "restoration" of the *Usus Antiquior*, but a "reform of the reform" of the Roman Rite. Fessio's dedication is to maintain the legitimacy both of *Sacrosanctum concilium* and the *Novus Ordo*, through a reform of the latter that would draw it closer to both the *forma* of the *Usus Antiquior* and the letter of council. Concerning the critical points to which this "reform of the reform" ought to attend, Fessio singles out two crucial issues: (1) the abandonment of *ad orientem* (to which we will turn below); and (2) the status of the three new "canons" (anaphoras) in the *Novus Ordo*.

Fessio reminds us that, prior to the promulgation of the *Novus Ordo* in 1969, the Church (East and West) had never known of a "choice of Eucharistic prayers".[108] According to the Byzantine Rite, for example, there are three anaphoras, that of the liturgies of Saint John Chrysostom, Saint Basil the Great, and Saint James, the uses of which are determined, not by the preference of the priest-celebrant, but by rubrics of use on particular feast days and in particular locations. In the Roman Rite, by contrast, there has only ever been one Eucharistic prayer, the Roman Canon, whose core dates back at least to the end of the fourth century.[109] In the form in which we now know it, the Canon was set by the time of Gregory the Great, at the end of the sixth century. According to Pope Benedict XIV, "No pope has added to or changed the Canon since Saint Gregory."[110] Henceforth the Canon remained the fixed center of the Latin liturgy, for which it was called the "Canon", meaning "rule"; indeed, for the Latin Church, it was understood as the supreme rule of orthodoxy, in the sense of both right worship and right opinion.

[107] Ibid., 49.
[108] Fessio, "Mass of Vatican II".
[109] Jungmann, *Mass of the Roman Rite*, 1:51–53.
[110] Benedict XIV, *De SS. Missae Sacrificio*, 162.

The esteem given to the Canon has to do not only with its use by the popes but with its mysterious and ancient origin, "wrapped in almost total darkness".[111] According to Louis Bouyer, neither "in East nor West is there any Eucharistic prayer remaining in use today that can boast such antiquity".[112] The earliest textual evidence of the Canon comes from Ambrose of Milan (ca. 340–397), who makes a protracted quotation from it in his *De Sacramentis*.[113] By the Middle Ages, with the exception of the Spanish Mozarabic Rite, the Roman Canon had become the core and fixed point of all Latin liturgies (and so not only for the Roman Rite, but also the Ambrosian Rite, the Sarum Rite, the Lyonese Rite, the Dominican Rite, and so on). And so from the time of Gregory the Great until the *Novus Ordo*, the Roman Canon held pride of place in a basically unaltered form at the heart of Latin liturgy—it is the one Canon known and prayed by Ambrose, Thomas Aquinas, Ignatius of Loyola, the Curé d'Ars, John Henry Newman, Padre Pio, Pope John XXIII, and so on. It is remarkable, given the perennial centrality of the Canon to the Roman Rite, that it was ever thought that such a unitive and uni-fying fact at the heart of the Church's liturgical life could be added to, rearranged, or shunted into the background of "optional use".[114]

In his *Catholic Dossier* essay, Fessio enumerates the new "canons" with brief commentary.[115] The first, "Eucharistic Prayer II", is an anaphora culled from the *Traditio Apostolica* (rediscovered at the end of the nineteenth century) and attributed to Hippolytus of Rome.[116] There have sometimes been claims that the anaphora is "the ear-liest [Roman anaphora] that has come down to us",[117] but recent

[111] Jungmann, *Mass of the Roman Rite* 1:49.

[112] As quoted in Alfredo Ottaviani and Antonio Bacci, *The Ottaviani Intervention: Short Crit-ical Study of the New Order of Mass*, trans. Anthony Cekada (Rockford, Ill.: Tan, 1992), 57n1.

[113] Ambrose, *De Sacramentis*, 4.5.21–25 (PL 16:443–45).

[114] In fact, worse was planned by the Consilium for the Roman Canon. There were three different plans for altering it significantly, but when the plans were given to Pope Paul VI, the pope refused to allow the changes. And so the Canon survived the *Novus Ordo*. See Enrico Mazza, *The Eucharistic Prayers of the Roman Rite*, trans. Matthew J. O'Connell (Collegeville, Minn.: Liturgical Press, 2004), 57.

[115] For a short narration of the process of the genesis of "canons" II and III, see Bouyer, *Memoirs*, 256–60.

[116] For the authoritative text, which we now have mostly in Latin translation, see Hip-polyte de Rome, *La Tradition Apostolique*, 4 (*Source chrétiennes* 11:48–52).

[117] Mazza, *Eucharistic Prayers*, 90.

scholarship would seem to undermine both the claim that it ever was a fixed anaphora and the claim that it has a Roman pedigree.[118] Originally written in Greek, the anaphoric text seems, rather, a descriptive account of how the Eucharist was celebrated, drawing on the celebration of the Eucharist in the Christian East and with no discernable connection to Rome or to the Latin liturgical tradition that later grew up in Rome sometime between the third century and the pontificate of Pope Damascus (366–384).[119] According to Lang, it "cannot be used as a source for Roman liturgical practice in this period because of uncertainties about its date, origin, and authorship."[120] A likely compilation of non-Roman and non-Latin liturgical fragments, according to Fessio, the anaphoric text of Hippolytus "was probably never used as a liturgical text because in the early days of the Church there was no final, written formalization of the liturgy, so this was [at most] an outline to be used by the celebrant."[121]

The new anaphora, then, likely never before used as a set anaphora, was introduced into the Roman Rite, at best, as a venerable ancient fragment of tradition, recently discovered after having been lost for more than a millennium and a half. It is difficult to see how precisely this introduction does not exemplify the "antiquarianism"

---

[118] Uwe Michael Lang, *The Voice of the Church at Prayer: Reflections on Liturgy and Language* (San Francisco: Ignatius Press, 2012), 55n22. Lang cites the following: B. Steimer, *Vertex traditionis: Die Gattung der altchristlichen Kirchenordnungen* (Berlin: de Gruyter, 1992); M. Metzger, "À propos des règlements ecclésiastiques et de la prétendue *Tradition apostolique*", *Revue des sciences religieuses* 66 (1992): 249–61; C. Markschies, "Wer schrieb die sogenannte Traditio Apostolica? Neue Beobachtungen und Hypothesen zu einer kaum lösbaren Frage aus der altkirchlichen Literaturgeschichte", in C. Markschies, W. Kinzig, and M. Vinzent, *Tauffragen und Bekenntnis: Studien zur sogenannten "Traditio Apostolica", zu den "Interrogationes de fide" und zum "Römischen Glaubensbekenntnis"* (Berlin: de Gruyter, 1999), 1–79; and P. F. Bradshaw, M. E. Johnson, and L. E. Philips, *The Apostolic Tradition: A Commentary* (Minneapolis, Minn.: Fortress Press, 2002). This most recent research, as Lang notes, confirms the intuition of Louis Bouyer; see his *Eucharist: Theology and Spirituality of the Eucharistic Prayer*, trans. C. U. Quinn (Notre Dame: University of Notre Dame Press, 1968), 188–91.

[119] Mazza, *Eucharistic Prayers*, 57. According to Jungmann, this translation from Greek to Latin was "not a sudden one" but must have already been well underway by the middle of the third century, since beginning with Pope Cornelius (d. 253), the inscriptions on the papal tombs are found in Latin, not in Greek. What is more, the transition from Greek to Latin was likely occurring at the very time of the transition from improvised to fixed formularies of the liturgy. See Jungmann, *Mass of the Roman Rite*, 1:50–51.

[120] Lang, *Voice of the Church at Prayer*, 55n22.

[121] Fessio, "Mass of Vatican II".

against which Pius XII had warned in *Mediator Dei*.[122] What is more, the anaphora, taken on its own, appears in the *Novus Ordo*, not as a replica of the text as it is found in the *Traditio Apostolica*, but in a form significantly modified and fashioned.[123] The foregoing, in all cases, makes it virtually impossible to see how the anaphora forms an organic part of the traditioned life of the Latin liturgy. This need not devalue the theological richness of the text itself, which should not be discounted.[124]

The case of "Eucharistic Prayer III", from the point of view of tradition, is more difficult still. This anaphora, theologically and liturgically rich as it is, was, as Fessio notes, an original composition of the Consilium charged by Pope Paul VI with the renovation of the Roman Rite after the council. It is well known that the principal author of the anaphora was Dom Cipriano Vagaggini.[125] That the anaphora is rooted in a wide-ranging and eminent knowledge of the tradition cannot be doubted, but neither can the fact that it has no organic basis in the liturgical life of the Roman Rite. Finally, "Eucharistic Prayer IV" is culled from an Eastern Egyptian anaphora still used today. If the theological richness of this anaphora cannot be questioned, neither can its traditioned quality: it is in fact organically generated from the original *traditio* living to this day. This notwithstanding, the transplanting of the Egyptian anaphora into the Roman Rite is not without its awkwardness, a fact evidenced by its practical disuse in contemporary celebrations of the *Novus Ordo*. The whole legitimacy of the new anaphoras of the Roman Rite, we can say, lies in the juridical and pastoral prerogative of Pope Paul VI to promulgate them as part of his missal in 1969. The legitimacy of this papal prerogative, for a Catholic, is difficult to dismiss without undermining the Catholic meaning of papal authority. The legitimacy of the papal prerogative of the reform of the Roman Rite notwithstanding, the particulars of the actual reform are hardly a settled matter. There

---

[122] *MD* 64.

[123] Evidence of the constructive and editorial work is quickly seen by comparing *Traditio Apostolica* (*Sources chrétiennes* 11:48–50) with "Eucharistic Prayer II". Cf. Bouyer, *Memoirs*, 258–59; and Mazza, *Eucharistic Prayers*, 95–96.

[124] For at least one point of theological richness that the anaphora brings, see my *Ecce Homo: On the Divine Unity of Christ* (Grand Rapids, Mich.: Eerdmans, 2016), 67–68.

[125] Mazza, *Eucharistic Prayers*, 125.

remain a range of legitimate questions and critiques that could be raised, not least those concerning the hegemonic displacement of the Canon by anaphoras that are, at best, only tenuously linked to the tradition of the Roman Rite.

In this regard, with respect to the new "canons", Fessio registers a twofold apprehension. First, with regard to the almost displacement of the Roman Canon by the second and third anaphoras, which has served to rupture the unitive tradition at the heart of the Latin Rite that stretches back more than a millennium and a half and, second, with respect to the instruction of *Sacrosanctum concilium* that "care must be taken that any new forms adopted should in some way grow organically from forms already existing",[126] Fessio implicitly raises the question of how the new anaphoras in fact pertain in an organic sense to the Roman Rite. Their status represents perhaps one of the most difficult problems facing a "reform of the reform", if that reform is meant to bring the *Novus Ordo* more deeply into contact with the *forma* of a liturgy "traditioned", and not "made" (whether through invention or archeological discovery).

4. Versus Deum per Iesum Christum

Martin Mosebach has noted how, "in the ancient world, if a ruler broke a tradition he was regarded as having committed an act of *tyrannis*."[127] For the ancients, in other words, tyranny was an act of violence that damaged a traditional form, a form of essential life handed down from one generation to the next.[128] Mosebach contends that the postconciliar "reform" of the Roman Rite was, accordingly, an act of *tyrannis* in this technical sense; it was not a *re*-form, in the sense of a humble return to an essential *forma*, but a violation of the *forma* of the Latin liturgical tradition and its genius, which is of divine origin. A warning of Joseph Ratzinger is here apt: "When the liturgy is self-made,... then it can no longer give us what its proper gift should

---

[126] SC 23 (*DH* 4023).

[127] Mosebach, *Heresy of Formlessness*, 24.

[128] Cf. Martin Mosebach, "Return to Form: The Fate of the Rite Is the Fate of the Church", *First Things* (April 2017), online at. https.//www.firstthings.com/article/2017/04/return-to-form.

be: the encounter with the mystery that is not our own product but rather our origin and the source of our life."[129]

Among the changes introduced into the Roman Rite by the "reform", one innovation stands out and encapsulates this *tyrannis*: the shift to the almost univocal posture of the priest *versus populum* throughout the liturgical celebration, even during the Consecration. According to Klaus Gamber, this shift of the celebrant toward the people poses the single greatest obstacle of continuity between the common practice of the *Novus Ordo* and the traditional form of the Roman Rite. As Gamber wagers: "the new position taken by the priest at the altar—which is without any doubt an innovation and not a return to a practice of the early Church—is based upon a new conception of the Mass: that of the 'eucharistic community around the table'."[130]

Most astonishingly, this iconic mark of the postconciliar "reform" is not only without precedence in the whole of the Christian tradition, but it is not mentioned in *Sacrosanctum concilium* (the constitution says nothing about liturgical posture), nor is it stipulated by any rubric of the *Novus Ordo*.

The unprecedented nature of the liturgical posture is demonstrated with meticulous documentation by Uwe Michael Lang.[131] Recapitulating and expanding the work of Gamber, along with Louis Bouyer[132] and J. A. Jungmann,[133] among others, Lang shows that, for the earliest Christians, the normal posture of prayer was to face toward the east, *ad orientem*. While Jews traditionally pray toward Jerusalem and Muslims toward Mecca, ancient Christians prayed toward the rising sun, from whence the Lord himself would return. Praying toward the east was justified on eschatological grounds. The witness to the authenticity of this posture in the ancient Church is impressive: the author of the *Shepherd of Hermas*, Tertullian, Clement of Alexandria,

[129]Joseph Ratzinger, *Milestones: Memoirs, 1927–1977*, trans. Erasmo Leiva-Merikakis (San Francisco: Ignatius Press, 1998), 148.

[130]Monsignor Klaus Gamber, *The Reform of the Roman Liturgy: Its Problems and Background*, with a back-cover quotation from Joseph Cardinal Ratzinger's preface to the French edition, trans. Klaus Grimm (Fort Collins, Col.: Roman Catholic Books, 1993), 118.

[131]Uwe Michael Lang, *Turning towards the Lord: Orientation in Liturgical Prayer*, with a foreword by Joseph Cardinal Ratzinger (San Francisco: Ignatius Press, 2004).

[132]Cf. Louis Bouyer, *Liturgy and Architecture* (Notre Dame, Ill.: University of Notre Dame Press, 1967).

[133]Cf. J. A. Jungmann, "Der neue Altar", *Der Seelsorger* 37 (1967): 374–81.

Origen, Augustine, and John of Damascus, all of whom explicitly write of facing east as the fitting posture of Christian prayer.[134] As Ratzinger states: "praying toward the east is a tradition that goes back to the beginning."[135] In the Middle Ages, Thomas Aquinas justified the traditional posture thus:

> There is a certain fittingness in adoring towards the east. First, because the Divine majesty is indicated in the movement of the heavens which is from the east. Secondly, because Paradise was situated in the east according to the Septuagint version of [Genesis 2:8], and so we signify our desire to return to Paradise. Thirdly, on account of Christ Who is *the light of the world* [John 8:12; 9:5], and is called *the Orient* [Zechariah 6:12]; *who mounteth above the heaven of heavens to the east* [Psalm 67:34], and is expected to come from the east, according to [Matthew 24:27], *As lightning cometh out of the east, and appeareth even into the west; so shall also the coming of the Son of Man be.*[136]

The traditional posture was a way of orientating our prayer toward the transcendent horizon of God and the eschatological future. In this way, not only were the priest-celebrant and congregation united, they were constitutively opened outward to a horizon of encounter beyond themselves. The posture is still maintained in the Eastern Orthodox tradition; and it obviously never had anything to do with the priest "turning his back" on the congregation.

The new Latin habit of celebrating *versus populum*, if it is without precedent both in the Roman Rite and the ancient rites of the East, does have an early modern precedence in the liturgical reconfigurations of the Reformation. Martin Luther, in a polemic against the

---

[134] See Lang, *Turning towards the Lord*, 43–55, who gives the textual references for these and more. Advocates of *versus populum* are quick to point to liturgical tradition in Rome, in which the altars of the great basilicas do face the congregation and the Canon has been for generations prayed *versus populum*. But this posture in the Roman basilicas was justified, never as a Mass celebrated *versus populum*, but as Mass celebrated *ad orientem* in a basilica that itself faces west, and not east, so that to pray the Canon *ad orientem* meant always to pray into the body of the basilica itself. See Lang, *Turning towards the Lord*, 78–80.

[135] Joseph Ratzinger, *The Spirit of the Liturgy*, trans. John Saward (San Francisco: Ignatius Press, 2000), 75.

[136] Thomas Aquinas, *Summa theologica* (hereafter cited as *ST*), trans. Fathers of the English Dominican Province, vol. 2 (New York et al.: Denziger Brothers, 1947), II II, q. 84, a. 3 ad 3, p. 1554. This passage is cited by Lang, *Turning towards the Lord*, 56.

Catholic Mass, stated that, "for the real Mass [that is, the Protestant Eucharist] among true Christians, the altar should not remain in its current form and the priest should always face the people—as, we can undoubtedly assume, Christ did during the Last Supper."[137]

Luther was deceived. First-century Palestinian-Jews did not eat sitting around a supper table facing one another like German Reformers or contemporary Europeans. Rather, as Lang notes, "*it was customary for the diners to recline* on couches arranged in a semicircle, with small tables being used for holding food and dishes. [In this arrangement,] the place of honour was on the right of the semicircle."[138] When the priest prays the most solemn prayer of the Church's liturgy, when he offers the Sacrifice of the Mass and consecrates the Eucharistic elements, he has never been understood as imitating the dining custom of Jesus at the Last Supper.[139] He is doing something greater: he is acting *in persona Christi*. And this means that the gesture he assumes is not a "re-playing" of a discrete action of Jesus, but an ultimate entering into the total gesture of Jesus' Paschal Mystery: a sacrifice that began with Jesus' offering of his perpetual presence in the Upper Room but that was not complete until he had "drunk at the hand of the LORD the cup of his wrath, who have drunk to the dregs the bowl of staggering" (Is 51:17) on the Cross of Calvary. For this reason, the priest was never supposed to have assumed the literal bodily gesture of Jesus, but rather one that recapitulates his total "Cruciform" of being. Accordingly, the most ancient and traditional posture for the priest was always to pray with his gaze fixed on the heavenly Father, *versus Deum* and, so, *cum populum*.

When the priest is orientated *versus Deum*, he allows the congregation to experience how they are fundamentally "with" him, captivated

---

[137] Martin Luther, *The German Mass and Order of Worship* (1526); quoted in Gamber, *Reform of the Roman Liturgy*, 139. Ironically, despite the injunction of Luther, *versus populum* was never universally taken up in the Lutheran tradition. See Lang, *Turning towards the Lord*, 94–95.

[138] Lang, *Turning towards the Lord*, 93 (italics mine). Lang continues: "From about the thirteenth century, depictions of the Last Supper adopted the *contemporary seating arrangement, with Jesus occupying* the place of honour in the middle of a large table and the apostles to his right and left, as, for example, in Leonardo da Vinci's famous fresco in Milan. *An image of this type may well have been in the mind of Martin Luther* when, in 1526, he suggested that the altar should not remain in its old position and that the priest should always face the people, as no doubt Christ did at the Last Supper" (93–94; italics mine).

[139] See Mazza, *Eucharistic Prayers*, 26–29.

by a gaze that looks higher, a gaze that seek always the face of the genuine and ultimate Other. It is a disposition especially suited to adoration.
By contrast, in the new arrangement, when the priest is positioned
univocally "facing the people", he comes himself to be the object of
the people's gaze, even in the moment of ultimate supplication. The
practice, thus, risks a certain clericalism. While the *versus Deum* position
implies that God is the center and focus, the *versus populum* posture suggests that the priest himself is the center of what is happening in the liturgy. The result is the replacement of adoration and supplication with
a "clerical-instructional interaction between the priest and the congregation".[140] In this way, the mystagogical encounter is undermined by
an arrangement that suggests—not the freedom of the encounter with
Christ—but an instruction and discourse about Christ, with the priest
as expert tutor.

The modern Catholic root of the celebration of the Mass *versus
populum* lies in the early twentieth century, in the Liturgical Movement, and is linked to the person of Romano Guardini.[141] Guardini
was one of the first priests to begin the practice, and he did so as early
as the 1920s, when he was associated with *Die deutsche Jugendbewegung*, a student youth scouting movement in Germany, which began
in 1896. When Guardini would celebrate Mass with the young people, he would celebrate a *missa recitata*, that is, a low Mass in which
the responses would be said aloud together by the congregation. It
was thus, perhaps, in part in order to lead the group in the *missa
recitata* that Guardini would celebrate *versus populum*. But more fundamental was Guardini's desire to proclaim the Word of God *to* the
young people. The rubrics of the low Mass here posed a problem,
since the priest was required in the low Mass to read the Epistle and
Gospel from the Missal set on the altar, and so facing the direction
he would presently pray the Canon. Guardini's solution, in order to

---

[140] Mosebach, "Return to Form".

[141] Gamber, *Reform of the Roman Liturgy*, 143. See Heinz R. Kuehn's firsthand account of
Guardini's practice in the introduction to *The Essential Guardini: An Anthology of the Writings
of Romano Guardini*, ed. Heinz R. Kuehn (Chicago: Liturgical Training Publications, 1997),
1–11. More generally on Guardini and the liturgy, see Alcuin Reid, O.S.B., *The Organic
Development of the Liturgy: Principles of Liturgical Reform and Their Relation to the Twentieth-
Century Liturgical Movement Prior to the Second Vatican Council*, 2nd ed. (San Francisco: Ignatius
Press, 2005), 92–95.

follow the rubrics as closely as possible, was to celebrate the whole Mass *versus populum* from behind a table altar. If this solution facilitated the *missa recitata* and made better sense of what it means to proclaim the Word intelligibly, it also emphasized, in terms of the Eucharist, the intimacy of the Mass as a "sacred banquet", something many associated with the Liturgical Movement felt had been forgotten before the council.[142] Guardini's Masses for the *Die deutsche Jugendbewegung* did indeed provoke among the students a new "impact of the sacred action",[143] and this new and positive experience had to do with the discovery of the liturgical meaning of *communio*, a communion in which the young people were implicated in a new way in the sacred action. But however significant the experience of the *missa recitata* may have been, the gesture, to the extent that it interprets the Mass as a "sacred banquet", misconstrues the liturgical meaning of *communio* or "synaxis".

The sacred action of the Mass does establish the Church's *communio*, and consciousness of this is integral to the genuine experience of the liturgy. In the first place, we can say that the liturgy is a "synaxis", since the Eucharist makes the Church and the Church gives the Eucharist.[144] The theological basis of this *communio sanctorum* is established by the prayers of the Mass itself and, in the first place, by the Roman Canon. According to von Balthasar, no "other thought is so persistent and so penetrating in the Roman Canon as the idea that the Church offers a sacrifice to God the Father."[145] And this sacrifice the Church offers, according to von Balthasar, on which the whole supplication of the Canon is based, is not a sacrifice strictly convertible with the once-and-for-all sacrifice of Calvary. Indeed, according to

---

[142] See Lang, *Turning towards the Lord*, 120–21.

[143] As Kuehn recounts: "He [Guardini] was a person who by his words and actions drew us into a world where the sacred became convincingly and literally tangible.... With him on the altar, the sacred table became the center of the universe.... The impact of the sacred action was all the more profound because Guardini celebrated the Mass *versus populum*—facing the people" (introduction to *The Essential Guardini*, 7–8).

[144] On the Eucharist as "synaxis", see Dionysius the Areopagite, *De ecclesiastica hierarchia* (PG 3:369–585), and Maximus the Confessor, *Mystagogia* (PG 91:658–722). Cf. Catherine Pickstock, "The Sacred Polis: Language as Synactic Event", *Literature and Theology* 8 (1994): 367–83.

[145] Hans Urs von Balthasar, "The Mass, a Sacrifice of the Church?" in *Explorations in Theology*, vol. 3, *Creator Spirit* (San Francisco: Ignatius Press, 1993), 185–243, at 185.

von Balthasar, the "uniqueness of the sacrifice of Christ" and its "permanent actuality" include something "difficult"—that "the Church and believers are admitted to share in the offering of this sacrifice."[146] And precisely insofar as the Church is admitted (indeed, required) to share in the oblation of Jesus, she shares in her own capacity and with her own sacrifice. For von Balthasar, indeed, the Mass is a sacrifice of the Church. In so being, the Sacrifice of the Mass is not a sacrifice autonomous from Christ's and is, indeed, bound to his sacrifice and is included within it, so much so that she cannot make her sacrifice without the memory and representation of the sacrifice of Calvary. And yet, properly, the Sacrifice of the Mass is hers, and hers to make; it is dependent on her freedom and so imbued with all the religious anxiety and urgency she expresses in the Canon, when she repeatedly begs that her sacrifice be made acceptable to God the Father.

The ultimate basis of the *offerimus* of the Church lies, according to von Balthasar, in the "answer to the offer love makes".[147] This, then, is the key to the Church's Sacrifice of the Mass. And what Love-Incarnate asks the spouse is that she would follow him to the gibbet of the Cross. That she would go with him to the altar of his ultimate sacrifice, where he will be both priest and victim. And there she is asked to do the impossible: she is asked to give her "consent" to the immolation of the sacred Victim. For von Balthasar, this is the necessary presence of the Blessed Virgin, invoked in the Canon of every Mass. She who was at the foot of the Cross is especially present at every celebration of the Mass. She is the original and immaculate collaborator with Christ and, so, the one in whom the Church must offer her own sacrifice in order that it be in communion with the sacrifice of Christ. Here the *communio* of the Church is established in the liturgy and in concerns entering into what Mary did when she "cooperated by love" in the work of redemption.[148] In other words, the Church must enter into the sacrifice of Mary, the piercing of her heart, which makes possible the sacrifice of the Church and the reality of which Saint Paul writes when he writes of being a "co-worker of God" (cf. 1 Cor 3:9; 1 Thess 3:2; and Col 4:11). In the "person"

---

[146] Ibid., 186–87.

[147] Ibid., 216.

[148] Augustine, *De Sancta Virginitate*, 6 (PL 40:399).

of Mary, the Church is an actor in the redemption wrought by the Son. But she is not an agent who "contributes" something additional or otherwise lacking in the sufficient sacrifice of Christ. Rather, she is an agent who comes with nothing but an "Amen" to give. But in a certain sense, this is everything. As von Balthasar writes: "nothing is harder for the one who truly loves than to let the beloved suffer, to 'permit' him to take the path he himself has chosen into suffering, abandonment by God, death and hell."[149] This is what Mary does: she permits and consents to the Cross. And this is what we do in the Sacrifice of the Mass. This unity with Christ through consent is the sacrifice of the Church offered to God. The archetype of this sacrifice is Mary: "[T]he Blessed Virgin ... faithfully persevered in her union with her Son unto the cross, where she stood, in keeping with the divine plan, grieving exceedingly with her only begotten Son, uniting herself with a maternal heart with His sacrifice, and lovingly consenting to the immolation of this Victim which she herself had brought forth."[150]

This for von Balthasar is the key to the anxious *offerimus* of the Roman Canon. In the liturgy of the Mass, the faithful are called to return with Mary to the foot of the Cross, to unite themselves in her *fiat* to the sacrifice of the Son, which is for her and us our own sacrifice, since "nothing is harder for the one who truly loves." This is the ultimate "synaxis", the true *communio* of love, which is *communio* with Jesus in his total gift of self. This *communio* is signified concretely when the priest unites himself *cum populo* in the Sacrifice of the Mass, when he turns with the people "together" *versus Deum per Iesum Christum*, to consent lovingly to the immolation of the Victim.

If this posture *versus Deum* is most adequate to signify the *communio* achieved through the Sacrifice of the Mass, it is important to note that, in the traditional form, this posture was never the univocal posture of the priest in the Mass, and neither is it today in the Eastern liturgies. Rather, the posture of the priest shifted throughout the liturgy, and only in key moments, and in the moments of ultimate supplication, did he assume the posture *versus Deum*. The priest, rather, assumed

---

[149] Balthasar, "Mass, a Sacrifice of the Church?" 217.

[150] Second Vatican Council, Dogmatic Constitution on the Church *Lumen gentium* (November 21, 1964), no. 58.

various concrete postures, some of which were *versus populum*, others *versus Deum*, each one specific and symbolically deliberate. The habit of the priest in the *Novus Ordo* is much more homogeneous. As Catherine Pickstock observes: "the Celebrant's position [in the traditional Roman Rite] was an ambiguous one, shifting between being on the side of the congregation [*ad orientem*] to being on the side of God [*versus populum*]. He was not simply 'above' the congregation, but had to request the *assistance* of the bystanders, and was subject to a permutation of identity which ... is integral to a liturgical characterization of the worshiping self."[151]

Thus the priest, requesting the *assistance* of the congregation, ascended to the altar in the name of the people, offering the sacrifice at the heart of the Mass on behalf of the congregation while remaining united with them *versus Deum per Iesum Christum*. In this way, he incarnated the interdependence of the many members of the body on one another and so signaled a *communio* that is not bureaucratic, but a complex nexus of interrelation and dependence.[152] The ultimate basis and end of this nexus is sacrifice: the gift of one's life for another, which generates and is generated from the radical gift of love at the origin of the *traditio* of Jesus himself.

This is the *communio* that truly unites the human being with God and is rooted in the *traditio* Jesus made of himself on Calvary in the Spirit to the Father. And so the *communio* of the liturgy is not a *communio* of the priest and the congregation "being together". It is a unity they discover through the more basic unity they have in being united to Christ in his sacrifice. The nature of this *communio* is made eloquent in the traditional offertory prayers of the Roman Rite. The first, the "Suscipe, sancte Pater", is a prayer to the Father to accept the sacrifice the priest will soon offer for himself on behalf of those present and on behalf of all Christians, living and dead, for salvation and for the remission of sins. The communion here is double: in the first place, it is the community of sinners (clerical and lay, living and dead, present and absent) and, in the second, the communion of

---

[151] Pickstock, *After Writing*, 173–74.
[152] This is resonant with what Victor Turner calls "communitas". See Lang on Turner in *Signs of the Holy*, 29–41; and cf. Victor Turner, "Passages, Margins, and Poverty", *Worship* 46 (1972): 390–412 and 482–94.

those sinners saved in the sacrifice the priest offers on behalf of himself and the community.

The next prayer, "Deus, qui humanae substantiae", is a petition
for deification, that through the sacred rites, God would make us
partakers of the Son's divine nature (*da nobis . . . eius divinitatis esse consortes*). This is the *mirabilius reformasti* to which the Mass opens us, the
ultimate *Mysterium* (here signified by the mingling of water and wine)
that, as Christ has participated to the depth in our human condition (*qui humanitatis nostrae fieri dignatus est particeps, Iesus Christus*), we
may through the sacred rites come to participate in his divinity. The
operative biblical text is 2 Peter 1:3–4, according to which God in
Jesus has given a share in his divine power to humanity in order that,
through knowledge of him we may "become partakers of the divine
nature [*divinae consortes naturae*]" (2 Pet 1:4). The prayer anticipates
a later prayer of the Mass, after the Consecration, when the priest
drops a portion of the consecrated Host into the chalice, entreating:
"Haec commixtio, et consecratio Corporis et Sanguinis Domini nos-
tri Iesu Christi, fiat accipientibus nobis in vitam aeternam." Here the
Mystery of becoming a partaker of the divine nature is made actual
in the real mixture of our human being with the consecrated Body
and Blood of Jesus; it is effectual for us unto eternal life, that is,
unto participation in the divine nature. These two prayers specify—
in an absolute way—the Christian theology of "synaxis", that the
true human *communio* of the Mystical Body is not a shared idea or
discourse, much less a common meal, but a deifying union actualized
through the sacred liturgy, whereby we are made "one" in Christ.
Christ, and no other, is the term of Christian communion.

But as soon we specify that, according to the prayers of the Roman
Rite, Jesus himself is the term of our "communion", we have to
return again to the essentially sacrificial character of the Mass. The
sacrificial character of the sacred rite was already clarified in the first
offertory prayer, which is now recapitulated in the following offertory prayers, beginning with the "Offerimus tibi, Domine", which
petitions God to accept the offering about to be made as an acceptable fragrance (*odore suavitatis*). Then, bowing, the priest asks again
that God would accept the gathered congregation and that God himself would grant that the sacrifice being offered be pleasing to him.
And then follows the epiclesis of the Roman Rite, in which the Holy

Spirit is called upon to bless this sacrifice. Following, after washing his hands, the priest prays the "Suscipe, sancta Trinitas", which specifies that the oblation being made will be made in memory of the Paschal Mystery of Jesus, in honor of Mary and all the saints, and to the end that it might achieve our salvation. Then, finally, the priest turns to the congregation and asks them to pray God that their common sacrifice (*ut meum ac vestrum sacrificium*) may be acceptable to God the Father.

What the traditional offertory prayers make clear is that sacrifice and communion are not counterpoised in the Mass, but, to the contrary, it is precisely the Sacrifice of the Mass that establishes the Christian character of the communion the Mass accomplishes.[153] For this reason, no *missa recitata*, no Mass *versus populum*, can adequately signify the Christian character of communion. There is no gesture that more fully signifies the "synaxis" of the liturgical action than does the unity of the priest with the congregation, *versus Deum per Iesum Christum*.

5. Christology and Liturgy

The loss of the gesture *ad orientem* illustrates a general confusion around the authentic Christological meaning of the liturgy. The liturgy does not worship an abstract divinity; neither is it an occasion of human togetherness: it is the act and adoration of God the Father by Jesus Christ himself, in which the Church participates through her unity with Christ. As Pope Pius XII put it: "The sacred liturgy is ... the public worship which our Redeemer as Head of the Church renders to the Father, as well as the worship which the community of the faithful renders to its Founder, and through Him to the heavenly Father. It is, in short, the worship rendered by the Mystical Body of Christ in the entirety of its Head and members."[154] In this light, the liturgy is a Christological fact. Hence, the insistence of Ratzinger

---

[153] On the internality of sacrifice and communion in the Eucharist, see the important work of Matthew Levering, *Sacrifice and Community: Jewish Offering and Christian Eucharist* (Oxford: Blackwell, 2005).

[154] *MD* 20 (*DH* 3841). Cf. *Catechism of the Catholic Church*, 2nd ed. (Vatican City: Libreria Editrice Vaticana; Washington, D.C.: United States Catholic Conference, 1997), 1069–70.

that only "a close connection with Christology can make possible a productive development of the ... practice of liturgy."[155]

A productive re-*form* of the liturgy, in this light, must begin from mindfulness of the newness of the Incarnation of the Son, which is the assumption of created form by the Creator. As Mosebach insists, this is the faith of Christianity:

> In Christ all the fullness of God dwells in bodily form, even in that of a dead body. Spirit takes form. From this point on, this form is inseparable from the Spirit; the Risen One and Savior, returning to his Father, retains for all eternity the wounds of his death by torture. The attributes of corporeality assume infinite significance. The Christian Rite, of which the Roman Rite is an ancient part, thus became an incessant repetition of the Incarnation, and just as there is no limb of the human body that can be removed without harm or detriment, the Council of Trent decreed that, with respect to the liturgy of the Church, none of its parts can be neglected as unimportant or inessential without damage to the whole.[156]

The liturgy, thus, is a distention of the form of the *missio* given to the Son by the Father in order that divinity itself might come carnally into the world. Jesus' form of being is the form of perfect human adoration of God the Father and, so, is the basis of Christian *latria*. As Pierre de Bérulle puts it:

> From all eternity, there has been a God infinitely adorable, but there was not yet an infinite adorer; there was a God infinitely worthy of being loved and served, but no man nor infinite servant capable of rendering a service and infinite love. You are now, O Jesus, this adorer, this man, this servant, infinite in power, in quality, in dignity, to satisfy this need fully and render this divine homage. You are this human, loving, adoring, and serving the supreme majesty as he deserves to be loved, served, and honored. And just as there is a God worthy of being adored, served, and loved, so there is also in you, O my Lord Jesus, a God adoring, loving, and serving him, to all eternity,

---

[155] Joseph Cardinal Ratzinger, *A New Song for the Lord: Faith in Christ and Liturgy Today*, trans. Martha M. Matesich (New York: Crossroad, 1997), x. Cf. Ratzinger, *Spirit of the Liturgy*, 29, 42, 67, 69, 76, 111, 140, 192, and 203.

[156] Mosebach, "Return to Form".

in the nature that was united to your person in the fullness of time....
[F]rom now on we have a God served and adored without any kind
of defect in this adoration and a God who adores without detracting
from his divinity![157]

This quote from Bérulle brings us to the very heart of the *novum* of
the Incarnation, wherein in Jesus the discrepancy between the human
being and God becomes the correspondence of adoration, a worthy
human rendering of *latria* to God the Father.

The generative origin of Christian liturgy is, in this light, wholly
sustained Christologically, in such a way that our human liturgy truly
is, in Christ, an *opus Dei* in which God himself takes the initiative so
that we may be "caught up" and redeemed in the initiative he has
taken *pro nobis*.[158] The method of this *opus Dei* is not an extrinsic *Deus
ex machina*, but rather a divine indwelling in our history that saves the
human being from within human history, through his *traditio*, the
generative source of a new history in which he is an incarnate presence. And so, for us, receptivity to the whole texture of the history
in which he has been traditioned is the first sign of fidelity to God.

The Christological paradigm that imbues our sense of what it
means to participate in the sacred action can be understood in a
twofold manner. In the first place, our liturgical disposition ought
to reflect the "enhypostatic" quality of Jesus' humanity as regards
his divine personhood, how his human nature exists and acts only
as it is united to the person of the *Logos*.[159] As Pius XII clarified:

---

[157] Pierre de Bérulle, *Discours de l'état et des Grandeurs de Jésus*, in *Pierre de Bérulle: Œuvres
Complètes*, vol. 7, ed. Michael Dupuy (Paris: Cerf, 1996), discours II, 123–24.

[158] Ratzinger, *New Song for the Lord*, 117.

[159] In modern theology, this doctrine is associated with Karl Barth; see his *Church Dogmatics*, I/2, *The Doctrine of the Word of God*, trans. G. T. Thompson and Harold Knight, ed. G. W.
Bromiley and T. F. Torrance (Edinburgh: T&T Clark, 1956), 163–65. For Barth, the doctrine
worked in terms of the *theologoumenon* of *anhypostasis—enhypostasis*, which designated for him
the negative and positive sides of one Christological doctrine. "*Anhypostasis* asserts the negative. Since in virtue of the ἐγένετο, i.e., in virtue of the *assumptio*, Christ's human nature has its
existence—the ancients said, its subsistence—in the existence of God, meaning in the mode
of being (*hypostasis*, 'person') of the Word, it does not possess it in and for itself, *in abstracto*.
Apart from the divine mode of being whose existence it acquires it has none of its own; i.e.,
apart from its concrete existence in God in the event of the *unio*, it had no existence of its
own, it is ἀνυπόστατος. *Enhypostasis* asserts the positive. In virtue of the ἐγένετο i.e., in virtue
of the *assumptio*, the human nature acquires existence (subsistence) in the existence of God,

Christ's human nature is not a *homo assumptus*, because his humanity is not a human "extent", it is not "something existing in its own right *(sui iuris)*".[160] The humanity of Jesus, Pius insists, exists only insofar as it subsists in the person of the Word, *inquantum subsistit in persona Verbi.*[161]

It follows from this that if the humanity of the Son of God is *verus homo*—even the unique instance of perfect humanity—this is because it is *instrumentum Divinitatis.*[162] The whole reality of Jesus' being, all he did and all that befell him, serves the divine *missio* the Son accepts from the Father, to "go to Jerusalem and suffer many things from the elders and chief priests and scribes, and be killed, and on the third day be raised" (Mt 16:21). The first Christological paradigm of liturgical action, then, concerns how the humanity of Christ "is" *verus homo* precisely because it is so perfectly rooted in the divine initiative so as to be one with it, *verus Deus*. So for us, as we participate in the liturgy, this means a disposition of grateful surrender to the *opus Dei* of the Holy Trinity, who has acted and acts in the Incarnation. Here everything points to the Marian *fiat mihi*, her ready waiting at the Annunciation and the sacrifice of the Yes she gives at the foot of the Cross. There is no room in the liturgy for *conceptio christiana*; the

---

meaning in the mode of being *(hypostasis,* 'person') of the Word. This divine mode of being gives it existence in the event of the *unio*, and in this way, it has a concrete existence of its own, it is ἐνυπόστατος" *(Church Dogmatics*, I/2, 163). As some patristic scholars have pointed out, Barth may have got his Greek wrong here, since ἐνυπόστατος is normally used in a way basically convertible with "existent" and not "existent-*in*". That this doctrine (if not the Greek) has a patristic pedigree, see the crucial article of Uwe Michael Lang, "Anhypostatos—Enhypostatos: Church Fathers, Protestant Orthodoxy and Karl Barth", *Journal of Theological Studies* 49 (1998): 630–57. For more recent scholarship on the patristic pedigree of the doctrine, see Benjamin Gleede, *The Development of the Term* ἐνυπόστατος *from Origen to John of Damascus* (Leiden: Brill, 2012), esp. 45–138.

[160] Pius XII, *Sempiternus Rex*, 31 *(DH* 3905). Pius expresses here precisely what Barth expresses in the quotation cited in the above note. On the importance of this Christology, see my *Ecce Homo, passim*.

[161] Cf. Pius XII, *Sempiternus Rex*, 31 *(DH* 3905): "Hi humanae Christi naturae statum et condicionem ita provehunt ut eadem reputari videatur subjectum quoddam sui iuris, quasi in ipsius Verbi persona non subsitstat."

[162] For the doctrine of Christ's human nature as *instrumentum Divinitatis*, see Aquinas, *ST* III, q. 19, a. 1, and for the definition of instrumental causality, see *ST* I, q. 45. a. 5. Further, cf. Theophil Tschipke, *L'humanité du Christ comme instrument de salut de la divinité*, trans. Philibert Secrétan (Fribourg: Academic Press Fribourg, 2003). Aquinas receives the doctrine from John of Damascus, *De fide orthodoxa* 3.15 *(PG* 94:1060a).

only valid attitude is that of receptive gratitude, *fides christiana* trustfully open to what has been handed down.

The second Christological paradigm, connected to the first, concerns the divine filiation that determines the Son's personhood and, so, his manner of being human. Jesus lives and exists wholly from his "constant communication with the Father".[163] If the center of Jesus' being is his communication with God the Father, then our communion in Christ, the supplication of the prayer "Deus, qui humanae substantiae", occurs wholly within this filial relation by which he is generatively constituted as the eternally begotten Son. To become partakers of the divine nature consists in adoptive filiation by grace, becoming *filii in Filio*, receiving the Spirit of adoption (cf. Rom 8:15).

This means that the whole basis and truth of our relation to God "in Jesus" consists in being in-formed by the indwelling Spirit, who turns us with Christ toward the Father. The pattern of *sequela Christi* is, in this way, made very concrete: rather than gathering together to follow Christ's moral example, we gather to follow Christ into the radical self-exteriorization he makes of himself *pro nobis* on the Cross. Here everything consists in the prayer of Jesus: "Abba Pater ... non quod ego volo, sed quod tu" (Mk 14:36). Because of the outpouring of the Spirit, this is now our prayer and so the heart of our Christian being: "accepistis Spiritum adoptionis filiorum in quo clamamus Abba Pater" (Rom 8:15). This determines for us a posture of ready waiting, of active receptivity, of freely determined passivity to the initiative of the divine Other.

God the Father, who led Christ in his earthly life by the Spirit, now leads the Church in the same Spirit.[164] In this light, the communion

---

[163] Joseph Ratzinger, *Behold the Pierced One: An Approach to a Spiritual Christology*, trans. Graham Harrison (San Francisco: Ignatius Press, 1986), 15; and cf. Joseph Ratzinger / Benedict XVI, *Jesus of Nazareth: From the Baptism in the Jordan to the Transfiguration*, trans. Adrian J. Walker (New York et al.: Doubleday, 2007), xiv.

[164] This is more than an invocation of Pentecost (cf. Acts 2:1–13); it is recognition that docility in the Spirit is the basis of Christian hope and the disposition of Christian being. As Paul puts it: "If the Spirit of him who raised Jesus from the dead dwells in you, he who raised Christ Jesus from the dead will give life to your mortal bodies also through his Spirit who dwells in you" (Rom 8:11). This is not on a vague idea of "spirit", but the concrete "form" of the Holy Spirit, who gives the human life of the incarnate Son its decisive shape and content. The Spirit is the term of Jesus' communication with the Father, who gives Jesus' mission its decisive orientation. He is the Spirit who incarnates Jesus in the womb of Mary (cf. Lk 1:35),

of the liturgical body comes from our being exposed and disposed toward the Holy Trinity.[165] The form of Christian prayer, in other words, is rooted in the Trinitarian reality, since the Spirit of adoption is the one who makes us "sons of God" and allows us to call on God the Father with the same intimate name with which Jesus addresses him: in Christ, he has become for us, too, "Abba Pater". This means that our gaze (and the whole infrastructure of our being) must become, like the gaze of Jesus, ever fixed on the initiative of the paternal origin, who eternally generates his Son in the Spirit (Love). Everything consists in our subsistence in the *traditio* of Son, which turns us *ad orientem* toward the Father in the Spirit who has been given us.

These two Christological factors determine an adequate disposition in the liturgy. The divine unity of Jesus, such that nothing of his human being exists *sui iuris*, must define our mode of being human in liturgy: fixed by the divine principle that acts (*opus Dei*). At the same time, the constitutive divine filiation of his being, his always and eternal generation in the Love (Spirit) of the Father and disposition to do his will, shows us that the end of our being in Christ is truly to pray the "Pater noster". To praise God in heaven, to beg for his Kingdom to come, and to pray that the Father's will be done is to enter into the depths of the inner mystery of who Jesus is.[166] The "decisive factor" of the liturgy, truly, "is the primacy of Christology".[167]

In this light, at the heart of the loss of the sacral character of the postconciliar Mass[168] lies an incapacity to see how man is meant

---

who alights on Jesus at his baptism (cf. Lk 3:22), who drives Jesus into the wilderness to be tempted (cf. Lk 4:1), in whom Jesus returns in power to begin his ministry (cf. Lk 4:14), who anoints Jesus to preach the good news (cf. Lk 4:18–21), by whom Jesus casts out demons (cf. Mt 12:28), who presumably leads Jesus ultimately to the Cross (cf. Lk 4:13; Mk 14:26; Gal 4:6; Rom 8:15), who is given up by Jesus to the Father at his death (cf. Lk 23:46), who is then sent by the Father to raise Jesus from the dead (Rom 8:11).

[165] Cf. Helmut Hoping, "Liturgy and the Triune God: Rethinking Trinitarian Theology", in Lang, *Authentic Liturgical Renewal*, 21–29.

[166] Cf. Joseph Ratzinger / Pope Benedict XVI, *Jesus of Nazareth*, pt. 2, *Holy Week: From the Entrance into Jerusalem to the Resurrection*, trans. Philip J. Whitmore (San Francisco: Ignatius Press, 2011), 157.

[167] Ratzinger, *New Song for the Lord*, 133.

[168] Cf. Joseph Cardinal Ratzinger with Vittorio Messori, *The Ratzinger Report: An Exclusive Interview on the State of the Church*, trans. Salvator Attanasio and Graham Harrison (San Francisco: Ignatius Press, 1986), 119–34.

thereby to be "caught up" into this double unity of Christ, into his hypostatic unity (which is the basis of our mystical union with him) and into his filial unity with the Father (which is the basis of our adoptive filiation). From this angle, Ratzinger understands the Christological underpinnings of the postconciliar liturgical crisis as both betraying and entailing a dualist Christology that dissociates the human factor from the divine unity of Christ. It implies a construal of the human being as if not only could he flourish without intimate communication with the divine, but more, that humanity and divinity are essentially contrastive and competitive, operationally speaking.[169] What is needed, according to Ratzinger, is new Christological concentration on the dyothelite unity of the Son's prayer, made dogma at the Council of Constantinople III.[170]

For Ratzinger, the chief advantage of the dyothelite unity of Jesus' two wills is its focus on the prayer of the Son, the locus of the most intimate aspect of his being: "Jesus's activity proceeded from the core of his personality ... his dialogue with the Father."[171] This is significant, not only because it specifies the oneness of Christ in his filial

---

[169] Ratzinger, *New Song for the Lord*, 8–9 and 27. In this regard, Ratzinger sets his analysis up in contrast to that of Karl Rahner. According to Rahner, the predicament of preconciliar Catholicism was broadly "monophysite", putatively emphasizing the divinity of Jesus at the expense of his humanity. See, for example, Rahner, "Current Problems in Christology", in *Theological Investigations*, vol. 1, trans. Cornelius Ernst (Baltimore: Helcon, 1963), 149–200, at 156 and 158–60; *Karl Rahner in Dialogue: Conversations and Interviews, 1965–1982*, ed. Paul Imhof and Hubert Biallowons (New York: Crossroad, 1986), 126–27; and *Foundations of Christian Faith: An Introduction to the Idea of Christianity*, trans. William V. Dych (New York: Crossroads, 2005), 298–302. Rahner sought in his Christology to correct what he perceived as the tendency toward monophysitism with what he called a "pure" (*reiner*) Chalcedonianism, by which he sought to reemphasize the *inconfuse, immutabiliter* side of the Chalcedonian definition (the abiding distinction of divinity and humanity in Christ), over and against the *indivise, inseparabiliter* side (the basic unity of the "one Christ"). According to Ratzinger, the crisis of modern Christology and contemporary liturgy is precisely the opposite, involving a tendency toward a dualistic view of the world in relation to God, and the human in relation to divinity. The danger of our epoch is not monophysitism, but a quasi-Nestorian dualism that juxtaposes the divine and human spheres and suggests that the more the human sphere is autonomous, the more it is "fully human". In this light, the liturgical crisis requires a Christological basis of the "fully human" that is fully doxological and counterpoised to the Rahnerian option in favor of this "pure" Chalcedonianism. On the limits of Rahner's Christological program, see my *Ecce Homo*, 9–15 and 70–74. On the negative impact of Rahner's theology on liturgical sensibility, see Lang, *Signs of the Holy One*, 43–50.

[170] See *Terminus* of Constantinople III (*DH* 556–58).

[171] Ratzinger, *Behold the Pierced One*, 17–18.

communication and activity, but also because, in the form of the "Pater noster", the filial communication of Jesus with the Father is precisely what Jesus "traditions" to his followers and, so, is the basis of Christian liturgy.

Genuine knowledge of Christ—true Christology—is thus liturgical, and it means participating in the prayer of Jesus through the *traditio* that stretches back to the original *traditio* and continually incarnates the presence of Jesus as a fact encountered at the heart of the life of the Church. The prayer of Jesus is thus the condition of the possibility of *ratio cognoscendi* in our speculative approach to the mystery both of who we are as human beings and of who God is as God.[172] Learning to call God "Father", then—which means turning toward the Father in Christ through the Spirit who intercedes on our behalf—is at once the discovery of our true creatureliness and our redemption: we are children in the Child (*filii in Filio*) for whom, as de Lubac put it, "beatitude is service, sacrifice is joy, vision is adoration, freedom is dependence."[173]

6. The Way of Beauty and the Cross

In *De Incarnatione Verbi Dei*, Athanasius of Alexandria, the great defender of Nicene orthodoxy and "true pillar of the Church",[174] declared that "it was precisely in order to be able to die that [the divine Logos] assumed a [human] body."[175] It is a remarkable declaration. By it Athanasius binds the Cross internally to the Incarnation, even rooting the latter in the former. The *missio* the Son receives from the Father is a *missio* to "tradition" his Divine Person into human flesh in order to "tradition" that flesh itself into the absolute self-gift that is the Paschal Mystery. The in-forming of

---

[172] See Johannes Hoff, "Self-Revelation as Hermeneutic Principle? The Rise and the Fall of the Kantian Paradigm of Modern Theology", in Conor Cunningham and Peter M. Candler, eds., *The Grandeur of Reason: Religion, Tradition and Universalism* (London: SCM, 2010), 167–217.

[173] Henri de Lubac, *Esprit et liberté dans la tradition théologique* suivi de *Petit catéchèse sur nature et grâce, Œuvres complètes*, vol. 14 (Paris: Cerf, 2013), 192; and cf. *Surnaturel*, 492.

[174] Gregory Nazianzen, *Oratio* 21.26 (SC 270:164).

[175] Athanasius of Alexandria, *De Incarnatione Verbi Dei*, 21 (PG 25:132b-c).

human being and human history by the divine Logos is directed to
an ultimate flourishing-point, the point at which the *forma* of the
Son's *missio* and his person are given iconic clarity. Here the whole
paradox of Christianity, and so the liturgy, comes to a tensive breaking point, but does not break. This fact is so basic to the narrative
structure of the Gospels that it forms the very basis of the Christian
claim: "I decided to know nothing among you except Jesus Christ
and him crucified" (1 Cor 2:2). Divine power is revealed in abject
fragility; the glory of human life is accomplished in the death of a
first-century Palestinian-Jew; and the divine love at the heart of
being is laid bare in the wounded face of the Crucified. Here is
the splendor of the Christian vision: the radiance of divine Love, "the
most sublime of beauties—a beauty crowned with thorns and crucified".[176] Thus beauty incarnate takes its decisive *forma*: the crucifix,
the quintessential symbol of the Latin Rite.

In this light, the crisis of the postconciliar reform of the Roman
Rite concerns perhaps above all the loss of the theological meaning
and experience of "cruciform beauty". If this is the case, in the first
place, it is due to the broader loss of beauty as transcendental perfection of being. As von Balthasar puts it, "Beauty is the disinterested
one, without which the ancient world refused to understand itself, a
word which both imperceptibly and yet unmistakably has bid fare-
well to our new world, a world of interests, leaving it to its own ava-
rice and sadness."[177] The loss of the transcendental meaning of beauty
is the loss of the internal attractiveness of the good and the true, and
this is a cultural situation disastrous for a rite that is an aesthetic participation in the Truth.

But on another level, the loss of the theological meaning of "cruciform beauty" is deeper yet and would seem to affirm the wider
aesthetic crisis of the "apotheosis of the ugly",[178] which is more than
mere forgetfulness of beauty's transcendental meaning. More than

---

[176] Hans Urs von Balthasar, *The Glory of the Lord: A Theological Aesthetics*, vol. 1, *Seeing the Form*, trans. Erasmo Leiva-Merikakis, ed. Joseph Fessio, S.J., and John Riches (San Francisco: Ignatius Press, 1982), 33.

[177] Ibid., 18.

[178] Lang, *Signs of the Holy One*, 97–105. The term the "apotheosis of the ugly" comes from the philosopher Remo Bodei (cf. *Le forme del bello* [Bologna: Il Mulino, 1995], *passim*, here at 120), who is here cited by Lang (at p. 100).

reducing the beautiful to the merely decorative, the "apotheosis of the ugly" is a principled decision of metaphysical significance, which decides that the very notion of the beautiful is a deception: "only the representation of what is crude, vulgar, and low is true."[179] Of course in the liturgy such a decision is not taken with the decisive boldness of the secular artist, but there is surely a broad aesthetic sense in the Church today that baroque art, Renaissance polyphony, and the elegant vestments of the preconciliar period are all worse than decorative distractions: they are an indulgence that cannot correspond to the humble poverty of the abject and crucified Jesus. But this is to misunderstand the liturgy at its root. The liturgy is not an imitation of Jesus, but a participative act of memory, of entering into the decisive event, the Paschal Mystery.[180] The liturgy makes explicit the certainty of the glory the Cross accomplished, which was veiled from human eyes at the time of its historical occurrence. In other words, the liturgy is analogous to the Transfiguration in the sense that it makes unambiguous to our senses the spiritual glory of the carnal Lord, which would be otherwise hidden. The liturgy clothes the memory of the Cross in the comeliness Christian faith judges to be its innermost truth: the beauty of Jesus loving us to the very end. And so, to eliminate beauty from the center of the liturgical event is to eliminate the resplendent *forma* and to substitute in its place a discourse on Christ (whether of doctrine or morality) in the place of the mystagogical encounter. It is to foreclose the possibility that the liturgy is not something about Christ but is truly a reality in-formed by the splendor of his presence. In this regard, what is needed, as Lang suggests, is a renewed appreciation of what Dostoyevsky meant in the word he gave to Prince Myshkin in *The Idiot* (1869): beauty will save the world. Of course, not just any beauty is meant here, but "the redemptive beauty of Christ".[181]

---

[179] Lang, *Signs of the Holy One*, 100.

[180] It is critical that the apostle Paul, at the end of his institution narrative, clarifies the meaning of this participative act of memory as having to do with Calvary: "as often as you eat this bread and drink the chalice, you proclaim the Lord's death until he comes" (1 Cor 11:26). The Roman Canon follows Paul here with precision: immediately following the words of Consecration, the Canon continues, "Unde et memores ... beatae passionis, nec non et ab inferis resurrectionis, sed et in caelos gloriosae ascensionis."

[181] Lang, *Signs of the Holy One*, 102.

The difficulty comes now when we look on the Cross, at what immediately does not appear to be beautiful. In fact, what we see would seem something close to the "apotheosis of the ugly", since the face of the Crucified—the face of Truth Incarnate—is a face of "no form or comeliness that we should look at him"; indeed he is of "no beauty", but is one "despised and rejected by men" (Is 53:2–3).[182] Yet from the point of view of Christian exegesis, this is always intimately cross-read with Psalm 45 (44), according to which Jesus is "the fairest of the sons of men", so much that "grace is poured upon [his] lips" (Ps 45:2).[183] Here again is the tensive paradox that threatens to break but does not. Jesus is a "paradoxical beauty".[184]

This realization of Christ's paradoxical beauty—a *forma* irreducible to any synthesis, any *conceptio*—points us toward a mystery that cannot be equalized. As de Lubac put it, "the Incarnation is the supreme Paradox: [Παράδοξος παράδοξων]."[185] Or as Mosebach puts it, it "belongs to the Catholic faith to endeavor to express the truth in irreducible paradoxes".[186] In the unity of Christ, who is of "no form or comeliness" and is "the fairest of the sons of men", we behold the *Forma* of the *forma* of beauty, which is the mystery of divine Love made flesh, made history, encountered as a carnal fact. It is the face of a God who is not ashamed to be our God (cf. Heb 11:16). As Lang puts it, the "totality of Christ's beauty is revealed to us when we contemplate the disfigured image of the crucified Savior, which shows us his 'love to the end' (cf. Jn 13:1)."[187] This is the salvific beauty that is the *forma* of the original *traditio*, and so it is the essential *forma* that must inform to its heart the liturgy. And this is the reason that the tradition of the Roman Rite grew over a millennium and a half in exquisite splendor and outward loveliness: because it was inwardly moved and captivated by the luminous fact of the original *traditio*, the

---

[182] Cf. Steven Fields, S.J., "The Beauty of the Ugly: Balthasar, the Crucifixion, Analogy and God", *International Journal of Systematic Theology* 9.2 (2007): 172–83.

[183] Here I am following Lang, who is referencing Joseph Ratzinger, "Wounded by the Arrow of Beauty: The Cross and the New 'Aesthetics' of Faith", in Ratzinger, *On the Way to Jesus Christ*, trans. M.J. Miller (San Francisco: Ignatius Press, 2005), 32–41, at 32–33.

[184] Lang, *Signs of the Holy One*, 103.

[185] Henri de Lubac, *Paradoxes of Faith*, trans. Paule Simon and Sadie Kreilkamp (San Francisco: Ignatius Press, 1987), 8.

[186] Mosebach, *Heresy of Formlessness*, 195.

[187] Lang, *Signs of the Holy One*, 103.

gesture of Christ *pro nobis*. "Greater love has no man than this, that a man lay down his life for his friends" (Jn 15:13). Only as long as *fides christiana* adheres to this fact can the liturgy be sustained in organic continuity with the origin. The rite that was forged over the centuries became so in-formed by the beauty of this gesture that it drew all things to itself to become a "complete consort dancing together",[188] a vital texture of history, of interconnected symbols, gestures, smells, silences, vestments, music, all of which work together to communicate the radiance of the *forma* that is their unity, the Mystery of incarnate love. This is the millennium and a half experience of the Roman Rite.

* * *

Now, fifty years after de Lubac's first glance at the new "canons" of the *Novus Ordo*, the original *traditio* of Jesus is yet valid for us, despite us, because it is constitutive of the Church. For this reason, the *forma* of the cruciform love traditioned in the *Usus Antiquior* is still, despite everything, a compelling fact that draws a people to itself. And so, it remains a privileged *forma*, where the presence of Christ is both given and received, a still valid *forma* of the liturgical encounter, valid as it has been generated at least since the time of Saint Ambrose. To achieve the end to which this *traditio* points is to achieve the grace of a "condition of *complete simplicity*" that must cost "not less than everything".[189] The adequate disposition of the heart is that of readiness, readiness to be conformed to the Cross received. It is capable of this only because it is not a "fabricated liturgy", but a mystagogical encounter with the brilliance of the very Love that flows, and continues to flow through two millennia, from the original *traditio*. Only the splendor of the gaze of Jesus makes sense of this adherence to him in this *forma*, which would dare ultimately to follow him into his death.

We may see this disposition in the life of de Lubac himself, who suffered at the service to the Church for the sake of this beauty that captivated him. He served in the Great War and sustained a terrible head wound that ravaged him with headaches for the rest of his life and frequently interrupted his studies and writing. During the Second World War, he dedicated himself to the clandestine journal *Témoignage*

---

[188] Eliot, *Four Quartets*, "Little Gidding", V, 10, in *Poems of T. S. Eliot*, 1:208.
[189] Ibid., V, 40 and 41, in *Poems of T. S. Eliot*, 1:209.

chrétien, which criticized Nazi ideology and the Vichy regime in France, charging them with being incompatible with Catholicism. And in the 1950s, he was silenced for his apparent unorthodoxy. While his orthodoxy was later vindicated, he yet suffered to witness in the last years of his life what he called an *apostasie immanente*.

It was in these final years, the years in which Father Fessio knew him, that, according to Father Georges Chantraine, he lived the "most difficult period" of his life.[190] The depth of the crisis at the heart of the Church filled Father de Lubac, we are told, "with an even greater agony than [what he had borne] in the preconciliar period", when the shadow of *Humani generis* clung to his name.[191] Even the honor of being elevated by Pope John Paul II to the College of Cardinals in 1983 could not assuage the sorrow of this son of Ignatius before what Cardinal Etchegaray once called the "silent schism" of the postconciliar epoch.[192] Mysteriously, however, this way of being *cum ecclesia*, in all that it entailed, was internal to how the *traditio* in-formed Father de Lubac and made him *homo ecclesiasticus*, as Father Fessio named him on the occasion of the cardinal's ninetieth birthday. A witness to the cruciform beauty of Christ, de Lubac's theology and person are a witness to the childlike receptivity that is the joy of being encountered by the Mystery-made-flesh. As he wrote near the end of his life: "Without claiming to refer to anything other than the Gospel such as the Church transmits it to me, I can ... make my own the words of [Johann Adam] Moehler on Jesus, with little concern for the whiff of pietism that some of our adult minds would criticize in them: 'I think I would no longer want to live if I were no longer to hear Him speak.'"[193]

---

[190] Chantraine, *Henri de Lubac*, 4:72.

[191] Ibid.

[192] It is a bitter irony of twentieth-century theological history that the final "rehabilitation" of de Lubac after *Humani generis*, completed by John Paul II, was nevertheless the occasion of a very tangible personal suffering. The culture of the "para-council" and the spirit of *Concilium* had so infused the Society of Jesus in Paris that the elevation of de Lubac to the cardinalate was not received by all of his Parisian Jesuit confrères as a cause of celebration. George Weigel narrates in his masterful biography of John Paul II how the Parisian Jesuits treated the elevation and consistory as "not their affair". Since they thus declined to assist the elder Jesuit with his preparations, de Lubac was forced to ask his younger friends at the French edition of the journal *Communio* to help him with the arrangements for his investiture. Upon his return from the consistory, Weigel tells us, the new Jesuit cardinal was given a reception by his Jesuit confrères, "at which only soft drinks were served". See George Weigel, *Witness to Hope: The Biography of Pope John Paul II* (New York: Harper Collins, 1999), 446, esp. see the note.

[193] De Lubac, *At the Service of the Church*, 148.

4

The Ratzinger Option: Introducing Christianity in a Postmodern Age

Michael Dauphinais

In the summer of 1967, a forty-year-old professor offered a series of lectures on the Catholic faith to faculty and students at the University of Tübingen. In 1968, these lectures would be published as a book under the title of *Einführung in das Christentum*, and then published in an English translation as *Introduction to Christianity* in 1969. Ignatius Press would reintroduce this magisterial work to a new generation of theologians and Catholics in the United States by republishing the work in 1990 and then offering a new edition with a new preface in 2004. The author, of course, was then Professor Joseph Ratzinger in the years before he became archbishop of Munich and Freising and cardinal in 1977, prefect of the Congregation for the Doctrine of the Faith in 1981, and eventually Pope Benedict XVI in 2005.

In this work, Ratzinger offers a re-presentation of the Apostles' Creed. Unlike other commentaries on the Creed earlier in the tradition, he is acutely aware of the fact that the Creed, and the Catholic faith it proclaims, is perceived by many in the postmodern world as fictional at best or an abuse of power at worst. He diagnoses many aberrant trends in contemporary theology as unhelpful strategies for making the faith accommodate prevailing world views. He sees these as inadequate not only for their failure to be faithful to divine revelation, but also for their failure to offer contemporary people a real answer to their existential situation. This paper will consider ways in which Ratzinger offers a presentation of the Catholic faith. To a postmodern age that has lost confidence in the human ability to discover truth and purpose, Ratzinger consistently defends the intelligibility of the revelation disclosed in the Creed and attempts to show how this intelligibility offers a meaningful existential alternative.

Introduction to Christianity encapsulates what I am calling the Ratzinger Option and approaches the central questions surrounding the Christian faith considered in their doctrinal perspective.[1] The central theme is how to present the mysteries of the faith in a way that assists their intelligibility in the modern world without disfiguring the mysteries by accommodating them to the standards of those who have rejected the faith or transcendent truths. A central conviction of this paper is that there are foundational intellectual obstacles to receiving the faith in the present age so that one aspect of the needed evangelical paradigm is to address those intellectual obstacles. Since faith is an assent of the intellect to the revealed truth about God, it requires an intelligibility, for the intellect cannot assent to what it believes to be false.[2] Ratzinger seeks to present this intelligibility without watering down the faith beyond its power to offer a meaningful alternative to the way of the world.

In his 1968 preface, Professor Ratzinger says that his book seeks to accomplish what Karl Adam's *Spirit of Catholicism* did for an earlier generation.[3] We might highlight distinct themes from Adam's work that help illuminate Ratzinger's work fifty years later.[4] In German,

---

[1] The reference to "the Ratzinger Option" is a deliberate play upon Rod Dreher's book, *The Benedict Option: A Strategy for Christians in a Post-Christian Nation* (New York: Penguin Random House, 2017).

[2] See Pope Benedict XVI, Encyclical Letter *Spe salvi* on Christian Hope (November 30, 2007), "Saint Thomas Aquinas, using the terminology of the philosophical tradition to which he belonged, explains it as follows: faith is a *habitus*, that is, a stable disposition of the spirit, through which eternal life takes root in us and *reason is led to consent* to what it does not see" (no. 7; emphasis added). See also Thomas Aquinas, *Summa theologica* (hereafter cited as *ST*), II-II, q. 4, aa. 1–2.

[3] Joseph Cardinal Ratzinger, *Introduction to Christianity*, trans. J.R. Foster and Michael J. Miller (San Francisco: Ignatius Press, 2004), 32.

[4] Karl Adam's theological contributions in the first half of the twentieth century are often recognized, but he has been criticized as well. See Robert A. Krieg, who writes, "Although Adam contributed to the theological renewal that led to Vatican II by stressing the humanity of Jesus Christ, the Church as a community, and the experiential dimension of Christian faith, he stood within the ecclesiological horizon of Vatican I when he rejected the modern idea of freedom", in "Karl Adam, National Socialism, and Christian Tradition", *Theological Studies* 60 (1999): 432–56, at 454. In this comment, at least, Krieg insufficiently distinguishes the modern idea of freedom from the more robust Christological anthropology of Vatican II.

the title is *Das Wesen des Katholizismus*. This is a deliberate echo of Adolf von Harnack's (in)famous work *Das Wesen des Christentums*, translated into English as *What Is Christianity*.[5] Claiming scientific history as the master discipline, von Harnack sought to separate the kernel of Christ's teaching from the husk of historical accretions in Catholicism. In responding to von Harnack, Adam offers a central claim: the Church is not something added onto Jesus, but it is Jesus himself who is the Church. Adam writes succinctly, "Christ is the subject of the Church", thus deliberately recovering the *totus Christus* theme present in the work of Saint Augustine and other patristic theologians. If Christ is seen as necessarily related to his Church, then Church as a distinctive reality is present from the beginning, even if much of its specificity develops later in time. The phenomenon of Christianity in its earliest stages, and even of Judaism in its stages until Jesus, as Adam observes, included three distinct and inseparable aspects: moral, creedal, and liturgical. All of these are necessarily understood "in Christ": morality is "in Christ"; the Creed is "in Christ"; and the liturgy is "in Christ". Christ and the Church form a whole.

Adam defends the affirmation inherent in the Catholic faith against all forms of reductionism associated with other approaches to Christianity or to human nature in general. Adam presents Catholicism as a bold affirmation of all that is human. It is modern ideology and Protestant theology that cleave man by separating his body and soul or his faith and reason. Against liberal Protestantism and historical reductionism, Adam offers a robust reaffirmation of the fullness of the Catholic faith in its creedal forms. He is not against historical work per se, but against historical work that reduces Christ and the Church into mere earthly realities. Moreover, he utilizes the work of historians to show that the early witnesses to Christ and to the Church were already of a supernatural form. In sum, Adam argues that only the Catholic Church witnesses to the whole Christ in service to the whole human being. The opposition to Catholicism, however, is not merely liberal Protestantism, but a modernity that has defined itself

---

[5] Pope Benedict identifies von Harnack as the central figure of the second stage of dehellenization in a lecture delivered on September 12, 2006, "Faith, Reason and the University: Memories and Reflections", popularly known as "The Regensburg Address".

as a negation, rejecting first the Church, then Christ, then God, and then finally human beings in their fullness.

Ratzinger's *Introduction to Christianity* recovers many of Adam's particular themes as well as much of his overall approach. He will affirm the supernatural dimension of the Church, note the limits of historical inquiry while embracing a historical argument for the fullness of the Church's faith in its earliest stages, a concern for continuity with respect to Christ and the Church. His overall approach considers various modern objections to the faith and then shows how the fullness of the Church's faith remains nonetheless intelligible. This allows him to show the existential meaningfulness of the Christian faith in the midst of a modern age that often finds the faith either false or irrelevant.[6] He contrasts the wholeness of creedal faith to the various reductions of human reason found in modernity.

An age of unbelief requires a suitable apologetic.[7] Apologetics here draws on the biblical theme from 1 Peter 3:15, but in a unique way. "Always be prepared to make a defense [*apologia*] to any one who calls you to account [*logos*] for the hope that is in you, yet do it with gentleness and reverence" (1 Pet 3:15). Before we address the key issue here with respect to *logos*, it is worthwhile to note that the biblical text directs that apologetics be offered with "gentleness and reverence". In Ratzinger's preface to the 1969 edition, he writes that

---

[6] Ratzinger begins *Introduction to Christianity* with Kierkegaard's story of the clown telling the village that the circus is on fire. The villagers find him amusing, perhaps, but do not believe him and end up losing their village to the fire. The theologian speaks a message moderns need to hear, and yet his speech as theology is hard for moderns to take seriously. In 2006, Pope Benedict continues to observe this skepticism of his atheistic colleagues at Regensburg, "It was once reported that a colleague had said there was something odd about our university: it had two faculties [of theology] devoted to something that did not exist: God" ("Faith, Reason and the University: Memories and Reflections", Lecture at the University of Regensburg, September 12, 2006).

[7] In an early 1958 essay, Ratzinger points out that an increasingly post-Christian society requires the Church to be more attentive in the way she presents her message. He writes, "The Church must ... [make] a distinction between missionary preaching, and preaching to the faithful." The faithful, however, are not the same as all those in the visible Church. Ratzinger recognizes "a change of consciousness among the faithful, which is a result of the fact of the increasing paganism within the Church [with respect to salvation in Christ alone]." Thus, apologetics is aimed both at those inside and outside the Church who find historical creedal claims incredible. See Ratzinger, "The New Pagans and the Church: A 1958 Lecture by Joseph Ratzinger", trans. Kenneth Baker, S.J., *Homiletic & Pastoral Review* (http://www.hprweb.com/2017/01/the-new-pagans-and-the-church/, accessed December 15, 2017).

he is filled with "gratitude and great joy" that his book "has been *helpful* to many people".[8] Ratzinger's apologetics is characterized by an attempt, not to humiliate unbelievers, but rather to "help" remove obstacles for those who struggle making the full assent of Christian faith.[9] Fundamental to this help is a continual focus on the problematic understanding of reason itself in the contemporary situation.[10]

Ratzinger judges that we must first address what reason is itself before we give a "reason", a *logos* or an account, for the faith. Ultimately, he discerns a reduction in reason that makes it impossible to give a reason for the faith from the point of view of this reduced reason. Ratzinger describes this reduced reason with multiple references— scientific reason, empirical reason, historical reason, et cetera—but he continually refers to the same opposition between a reduced reason versus an expanded reason or a *logos* open to the fullness of reality. This essay will identify selected areas in which Ratzinger employs the two understandings of *logos*—reduced and holistic—to assist in the presentation of the Christian faith as intelligible: first, technological reason; second, scientific reason; third, historical reason; fourth, mythological reason; and, fifth, whole Christian reason.[11]

---

[8] Ratzinger, *Introduction to Christianity*, 35, italics added.

[9] Lawrence Cunningham connects the theme of apologetics to the particular university audience of the original 1967 lectures: "he was speaking to both believers and nonbelievers. In that sense at least he intended to give a fair account of the Christian faith that would have the ring of both catechesis and apology", in "Reflections on *Introduction to Christianity*", *Explorations in the Theology of Benedict XVI*, ed. John Cavadini (Notre Dame, Ind.: University of Notre Dame Press, 2012), 142–54, at 153. Cunningham further distinguishes between Karl Adam's word "essence" (*Wesen*) and Ratzinger's word "introduction" (*Einführung*): "[Ratzinger intends] to draw his audience into a sympathetic understanding of the Christian faith, not simply provide a sympathetic superficial account of Christianity's main doctrinal points. It has always seemed to me that Ratzinger understood his vocation as a theologian not as a disinterested but learned purveyor of facts but rather as someone who was a pilgrim of faith inviting others to join that journey" (144).

[10] In a 1970 book review of *Introduction to Christianity*, Patrick Hannon concludes, "I think it represents modern theology at its best—faithful to the traditional faith but taking its cue from the real questions of the real world, and facing them in a way which does justice both to Christian belief and to our time", *The Furrow*, vol. 21, no. 11 (1970): 734–36.

[11] This essay includes largely equivalent references to *logos*, reason, rationality, and such. By way of reference, Ratzinger employs the following original German terms: *Vernunft*, which is translated both as reason and as rationality; *Wahrheit*, truth; *Sinn*, meaning; *Gedanke*, thought; *Denken*, thinking; *Gewissheit*, certainty; *Vernunftgewissheit*, intellectual certainty; *wissbar*, knowable; *Machbarkeitswissen*, practical knowledge; *Wissen*, knowledge; *Verstehen*, understanding. He often leaves *logos* untranslated, as he sometimes does with *ratio*.

The Technological Reduction of Logos

The first area that will be addressed is technical reason, or, more precisely, the directing of reason away from truth and toward technical production. Ratzinger offers multiple stages in this transformation. He proposes that the human spirit in its encounter with reality moved historically through three dominant modes that he summarizes briefly as "the magical, the metaphysical, and finally today the scientific".[12] The term "magical" here is not used derogatively, but rather indicates an attempt to manipulate and respond to the world around man on the basis of the cumulative experience of trial and errors without a concomitant inquiry into the real causes of things. The metaphysical attitude characterizes parts of the ancient and the medieval world in their conviction that the world is intelligible as coming from an intelligent first principle, or Creator. Ratzinger summarizes this approach as *"verum est ens* (being is truth)."[13] The Creator of the world fashions the world into being through the Creator's own intelligent creative activity; thus, *verum est ens.* In a triangular harmony, the intelligent human mind is capable of discovering the intelligible causes of created beings, which were created by an intelligent cause. As Ratzinger expresses this interrelation, "since all being is thought, all being is meaningful, *logos,* truth."[14] The unity of being and truth respects an understanding of reason that is open to the fullness of being.

Ratzinger identifies the rejection of this classical conception of reason with the correlative rise of technical, or technological, reason.[15] He will chart this transformation of reason in two stages. First, he identifies a rejection of *verum est ens* in varying developments in the philosophical work of Descartes, Kant, and Vico. According to Ratzinger, Descartes "models this intellectual certainty on

---

[12] Ratzinger, *Introduction to Christianity,* 57. Ratzinger explains in a parenthetical comment that " 'scientific' (*wissenschaftliche*) here is being used in the sense in which we speak of the natural sciences (*Naturwissenschaften*)."

[13] Ibid., 59.

[14] Ibid. Ratzinger clarifies in a footnote that this approach is "only fully true of Christian thinking, which with the idea of the *creatio ex nihilo* attributes to God the material, too; for the ancient world, this remained the a-logical element, the universal matter alien to the divine, thus also marking the limit to which reality could be comprehended" (59n9).

[15] The terms "technical" and "technological" share the root of the Greek word *techne* and show human reason as applied to the making of things as opposed to *sophia* as wisdom.

mathematical certainty and elevates mathematics to the position of the prototype of all rational thinking".[16] Against this backdrop, Vico moves in an opposing direction and "advances his own formula, *verum quia factum*", or truth is what has been made by man.[17] Ratzinger sees in these a common dual movement at work in the modern period shaped by Descartes and Vico in which "complete, demonstrable knowledge is attainable only within the bounds of mathematics and in the field of history, which is the realm of man's own activities and can therefore be known by him."[18] The rise of history as a master discipline can be seen in various fields: F. C. Baur in historical-critical theology; Marx in historical-dialectical economics; and Darwin in historical-evolutionary biology.[19]

Ratzinger adds then a second stage in which the dominance of history or the factum yields to the technological reason. He labels it *verum quia faciendum*, or "truth is what is makeable." This necessitates a future-oriented standard of truth. Reason no longer has the task of discovering truth or remembering, refining, and passing on human wisdom; instead, reason is a tool used by the will in order to manipulate the world—and man as part of the world—into what we deem useful and comfortable.[20] Not only does this view of reason reduce our understanding of the mystery of man, it also limits the ability to refer to God in any meaningful manner. God is simply the unlimited future possibility of our development. Ratzinger writes

[16] Ratzinger, *Introduction to Christianity*, 61.

[17] Ibid., 59.

[18] Ibid., 61.

[19] Ibid., 62.

[20] See also Ratzinger's 1988 address entitled "Consumer Materialism and Christian Hope", in which he links the loss of the natural moral law to the resulting lack of limits on what humans may do to each other and to the world: "This reduction of nature to demonstrable and thus pliable facts has consequences: no moral message outside of ourselves can reach us anymore.... [C. S.] Lewis raised this warning during the Second World War because he saw how, with the destruction of morality, the very capacity to defend his nation against the onslaught of barbarism was imperiled.... This seems to me to be a comment of great import: the opposing worldviews of today have a common starting point in the rejection of the natural moral law and the reduction of the world to 'mere' acts.... The 'abolition of man' which follows from making absolute one method of coming to knowledge is the clear distortion of this worldview as well." (Text available at http://catholicexchange.com/framing-benedict, accessed August 1, 2016.) This public lecture at Cambridge was further developed in a published article that may be found in *A Turning Point for Europe?* (San Francisco: Ignatius Press, 2010).

that the modern man under the spell of technological reason "does not need to regard it as impossible to make himself into the God who now stands at the end as *faciendum*, as something makable, not at the beginning, as *logos*, meaning".[21] Both man and God are eclipsed in this reduction of reason. Ratzinger also shows how these two stages are one continuous devolution of reason: "The reduction of man to a 'fact' is the precondition for understanding him as a *faciendum*, which is to be led out of its own resources into a new future."[22]

Christian belief becomes the alternative to technological reason. This has two apologetic notes: first, the Christian faith is not opposed to reason per se, but only to the technological reduction of reason; second, the Christian faith itself is what gives importance to history (in the *factum*) and the future (in the *faciendum*). It would be an erroneous and unhelpful apologetics that would shift Christianity to mere practical reason in order to conform it to the contemporary technological mentality. On the other hand, it would be unhelpful to present the Christian faith as merely an intellectual ascent into the truth of being. Ratzinger, instead, describes Christian belief as a decision to take a stand, yet one that remains oriented to the truth as theoretical knowledge and not merely to utility as practical knowledge. Belief, however, is "not a blind surrender to the irrational. On the contrary, it is a movement toward the *logos*, the *ratio*, toward meaning and so toward truth itself, for in the final analysis the ground on which man takes his stand cannot possibly be anything else but the truth revealing itself."[23] Ratzinger tries to help his audience to see that it is not against reason to commit oneself to a truth that exceeds what we ourselves can make. What we can discover is greater than what we can make.

In modernity, Ratzinger discerns a temptation to allow the loss of theoretical reason to distort the proclamation of Christianity.[24] In

---

[21] Ratzinger, *Introduction to Christianity*, 66.

[22] Ibid.

[23] Ibid., 75.

[24] In his *Principles of Catholic Theology*, Ratzinger affirms the primacy of theoretical knowledge within Christianity: "[Theology] must preserve the primacy of that truth that is self-subsistent and that must be discovered in its selfness before it can be measured in terms of its usefulness to mankind." *Principles of Catholic Theology: Building Stones for a Fundamental Theology*, trans. Sister Mary Frances McCarthy, S.N.D. (San Francisco: Ignatius Press, 1987), 320.

this mode, Christianity is reduced to the level of practical knowledge so that belief would merely be a decision to make a new future on either the individual or societal level. Ratzinger, however, maintains that belief must be an act of a reason capable of attaining the truth of the being of things and of the source of all things. He describes

> one last antithesis between practical knowledge and belief. Practical knowledge must—as we have already seen—by its own intrinsic aim be positivistic; it must be confined to what is given and can be measured. But the consequence of this is that it no longer inquires after truth. It achieves its successes precisely by renouncing the quest for truth itself and by directing its attention to the "rightness", the "soundness" of the system whose hypothetical design must prove itself in the functioning of the experiment. In other words, practical knowledge does not inquire what things are like on their own and *in themselves*, but only whether they will function *for us*.[25]

Christian belief can never be judged by how it will function for us but only by how it helps us conform to reality.

Christian belief always remains a decision in favor of the truth discovered. Ratzinger writes, "Truth is the only ground suitable for man to stand upon. Thus the Christian act of faith intrinsically includes the conviction that the meaningful ground, the *logos*, on which we take our stand, precisely because it is meaning, is also truth."[26] Here Ratzinger emphasizes the intrinsically intellectual dimension of the human person in assenting to the truth of faith. Ratzinger shows that this orientation to truth is present in both the biblical and the Greek view of the world: "The indivisibility of meaning, ground, and truth that is expressed both in the Hebrew word 'Amen' and

---

[25] Ratzinger, *Introduction to Christianity*, 75. Then-Cardinal Joseph Ratzinger explicitly links this technological reduction of reason to life issues in this preface to the 2004 edition of *Introduction to Christianity*: "Man is becoming a technological object while vanishing to an ever greater degree as a human subject, and he has only himself to blame. When human embryos are artificially 'cultivated' so as to have 'research material' and to obtain a supply of organs, which then are supposed to benefit other human beings, there is scarcely an outcry, because so few are horrified any more" (17).

[26] Ibid., 76. This sentence has the following footnote: "The Greek word *logos* displays in its range of meanings a certain correspondence with the Hebrew root *'mn* ("Amen"): word, meaning, rationality, truth [*Wort, Sinn, Vernunft, Wahrheit*] are all included in its semantic range."

in the Greek *logos* at the same times intimates a whole view of the world."[27] This whole dimension of human life and the discovery of meaning is what is eclipsed by the reduction to technological or practical reason: "It is certainly true that belief or faith is not knowledge in the sense of practical knowledge and its particular kind of calculability.... But the reverse is also true: calculable practical knowledge is limited by its very nature to the apparent, to what functions, and does not represent the way in which to find truth in itself, which by its very method it has renounced."[28] Ratzinger suggests that there are differing modes of our intellectual encounter with the world: "The tool with which man is equipped to deal with the truth of being is not *knowledge* but *understanding*: understanding of the meaning to which he has entrusted himself."[29] Knowledge of how to manipulate the world around us is part of the beauty of man and his ability to live in society. Nonetheless, such manipulative knowledge needs to be grounded in the truth of things, a truth that such knowledge cannot itself provide. Ratzinger observes, "Knowledge of the functional aspect of the world, as procured for us so splendidly by present-day technical and scientific thinking, brings with it no understanding of the world and of being."[30] Ratzinger attempts to show that Christianity itself, and not mere technology, offers this desired understanding.[31]

The Scientific Reduction of Logos

Scientific reason may be distinguished from technological reason. Scientific reason looks to the truth of the universe. Nonetheless, even when reason is open to the discovery of scientific truth, there exists

[27] Ibid., 76.

[28] Ibid., 77.

[29] Ibid. See also the way in which Josef Pieper distinguishes between reason or *ratio* and understanding or *intellectus* in *Leisure: The Basis of Culture* (San Francisco: Ignatius Press, 2009).

[30] Ratzinger, *Introduction to Christianity*, 77.

[31] Michael Hanby reflects at length on Ratzinger's theme of the technological reduction of reason in his "*Homo Faber* and/or *Homo Adorans*: On the Place of Human Making in a Sacramental Cosmos", *Communio* 38 (2011): 198–236. Drawing explicitly on Ratzinger's *Introduction to Christianity*, Hanby writes, "As nature becomes artifice, knowledge effectively becomes engineering" (209).

a significant danger in the reduction of reason to what is empirically verifiable or demonstrable via mathematical reasoning.[32]

Scientific reasoning may affirm the existence of God as the source of creation. Ratzinger recalls how Einstein came to affirm the existence of an intelligence and quotes Einstein in saying that in the laws of nature "an intelligence so superior is revealed that in comparison all the significance of human thinking and human arrangements is a completely worthless reflection."[33] Yet, Einstein saw this greatness of the intelligence displayed in the universe as incompatible with any human projections. Thus, Ratzinger notes how Einstein eschews the anthropomorphism and morality associated with revealed accounts of God. Ratzinger then considers the view of a famous mathematician who likewise affirms the existence of an intelligent source of the mathematical principles that underlie the universe and our ability to understand these principles.

Ratzinger, however, goes farther to show that this scientific and mathematical reasoning is not adequate to the fullness of being. In a lapidary manner, Ratzinger observes the irony in the idea that a physicist sees the physics in the universe and "the mathematician discovers the mathematics of the cosmos, the being-thought-ness of things; but no more."[34] In so doing, they admit a physicist mind and a mathematical mind behind the universe. Yet, it is hardly surprising that this is all they see since they are only looking through the lens of scientific reasoning. Ratzinger queries, "Can the mathematician who looks at the world mathematically find anything else but mathematics in the universe?"[35] The language of mathematics does not itself express morality or aesthetics and so may only affirm a divine being that is true, yet not one that is good or beautiful. Here Ratzinger suggests that this view is not the true view, but actually a diminution of the full truth of being, which must include the true, the good, and the beautiful since it provides the ground of human meaning.

As Ratzinger develops his analysis, he shows how scientific reasoning fails to be an adequate account of the human experience of

---

[32] Ratzinger reflects on how the natural scientific mode of reasoning has been employed in Christian theology and decisively rejects such a "scientific theology" in his *Principles of Catholic Theology*, 322ff.

[33] Ratzinger, *Introduction to Christianity*, 153, citing A. Einstein, *Mein Weltbild*.

[34] Ibid., 154.

[35] Ibid.

understanding the world around us. Ratzinger begins with the scientist's own experience of wonder: "[Has he] never seen an apple tree in blossom and wondered why the process of fertilization by the interplay between bees and tree is not effected otherwise than through the roundabout way of the blossom, thus including the completely superfluous wonder of beauty ...?"[36] Ratzinger here invites the scientist to be attentive to the scientist's own process of reasoning and to discover that there is more than may be explained mathematically. It is not accidentally that Ratzinger adduces living things interacting in their complex environments. Life itself presents itself to us as a recognizable reality; living beings likewise present themselves as recognizably distinct.

Ratzinger reflects upon the experience of the scientist through the language of form, or *Gestalt*. The language of form has been used by the philosophical tradition to identify that unity of operation which hallmarks the intelligibility of distinct living things as well as their complex interactions. When man looks at the world, he does not perceive simply discrete data, but perceives living wholes that bring unity to the discrete matter of the universe. Ratzinger thus asks whether it is truly rational to deny validity to this human experience and answers "no". Instead, the truly rational response is to see that the human creature is irreducibly capable of recognizing—and beholding—forms of things in our environment. These forms present themselves as vital and real. In so doing, they tell us something about the nature of our reasoning that recognizes them as well as about the source of the universe that must somehow be the source not only of the laws of nature but also of these forms of living beings that are recognized as beautiful and good. In a gentle, yet forceful, apologetic move, Ratzinger presents the experience to the person under the spell of scientific reasoning: "In the world we find present, without doubt, objective mathematics; but we also find equally present in the world unparalleled and unexplained wonders of beauty, or, to be more accurate, there are events that appear to the apprehending mind of man in the form of beauty, so that he is bound to say that the mathematician responsible for these events has displayed an unparalleled degree of creative imagination."[37]

[36] Ibid.
[37] Ibid., 155.

Ratzinger further questions the limitation to scientific reasoning based upon the understanding of freedom, both human and divine. Arguing that the human perception of forms of life and beauty point to the presence of those forms in the source of the universe and the human creatures within it, he draws the audience away from exclusive mathematical necessity to the reality of loving freedom. He writes, "If the *logos* of all being, the being that upholds and encompasses everything, is consciousness, freedom, and love, then it follows automatically that the supreme factor in the world is not cosmic necessity but freedom."[38] If there is freedom in the source of the universe and an echo of that freedom in the human creature, then "the world can never—if this is the position—be completely reduced to mathematical logic."[39] Ratzinger, moreover, connects this truth to the human experience of good and evil. Again, we observe his apologetic approach by inviting the scientist to consider his own desire to foster the good and resist evil, however it is understood by the given individual. The scientific reduction of reasoning would remove the very ground for moral approbation and indignation.[40] Ratzinger draws the connection as follows: "a world created and willed on the risk of freedom and love is no longer just mathematics. As the arena of love it is also the playground of freedom and incurs the risk of evil."[41] Only a human reason that is open to moral and aesthetic truths is adequate to respond to the reality of the human drama of good and evil.[42]

---

[38] Ibid., 159.

[39] Ibid., 160.

[40] In his preface to the 2004 edition of *Introduction to Christianity*, Ratzinger explicitly connects the reduction of reason with the loss of moral truths: "If the world and man do not come from a creative intelligence, which stores within itself their measures and plots the path of human existence, then all that is left are traffic rules for human behavior, which can be discarded or maintained according to their usefulness.... The problem of moral values is on the order of the day in our time, and it is an item of great urgency. Faith in the Logos, the Word in the beginning, understands moral values as *responsibility*, as a response to the Word, and thus gives them their intelligibility as well as their essential orientation" (27).

[41] Ibid., 160.

[42] In addition to the specifically moral dimension, such an approach eclipses the majority of human experiences. Pablo Blanco Sarto writes, "Ratzinger proposes a 'truthful reason'—not a technical and purely mathematical reason—that has a universal openness to faith, as well as to the world of feelings and other human activities", in "*Logos* and *Dia-Logos*: Faith, Reason, (and Love) according to Joseph Ratzinger", *Anglican Theological Review*, vol. 92, no. 3 (2010): 499–509, 507.

The Historical Reduction of Logos

What is an authentic historical science, and how does it assist the reception and proclamation of the Christian faith? Is history the living encounter of human beings with God in the covenants handed down from one generation to the next? Or is history only what we can know with documentary verification? Ratzinger discerns an erroneous reduction of the domain of history to what can be verified as historical.[43] This places enormous strain on the Creed, since it has irreducibly historical claims about the Incarnation, death, Resurrection, and Second Coming of Jesus Christ. Jesus Christ is no longer one but has been separated in strains of modern theology into the Jesus of history and the Christ of faith. Ratzinger argues that this separation is not only injurious to the intelligibility of the Creed but is also based upon an overly simplistic quasi-scientific view of history.

How should reason stand before history? Ratzinger avers that the historico-critical method is unduly influenced by the scientific method associated with the natural sciences. The modern scientific method is based upon repetition, and thus its application to historical matters is more complicated than might appear at first glance. Repeated experiments to test hypotheses and conclusions yield verification. Ratzinger notes, however, that, "the historian is denied this satisfaction; past history cannot be reenacted, and verification must be content with the demonstrable soundness of the evidence on which the historian bases his view."[44] Ratzinger argues that the case for scientific history is even weaker than the impossibility of repetition. While physics has observable reality ever before it, history must "rely on the availability of documents, that is, on chance statements".[45] Moreover, unlike the disclosure of material reality as investigated by physics, when human experience is recorded in documentary evidence, much of the richness of human experience is lost and much of that meaning will involve the experience of the human interpreter.[46] History has an empirical dimension, but its presence is not before us as an

[43] For additional reflection on the connection between salvation and history, see Ratzinger, *Principles of Catholic Theology*, 153ff.

[44] Ratzinger, *Introduction to Christianity*, 195.

[45] Ibid.

[46] Ibid., 196.

empirical reality. Attempts, therefore, to apply the experimental scientific method to the study of history will inevitably lead to a certain kind of distortion before the truth of history.

The lens through which we observe reality shapes what we will see and what we will miss. When we query the origins of the universe through physics, we will exclude features of our existence such as meaning, hope, goodness, and evil. So also, when we query the origins of Christianity through the lens of the modern historico-critical method, we will miss the living tradition of the Church, the stories of meaning, hope, goodness, and evil. Ratzinger draws the parallel in an explicit manner: "Just as in physics being retires behind appearance, so here to a large extent the only past events that are still accepted as valid are those that are presented as 'historical', that is, tested and passed by historical methods. It is quite often forgotten that the full truth of history eludes documentary verification just as much as the truth of being escapes the experimental approach."[47] The constrictions of reason to physics and historical science, if allowed to have the final word, eliminate much of the truth of being and history. Just as Ratzinger would not eschew physics as a splendid mode of inquiry, he does not eschew historical studies. He refuses, however, to let either physics or historical studies be the only scope of reason as it investigates reality and the claims presented in the Christian Creed.

Modern historical science falters before the Christian claims. Ratzinger suggests that such a historical rationality "not only reveals but also conceals history".[48] This approach "can see the man Jesus all right but can only with difficulty discover Christ in him, which as a truth of history cannot simply be checked as right or wrong by reference to the documentary evidence."[49] The question of whether God was in Jesus Christ cannot be settled by the historico-critical method since God as such could never appear as a piece of documentary history.

Yet, what if God did enter history? Ratzinger emphasizes that we are not left in an impossible situation in which we must remain cut off from a God who cannot enter into our historical existence. He

[47] Ibid.
[48] Ibid.
[49] Ibid.

goes farther to suggest that strains in modern thought would prefer a God who stayed outside of history. Although the divine presence cannot be verified in historical artifacts by means of historical science, the divine presence does in fact come into history in specific forms stemming from God's covenantal relationship with human beings. Ratzinger observes, "It irritates us [today] that God should have to be mediated through outward forms: through Church, sacrament, dogma, or even just through the Gospel (kerygma), to which people like to withdraw to reduce the irritation and which is nevertheless itself something external."[50] Each outward form appears as a historically recognizable phenomenon and yet communicates an internal divine presence.[51]

God's presence in history dispels the modern myth of the individual. We are historical and communal beings who discover meaning from others and for others, both those who live now and those in the past. Ratzinger connects a fulsome understanding of history to the order of each person within the greater whole of the Church: "Christian faith is not based on the atomized individual but comes from the knowledge that there is no such thing as the mere individual, that, on the contrary, man is himself only when he is fitted into the whole: into mankind, into history, into the cosmos, as is right and proper for a being who is 'spirit in body'."[52] Once the narrow lens of modern historical science has been broadened, history is the means by which we encounter Christ's presence in the Church. Ratzinger presents the very scandal of the uniqueness of God's revelation in Jesus Christ and in his Church as the manner in which God's revelation becomes existentially meaningful for each person: "Christianity proceeds from the principle of 'corporeality' (historicity), that it is to be thought of

---

[50] Ibid., 244.

[51] This same pattern may be seen in Ratzinger's treatment of the intelligible unity of Scripture in other of his writings. Aaron Pidel, S.J., writes, "On Ratzinger's view, Scripture intends to affirm its own expressions only as pointing beyond themselves, that is, as a material witness to the single complex truth that is God's self-disclosure in Christ. He does not, however, narrow the inerrancy of Scripture to matters of faith and morals. Rather, because Christ, the incarnate Logos, grounds all rationality, the intention of Scripture must also encompass scientific, historical and religious claims—though only to the extent that each bears upon faith in Christ": see Pidel, "Joseph Ratzinger on Biblical Inerrancy", *Nova et Vetera*, English ed., vol. 12, no. 1 (2014): 307–30, at 322.

[52] Ratzinger, *Introduction to Christianity*, 245.

on the plane of 'the whole' and has meaning only on this plane, and that nevertheless for this very reason it sets up and must set up the 'individual' as a principle, which is its scandal, the intrinsic necessity and rationality of which are nevertheless evident here."[53] The Church then exists necessarily with historical and theological dimensions.

When Ratzinger addresses the Creed's confession of faith in the Holy Spirit, he deliberately intertwines a metaphysical perspective with a historical viewpoint. The tripartite division of the Creed first tells the story of salvation moving from the one God in creation and the covenants with Israel, through the saving actions of Jesus Christ, and then to the extension of those saving actions in the Spirit and his presence in the Church. And, yet, the Creed also speaks of the three Persons of the Trinity, who exist as one God from all eternity. Here Ratzinger discerns two approaches that need to be distinguished in order to be united: "the interplay of 'salvation history' and trinitarian viewpoints is characteristic of the oldest stages of Christian thought."[54] It was only later that an unfortunate division arose between "theological metaphysics, on the one side, and theology of history, on the other". An urgent task today is to recover this "original unity of Christian thought.... [a unity] molded by the unity of history and being".[55] Ratzinger thinks that the reduction of history to modern historical science has prevented Christianity from being able to offer meaning to the modern person. With some irony, Ratzinger suggests that the more Christianity is presented in the fullness of its creedal claims seen through this unity of history and being, the more Christianity becomes a path of meaning.[56]

The Mythological Reduction of Logos

God's entrance into history simultaneously needs to avoid the mythological reduction of God to a historical being within the world.

---

[53] Ibid., 251.

[54] Ibid., 332.

[55] Ibid.

[56] In his *Principles of Catholic Theology*, Ratzinger writes forcefully, "In view of the fundamental meaning of this 'is' [as in: God 'is' man], I would stress more strongly today than I have in these pages the irreplaceability and preeminence of the ontological aspect and, therefore, of metaphysics as the basis of any history" (190n172).

Ratzinger reflects upon the encounter of intertestamental Judaism and the early Church with the Greco-Roman philosophy, religion, and society. That encounter forced these communities to determine their fundamental stance vis-à-vis human nature and culture. Ratzinger writes, "early Christianity boldly and resolutely made its choice and carried out its purification by deciding *for* the God of the philosophers and *against* the gods of the various religions."[57] God could not be understood as a being in the cosmos, but only as being itself that shares its being with the cosmos. Ratzinger roots this affirmation in the early Old Testament revelation of a personal God (*numen personale*) rather than a local God (*numen locale*). He thus connects the early religion of Israel to the faith expressed in the New Testament: "the emanation of God's personality, the understanding of God on the plane defined by the I-and-You relationship".[58] Ancient mythological religion formed a horizon of thinking about gods that eclipsed the Creator God. The early Christians thus set aside Zeus and Hermes as lenses through which to think about God, but they did not set aside Being itself. Ratzinger describes their judgment: "When we say God,... we mean only Being itself, what the philosophers have expounded as the ground of all being, as the God above all powers—that alone is our God."[59] Ratzinger consistently draws upon the Christian practice of affirming the Greek *logos*, while eschewing the Greek *mythos*.[60]

Ratzinger observes that the affirmation of *logos* against *mythos* formed part of the original dynamic of Greek philosophy. He goes farther to suggest that Greek and Roman cultures and societies suffered from this separation of *logos* and *mythos* and the resulting separation of reason and piety: "The ancient religion did eventually break up because of the gulf between the God of faith and the God of the philosophers, because of the total dichotomy between reason and

[57] Ratzinger, *Introduction to Christianity*, 137.

[58] Ibid., 124.

[59] Ibid., 138.

[60] Thomas G. Guarino ably summarizes Ratzinger's approach: "Again in the early Church, the Pope insists, a choice was boldly made for utilizing and purifying the God of the philosopher, even while rejecting the gods of various mythic religions. Our God, the early Christian writers say, is the highest being of whom your philosophers speak.... What occurs here is the triumph of *logos* over *mythos*, of existing actuality over fiction and fable", in "The God of Philosophy and of the Bible: Theological Reflections on Regensburg", *Logos: A Journal of Catholic Thought and Culture*, vol. 10, no. 4 (2007): 120–30, at 123.

piety."[61] Ratzinger transfers this post-mortem to the circumstance of Christianity in the face of modernity.

As was the case in the Greco-Roman world, there exists in certain modern strains of Christian theology a strong separation of reason and piety. This is the mythological reduction of reason. Ratzinger strives to elevate piety or mythos so that it can participate in reason. He does so for two reasons. First, he draws upon the parallel to the collapse of ancient religion to offer a prognosis for Christianity were it to follow the same separation: "The Christian religion would have to expect just the same fate if it were to accept a similar amputation of reason and were to embark on a corresponding withdrawal into the purely religious, as advocated by Schleiermacher and present, paradoxically enough, in a certain sense in Schleiermacher's great critic and opponent Karl Barth."[62] Reason and piety need to go hand-in-hand in order for either reason or piety to be channels of existential meaningfulness. Attempts to separate them within Christianity render the Christian faith sterile, ironically without reason or piety. Ratzinger observes that the ancient religion "did not go the way of *logos* but lingered in myths already seen to be devoid of reality".[63] Ratzinger's approach throughout his *Introduction* is to avoid this unreality of religion in the modern world by showing how reason is elevated and actualized in confessing the Christian faith.

Second, piety must embrace reason since the *logos* became *sarx*. Christology thus unites piety and reason despite many misguided attempts within Christianity to separate them. The fullness of reason can see in the true historical revelation of Jesus Christ the divine presence. The Christological confession of the Apostles' Creed and later creeds resist reduction into the world of pagan mythology. Ratzinger thus contrasts dogma with myth: "Developed christological dogma acknowledges that the radical Christship of Jesus presupposes the Sonship and that the Sonship includes the Godship; only if it is thus understood does it remain 'logos-like', that is, a rational statement; without this logical consistency, one sinks into myth."[64] The story of

---

[61] Ratzinger, *Introduction to Christianity*, 139.
[62] Ibid., 139.
[63] Ibid., 140.
[64] Ibid., 211.

Jesus Christ as confessed in the Creed is not one myth alongside other myths but is the disclosure of God's myth. As God's myth, it is fully reasonable; in fact, it is reason itself manifested in history.

Ratzinger repeatedly affirms the role of reason in the earliest stages of the communication of the Christian proclamation.[65] He presents theology as *logos*-based discussion of God and affirms theology as "the basis of the inalienable right of Greek thought to a place in Christianity. I am convinced that at bottom it was no mere accident that the Christian message, in the period when it was taking shape, first entered the Greek world and there merged with the inquiry into understanding, into truth."[66] The proper proclamation of the Christian faith needs to avoid the reduction of reason into myth but must, rather, see that reason finds in Jesus Christ truth himself. Ratzinger writes, "Man can rethink the *logos*, the meaning of being, because his own *logos*, his own reason, is *logos* of the one *logos*, thought of the original thought, of the creative spirit that permeates and governs his being."[67] The doctrine of creation appears as the antidote to the reduction of reason. Creation no longer is something mythological that happened in the distant past. Creation, instead, is presently known in the intelligible response to the intelligibility of the universe as it is received by the unique creature called *homo sapiens*.

Christian Reason: The Wholeness of Logos

Although the Greek *logos* is more expansive than the modern reductions associated with technological, scientific, and historical modes of reasoning, it too must be distinguished from the fullness of reason in the biblical revelation. I will focus on two central themes presented by Ratzinger in which Christian theology must hold on to the

[65] In his *Principles of Catholic Theology*, Ratzinger affirms Romano Guardini's "primacy of *logos* over *ethos*" and Aquinas' theology as first a "*scientia speculativa*" (319). Ratzinger continues, "we fail to understand the meaning of Christology precisely when it remains locked in a historico-anthropological circle and does not become a real theo-logy, in which the metaphysical reality of God is what is discussed" (319).

[66] Ratzinger, *Introduction to Christianity*, 78.

[67] Ibid., 59 (Der Mensch aber kann dem Logos, dem Sinn des Seins, nachdenken, weil sein eigener Logos, seine eigene Vernunft, Logos des einen Logos, Gedanke des Urgedankens ist, des Schöpfergeistes, der das Sein durchwaltet).

fullness of biblical *logos*: first, the source of the universe is not only being and intelligence but is also personal and loving; and, second, the source of the universe manifests himself as grace and gift.

Biblical revelation transforms, but does not destroy, the Greek understanding of being itself as the source of the universe. A deeper element is revealed, but the metaphysical approach remains.

Biblical revelation here transforms but does not destroy. Once God reveals himself as personal, the human creature's relationship to God is ever changed. Ratzinger contrasts the concept of God to the name of God. We are no longer discovering the truth of being as a human endeavor but, instead, are responding to the divine initiative. Ratzinger writes, "The concept tries to perceive the nature of the thing as it is in itself. The name, on the other hand, does not ask after the nature of the thing as it exists independently of me; it is concerned to make the thing nameable, that is, 'invocable', to establish a relation to it."[68] When God reveals himself to human beings, he is thus inviting them not only to understand him but, above all, to call upon him.

This approach allows Ratzinger to perceive a profound unity between Old Testament and New Testament revelation. The unity is not an arbitrary imposition but is rooted in the intelligibility of divine revelation as coming from the divine *logos* to human *logos*. The revelation of the name to Moses enabled a new mode of divine presence in the world in which God "enters into coexistence with them".[69] Yet, this is the same theme manifested in Jesus Christ. Ratzinger makes this connection explicitly: "God is one of us. Thus what had been meant since the episode of the burning bush by the idea of the name is really fulfilled in him who as God is man and as man is God. God has become one of us and so has become truly nameable, standing in coexistence with us."[70] The biblical *logos* adds to the Greek *logos* the dimension of name, yet the name is not arbitrary or irrational since it allows human beings to enter into relation with being itself.

Biblical revelation teaches that the path of knowledge and wisdom requires conversion. As fallen human beings, we are oriented to false

[68] Ibid., 134.
[69] Ibid.
[70] Ibid., 135.

gods within creation. We have a penchant for idolatry and may only arrive at an iconic view of creation through a deliberate renunciation. Ratzinger develops this theme by considering the fundamental creedal affirmation of faith in one God, an echo of the earlier Israelite *Shema* (Deut 6:4–9). The affirmation of the one God simultaneously renounces "the worship of bread, the worship of love, and the idolization of power". Thus, "it is a profession in the fullest sense of this word, that is, it is not the registration of one view alongside others but an existential decision."[71] Conversion here begets understanding: "Understanding grows only out of belief. That is why theology as the understanding, *logos-like* (= rational, understanding through reason) discussion of God is a fundamental task of Christian faith."[72] Conversion is not the rejection of human reason; reason needs the assistance of the will assisted by grace in order to perceive reality in its full theological dimension.[73]

The biblical vision thus opens up a new view of creation, especially of the human creature. The world comes from reason, but it also comes from love. Therefore, being, both in God and in creatures, manifests itself as a being-from and being-for.[74] Ratzinger here draws a distinction between the Greek view of the cosmos and the Christian view:

> Greek thought always regarded the many individual creatures, including the many individual human beings, only as individuals, arising out of the splitting up of the idea in matter. The reproductions are

---

[71] Ibid., 111.

[72] Ibid., 77–78.

[73] Aidan Nichols, O.P., connects Ratzinger's decision to follow the Creed as decisive for the role of belief and conversion. "[The Apostles' Creed] is the Church's own formulation of faith for the candidate entering upon the life of faith by baptism.... Ratzinger points out that the triform, Trinitarian patter of this creed corresponds to a threefold renunciation, of the world, the flesh and the Devil, asked of the neophyte. Doctrine is inseparable from the conversion of one's whole being", in *The Thought of Pope Benedict XVI: An Introduction to the Theology of Joseph Ratzinger*, new ed. (New York: Burns & Oates, 2007), 76–77.

[74] In his preface to the 2004 edition of *Introduction to Christianity*, Ratzinger accentuates this connection between reason and love: "The God who is *logos* guarantees the intelligibility of the world, the intelligibility of our existence, the aptitude of reason to know God [*die Gottgemäßheit der Vernunft*] and the reasonableness of God [*die Vernunftgemäßheit Gottes*], even though his understanding infinitely surpasses ours and to us may so often appear to be darkness. The world comes from reason, and this reason is a Person, is Love—this is what our biblical faith tells us about God" (26).

thus always secondary; the real thing is the one and universal. The Christian sees in man, not an individual, but a person; and it seems to me that this passage from the individual to person contains the whole span of the transition from antiquity to Christianity, from Platonism to faith.[75]

If God is personal, and if the personal God has taken on the fullness of human nature in Jesus Christ, then each human person exercises an unrepeatable role in the drama of creation and redemption.

If God is personal, then it is not surprising that this God loves, acts, and gives himself in our history. This changes the fundamental characteristic of all biblical thought versus Greek thought. Ratzinger states concisely, "One could say epigrammatically that faith does in fact come from 'hearing', not—like philosophy—from 'reflection'."[76] Ratzinger, however, does not present this as a destruction or as mere antagonism, but as a transformation: "The assertion 'faith comes from what is heard' [Rom 10:17] ... illuminates the fundamental differences between faith and mere philosophy, a difference that does not prevent faith, in its core, from setting the philosophical search for truth in motion again."[77] Biblical reasoning is always in the mode of receptivity to God's revelation, but both are guided by a desire for truth.

God reveals himself not only as personal but also as gift. The personal *logos* is gift. Ratzinger thus develops *logos* as the means by which human beings might receive the gift of the divine love. In summarizing the meaningfulness of the creedal confession of Jesus Christ, Ratzinger writes, "The primacy of acceptance includes Christian positivity and shows its intrinsic necessity."[78] If Christian positivity necessitates the primacy of acceptance from the standpoint of the Christian, then reason alone is never sufficient. He writes, "our relation to God ultimately cannot rest on our own planning, on a speculative knowledge, but demands the positivity of what confronts us, what comes to us as something positive, something to be received."[79]

[75] Ratzinger, *Introduction to Christianity*, 160.
[76] Ibid., 91.
[77] Ibid.
[78] Ibid., 268.
[79] Ibid.

Ratzinger expands on this theme of gift when he contrasts the biblical account of grace to the Greek account of ethos. "To the Bible, the limits of human righteousness, of human capabilities as a whole, become an indication of the way in which man is thrown back upon the unquestioning gift of love, a gift that unexpectedly opens itself to him and thereby opens up man himself, and without which man would remain shut up in all his 'righteousness' and thus unrighteous."[80] *Logos* thus not only discovers meaning, but it receives unmerited forgiveness and love.

Forgiveness and love enter into human history as a gift. Ratzinger develops this theme by reflecting upon the Creed's united confession of belief in the Holy Spirit and the Church: "This sacramental approach produces a completely theocentric understanding of the Church: the foreground is occupied, not by the group of men composing her, but by the gift of God that turns man around toward a new being that he cannot give to himself, to a communion that he can only receive as a gift."[81] Human beings are called to communion, but not to a communion that can be achieved via the development of natural virtue. The Greek account of ethos is thus both fulfilled and radically transformed through the Christian notion of gift and grace.

Ratzinger develops the language of gift through its excessiveness. He points to the miracles of the multiplication of loaves and fish and to the transformation of water into wine as manifesting "the divine excess or abundance, which infinitely surpasses all needs and legitimate demands".[82] This reality of excessive gift is the true character of Christian worship. Ratzinger observes that these two miracles of excess also are signs of the multiplication and transformation of bread and wine in the Eucharist. Thus Christ himself is the cornerstone of the excessive love of God. Ratzinger contrasts the law of excess that can see creation as an icon of the giving God versus the law of calculation that sees creation as idols in competition for scarce resources: "So excess or superfluity—let us repeat—is the real definition or mark of the history of salvation. The purely calculating mind will always find it absurd that for man God himself should be expended.

[80] Ibid., 259.
[81] Ibid., 336.
[82] Ibid., 261.

Only the lover can understand the folly of a love to which prodigality is a law and excess alone is sufficient."[83] Reason alone, however open it is to the true being of things, will never realize the inner logic of human history in which the gift of salvation is offered to those who are unworthy in order to make them worthy in this life and the next.

The nature of the gift grounds the mutual independence of faith and love. Faith without love risks a dry speculation; love without faith risks a false claim that man can attain his true end in this life. Ratzinger writes, "for without faith, which we have come to understand as a term expressing man's ultimate need to receive and the inadequacy of all personal achievements, love becomes an arbitrary deed. It cancels itself out and becomes self-righteousness."[84] Human love must necessarily recognize its imperfection. Love combined with faith acknowledges the giftedness of human life at every point in our personal and communal histories. Christianity, however, must avoid the opposite error of privileging faith apart from love. The same Christ who invites faith also comes as judge of our works. Drawing upon Matthew 25, Ratzinger writes, "to profess one's faith in Christ means to recognize the man who needs me as the Christ in the form in which he comes to meet me here and now; it means understanding the challenge of love as the challenge of faith."[85] As Ratzinger has argued for the unity of Jesus and Christ, here he affirms the unity of love and faith: "faith that is not love is not a really *Christian* faith; ... a fact that must redound both against any doctrinalistic misunderstanding of the Catholic concept of faith and against the secularization of love that proceeds in Luther from the notion of justification exclusively by faith."[86] Just as the gift needs to be received in faith and returned in faith, the gift of salvation needs to be received in love and returned in love.[87]

Ratzinger emphasizes the fullness of being in its personal dimension to address certain problems within Christological debates. He

---

[83] Ibid., 262.

[84] Ibid., 270.

[85] Ibid., 209.

[86] Ibid.

[87] In a 2008 address, then-Pope Benedict presents the intrinsic unity of goodness and truth. He writes, "This is also the meaning of Socratic enquiry: What is the good which makes us true? The truth makes us good and the good is true: this is the optimism that shapes the Christian faith, because this faith has been granted the vision of the *Logos*, of creative Reason which, in God's incarnation, revealed itself as the Good, as Goodness itself", in the Lecture by the Holy Father Benedict XVI at the University of Rome "La Sapienza" (January 17, 2008).

diagnoses an unhelpful separation that has occurred in modern theology between the theology of the Incarnation and the theology
of the Cross. This separation finds its roots in a philosophical separation of being and event. Yet, the philosophical notion of being,
once illumined by the perspective of faith, allows for a full actuality
even within the horizon of history. This approach excludes both an
unnecessary separation and a false identity in his treatment of the
theologies of the Incarnation and of the Cross. They need to be both
distinguished and united. Ratzinger describes this unity of polarities
as follows: "the *being* of Christ ('Incarnation' theology!) is *actualitas*,
stepping beyond itself, the exodus of going out from self; it is, not
a being that rests in itself, but the act of being sent, of being son, of
serving. Conversely, this 'doing' is not just 'doing' but 'being'; it
reaches down into the depths of being and coincides with it. This
being is exodus, transformation."[88] The metaphysical perfection
of being and actuality enters into history in a decisive manner that
transforms and redeems history.

Being enters history. Thus reason must be open to discovering
truth in both metaphysical and historical reflections on what God has
done in Jesus Christ. Ratzinger pauses to reflect on the utter newness
of this entrance of the timeless Word into history: "Although faith in
the *logos*, the meaningfulness of being, corresponds perfectly with a
tendency in the human reason, this second article of the Creed proclaims the absolutely staggering alliance of *logos* and *sarx*, of meaning
and a single historical figure."[89] Being is united to a being; history
is united to a historical instance; the intelligibility of the cosmos is
united to a distinct part of the cosmos. Ratzinger emphasizes that
human reason is open to receiving this disclosure that exceeds all
expectation of reason.

Conclusion: Logos and the Communication of the Faith

Ratzinger proposes that creedal faith elevates human reason and offers
a living antidote to the various reductions of human reason preva-
lent within modern and postmodern society. He roots theological

---

[88] Ratzinger, *Introduction to Christianity*, 230.
[89] Ibid., 193.

reflection and apologetic engagement in the revelation of Jesus Christ as communicated in the Creed. The Creed and *logos* are thus inseparable. The communication of the Creed requires the *Logos* it reveals and the *logos* by which it is received. Moreover, *logos* requires in turn that the faith be communicated in a creedal manner capable of expressing saving truths about God and man. Ratzinger offers an approach to Christian teaching and apologetics with a bold affirmation of the wholeness of the *logos* that professes faith in the wholeness of the Christian Creed. Faith perfects human reason.

As prefect of the Congregation for the Doctrine of the Faith, in 1990, he would write in *Donum veritatis* that the principles of theology are revealed and as such have the force of givens.[90] The principles of theology are the articles of the Creed, above all the revelation of the great mysteries of the Incarnation and the Trinity.[91] The Creed has a unity grounded in the unity of God's actions in creation and redemption as revealed in Scripture. The articles of the Creed allow for communion with the mystery they reveal. Thomas Aquinas affirms that the act of the believer terminates, not in the proposition, but in the reality. One does not merely profess the Creed; one comes to know and love the God professed. Ratzinger seeks to communicate this same reality. Through the Creed, when one embraces it through the wholeness of graced human reason, we come to know and love the source of our reason and love. Thus, the Creed is the midpoint between the entirety of the breadth and depth of Sacred Scripture and the Triune God with whom mankind has entered a covenantal communion through the Incarnation of the Son of God.

---

[90] *Donum veritatis*, no. 12, "In theology this freedom of inquiry is the hallmark of a rational discipline whose object is given by Revelation, handed on and interpreted in the Church under the authority of the Magisterium, and received by faith. These givens have the force of principles. To eliminate them would mean to cease doing theology."

[91] In his preface to the 2004 edition of *Introduction to Christianity*, Ratzinger reaffirms his approach: "I believe that I was not mistaken as to the fundamental approach, in that I put the question of God and the question about Christ in the very center" (29).

5

Hans Urs von Balthasar and His Path to Reinhold Schneider

Peter Casarella

L'heure n'est aux déserteurs timorés, mais aux hommes courageux qui resistent et qui dirigent.

—Hans Urs von Balthasar

Anyone who delves into the work of the Swiss Catholic theologian Hans Urs von Balthasar quickly finds a confirmation of the judgment of Henri de Lubac that he was indeed the most learned man in Christendom. But this very approbation fuels concerns raised by his critics that his sweeping vision of Christian faith barely transcends that of a high-minded Romanticizing poet when it comes to the question of how Christian faith shapes our understanding of culture and politics. It is somewhat ironic that the figure of Hans Urs von Balthasar has been dragged into the new culture wars. Von Balthasar himself was

Part of the last section of this essay on the Christological *analogia entis* has already appeared in my contribution to *The Analogy of Being: Invention of the Antichrist or the Wisdom of God?* ed. Thomas Joseph White, O.P. (Grand Rapids, Mich.: Eerdmans, 2011), 192–206.

The epigraph reads: "This is no time for timid deserters but for men of courage who resist and guide others." Hans Urs von Balthasar, "Sur les conditions d'une culture", *Comprendre: Revue de Société Européene de Culture* (1950): 196. Interestingly, Balthasar is referring here to James Joyce, Picasso, and "the Faust of Thomas Mann". His hero for the spiritual revitalization of Europe in this lecture is, however, Goethe.

only an occasional polemicist. For example, his small book *Cordula oder der Ernstfall* (*The Moment of Christian Witness*) contains a penetrating caricature of Karl Rahner's notion of an anonymous Christianity.[1] But his most well-known works, like the monumental triptych on theological aesthetics, theo-drama, and theo-logic, betray little interest in engaging his opponents or provoking controversy. Here the transcendentals of beauty, goodness, and truth are recovered as starting points for a synoptic vision of the glory of the Lord in God's self-revelation and as an articulation of the fundamental truth that Christ offered himself for the sake of witnessing to a truth regarding the wondrous immensity of divine goodness and mercy.

By the same token, it is pretty clear why von Balthasar has received such vociferous criticism from certain quarters. He was suspicious of most attempts by modern theologians to create artificial bridges between the legitimate insights of the secular world and the wisdom gained from Christ. After some initial attempts to build up his theology on the basis of the question of God as posed by modern man, von Balthasar turned to a more direct form of engagement with the culture, both in his many writings and in his own arduous and somewhat conflicted search for a proper state of life in the Church.

What is the distinguishing characteristic of his mature theology of culture? Given the enormous scope of his vision and sheer volume of his works, I would begin by highlighting a single feature. The Christian vision of faith and of the world for von Balthasar demands that all things be submitted to Christ. No Christian response to the prevailing culture can ignore the fact that Christ is both the firstborn of all creation (Col 1:18) and the all-holy wisdom of God. The task of engaging culture is thus (to paraphrase a title of a work of Saint Bonaventure that he himself invoked) a re-tracing (*reductio*) of all the disciplines back to their proper abode within the highest wisdom of God. Bonaventure's term *reductio* carries with it an assumption that disciplines are not at all stripped of their integrity as intellectual or even practical forms of inquiry on the way back to their origins. On the contrary, the path back to the highest wisdom demands guidance from one who not only is wise as to

---

[1] Hans Urs von Balthasar, *The Moment of Christian Witness*, trans. Richard Beckley (San Francisco: Ignatius Press, 1994).

what constitutes the unity of the disciplines, but also represents a living witness to Christ's own holiness.

Von Balthasar submitted all things to Christ, and he never himself submitted to the kind of rigorous intellectual scrutiny that comes from being a member of an academic community. Although he spent his life lecturing to university audiences and was offered such positions more than once, he was never a university professor. With this remark, I am not in any way suggesting that his works are naïve or uncritical. Nor would I proffer the opinion that the research university always lives up to its own ideal of critical inquiry in the area of theology and culture. But there is a point to looking seriously at the charges made against von Balthasar since his followers have sometimes considered his non-affiliation with academic theology as a way of warding off the criticisms made against his thought.

What do von Balthasar's critics find to be the principal shortcomings in his theology of culture? The list of grievances is long and varied, but I will attempt to summarize with three points: the charge of elitism, the theology of history, and the apparent opposition to all forms of political and social liberation. Regarding the first point, von Balthasar himself readily admitted to the odd tone of his own writings in the setting of a largely progressive, postconciliar Catholicism. For example, in the preface he wrote to an interview with then theologian Angelo Scola (now Cardinal Scola and retired archbishop of Milan) that took place two years before his death, he comments on how his own words must sound to the average Catholic today:

> Much will have to be said that sounds harsh; may I be pardoned for this and may it be attributed to my shortsightedness. Or, if you will, to my age and backwardness, which show little relish for the latest novelties. Or again, to my love for a Church that has endured for two millennia, has retained her vigor throughout and thus was not born suddenly as a "postconciliar" Church. This could be the true reason why some things may sound harsh; if one knows a bit about the history of the apostolic and holy Church, one measures them against her greatness, and then they appear in a format too flimsy for her catholicity. By holding such views, one risks being labeled "preconciliar" (as if there were such a thing) and pessimistic (which Ratzinger certainly is not; he is merely a realist). I, too, am anything but pessimistic, for the Church, assailed as she is from without and within, demonstrates

by that very fact that she possesses a vitality that is unbearable for the godless world. Amidst the present din of battle, I can clearly sense this vitality, which is bursting forth with renewed life.[2]

But the critics are not merely concerned about the tone of von Balthasar's remarks. Recently, for example, as sympathetic an admirer as John Milbank made the charge in his book *The Suspended Middle* (a title that he in fact borrowed from a comment by von Balthasar) that von Balthasar's works seem marked with elitism when compared to the more ample and generous vision of his teacher Henri de Lubac.[3] Elitism or a certain aloofness to the latest novelties thus remains a leitmotif in virtually every criticism written of the Swiss theologian, and von Balthasar himself concedes that his own writings sometimes generate this impression but maintains that there is more there than meets the eye.

The question of the theology of history is more substantial. Von Balthasar wrote a number of books exactly on this topic, but that fact has not stopped his challengers. This criticism has arisen in a number of different quarters: Thomas Dalzell, Vincent Holzer, Stephan Lösel (a student of Jürgen Moltmann), Frederick Bauerschmidt, and even to a certain degree Karl Rahner, who once claimed in a radio interview that his friend whom he greatly admired incorporated aspects of a Gnostic way of thinking into his theology of Holy Saturday.[4] In its generalized form, the criticism is that von Balthasar locates the event character of the Trinity in a lofty, supratemporal realm and never adequately works out the proper unfolding of the self-manifestation of the Triune God in the actual realm of concrete history. This charge would seem like a caricature were it not for the fact that von Balthasar does maintain that the divine life is enriched by virtue of the self-emptying of an eternal Trinitarian event. In this case, the term "to enrich" (*bereichern*) presupposes that the Kingdom of God (*ta basileia tou theou, das Reich Gottes*) is always already infinitely rich.

---

[2] Hans Urs von Balthasar, *Test Everything, Hold Fast to What Is Good: An Interview with Hans Urs von Balthasar*, trans. Maria Shrady (San Francisco: Ignatius Press, 1989), 7–8.

[3] John Milbank, *The Suspended Middle: Henri de Lubac and the Debate concerning the Supernatural* (Grand Rapids, Mich.: Eerdmans, 2005).

[4] Cf. Cyril O'Regan, *The Anatomy of Misremembering: Von Balthasar's Response to Philosophical Modernity*, vol. 1, *Hegel* (New York: Crossroad, 2014).

Divine enrichment is not a matter of combining God with something other than God to create a third entity. God gets nothing from the world that is not already given to the world from within the infinite generosity of the divine life. It is thus a matter of understanding the divine receptivity to the creaturely offering of freedom as the expression in a finite form of Trinitarian self-enrichment. Von Balthasar can be said to defend the immutability of divine self-enrichment even while acknowledging the emergence of such novelties as "joy" and "surprise" within the immanent Trinity. This is just a very brief response to one of the most difficult questions of interpretation in von Balthasar's thought. I have tried here simply to lay out why it might be construed as a disputed question.

The third major concern follows directly from the second. If history is not taken seriously as the prime locus for the unfolding of God's self-revelation, then it would seem to be a direct consequence of this Christology and Trinitarian failing that theology would not be able to respond to the cry for political liberation from those who are being oppressed by unjust social structures. Von Balthasar opposed many forms of political and liberation theology in ways that only confirmed the charge of elitism. I will return to this question at the end of my chapter.

My intent in what follows is to offer a deeper understanding of von Balthasar's thought in light of these particular charges. In this essay I will address three neglected aspects of a response to these charges: (1) the social and political context out of which his early thinking developed, (2) his engagement with the German writer and social critic Reinhold Schneider, and (3) a brief glance at his response to liberation theology.

Some Aspects of Von Balthasar's Early Cultural Milieu

Von Balthasar's critics generally avoid looking at his thought in its own social and political context. They present his recovery of wisdom from the past as if it were conceived in a vacuum. *Ressourcement* theology thus becomes opposed to social engagement. It would be equally shortsighted to make the opposite mistake of turning von Balthasar into a quiet revolutionary; however, there is more to the story about his social and political education, as one begins to see if one peruses the recent biographical volumes on his early development written by Aidan Nichols.[5]

Let me offer a brief glimpse into how even the patristic scholarship of von Balthasar was conditioned by social upheaval. Werner Löser, in his still valuable book *Im Geiste des Origenes: Hans Urs von Balthasar as Interpret der Theologie der Kirchenväter*, characterizes von Balthasar's patristic hermeneutics as a theological phenomenology.[6] Brian Daley, by contrast, says that von Balthasar discovered in the Fathers an objectivity missing from Gnosticism and German idealism.[7] Regarding the philosophical vintage of von Balthasar's own hermeneutics, Daley perceives "an uneasy mixture of Hegel and neo-Thomism" in the book on Gregory of Nyssa.[8] He furthermore maintains that the Swiss theologian "oddly juxtaposed lenses of Thomist ontology and Hegelian logic" in the book on Maximus the Confessor, *Cosmic Liturgy*.[9] These variant descriptions, one in praise of a Husserlian-inspired innovation and another expressing more skepticism at the synthesis, are not necessarily at odds with one another.[10] But a review of the circumstances out of which von Balthasar forged his patristic hermeneutics might shed additional light on the question about how such a seemingly eclectic reading method came into being in the first place.

Once he was introduced to the Fathers, von Balthasar began a lifetime of theological work in service to *their* witness to Christ and the Church. On the other hand, the original research on the Fathers mainly took place in the period between his studies in Lyon (which began in the fall of 1933 and lasted until the middle of 1937) and the

---

[5] See, for example, Aidan Nichols, *Scattering the Seed: A Guide through Balthasar's Early Writings on Philosophy and the Arts* (Washington, D.C.: Catholic University Press of America, 2006).

[6] Werner Löser, *Im Geiste des Origenes: Hans Urs von Balthasar als Interpret der Theologie der Kirchenväter* (Frankfurt am Main: Knecht, 1976).

[7] Brian E. Daley, "Balthasar's Reading of the Church Fathers", in *The Cambridge Companion to Hans Urs von Balthasar*, ed. Edward T. Oakes, S.J., and David Moss (Cambridge: Cambridge University Press, 2004), 201.

[8] Ibid., 197.

[9] Ibid., 198. He is referring to Hans Urs von Balthasar, *Cosmic Liturgy: The University according to Maximus the Confessor* (San Francisco: Ignatius Press, 2003), which Daley himself translated.

[10] The influence of Husserl on von Balthasar, particularly with regard to the original publication of *Wahrheit der Welt* in 1947, still needs a closer examination.

early period of his service as a Catholic chaplain in Basel. In fact, after the publication in 1942 of *Présence et pensée: Essai sur la philosophie religieuse de Grégoire de Nysse*, von Balthasar's labors on behalf of the Fathers usually took a form that would not be recognized today as original research—that is, putting together a collection of excerpts, revising an old monograph, laying out the theological styles of Augustine, Irenaeus, or Dionysius (Denys) as contributions to a theological aesthetics (in the *Glory of the Lord*, volume 2), or providing a new set of German translations (especially in the case of Augustine). This is not to say that his interest in the Fathers waned after the end of World War II. On the contrary, the theological aesthetics and other mature projects demonstrate the ongoing relevance of patristic theology. At the same time there was a focus by von Balthasar in the late 1930s and early 1940s on patristic *scholarship* that deserves some attention in its own right. In other words, the period between 1933 and 1942 was the period in which von Balthasar came to terms, and not without serious reservations, with his identity as "a patrologist".[11] Even after he decided not to adopt that label, he continued to labor in the vineyards of the Fathers.

What was the context out of which he came to read the Fathers? More needs to be investigated in this regard. For that reason, we turn our attention to the essay "The Fathers, the Scholastics, and Ourselves", which appeared in 1939 in the journal based in Vienna called *Theologie der Zeit*.[12] Von Balthasar was connected to the city of Vienna through his years as a student in that city and in particular with the musically inclined Catholic psychologist Rudolf Allers.[13] Moreover, the year 1939 was a pivotal one in the life of von Balthasar and in the life of Europe. Von Balthasar had been ordained in Munich on July 26, 1936, by Michael Cardinal Faulhaber. The cardinal (who also ordained the two Ratzinger brothers) was an aristocratic opponent of

---

[11] He uses this term in a very disparaging way in "The Fathers, the Scholastics, and Ourselves", *Communio: International Catholic Review* 24 (1997): 349: "And so we easily let ourselves be convinced that Scholasticism is not only unmodern and unpractical but is also more or less guilty for bringing us to this current impasse. In not much time at all, we have worked our way back one more step ... and have become ... 'patrologists'."

[12] Ibid., 347–96. The original was published as "Patristik, Scholastik, und wir", *Theologie der Zeit* 3 (1939): 65–104. The English translation was done by Edward T. Oakes, S.J.

[13] Cf. Thomas Krenski, *Hans Urs von Balthasar: Das Gottesdrama* (Mainz: Matthias Grünewald-Verlag, 1995), 14–33.

the ethos of the Third Reich. In fact, Faulhaber worked with then Cardinal Pacelli (later Pope Pius XII) in 1933 to sign a *Reichskonkordat* with the Nazis. The alternative, Faulhaber thought, would have been the wholescale extermination of Catholics. In the very same year, Faulhaber preached that salvation comes, not from German blood, but from the blood of Christ, a statement taken by the security forces of the regime as a provocation in favor of the Jews. Similarly, when he condemned the racism of *Kristallnacht* in 1938, a Nazi mob broke the windows of his episcopal residence.

In fact, von Balthasar returned to France after his ordination to finish his studies in theology.[14] From the middle of 1937 until the beginning of 1940, von Balthasar was sent back to Munich. The times were tense. Von Balthasar wrote to his father on December 20, 1938 (just days before the signing of the Munich agreement that forced the Czechoslovak Republic to cede the Sudetenland, including key military defense positions, to Nazi Germany): "Who knows how the situation here will develop and if I won't have to return one fine day to Switzerland?"[15] In Munich, von Balthasar undertook his tertianship (the final phase of Jesuit formation) under the direction of Father Albert Steger, one of the first German Jesuits to interpret Ignatius more as a mystical and less as an ascetical theologian.[16] During this period, he collaborated with Karl Rahner on a plan for a new dogmatics and spoke at length with Hugo Rahner about their common interests in the Fathers. He also revised his dissertation for publication. On February 22, 1939, von Balthasar wrote again to his father. He makes it clear that he does not expect to stay very long in Munich:

> Some new forces [presumably new priests] will arrive here since the suppression of Saint Blasien and of Godesberg [both are sites of Jesuit *Gymnasien* that had presumably been closed by the Nazis] will free up as many forces as we want. Of course, one has to wonder how long we ourselves will survive here. You've caught wind of the closing of the faculty of Catholic theology here at Munich. For the moment I have a mountain of book reviews and a bunch of articles for *Stimmen*

---

[14] For what follows, see Elio Guerriero, *Hans Urs von Balthasar* (Milan: Paoline, 1991).

[15] Letter to his father, December 20, 1938, as cited in ibid., 83.

[16] Peter Henrici, "Erster Blick auf Hans Urs von Balthasar", in *Hans Urs von Balthasar: Gestalt und Werk* (Cologne: Communio, 1989), 27.

[*der Zeit*] and other journals that will require of me one or two months
of time. Probably before the fall, when the tertianship begins, I will
not get involved in another monumental task (*altro lavoro di grosso res-
piro*) because who knows what will transpire then?[17]

That summer von Balthasar moved back into the Jesuit residence in
Pullach bei München to start his tertianship. In fact, it was only a
matter of a few months before he took up the position as Catholic
chaplain in Basel and turned down an offer to teach ecumenical theology at the Pontifical Gregorianum University in Rome.[18]

In early 1939, von Balthasar was thus in Munich writing articles
and book reviews for *Stimmen der Zeit*. The newly documented history of that journal also speaks directly to the troubling signs of the
times that were then in play. This would eventually lead to hard times
for the Jesuits in Munich and the suppression of the journal. Already
in November of 1935, the Jesuit Peter Lippert had written an article in *Stimmen der Zeit* entitled "With Force—With Forbearance".
Church historian Martin Ederer describes the effect of this piece,
which was part of a larger program of strategic resistance devised by
the contributors, who were being guided by Erich Przywara, S.J.:

> Lippert advocated achieving goals through patience and without
> force: "You see now, my friends, why we cannot operate by using
> power, through brute force, through threats, through reproaches, and
> through beatings into submission as does another method." He also
> reminded his readers that "*It is truth that triumphs, not merely a thought or
> a spoken reality, not an empty system, not an idea or ideology, but what really
> exists.*" The insinuation was all too clear to the government censors.
> As a result, the Reich government forced *Stimmen der Zeit* to sus-
> pend publishing operations until April of 1936. Format and ideology
> remained unchanged, but *Stimmen der Zeit*'s more blunted criticisms
> of Nazi ideology indicate that its editorial staff recognized it had to be
> more cautious if it were to survive at all. Its first serious confrontation
> [was] a telling episode about the dynamics and the realities of sur-
> vival under totalitarian regimes. With the German invasion of Poland
> in September of 1939 and Germany's subsequent shift to a wartime

---

[17] Letter to his father, February 22, 1939, following the Italian translation in Guerriero,
Hans Urs von Balthasar, 84.

[18] Henrici, "Erster Blick auf Hans Urs von Balthasar", 27.

economy, *Stimmen der Zeit* was obliged by government order to publish six double small-print issues per year rather than the usual twelve
because of the wartime paper shortage. *Stimmen der Zeit* ultimately
lasted until April,1941, when the Gestapo stormed and closed down
its editorial office in Munich for the remainder of the war. The reason: Peter Lippert's 1935 article. It was a dubious explanation since
by 1941 Lippert had been dead for almost five years. The authorities
later explained their actions by citing the wartime paper shortage, a
somewhat more credible reason. But for a totalitarian regime at war,
no reasons were really needed, and *Stimmen der Zeit* ultimately met
the same fate as so many other journals that did not conform fervently
enough to the aims and ideals of the Third Reich. For the Nazis who
found *Stimmen der Zeit* politically suspect, wartime hardship easily
justified—if it did not adequately explain—what peacetime prosperity
could not.[19]

In other words, these facts explain the situation in which von
Balthasar found himself in 1939 as a thirty-four-year-old Jesuit priest
from Switzerland. His own account in an essay of 1945 confirms his
real sense of impending danger:

> Everything, then, was running true to course, and it seemed that I, as
> a collaborator of a periodical in Munich, was destined to become the
> perpetual student of the intellectual sciences. But the boots of the SS
> sounded ever more loudly from the nearby Ludwigstrasse, and no ear
> could escape the loudspeakers that were set up everywhere in the city.
> The area around the old Hofbräuhaus became eerie and terrible, and I
> was glad to be offered the position in Switzerland that transferred me
> to direct pastoral work.[20]

I do not want to overplay the role of politics in von Balthasar's
early Jesuit formation. Rupert Mayer, S.J., had been sent to a concentration camp for public resistance in 1939. Von Balthasar, by

[19] Martin F. Ederer, "Propaganda Wars: *Stimmen der Zeit* and the Nazis, 1933–1935", *The
Catholic Historical Review* 90, 3 (July 2004): 456–72, here at 471–72. More details on this matter, in the light of a recent, hastily composed provocation, can be found in Aaron Pidel, S.J.,
"Erich Przywara, S.J., and 'Catholic Fascism': A Response to Paul Silas Peterson", *Journal
for the History of Modern Theology / Zeitschrift für Neuere Theologiegeschichte* 23, 1 (2016): 27–55.
[20] Hans Urs von Balthasar, *My Work: In Retrospect* (San Francisco: Communio Books,
1993), 13.

contrast, was not by nature an activist of any sort, and under these circumstances overt resistance like that of Mayer was not going to be an option. Von Balthasar spent most these days in Munich rewriting his dissertation and reviewing new scholarship on European poets. There was indeed a cultural program for renewal in this work, as I will demonstrate shortly. In sum, his engagement from a distance with the embattled journal shows his attunement, in spite of his natural inclinations, to the social and political circumstances that surrounded him. What was taking place in politics and society should not be disassociated from his rapidly growing sense of a vocation as a theologian and as a one called to serve in the Church. Von Balthasar was seeking a new path for Church and society and could not ignore what was taking place around him.

Returning to "The Fathers, the Scholastics, and Ourselves", I would first note that the essay begins with a then familiar image of the twilight of the idols.[21] The questioning of the vast regions of the West is likened by von Balthasar to a forest scene in the autumn: "The tree of culture is now being stripped of its leaves."[22] We are told that the leaves on the ground are not historical artifacts. These living memories of two millennia of Christianity are expressive forms that served as the dwelling places and vestments of Christian life. The autumnal state is thus a time of introspection and a *kairos*, a moment to reflect upon one's own stance in relationship to the dropping bower, the decaying leaves of Western culture, and the boots of the SS from the nearby Ludwigstrasse. Culture and politics both signal the reality of decay.

We can identify fairly precisely some of the literary precedents for von Balthasar's metaphor. In the 1930 edition of his dissertation, *Geschichte des eschatologischen Problems in der modernen deutschen Literatur*, von Balthasar cites a number of literary and musical figures

---

[21] No one to my knowledge has ever thought to compare von Balthasar's early development to that of the Lausanne-born writer Alejo Carpentier, who, like the young von Balthasar, was under the sway of Spenglerian disgust with the modern West. In 1939, Carpentier abandoned France and his advocacy for the modernist poetry of French surrealism to emigrate to his homeland of Cuba and dedicate himself to chronicling in novelistic form the religiosity of the indigenous in Latin America. On this development, one may consult Alexander Nava, *Wonder and Exile in the New World* (College Station: University of Pennsylvania Press, 2013).

[22] Von Balthasar, "Fathers, the Scholastics, and Ourselves", 34.

who thematize the *topos* of autumnality. Preeminent in this group of metaphysically homeless and existentially alienated artists is the poet Georg Trakl and especially a book of poems he published in 1915. What attracts von Balthasar to Trakl's vision of the fall of the West is his very un-Nietzschean attitude that an *inner* sense of what is just and what is evil—even if these notions have been stripped of their *outer* content—must still be invoked as the proper way to make a judgment about history.[23] Moreover, in 1919, Johann Huizinga published his influential *Herfsttij der Middeleeuwen* ("The Autumn of the Middle Ages"), a work that von Balthasar seems to have read and whose allusion to cultural decay in an earlier epoch draws upon the same theme as that evoked by Trakl.[24] Herein lies the analogical leitmotif that will guide the posing of the central problem of the interpretation of history in the essay: "[A]ll of history is an event and possesses a tendency. Therefore, we must isolate the meaning of the great epochs as well as try to understand them in their respective contexts."[25] In short, presentism and anti-presentism are both set aside while all epochs are subjected to the same form of scrutiny. The *kairos* of the present crisis thoroughly penetrates every attempt to read the past without shackling the past to the present. As a keen student of literary history, von Balthasar was well aware that there is both non-identity and otherness in the retrieval of the greatness of each past epoch, which is what necessitates the explicitly "analogical" approach to history he will adopt. There is no avoiding of the hermeneutical problem even though—interestingly—the last word lies, not with the then regnant Heideggerian hermeneutical circle, but with the newly discovered Ignatian encircling of the discernment of spirits.[26]

The first section of the essay includes a brief and somewhat mocking reference to the newly discovered exemplarity of Eastern Orthodoxy. Von Balthasar states that an extraordinary interest is being paid to various forms of Orthodox Christianity, a development to which he devoted a lengthy article in *Stimmen der Zeit* earlier in 1939 ("Die

---

[23] *Geschichte des eschatologischen Problems in der modernen deutschen Literatur* (Freiburg: Johannes, 1998), 158–61, 197.

[24] Cf. Guerriero, *Hans Urs von Balthasar*, 85.

[25] Von Balthasar, "Fathers, the Scholastics, and Ourselves", 352.

[26] Cf. *Geschichte des eschatologischen Problems*, 15–20.

Wendung nach Osten"). His point about Eastern Orthodoxy remains the same as his analysis of the West. We cannot idealize the past, and we cannot pretend that Russian Orthodoxy today adequately preserves the heritage of the Fathers through "an ecstatic slumber of timelessness".[27]

The method begins and ends with a consideration of "a total structure". What appears at first glance as a Hegelian *Aufhebung* (a complete resolution into a final, closed synthesis) of three dialectically interrelated images of the cosmos is actually a much more fluid system held in dynamic tension by the principle—drawn from the diary of Hegel's most astute opponent, Søren Kierkegaard—of the law of conversion.[28]

> With every step forward that man makes, God becomes even more infinitely exalted, and thereby man becomes smaller, even if this happens by virtue of the progress he makes.... If I might put it this way, it is a kind of "reticence" on God's part because of His majesty. Precisely because he surrenders Himself more and enters more into commerce with man, precisely there will man be demoted [*degradiert*], however elevated he be at the same time.
>
> Yes, he is still being elevated but he is being elevated by virtue of the fact that he receives an infinitely higher vision of what God is, and so he is demoted. How exalting! No human sovereign can guard himself in this way against the press of his subjects. "He must increase, while I decrease": That is the law for everyone who approaches God. If God had been separated from us by a million steps on a staircase, He would never be able to guard against the urgent press of man, for steps, however many, can eventually be climbed. But the law of conversion assures us that the approach is ever-distant: Infinite majesty! "But that means," you say, "that, in a way I lose God!" How? He is still increasing! No, I am losing something all right: I am losing myself, my self-possession, until finally I find my whole blessedness in this worship: He must increase while I decrease. But this is of course already the law for all true love![29]

God becomes ever greater with each step forward that man makes in his religious quest. Conversion is not inversion. The placing of

---

[27] Von Balthasar, "Fathers, the Scholastics, and Ourselves", 350.
[28] Ibid., 361.
[29] Ibid.

this law of distance within the total structure of Christian development prevents the Kierkegaardian inheritance from becoming a bare
dialectical principle unaffected by the analogical rhythm of the total
structure.[30] The presence of the law of conversion is thus a guide-
post to the total structure, one that prevents the total structure from
becoming static, self-enclosed, and a violation of the always greater
majesty of God's self-revelation.

Von Balthasar's method for approaching the history of the Church
draws upon the theory of expression that he had been crafting since
his publication in 1925, as a mere twenty-year-old student of literature and the arts, of *Die Entwicklung der musikalischen Idee*.[31] There
his insight was quite rudimentary: cultural forms vary in different
lands and in different epochs. These forms become concrete through
the *material signata* of the arts, which still leaves room for a unity to
those arts that is best expressed in the idea of musical integration
with separate consideration of the rhythm and the tone of the diverse
components. That text underscores organic development without
paying much attention to the normative quality of tradition except
to say in a highly Romantic vein that all development in the arts is
guided by the *Information Gottes*, God's lending of meaningful form
to the dynamic development of the world. By 1939, von Balthasar
had purified his youthful vision of development of its radical dependence upon a Romantic theology of expression without abandoning
the original insight altogether. Ignatian hope for new growth had
supplanted a purely aesthetic dependence on aimless, Traklian wan-
dering. The seed for his social engagement lay precisely in this overcoming of the aesthetic.

Von Balthasar's recipe for evaluating the fact that Christians are
inevitably beholden to the present is to treat the legacy of the Christian past as a veritable strength and to overcome the forgetfulness of

---

[30] This tension already foreshadows the very complex debate that both von Balthasar
and his teacher Erich Przywara undertook in the 1940s with Karl Barth on the relationship
between analogy and dialectic. Although I return at the end of this essay to those considerations, I have dealt with that issue at greater length in my essay: "Hans Urs von Balthasar,
Erich Przywara's *Analogia Entis*, and the Problem of a Catholic Denkform", in *The Analogy of
Being: Invention of the Antichrist or the Wisdom of God?* ed. Thomas Joseph White, O.P. (Grand
Rapids, Mich.: Eerdmans Press, 2011), 192–206.

[31] Hans Urs von Balthasar, *Die Entwicklung der musikalischen Idee* (Einsiedeln: Johannes Verlag, 1998).

tradition by recovering the "internal law" that governs each epoch of the past. He states:

> In order soberly to discuss the meaning of the three great spiritual periods of the Church (patristic, scholastic, and modern) to the extent possible in an essay, it seems to us that there is only one way to reach this goal: To press on past all external and superficial features of each epoch, to focus on its innermost structural law, and then to measure each respective formal law according to the structural law of what is essentially Christian as we encounter this norm in the Gospel. We are not doubting of course that this essential "idea" of Christianity does not hover like some abstract universal law over history and its changes but rather expresses itself in the level of history in ever-new forms without our being able thereby to call any one of these forms the absolute one.[32]

Is he a modernizing, a-historical essentialist? In fact, this statement is a repudiation of the essentialism of Adolf von Harnack and others who pursued that goal at the turn of the twentieth century and represents the recent efforts of many German-speaking Catholic intellectuals to do the same. The discernment of an internal "structural law" is not the same as picking out an essence from an array of diverse characteristics. Von Balthasar believes that an idea about the relationship between God and the world can be extracted from every epoch, but he does not believe that it is the task of the theologian to prioritize or synthesize the value of patristic, Scholastic, or modern ideas. As in the early work on music, the emphasis is still placed on the organic flow of ideas from one epoch to the next. There is a difference for von Balthasar between an abstract and purely notional essence and an inner form that can only be expressed in and through a variety of particular forms. The supposition in "The Fathers, the Scholastics, and Ourselves" of an idea that synthesizes all the life and work of an epoch—however idealist that may sound—is still being determined in the context of the concrete development of specific forms of Christian existence. Once again, the law of conversion—inspired, but not defined, by Kierkegaard—is designed to prevent any flight into the Hegelian stratosphere.

---

[32] Von Balthasar, "Fathers, the Scholastics, and Ourselves", 352.

Coming from a country where the ban on Jesuits would not be lifted until the 1970s and having discovered his vocation from afar (that is, while a student of the humanities), von Balthasar was consequently an ardently Ignatian Jesuit. There is no one source for von Balthasar's Ignatian roots, but one important one needs to be mentioned here. In 1938, Erich Przywara published the first edition of his multi-volume commentary on the Spiritual Exercises of Saint Ignatius of Loyola called *Deus semper maior: Theologie der Exerzitien*.[33] Von Balthasar either had read the book by 1939 or was at least familiar with the basic outline of Przywara's reading of Ignatius since Przywara was not only his teacher and close friend but also an editor of *Stimmen der Zeit*. The section of the essay on the law of Christ emphasizes in the spirit of *Deus Semper Maior* (and the pertinent decree of the Fourth Lateran Council made famous by Przywara) that the difference between Creator and creature is always greater than any similarity without ruling out the real possibility of thinking analogically about the God-world relationship.

While studying at Fourvière from 1933 to 1937, von Balthasar made the acquaintance of Henri de Lubac, S.J. In these years, de Lubac was teaching fundamental theology at the Catholic University of Lyon and researching, as well as teaching (between 1935 and 1940) one course at the Jesuit seminary at Fourvière, where he also lived starting in 1934. The encounters with de Lubac were a key to von Balthasar's development. In 1938, de Lubac published *Catholicisme*, a groundbreaking text that makes a very timely argument for submitting all things to Christ.[34] The influence of de Lubac is present in von Balthasar's essay if one reads carefully, for von Balthasar also highlights throughout the essay the natural orientation of the rational creature to a supernatural end in the divine life of God. This is precisely the point where von Balthasar's theology of the Fathers intersected with the developing systematic thought of one of the key theologians who introduced von Balthasar to the thought of the Fathers.

---

[33] Erich Przywara, S.J., *Deus Semper Maior: Theologie der Exerzitien* (Freiburg: Herder, 1938), vols. 1–3.

[34] Henri de Lubac, *Catholicisme: les aspects sociaux du dogme* (Paris, 1938: seven editions were published, the last in 1983), English trans.: *Catholicism: Christ and the Common Destiny of Man*, trans. Lancelot C. Sheppard and Sister Elizabeth Englund, O.C.D. (San Francisco: Ignatius Press, 1988).

The fourth and fifth sections of the essay, entitled "The Basic Law of Christianity: In the Church" and "Rules of Discernment", are even more thoroughly Ignatian.[35] He underscores the claim that even the supernatural origin of the Church "from above" in no way diminishes the fact that "the Church, in her being sent out to the world, is herself fundamentally a part of the world."[36] This means there is "an essential visibility" and a "decisive naturalness" to the way in which Church engages the world. The Church stands with the world before God, not alongside God and above the world. This starting point also does not diminish the difference between Church and world but calls upon the Church to remain radically humble when she undertakes all of her varied tasks in the worldly realm.

The next section delves into "The Law of Patristics". Von Balthasar prescinds from any simpleminded historical summaries or a narrow focus on a couple of key figures. Instead, he isolates a "Platonizing" pattern whereby the soul is led from below (nature) to above.[37] He does not disparage this pattern or wish to excise it altogether. It is, however, the exact opposite of the Ignatian pattern of considering how the exercitant is called "from above" to engage in a mission in the world. It also falls in line with the caricature of Platonism that you find in Friedrich Nietzsche and other masters of suspicion. Von Balthasar's subsequent studies of particular patristic authors contain nothing of this paper tiger. So let us examine carefully how this moderated anti-Platonism fits into his overall evaluation of the Fathers. Specifically, these are among the distinct tendencies that we encounter in the Church Fathers:

> The ceaseless reduction of the levels of being to the highest Being (an insight that lies at the heart of Platonic logic); its transcendence from all merely participating being; a deep ontological piety according to which existence itself is a prayer (as the corresponding echo of this

[35] For a mature treatment of Balthasar's take on the Ignatian discernment of spirits, see *Theologik III: Der Geist der Wahrheit* (Einsiedeln: Johannes Verlag, 1987), 360–62; English trans.: *Theo-Logic III: The Spirit of Truth*, trans. Graham Harrison (San Francisco: Ignatius Press, 2005), 390–92, and Mark A. McIntosh, *Christology from Within: Spirituality and Incarnation in Hans Urs von Balthasar* (Notre Dame: University of Notre Dame Press, 1996).

[36] Von Balthasar, "Fathers, the Scholastics, and Ourselves", 363.

[37] Ibid., 379. "The Platonic schema shows the formal outline of the God-creature relationship too simplistically."

presence of being in the realm of consciousness); the feeling for the
fact that the creature is nothing other than the presentation and representation of God outside of himself; and thus a deep understanding
of the cultic, of the objectivity of the symbolic and sacramental world
order: All of these are the eternal values of the patristic era.[38]

The Platonism of the Fathers will be tempered by the Aristotelianism
of the greatest of the Scholastics. But this binary contrast, he says,
hardly covers the dialectic that will finally contribute to the total structure. Instead the "world-condemning" dying to the world found in
patristic attitudes of prayer, worship, and sacramental symbolism need
to be radically transformed into a new idiom of a "world-affirming"
dying to the world. Surprisingly, mortification is the perduring element, but only of a certain kind.[39] Von Balthasar recognizes with
great clarity that the ontological grounding laid by the Fathers cannot
be abandoned for the sake of modern subjectivism. Nor must one
abandon all they bequeathed regarding the Christian praxis of *askesis*,
especially in the contemplative life. In fact, more weight needs to
be placed on the spiritual significance of the natural and the finite
as precisely in order to send finite beings into the abyss of modern
apathy with a sense of destiny and purpose. The Fathers understand
perfectly well and in an exemplary fashion the whither of Christian
life. More is still needed about the individual dynamics of the way
itself and the reasons for embarking upon the paths that the Fathers
clearly delineated.

Section 7 on "The Law of the Scholastics" would seem to be of
little value to a truly dynamic and fluid synthesis of Christianity's history. Von Balthasar is aware that his emerging style is least like that of
the Scholastic Fathers and takes pain to absolve Aristotelianism of any
guilt in the history of decline. He notes that Saint Thomas as a theologian of "nature" did speak to the "self-subsistence of created being
that is *presupposed* before any gracious and unmerited participation in
God can take place".[40] The investigation of nature in this properly

---

[38] Ibid., 391.

[39] Ibid., 391–92. For a specific example of world-affirming dying to the world from a
different vantage point, one that seems to meet this description or at least to move in this
direction, see James LeGrys, "Blondel's Idea of Assimilation to God through Mortification of
Self", *Gregorianum* 77, 2 (1996): 309–31.

[40] Von Balthasar, "Fathers, the Scholastics, and Ourselves", 381.

Thomistic key thus becomes a signature achievement within the living legacy of Scholasticism:

> This provides theology with a way for expressing a most fundamental fact of the Christian dispensation, that every relationship of the creature to God is to be constructed only on the basis of a mutual otherness that is always more predominant. Furthermore, it says that *only* this basis of ever-greater difference suffices to support and make possible the highest unity. Thomas saw the paradox in all its starkness when he asserted the principle that: The nearer a creature stands to God, the more it is capable of moving by virtue of its own powers.
>
> It is clear that with this fundamental change, in principle at least, all those dangers fall away that came with the Platonic schema. For no longer do the levels of being (spirit-soul-body; or man-animal-plant-matter) have the exclusive character of a step-by-step depotentializing of being and of a progressive alienation from the central fire of life. In place of the Great Chain of Being there emerges the rounded, ordered cosmos closed in on itself in which every individual thing possesses its worth and dignity and no single thing—including inert and dead matter—is permitted to be dispensable to the whole.[41]

In sum, Scholasticism was decadent as far as its dominant form of expression goes but permanently fecund as far as its genuine metaphysical insights are concerned.

The Law of the Modern (section no. 8) is by contrast with Thomism not an original structure. It is rather a synthesis of past structures, one that emphasizes that

> the world into which the incarnation has taken place is a truly worldly world: Not, for example, a shadowy and symbolic copy of a higher, spiritual, ideal and universal world but rather a world in which there are unique individual persons and situations, in which time and space are the bases of qualitative differences, differences which cannot be reduced to a general concept without robbing the particular of something essential to itself. This is a world, then, in which there is a true history.[42]

The Platonic legacy of prioritizing the universal over the individual to the point of the absorption of the latter into the former has been

---

[41] Ibid.
[42] Ibid., 388.

finally surpassed. But the happy result is not an atomistic world that remains blind to any glimpse of universal truth. Christ's presence in the natural world is now the starting point for reflection upon a theology of culture and the point from which believers and non-believers alike can join him in this descent into the world.

The final section of the essay deals in a new way with the "total structure" of Christianity's organic unfolding in history. That dynamic totality is greater than the sum of its parts, but only when grasped in a distinctively spiritual and anti-Hegelian way. The final synthesis is thus an Ignatian corrective to the excesses of the patristic and Scholastic ideas that are then given greater cogency through the affective language of modern personalism. In fact, the approach to structure through contrapuntal rhythms echoes the early philosophical thought of Munich theologian Romano Guardini.[43]

> The modification in the spiritual attitude that is contained in this transition from patristic to modern piety can be described as the change from a world-*condemning* "dying to the world" to a world-*affirming* "dying to the world." In other words, in modernity what comes unmistakably to the fore is that even the factor of the Christian mortification to the world stands under the more comprehensive sign of mission. Christian death should not lead us to abandon our natural post in the world where revelation and the order of salvation have placed us; rather, our dying must itself be suffered through *while* we maintain our post. The patristic sense for objectivity and representation need not give way, then, to a more predominant subjectivism and anthropocentrism (as the line is always being incorrectly drawn). Rather, in the principle of the modern, this feeling for objectivity and representation comes precisely to its fulfillment, at least when every "subjectivity" of ecstatic ascent to God remains encompassed by the meaning and consciousness of Christian mission.[44]

Herein lies the true and living *Aufhebung*, one that bears only a superficial resemblance to the Hegelian one. In the mortifying encounter

---

[43] Romano Guardini, *Der Gegensatz: Versuche zu einer Philosophie des Lebendig-Konkreten* (Mainz: Matthias Grünewald, 1925). This work rewrites a text that is critical of Kierkegaard that was begun in 1914. Von Balthasar had studied with Guardini in Berlin in the 1920s and discusses the methodological importance of this particular text in Hans Urs von Balthasar, *Romano Guardini: Reform from the Source*, trans. Albert K. Wimmer and D. C. Schindler (San Francisco: Ignatius Press, 2010), 23–24.

[44] Von Balthasar, "Fathers, the Scholastics, and Ourselves", 391–92.

with one's own radical finitude, the option for going to the peripheries comes to the fore. The choice therefore exceeds that between individual and community. The believer opts to go out for the sake of the world even though all the worldly evidence points to the likelihood of being consumed by the world. In the light of this outright paradox, von Balthasar realized that new models of holiness and ecclesial witnessing were needed for the contemporary believer.

Theology and Holiness in Reinhold Schneider

We can now speak about the role of the witness of Reinhold Schneider in von Balthasar's early development. Its importance has been sadly overlooked in most of the literature. Schneider, however, was a towering figure in the postwar German consciousness. For German Catholics, he was far more important than Dietrich Bonhoeffer as a symbol of spiritual resistance to the regime. In fact, Schneider has been called the conscience of the German nation by both Walter Kasper and Joseph Ratzinger, but sadly his witness and literary output have already faded from the memory of even contemporary Germans. Von Balthasar considered his stance so essential that he wrote a lengthy book about him in 1953 (only two years after the first edition of his book on Barth) and then republished the work under the title *Nochmals: Reinhold Schneider* (Once again: Reinhold Schneider) toward the end of his life.[45] The English editors translated this nondescript title with the more evocative *Tragedy under Grace: Reinhold Schneider and the Experience of the West*, adopting a pessimistic phrase drawn from a writing of Schneider but also augmenting the problem of elitism that von Balthasar himself seemed to have avoided with his title.

Schneider was a poet and novelist who embodied the synthesis of theology and holiness that von Balthasar thought was absent in the discourse of academic theology. Von Balthasar later wrote about French poets (Paul Claudel, Charles Péguy, Georges Bernanos, even Simone Weil) and his fellow partner in the Ignatian realm, Gerard Manley Hopkins, but Schneider was a contemporary Christian witness

---

[45] *Tragedy under Grace: Reinhold Schneider on the Experience of the West*, trans. Brian McNeil, C.R.V. (San Francisco: Ignatius Press, 1997).

from the public domain who captivated von Balthasar's ample literary imagination from a very early stage. The original book from 1953 represents a historical and literary map of European cultural renewal, the very task that von Balthasar undertook as a chaplain, translator, and publisher for the rest of his life. In this engagement as well as the later ones, von Balthasar struggles to articulate the worldly engagement of the Christian even as he becomes more and more convinced of the utter fragility of all attempts to enter into solidarity with the political currents that arose after World War II and then later with postconciliar ecclesial currents.

Schneider was a quintessentially tortured soul who read and reread Kierkegaard, Schopenhauer, Nietzsche, and Unamuno and considered at one point in his life becoming Buddhist. His literary output was enormous; it might even have exceeded that of von Balthasar. The Schneider bibliography appended to the 1991 edition of his book includes 164 book titles. I will focus on aspects of Schneider's witness that speak directly to the issues at hand regarding society and politics: his notion of a spiritual aristocracy and his opposition after 1945 to German rearmament.

Schneider wrote, for example, about the coronation of emperors in the Middle Ages. He came from an aristocratic family, but the estate (Hotel Messner) was destroyed in 1956–1957, which elicited a profound sense of resignation and became the occasion for the new last chapter in the second edition of von Balthasar's book. That section was fittingly entitled "Curtain". Schneider idolized an idealized form of spiritual knighthood—whether it was found in the religious vocation of feudal knights, Shakespeare's self-renunciatory kings, or the Dominican Bartolomé de Las Casas, whose defense of the Indians was the subject of one of his most popular books. Part of Schneider's interest in extending the category of an old-world aristocracy to the saints of the modern world was to recover a vocabulary that deliberately repudiated the banality of bourgeois civilization. It was as much a reworking as an extension. In renouncing the colonial urge to amass power and wealth, Schneider sees an underlying ethos that paradoxically has been lost but still needs to be restated so that it can play a role in society once again: "The knightly idea is open: Christian existence lives on the basis of mission and loses its *raison d'être* if it loses its mission. 'It is not the "West" as a cultural area that is the ground that will bear us; but Western Christianity will bear us. Christianity is opened up to the world, for it must bear responsibility for the world.' "[46] Schneider realized that systemic violence was written into the script of colonial expansion. The antidote lies not in sanitized histories that ignore the massacres or in the Christian fortitude of a Las Casas. The challenge lies in marshalling "an equally unheard-of massing of Christian, supernatural powers".[47] Which Christian saints have been formed who witness to the self-renunciation in the individual soul and in the social body that can overcome this systemic corruption of the West? On this very point, he cites Saint Francis of Assisi, Saint Ignatius of Loyola, and John Henry Cardinal Newman.[48] The question of theology and sanctity is the one to which Schneider constantly returns, and that is why he still harbors a hope that some very modern and democratic form of spiritual aristocracy could once again animate the Christian conscience.

Schneider opposed German rearmament but remained "selective and guarded" toward the end of his life with the label of pacifism.[49] Cheap pacifism that did not consider the consequences for the exercise of power in the face of genuine oppression Schneider considered "a No to life". "An entire people", he once said, "cannot be medical orderlies." In other words, he called the problem of peace "one of the most tragic problems of history".[50] He considered power to be indispensable in the construction of a state worthy of man and knew that the granting of power was inevitable, ambiguous, and dangerous. After the fall of Hitler, whom he adamantly opposed in writings that were carried by soldiers of the resistance into the battlefield, Schneider knew that his love for a spiritual crown had to be drastically rewritten. This "spiritual crown" becomes translated, according to von Balthasar, into three words: freedom, conscience, and responsibility. The language smacks of a universal ethics, for its terms could very well derive from the terms of the world. But von Balthasar remains convinced that catholicity of the mission to

---

[46] Ibid., 249, quoting Reinhold Schneider, *Erbe im Feuer: Betrachtungen und Rufe* (Freiburg: Herder, 1946), 151.

[47] Von Balthasar, *Tragedy under Grace*, 249.

[48] Ibid., 248.

[49] Ibid., 278–79.

[50] Ibid., 279.

interiorize freedom, conscience, and responsibility—especially in an ethics that denounces violence as radically as had Schneider—places a unique claim upon the Christian believer. The believer is called to live out this mandate with a courage that cannot be derived from the terms set by the world. Recourse to traditional formulae does little good in the light of the loneliness that the Christian faces in embodying this ethic of responsibility. One remains in communion with the Church and through the Church with the very heart of the world, but the personal anguish of the task is not thereby diminished.

A Brief Excursus on Liberation Theology

Von Balthasar did not oppose all forms of social and political liberation, but his suspicions of political and social liberation went straight to the core convictions of their adherents. Before concluding, I would like to examine just one remark he made about this issue. The resolution of the debate between Balthasarians and political theologians like Johannes Baptist Metz must be dealt with in another context.[51]

In his 1986 interview with Angelo Scola, von Balthasar returns to the question of a Christian culture and affirms the need to consider the conditions for its revival in our secular age. After noting the degradation of humanity that had taken place through the illusory promise of freedom through a technical civilization and "pseudo-human bureaucratic machinery", he makes the following pithy remark:

> How should one go about freeing man from a prison he has built for himself and create an authentic Christian culture? How can we free him from a contrivance of worldwide dimensions, which is almost automatically self-perfecting? Politics and economics are so inextricably entangled that no one apparently is able to bring this wheel-work to a standstill. One cannot help wondering whether the liberation theologians sufficiently accounted for the global proportions of this phenomenon. In the foreground one can certainly divide people into the "oppressors" and the "oppressed". But is it taken into consideration

---

[51] Besides the work of O'Regan cited above, an original contribution to this debate is also made in Todd Walatka, *Von Balthasar and the Option for the Poor: Theodramatics in the Light of Liberation Theology* (Washington, D.C.: Catholic University of America Press, 2017).

that the oppressors in the foreground are or may be themselves the oppressed in the background and that it will be difficult indeed from here on to find the Ultimate Oppressor? Perhaps they all belong to the oppressing oppressed—which in no way should imply that everyone is an innocent lamb.[52]

This is a provocative remark that could take on a meaning it did not intend to convey when extracted from the context of an open exchange with an admiring pupil. But it also gets to the heart of von Balthasar's concern about the theology of liberation, which is expressed elsewhere in the same interview in the form of a detailed critique of Leonardo Boff's Christology and Mariology in his *Passion of Christ, Passion of the World*.[53]

The central problem with certain programs for social liberation according to von Balthasar is that they fail to undertake a thorough criticism of the Prometheanism of the modern age. If our age is characterized in a fundamental way by the hubris of stealing fire from the gods in order to create a society that can perfect itself as an image of the divinity, then no program for social liberation can fail to deplore the miserable consequences of the illusion of self-perfection. Von Balthasar does not soften the blow by noting that the poor do not themselves stand in need of criticisms of Prometheanism when they are caught in the machinery of modern bureaucracy. If anything, he displays what some would consider an insensitivity to the plight of the poor by claiming that some advocates of their social liberation incorporate into their schemes for liberation the very mechanism that causes the oppression in the first place. He is not denying that there are victims of social structures of sin and taking recourse in a kind of libertarian scheme of individual salvation. On the contrary, his seemingly dialectical understanding of the relationship between the corporate dimension of Christian hope and the false hope of a man-made utopia seems at first glance insuperable. He is by no means ruling out political interpretations of the Old and New Testament for theology or the Church. His main point is to avoid the premature

[52] Von Balthasar, *Test Everything*, 49–50.
[53] See Leonardo Boff, *Passion of Christ, Passion of the World: The Facts, Their Interpretation, and Their Meaning Yesterday and Today*, trans. Robert R. Barr (Maryknoll, N.Y.: Orbis Books, 1987).

baptizing of a particular man-made ethos—modern secularism, politics of identity, and so on—that would in the end resemble Hitler's "German Christians".

Conclusion

I began by talking about the submitting of all things to Christ. I will conclude by looking at one of the mature formulations of this same idea. In 1978, von Balthasar returned to the question of the *analogia entis* while writing *Theodramatik*, vol. 3, part 2 (= *Theo-Drama*, vol. 3).[54] The brief treatment of analogy in this text is extremely elucidating not only for understanding his own path to the theory of analogy but for grasping the ultimate foundations of his theology of culture as well. The basic development concerns the explicitly Christological frame for the problem of the *analogia entis* that was already present in his essay from 1939 but is now placed front and center.

Von Balthasar begins by stating that "between the divine and created natures there is an essential abyss."[55] The Barth book already included the proposal to think of the *duplex ordo cognitionis* of Vatican I as ultimately identical with the two natures of the Chalcedonian decree.[56] In that same context, von Balthasar states that Maximus the Confessor preserved the soteriological essence of that decree with the dictum "Christ can 'save' humans only by 'safe-guarding' them", a maxim that points to the final pattern of human redemption within the unity of Christ's two natures.[57]

Von Balthasar then connects the wholly Otherness of the unmixed natures to the question of the principle of analogy in this way:

> However *analogia entis* may be defined in philosophical detail, it means that the terms employed cannot be traced back to a generic concept (for example, as if both God and the creature were to fall *under* the

[54] Hans Urs Von Balthasar, *Theo-Drama*, vol. 3, *Dramatis Personae: Persons in Christ*, trans. Graham Harrison (San Francisco: Ignatius Press, 1992).

[55] Ibid., 3:220.

[56] Hans Urs Von Balthasar, *The Theology of Karl Barth: Exposition and Interpretation*, trans. Edward T. Oakes, S.J. (Communio Books; San Francisco: Ignatius Press, 1992), 272.

[57] Ibid., 271.

heading of "being as such": this is the danger of Scotism and late Scholastic rationalism).... Quite simply, this means that the person of the Logos in whom the hypostatic union takes place cannot function, in any way, as the ("higher") unity between God and man; this person, as such, is God. Since the person of the Logos is the ultimate union of divine and created being, it must constitute the final proportion [*Mass*] between the two and hence must be the "concrete *analogia entis*" itself. However, it must not in any way overstep this analogy in the direction of identity.[58]

The phrase "concrete *analogia entis*" signifies here that the one person of the two natures tolerates no *Aufhebung* of humanity and divinity, a principle with which we are already well familiar. To admit such an overcoming of the difference within the union makes meaningless "the very presuppositions of the *pro nobis*".[59] Different conceptualities arose in the theological tradition to make this crucial point. Maximus the Confessor spoke of a chasm or abyss between the divine and created natures, and Scholastic theologians (*a fortiori* Nicholas of Cusa) denied any *proportio* (or comparative relation) of the infinite to the finite.[60] Interestingly, the "synthesis" of natures in one person invented by Antiochene theologians and carefully refined by Maximus, Peter Lombard, and Thomas Aquinas is not the last word for the mature von Balthasar, a point that may reflect his perduring debt to Barth. Here von Balthasar maintains that the view of a synthetic person in the tradition is of less value for a Christology of mission than *a free act of union by a Divine Person*. In other words, the dogmatic inadmissibility of a notional ascent *from* two natures *to* one person opens up the domain of freedom. According to von Balthasar, the "must" of Jesus' fulfillment of a mission from the Father remains a wholly *free* act of obedience. In order to shed light on the Ignatian question of how freedom and obedience come into play with one another, von Balthasar provides an analogy drawn no doubt from his own experience as a composer and as an author: "It is like the artist or scholar who is so possessed by his vocation that he only feels free,

---

[58] Von Balthasar, *Theo-Drama*, 3:221–22, citing *Theologie der Geschichte* (Einsiedeln: Johannes Verlag, 1959), 53–54.

[59] Von Balthasar, *Theo-Drama*, 3:221

[60] Ibid., 222–23.

only feels totally himself, when he is able to pursue this task that is so much his own."[61]

There is much more that could be said about the notion of a Christological analogy of being in *Theo-Drama*. As Pope Benedict XVI implied in his Regensburg address, the proper way of asking the question of being is the bulwark to defend against any nominalistic attempt to turn the singularity of Christ's sending as the determinative act in the history of salvation into a theory of an arbitrary, wholly irrational imposition of a divine will. Przywara recognizes the necessity and the limits of a philosophy of being within the concrete order of creation. Przywara preserves the Chalcedonian balance between similarity and difference in an overarching metaphysics of unity. So far von Balthasar is only repeating what has already been developed in the book on Barth. Here he also notes there is something slightly exaggerated in Przywara's thesis regarding the law of being, an interesting formulation in the light of the analysis of structural laws just examined. A footnote attempts to clarify the point.[62] The footnote states that Przywara relied upon the text of the Fourth Lateran Council and says that the phrase *tanta similitudo* ("an even greater likeness") that Przywara took in an Ignatian fashion to signify that there is difference no matter how great the similarity has been altered in the new edition of Denzinger to simply *similitudo*. More to the point, von Balthasar adds: "It is no accident that Przywara never produced a Christology."

So here we finally encounter the problem that von Balthasar sees in the thought of Erich Przywara. He clearly does not intend to deliver a fatal blow to either Przywara's systematizing of analogy or to that of other Catholic thinkers. But a new accent has now been placed upon the work of Przywara. Przywara's metaphysics can be a great aid to a theologian in seeing the order of being in creation with Christ as its ground. His theory of analogy is grounded in the concreteness of revelation, but the living form of Christ and the Christological determinations of the analogy of being are still too vague. In other words, von Balthasar's final verdict seems to be that Przywara can take the theologian to this mountain, but he himself did not make the ascent.

[61] Ibid., 225.
[62] Ibid., 220n51.

I began this essay with the assertion that for von Balthasar all things must be submitted to Christ, and I have just alluded to the development of a Christological *analogia entis* in conversation with Barth and Przywara as a further elaboration of this claim. In *Theo-Drama*, von Balthasar suggests that Przywara's *analogia entis* is inadequate to the task of articulating a Christology of mission that is robustly Trinitarian and that simultaneously addresses fully the dilemma of human freedom as it needs to be understood today. Some sort of analogy of being needs to be incorporated into Christology, but Przywara's is only a first step to reaching that goal. The study of the total structure made in 1939 seems to suggest a similar conclusion, even though the actual critical debate with Przywara's thought would not come into full view until much later.

What is the final step that brings together holiness, culture, and politics and also responds to the charge of elitism among his critics? I would like to suggest that the idea of a centrifugal integration permeates von Balthasar's mature thought and unveils the hidden key ignored by so many of his critics.[63] The question of integration is quite central to von Balthasar's project and only seldom gets mentioned by scholars working on his thought. In sum, von Balthasar conceives of the whole truth about God and man as a symphony whose unity is greater than its parts. Przywara's principle of analogy is certainly one fragment of that whole and is a fragment in which one can even begin to view the whole as a whole. Von Balthasar argues, quite effectively in my estimation, that you cannot drive a wedge between Przywara's religious metaphysics and a Christocentric theology. Many of the resources needed for integrating the two are already present in Przywara.

What von Balthasar adds to Przywara's Ignatian metaphysics of the rhythm of creation—which already contains a seed for mission—is his own understanding of the outwardly directed catholicity of the

---

[63] The idea of centrifugality is found in an early writing but applies throughout. It refers to the stance of moving from the Church into the world and not vice versa (*centripetality*). I am taking it from "Sull'Idea di Una Casa Editrice Cattolica" (originally published in German in *Renaissance, Gespräche und Mitteilungen*, quaderno no. 1, 1952–1953), as translated into Italian in Guerriero, *Hans Urs von Balthasar*, 387–93. Joseph Fessio, S.J., to whom this volume is being offered, embodies the principle of Catholic centrifugality better than anyone alive today.

Church. Here is where the social and political witness of a Reinhold Schneider is so pivotal. One theme that recurs in von Balthasar's writings is that of the *Weltauftrag* of the Christian: What is the Christian commissioned to do in the world of which he is not a part? Flight from the worldliness of the world is not an option, and the choice made by von Balthasar together with Adrienne von Speyr of founding a secular institute as opposed to living in monastic seclusion is but a practical confirmation of this conviction. According to von Balthasar, all theology that takes the mission of the Church seriously presupposes the localized universality of both theology and the Church. Von Balthasar's critics seldom acknowledge this theme in his writings. More importantly, few of us, I think, have thought through all the implications for theological and ecclesial reflection of the fundamental homelessness of the Christian in the world in which we find ourselves. Von Balthasar's insight here might harbor vestiges of a kind of elitism, but it never rests upon a self-satisfied attitude of indifference to either the depth of the spiritual predicament of our age or the urgency of responding to the cry of those who suffer.

6

From Classic to Patristic:
Von Balthasar, Rahner, and the
Origins of Analogy

Stephen M. Fields, S.J.

The relation between the analogy of being and the analogy of faith has occupied the attention of both Hans Urs von Balthasar and Karl Rahner. The analogy of being, a philosophical doctrine, posits that reality is neither equivocal nor univocal, but that its finite and infinite modes subsist harmoniously in a unity-in-difference. The analogy of faith, a theological doctrine, amplifies and develops the analogy of being with the data of faith known through a freely offered divine revelation. The key question raised by these analogies concerns how they are coherently related. Catholic theology has traditionally maintained the fructifying reciprocity between reason and faith, in such a way that faith's truth claims can never be non-rational, however much their supra-rationality can be defended as ensuing from a divinely infused virtue. We see this tradition in the Greek East at least as early as Justin the Apologist, who asserts in the *logos spermatikos* that wherever truth is found, the Logos who is the source of truth must implicitly be immanent.[1] In the Latin West, Augustine's famous adage *crede ut intelligas* boldly asserts the same message.[2]

The origins of the fusion between these analogies lie in the patristic age when Christianity began to confront the forms of Platonism

---

[1] Justin, *Apology* I, ed. and trans. Edward Rochie Hardy, in *Early Christian Fathers*, ed. Cyril C. Richardson et al. (New York: Macmillan, 1970), 225–89, at 233.

[2] Augustine, *Tractates on the Gospel of John*, 29.6, in vol. 35 of J.-P. Migne, ed., *Patrologia cursus completus: Series latina*, 220 vols. (Paris: 1844–1864).

deliberately and systematically. For his part, von Balthasar, in studying Plato and Plotinus in the fourth volume of *The Glory of the Lord*,
does not expressly lay out their understandings of the analogy of
being. The same can be said of the analogy of faith in his treatment
of the fifth-century Dionysius (Denys) the Pseudo-Areopagite in this
work's second volume. Nonetheless, both analogies are implicitly
disclosed there. Our project here will explicate these analogies while
showing how they come into a synthesis. For his part, Rahner, in
his seminal study of the Trinity, innovatively conceives the relation
between the analogies in the distinction between the "logical", or
dogmatic, and the "ontic", or secular, use of expressions. We will
use this distinction to shed light on the patristic development of the
doctrine of the Trinity.[3]

Heidegger offers our endeavor an encouraging word. Although
neither a theologian nor a proponent of the analogy of being as clas-
sically conceived, he nonetheless reminds us of the importance of
attending to the origin of ideas. An origin represents the "distinctive
way in which truth" manifests itself historically. Following his lead,
these reflections hope to help us peer more incisively into the essence
or nature of Christianity's self-understanding and to draw from it a
lesson for contemporary application.[4]

Plato

Given the seminal nature of Plato's thought spread throughout diverse
works, von Balthasar's wide-ranging study first explores the analogy's
inner tensions before seeking their coherent resolution.[5] These tensions make sense only when seen against Plato's own vision of truth,
which, for von Balthasar, consistently drives his dialogues. This vision
led to his break with the poets. However much he loved them, the

---

[3] Whereas I am indebted to Rahner for the distinction between logical and ontic expressions, I am responsible for using it to study the Trinitarian dogma.

[4] Martin Heidegger, "The Origin of the Work of Art", in *Poetry, Language, Thought*, ed.
and trans. Albert Hofstadter (New York: Harper and Row, 1971), 17, 78.

[5] Hans Urs von Balthasar, "Plato", in *The Realm of Metaphysics in Antiquity*, trans. Brian
McNeil, C.R.V., et al., ed. John Riches, vol. 4 of *The Glory of the Lord: A Theological Aesthetics*, ed. Joseph Fessio, S.J., et al. (San Francisco: Ignatius Press, 1989), 166–215.

death of Socrates made it clear that "tragedy had been carried over from the stage into reality."[6] Causing his dramatic fall, philosophy's radical commitment to the truth entails the mind's ascent to the wisdom that contemplates the Forms. This ascent decisively divides humanity into two casts: those who serve this truth and those who live by power. Yet, as Socrates' death also shows, the true philosopher does not retreat into an isolated hermitage but, actively engaged in the polis, he gives social witness to the truth. Accordingly, von Balthasar reminds us that, in the *Republic's* "allegory of the cave", the escapee, having reached the light at the summit, returns into darkness to announce the good news to those still imprisoned. But here, ironically, he faces only hostility and derision. Nonetheless, truth, as the consummate good, is worth all sacrifices. When the lover of wisdom serves it, delusion, mere opinion, and relativism are challenged so that "the greatest possible good accrues to the state."[7] Still, however social its ambit, truth is assimilated only by means of the philosopher's own inner vision, which, when arduously obtained, demands in turn the equally arduous descent to *praxis*.[8]

Von Balthasar opines that Plato understands the pure vision of truth more as an ideal, not utterly impossible to incarnate, but dependent on the rare appearance of a messiah-like figure. Such a hero would need to dispense with private property and even marriage, not only for himself but for the commonwealth as a whole, so that the "merciless systematic" of truth could obtain in the polis.[9] As von Balthasar says, Plato must have perceived that these attempts to make "heaven on earth" would turn into "a caricature".[10] Because the stark tension thus remains between the mind's flight to the eternal and its return into history, we find ourselves forced to ask whether either aspect of the dialectic is efficacious. In other words, can the polarity be resolved only by the tragedy of Socrates' death? Such an option,

---

[6] Ibid., 168.

[7] Ibid., 173.

[8] D. C. Schindler notes that Balthasar, integrating Socrates' witness to truth unto death in his own work, claims that such witness confirms truth's objectivity. See *Hans Urs von Balthasar and the Dramatic Structure of Truth: A Philosophical Investigation* (New York: Fordham University Press, 2004), 308; citing *Truth of the World*, trans. Adrian J. Walker, vol. 1 of von Balthasar, *Theo-Logic: Theological Logical Theory* (San Francisco: Ignatius Press, 2000), 120–30.

[9] Von Balthasar, "Plato", 175.

[10] Ibid.

we might claim, remains all that the Greek ethos finally offers, as the plights of Antigone and Oedipus further suggest.

Turning to the tensions inherent in Plato's view of knowledge, von Balthasar underscores its necessary orientation to the universal reality extrinsic to the subject. Humanity is not "the measure"; on the contrary, this lies in the submission of the knowing spirit to a purposeful world that discloses itself as something of an epiphany.[11] Knowledge transcends imagination and concepts, even the objects of reality themselves. Plato supports this claim with the notion of form, an important component in his reconciliation of being, or permanent identity, and becoming, or contingent flux. In everything that changes, the light of being radiates precisely in and through the particular way that every existent is. This light is the Good that, as the cause of knowledge and truth, is prior to both. As von Balthasar says, because of the participation of all that is in the Good, we have something more than a mere categorical "*a priori* at the heart of reason".[12] Because knowledge of this participation results only from the mind's dialectical journey upward, truth itself exceeds all divisions of knowledge into distinct sciences, even though these bathe immanently in it.

Von Balthasar diagnoses three modes by which Plato explains the light of knowledge; each mode contains its own inner tensions. The first, the well-known *anamnesis*, or recollection, means that all knowledge of universals results from the preexistent soul's gazing upon the Forms prior to its fall into materiality. Because as sources of knowledge the Forms participate in the meta-unification of the Good, it follows that, for the philosopher, the divine aspect of humanity, so often mentioned by Plato, consists in its rationality. It further follows that piety, true devotion to the divine, consists in the full and consistent exercise of the mind's ascent. In it, the divine and the human blend in a homogeneity of rational subject and rational object.

Plato refers to "eros" and "daimonion" as the second mode of explaining the light of knowledge. They consist in a divine-like inspiration that causes in the soul infatuations that range widely from beautiful persons to the highest wisdom. They powerfully agitate the soul to remember the beauty and truth that it beheld in

[11] Ibid., 176.
[12] Ibid., 180.

its preexistence. Yet, as Socrates learns in the *Symposium* from the goddess Diotima, eros is neither divine nor human; it is rather a burning to acquire something lacking. It therefore obtains as an "'in between'",[13] a medium that carries the mortal to the immortal.[14] Eros leads to a reposing "with and in the presence of" truth, even more to a "'begetting'"[15] of truth in the soul.[16] Nonetheless, for all its power, the daimonion of Socrates, affirms von Balthasar, remains for Plato personal, even idiosyncratic. It cannot be identified as "a new stage of spiritual self-consciousness".[17] Effective as it might be in leading us to the universal, it remains always subordinate to it.

The third mode is myth, which for Plato, according to von Balthasar, begins where "the lines drawn by philosophical reflection stretch beyond its grasp."[18] Thus, we find Plato creating a personal creator-god in the *Timaeus*, who is set between lesser gods, on the one hand, and the Form of the Good, on the other. Here myth and philosophy sit uneasily juxtaposed, even as we might wonder how the soul harmonizes prayer to the personal divinity with reason's ascent to its telos. Ironically, therefore, the myth undercuts philosophy. If the myth somehow transcends *theoria* yet also nourishes it, then "in the context of human totality", philosophy, as the "queen of the sciences", seems forced to abdicate.[19]

Considering these modes, von Balthasar inquires more deeply into the transcendence that for Plato consummates knowledge. As the soul's act of judgment that grasps being in the midst of change, knowledge must lead to a passing of the mind into pure being. But von Balthasar sees Plato adding an important caveat. Unlike the undifferentiated being of Parmenides, being's authentic notion must contain an implicit analogy; it must be understood as absorbing "becoming" within itself. On the one hand, the realities of the world are "shot through in [their] innermost being with the non-existent [that is,

---

[13] Ibid., 189.
[14] Plato, *Symposium* 202A, in *Lysis / Symposium / Gorgias*, trans. W. R. M. Lamb, Loeb Classical Library 166 (Cambridge, Mass.: Harvard University Press, 1975).
[15] Von Balthasar, "Plato", 191.
[16] Plato, *Symposium*, 212AB.
[17] Von Balthasar, "Plato", 194.
[18] Ibid., 195.
[19] Ibid., 197.

becoming]".[20] Every reality "is negated in so far as it is opposed to itself in its parts".[21] On the other hand, absolute transcendence, as the necessary object of participation of all finitude, dynamically holds contingency in itself. The upshot is that, in a sense, being for Plato is not static, but immanently dynamic. Only through the finite world marked by becoming can the philosophical soul receive the daimonion that carries it to the all-embracing transcendence that explains becoming. The soul must yearn unfulfilled in contingency for its principle of surcease. According to von Balthasar, this principle for Plato is the Good, convertible with pure being and the beautiful.

Von Balthasar sees Plato defining the beautiful as the cause of what is fitting and appropriate to being and hence as the principle of any particular existent's integrity. For Socrates, it is unacceptable to divorce the beautiful from the good; otherwise, we could absurdly "conceive of a good which might not be beautiful".[22] For this reason, in the *Cratylus*, when Socrates "'dreamt'" of the Forms, he saw "'the beautiful and the good in Itself'".[23] Yet if they are not separable, the beautiful and the good can nonetheless be distinguished within their unity. In the *Timaeus*, which Balthasar sees as Plato's decisive word on aesthetics, beauty means, above all, the inner measure that obtains in every level of reality: in the body's grace, the soul's morals, the cosmos' harmony, and the divine's grandeur. Aggressively, Plato thus overthrows any merely subjective view of beauty as giving pleasure to personal taste. Still, when beauty is encountered and assimilated, it does confer on a person its distinctively satisfying joy of inner justice. Moreover, because of beauty's identity with the Good, Plato affirms that "what is aesthetically right is only discoverable in the context of what is ethically right."[24] Only the soul purified by virtue can mount to the summit of reality's objective telos.

The relation between this objective telos and the finite world comes into clear vision for von Balthasar in the *Timaeus* creation

---

[20] Ibid., 199.

[21] Ibid.

[22] Ibid., 203.

[23] Plato, *Cratylus* 439C, in *Cratylus / Parmenides / Greater Hippias / Lesser Hippias*, trans. Harold North Fowler (Cambridge, Mass.: Harvard University Press, 1926); Loeb Classical Library 167. Quoted in von Balthasar, "Plato", 204.

[24] Von Balthasar, "Plato", 208.

myth. Here we see that the difference between transcendence and finitude is ultimately absorbed "within the identically divine".[25] The world represents, not merely an ontologically diminished image of the plenitude of its archetype, but "a quasi-sacramental representation of the gods".[26] As a result, fashioned under the Good, the cosmos stands "in its glory 'self-sufficient', indeed 'a blessed god' " itself.[27] It follows that the ascending soul, in knowing truth, can therefore reach into the inner essence of the Good and so merge into it. Becoming is thus consummated in the transcendental unity that makes it possible.

Nor is this thesis confined to the *Timaeus*. In the *Laws*, avers von Balthasar, Plato yokes divine and human into a "final identity" of harmony and balance, making it apparent that any gratuitously offered supernatural revelation would be redundant to what already "is accessible to" philosophy.[28] Similarly, in the *Epinomis*, Plato affirms that the lover of wisdom, having intuited the proportioned regularity of reality, receives a " 'revelation of a single bond of natural connection between all being' ", which is "God".[29] Consequently, we are led by von Balthasar to wonder whether in Plato any proper analogy of being between finite and infinite remains, or whether it has effectively collapsed into an ontological univocity. Undoubtedly, this is precisely what von Balthasar, as a skeptic of ontologism and pantheism, would have us ask.

Plotinus

Von Balthasar's reading of Plotinus manifests how the tensions in the Academy's analogy of being find a more satisfying reconciliation in this great student of Ammonius Saccas.[30] A central tension, as we

[25] Ibid., 210.

[26] Ibid., 211.

[27] Plato, *Timaeus* 33D, 34B, in *Timaeus / Critias / Cleitophon / Menexenus / Epistles*, trans. R. G. Bury, Loeb Classical Library 234 (Cambridge, Mass.: Harvard University Press, 1929). Quoted in von Balthasar, "Plato", 210.

[28] Von Balthasar, "Plato", 213.

[29] Plato, *Epinomis* 991E–992B, in *Charmides / Alcibiades / Hipparchus / Lovers / Theages / Minos / Epinomis*, trans. W. R. M. Lamb, Loeb Classical Library 201 (Cambridge, Mass.: Harvard University Press, 1927). Quoted in von Balthasar, "Plato", 215.

[30] Hans Urs von Balthasar, "Plotinus", in *Realm of Metaphysics in Antiquity*, 280–313.

have seen, concerns the cleavage between myth and philosophy. Plato uneasily juxtaposes them so that the ascent of the soul to the Forms seems undercut by the gods' creation narrative. By contrast, Plotinus understands religion to sum up the value of all myth, even as philosophy absorbs religion. Being itself constitutes the divine revelation that "outshines all the splendours of particular myths".[31] "A vast ensouled organism", the cosmos of being finds its source in the One that, as the Good, generates all grades of reality as its own unfolding explication, even as its own absolute transcendence remains uncompromised.[32] The divine realities of Intellect (Nous) and World-Soul (Psyche), flowing from the One prior to the ranges of finitude, do not represent, avers von Balthasar, "a falling-away from primitive purity". Because they "are not temporally" emanated, they stand "perfectly good and beautiful just as they are".[33] Nous *en*folds the multiplicity of all forms within its own infinite unity, whereas Psyche *un*folds these individually into history, where the Good can thus shine with remote luster through time. Because being is explicated holistically, no detrimental "fall" obtains in the Plotinian "creation". On the contrary, "individuality is ... thoroughly positive", even as flesh, congenial to spirit, draws bodily sensibility into itself by virtue of the power that it receives from above.[34]

Another tension concerns the origin of the finite cosmos. If Plato never satisfactorily resolves the polarity between its deformation by change and its divine sacramentality, Plotinus speaks of the " 'overflowing potency' " of the One, which grounds all else, as "simply the expression of his perfection".[35] Although it is frequently claimed that the Good generates because, as *diffusivum sui*, it must, still, strictly

[31] Ibid., 280.

[32] Ibid., 282.

[33] Ibid., 284.

[34] Ibid.

[35] Von Balthasar cites Plotinus' works, as far as possible, from the first three volumes of *Plotinus Schriften*, trans. Richard Harder et al. (Hamburg: Verlag Felix Meiner, 1956–1971). He also uses *Plotini Opera, editio minor*, ed. Paul Henry and Hans-Rudolf Schwyzer, 3 vols. (Oxford: Clarendon Press, 1964–82), supplemented by Plotin, *Ennéades*, ed. Émile Bréhier, 6 vols. (Paris: Les Belles Lettres, 1924–1938). Citations are translated to reflect the structure of the German versions that he uses checked against available English translations such as Plotinus, *Enneads*, ed. Arthur H. Armstrong, 7 vols., Loeb Classical Library 440–45 (Cambridge, Mass.: Harvard University Press, 1966–1988), 468. VI.8.10, quoted in von Balthasar, "Plotinus", 288.

speaking, no necessity can obtain in the One. It rises so "'beyond reason'" and so "'beyond will'", transcending any implication of form, that it remains totally alien even to what emerges "'from its own self'".[36] Thus, "so 'wholly other'" as to "be called 'not-other'", its "'superabundant power'", by potentiating itself, "wills" itself to be what it is.[37] Consequently, the One's creativity never suffers depletion or succumbs to any need, nor do its products constitute accidents of its supreme subsistence. Each rank of unfolding possesses the ontological "urge to bring forth" the rank next in order to it.[38] Yet the explicating level inheres in the explicated level until the final level is reached, matter, which alone is wholly other to the One.[39] It therefore follows that the One insinuates itself as ever present in all other emanations, endowing them with "'a share in the being of the Good'".[40] These, in their cosmic "totality", build the One's "'throne'", metaphorizes Plotinus, which manifests the "ultimate essence of [the One's] beauty".[41]

A third tension concerns the relation between the Good, on the one hand, and being-form-truth, on the other. Plato views truth at times as the consummate good and at other times as a function of contemplating the Forms transcendentally unified by the Good. By contrast, Plotinus clearly originates being-form-truth in Nous, which can be done only because Nous subsists precisely in the Good. Nous constitutes the "unity-in-duality" of *noesis* (pure knowing) and *noemata* (the object known).[42] Because it grasps all that is and can be, "every potential ... is always already actual" in it.[43] Moreover, because Nous unfolds its unity-in-duality through Psyche in the spatio-temporal world, it explains the ontological possibility of the division between the thinking subject, on the one hand, and the material objects that human intelligence knows, on the other. In Nous, according to von Balthasar, Plotinus therefore posits an

[36] V.3.13, quoted in von Balthasar, "Plotinus", 287.

[37] VI.8.9, quoted in von Balthasar, "Plotinus", 288; VI.9.8, quoted in Balthasar, "Plotinus", 290.

[38] Von Balthasar, "Plotinus", 290.

[39] Ibid., 291.

[40] IV.8.6, quoted in von Balthasar, "Plotinus", 291.

[41] V.5.3, quoted in von Balthasar, "Plotinus", 290.

[42] Von Balthasar, "Plotinus", 292.

[43] Ibid., 293.

"objective realism" or an "'ideal-realism'", which grounds being in a form capable of our perception and affirmation.[44]

Yet, as von Balthasar trenchantly observes, Nous' distinctive integrity results only because the One, although immanent in Nous, rises transcendently above it. Precisely because "intellect and being are thus boundless and infinite in their inextricable mutuality", Nous participates in the One. It strains toward the One, seeking it as the telos of its own "endless journey through" its myriad of enfolded forms.[45] Nonetheless, its own pleroma gives it a certain rest, because "'its thinking is not seeking but possessing ... eternally all things'."[46] Thus ironically, as von Balthasar notes, Nous pines for what it already contains from its eternal initiation, the One, whose epiphany it represents.

When through Psyche Nous fractures its unity-in-diversity in history, it initiates the dynamism constituting the person's dialectical ascent. The mind's eros yearns to return to the source of its explication, which is finally the One, immanent in the divine emanations ontologically more proximate to it. In this ascent, "the intellect perceives beyond its own being something marvellous, ... something sublimely worthy of veneration."[47] Because no concept can accommodate this perception, it can only be guessed. Although being-form-truth leads us to this grand horizon, intellect must be abandoned for the "'upward leap'",[48] the "'dreadful yearning'" of a solitary encounter.[49] "[Purified] from what is earthly",[50] we can "'lay hold of that One with our whole self, and there is no part in us with which we do not touch God'."[51]

In the penultimate stage of the ascent, when the soul has not yet seen the One, "'the Good is the object of striving'" for which it longs and pants; but when its sight is ultimately caught, the Good's sheer beauty, as "'the object of astonishment'", amazes the soul.[52] And yet, because beauty belongs properly to being-form-truth and

[44] Ibid.
[45] Ibid., 295.
[46] V.1.4, quoted in von Balthasar, "Plotinus", 296.
[47] Von Balthasar, "Plotinus", 303.
[48] V.5.4, quoted in von Balthasar, "Plotinus", 304.
[49] VI.7.34, quoted in von Balthasar, "Plotinus", 304–5.
[50] VI.9.4 et al., quoted in von Balthasar, "Plotinus", 305, see n. 391.
[51] VI.9.9, quoted in von Balthasar, "Plotinus", 305–6.
[52] I.6.7, quoted in von Balthasar, "Plotinus", 306.

thus to Nous; and because therefore "the One 'does not deign to be beautiful'", the summit of the ascent is not, as in the *Symposium*, accurately defined as beautiful.[53] Nonetheless, beauty is part of it, because the soul, resting in the beautiful pleroma of Nous, grasps in it beauty's formless source. In a sense, then, the beauty of Nous' being-form-truth mediates immediately its transcendent source immanent in it.

If von Balthasar suggests that Plato, despite adumbrating an analogy of being, effectively collapses infinite and finite into a univocity, still his study of Plotinus outlines an authentic analogy subsequently beneficial to Christianity. Differentiation irreducibly obtains in the grades of the Plotinian cosmos, because each explicated image manifests its explicating archetype in a diminished but authentic form. Yet the originating Good, suffusing all grades, is never "'distant from us'".[54] Vitally important, the analogy firmly preserves the One's transcendence within its emanations. It breaks into the finite world of being-form-truth with the gratuitous glory of its formless potency. Being as such thus becomes an epiphanous symbol of an absolute "light" glimpsed indirectly in forms. These, while sharing its luster, at the same time negate themselves by pointing away from their own reality to it. Von Balthasar calls this dimension of the Plotinian system "theological".[55] He means that human intelligence perceives in the world of our sensibly conditioned experience a pure gift that both sustains and defies it. Yet, whereas intellect may touch it by means of a natural connection, the One remains paradoxically so totally other-and-not-other that any univocity between human and divine is utterly unthinkable.

Dionysius

In the corpus attributed to Dionysius the Pseudo-Areopagite, von Balthasar shows us a Greek theologian whose "explosive and yet constructive originality" adapts the analogy of being to the analogy of

---

[53] V.8.8, quoted in von Balthasar, "Plotinus", 306.
[54] VI.5.1, quoted in von Balthasar, "Plotinus", 287.
[55] Von Balthasar, "Plotinus", 301.

faith.[56] Whereas Dionysius borrows much of the first analogy from the Plotinian explication of reality out of the absolutely transcendent, he modifies the Neoplatonic doctrine of the One in light of Christian revelation in order to fashion the second.[57] In turn, this modification expands nature by suffusing it with grace, even as nature retains its own integrity. A highly original vision of reality results, rich in nuance and coherent in its subtle differentiations.

The cosmos of being, dynamically proceeding from and returning to God, constitutes a manifestation of its hidden origin. According to von Balthasar, Dionysius thus sees the emerging world as an artifact entailing an analogy between its own spatio-temporality and its sublimely generating source. Between finite and infinite, this analogy establishes a simultaneous relation of affirmation, or kataphasis, and negation, or apophasis. Although God remains immanent in the world, all predicates drawn from it that affirm God must be negated, even to the point of "frenzy", because divinity exceeds rational reduction.[58] Nonetheless, in Dionysius, opines von Balthasar, even more than in Plotinus, the mind's ascent to God by means of denial "is kindled only" by God's self-effusive descent to the world.[59] In fact, Dionysius underscores this descent so strongly that "any flight from the world is unthinkable, even for the most exalted mysticism."[60] As a result, von Balthasar confidently asserts that Dionysius resists definition as "the advocate and architect of all negative theology, the mystical iconoclast, as he is generally thought to be".[61]

If the divine kataphasis establishes the analogy of being, still, because God's reality is utterly "inimitable", God and the world constitute a

---

[56] Hans Urs von Balthasar, "Denys", in *Studies in Theological Styles: Clerical Styles*, trans. Andrew Louth et al., ed. John Riches, vol. 2 of *The Glory of the Lord* (San Francisco: Ignatius Press, 1984), 144–210, at 147.

[57] Although Dionysius' "dependence on Neo-Platonic forms of thought is so obvious", still Balthasar mentions other influences like the Alexandrians, Gregory of Nyssa, Philo, Proclus, and the Areopagite's own teacher, Hierotheus. About these, Balthasar pays a moving tribute to Dionysius, who "does not want to borrow, but rather to return what has been borrowed to its true owner" (the true God revealed in Christ) (ibid., 208).

[58] *De Mystica Theologia* (hereafter cited as *MT*), end; von Balthasar, "Denys", 165n43.

[59] Von Balthasar, "Denys", 165.

[60] Ibid., 166.

[61] Ibid., 179.

"like unlikeness and an unlike likeness".[62] This paradox results from the distinction, von Balthasar claims, that Dionysius draws between God's self-communication, which grounds the finite order, and the reality of God, who communicates. God communicates being to the visible reality through, or by means of, his own being. This act of self-revelation, which bridges finite and infinite modes, grounds the simultaneous similarity and dissimilarity between them. At once, this act flows forth from God while it creates the cosmos that, in its contingency, stands radically other than God. Consequently, on the one hand, the being of God instrumentally causes creation and thus provides the ground for the divine names. On the other hand, because creation exists "by God's *allowing* it *to share* ... that 'which cannot be shared'",[63] creation participates in God "'while not participating'".[64] Here for the first time, von Balthasar helps us to glimpse Dionysius' introduction of something new into the schema of Plotinus to which he is so indebted: a notion of divine freedom radically other than the great Neoplatonist's. Accordingly, we see what in Dionysius is perhaps the precise point of transition from the analogy of being to the analogy of faith. Through the mediation of grace alone "can the sensible symbols speak of God['s]" authentic freedom.[65] In so doing, they allow us to see "through the sacred veil of the temporal revelations to perceive in rapt contemplation the eternal mysteries".[66]

Dionysius develops his innovative doctrine of God by subordinating being to eros (extroverted love), which is "of equal rank and the same meaning" as the good and the beautiful.[67] He thus fuses into Christian monotheism three predicates that Plotinus distributes between the One (good) and Nous (being, beauty), even as he adds

---

[62] Dionysius, *Epistolae* 2, 9.1, in vol. 3 of J.-P. Migne, ed., *Patrologia cursus completus: Series graeca*, 161 vols. (Paris, 1857–66), 1068A–1069A, 1105D. Unless noted, the works of Dionysius are cited with the pagination from Migne. Quoted in von Balthasar, "Denys", 180; see also 202.

[63] *De Divinis Nominibus* (hereafter cited as *DN*): V.8 (824C).

[64] Dionysius, *DN* II.5 (644A), quoted in von Balthasar, "Denys", 186. For an analysis of the role of participation in Balthasar's study of Dionysius, see Junius Johnson, *Christ and Analogy: The Christocentric Metaphysics of Hans Urs von Balthasar* (Minneapolis, Minn.: Fortress Press, 2013), 91–95.

[65] Von Balthasar, "Denys", 184.

[66] Ibid., 153.

[67] Dionysius, *DN* IV; quoted in von Balthasar, "Denys", 189.

a fourth (eros).[68] In deference to the Plotinian One, he affirms that the name of God embracing all being is the good. But "the good", he avers, "is celebrated ... as beauty" because goodness "causes the consonance and splendor of all".[69] Moreover, the divine goodness is eros because it does not "abide in itself but has moved [to] the generative thrusting forth of all beings", especially the Incarnation, its "preeminent ecstasis".[70] Eros, goodness, and beauty thus constitute " 'the cause of all initiation' ",[71] even as they "express the power of the primordial Godhead in radiance and affirmation".[72] It therefore follows that they mediate the divine being that creates; in them being subsists, and from them flow " 'both being and well-being to all that is.' "[73] If God's goodness is loving, then God is free. If eros generates being, then being is freely loving. In the union of goodness, beauty, eros, and being, Dionysius incorporates the philosophical analogy into the analogy of faith. In so doing, he augments what Plotinus, transforming Plato, bequeathed to him. Indeed, claims von Balthasar, Dionysius' "Christianizing of the Neo-Platonic *milieu* [is but] a side-effect of his own properly theological endeavour."[74]

We see this Christianizing perhaps most forcefully in the adaptations that Dionysius' innovative genius makes to the Platonic ascent of the mind to transcendence. In its mounting ecstasy driven by eros, the soul, in contrast to what we find in Plato and Plotinus, imitates the free ecstasy of the divine eros, "which out of love goes out of itself into the multiplicity of the world".[75] God's eros confers

---

[68] "Denys ... avoids speaking in a Plotinian way of a world-soul" (Psyche) (von Balthasar, "Denys", 161).

[69] Dionysius, *DN* IV.7 (701C); in Pseudo-Dionysius the Areopagite, *The Divine Names and Mystical Theology*, trans. John D. Jones (Milwaukee, Wis.: Marquette University Press, 1980), 138.

[70] Dionysius, *DN* IV.10 (708B); in Jones, *Divine Names*, 142–43; Jones, introduction, *Divine Names*, 15–103, at 59. Nonetheless, Balthasar refers to "Roques' systematic account" claiming that "christology appears as a kind of appendix" in Dionysius; "Denys", 162.

[71] Von Balthasar, "Denys", 196.

[72] Dionysius, *De Coelesti Hierarchia* (hereafter cited as *CH*) III.1 (164D), quoted in von Balthasar, "Denys", 191. Citations of this text take vol. 58 of *Sources Chrétiennes* as a basis [*La Hiérarchie céleste*, ed. and trans. R. Roques et al. (Paris: Éditions du Cerf, 1958)]. Roques follows Migne's numbering and keeps to his lines.

[73] *De Ecclesiastica Hierarchia* I.3 (373 CD), quoted in von Balthasar, "Denys", 200.

[74] Von Balthasar, "Denys", 149.

[75] Ibid., 205.

an aesthetic significance on creation absent in Platonism. Although Plotinus would agree that all existents "'carry within themselves ... the image of their causes [in the good and the beautiful, which] are transcendent over their effects' ", still Dionysius, by deriving all reality from the divine freedom, makes human beings capable of a mutual relation of love with their supreme artisan.[76] If this relation is consummated when the soul's ascent enters into mysticism, then, as von Balthasar notes, Dionysius stands "far removed from Plato's 'conversion' from aesthetics to philosophy". Von Balthasar means that any ascent into the transcendent "'much more'" can never abandon humanity's radical engagement with "form and what it expresses".[77] Even as the apophatic mystic is "peeling off" the layers of sensible existence, he must realize that God exceeds apophasis even as God exceeds kataphasis.[78] Crucially, therefore, the ascent of the analogy of faith "demands both a deeper penetration *into* the [sensible form of beings] and also a more sublime transcendence *beyond* it". They "are more fully integrated, the more perfectly [each act is] achieved".[79]

Yet *how* is this integration to be achieved? Certainly, Dionysius posits the immanence of the Incomprehensible in the comprehensible, because God, who transcends comprehension, "makes himself comprehensible in his communications".[80] Nonetheless, von Balthasar subtly diagnoses in this paradox the same tension between the mind's flight to the eternal and its return into history that emerges in Plato. In Dionysius, mankind's greatness and tragedy both entail its immersion "in the aesthetics of the world of images [forms] and at the same time" its irresistible exigency "to dissolve all images in the light of the unimaginable".[81] In Plato, the resolution entails an ontologically univocal merging between finite and infinite. In Plotinus, it entails the mystical passing-over of the soul from form in its return to the One who transcends being, truth, and beauty. Christianity precludes both solutions because, as von Balthasar claims, no immediate knowledge of God, however analogous, is possible, at least in this life,

---

[76] Dionysius, *DN* II.8 (645 CD); quoted in von Balthasar, "Denys", 168–69n52.
[77] Von Balthasar, "Denys", 168.
[78] Ibid., 206.
[79] Ibid., 169.
[80] Ibid., 185.
[81] Ibid., 179.

not even for Moses and the apostle Paul.[82] Par excellence, the Incarnation mediates divine knowledge when it suddenly radiates "into the darkness of human existence" precisely to embrace form and give it divine value.[83] In Christianity, therefore, philosophy alone remains impotent to give surcease to the dialectic in the core of Platonism.

It is only the Church, embodying the analogy of faith in "the heart of the world", that, in her sacraments, lifts the veil covering being's conundrum.[84] Although the sacramental signs drawn from created realities hide their sacred meaning, they do so "only in order to initiate [us] more perfectly". If the Eucharist makes the Church even as the Church makes it, then by "ascending the steps of the shrine [we] can draw yet nearer to the mystery."[85] Its natural elements of bread and wine, from the beginning of the liturgy, are placed within the context of the " 'holy myth' " of the Paschal events that, in grace, they reenact.[86] Their consecration by the priest results in a sacred "destruction of the image for the sake of the pure concept", the presence of Christ as their essential meaning. In their subsequent consumption, when the finality of the sacrament is realized, a "mystical union" ensues that subsumes the human into the divine.[87] Faith, consenting where the senses fail, renders speech inaudible before the blessed elements, even as in them faith's uttered word " 'becomes completely one with the Inexpressible. '"[88] Ultimately, then, Dionysius does accomplish the merging between the One and the many that Plato and Plotinus effect by pure metaphysics. But in Christianity, this quasi-univocity can only obtain by the One's freely self-revealed eros.

Von Balthasar views Dionysius as tethering any mystical ascent to the Church, whose praise of God in the Mass it extends. If the mystic communes with "the heavenly court", he can do so only because the Church, by grace that builds on nature, represents the ineffable in history.[89] Because in the Eucharist the Church partakes of her

---

[82] Ibid., 206–7.
[83] Ibid., 193.
[84] Ibid., 166.
[85] Ibid., 173.
[86] Ibid., 183.
[87] Ibid.
[88] *MT* IIIe (1033BC), quoted in von Balthasar, "Denys", 174.
[89] Von Balthasar, "Denys", 166.

own essence, it follows that mysticism finds its rightful center in the sensible form of this premier sacrament, where it inescapably abides, even as it imports the Eucharist's effects into time and space for the building up of the one body in love. Furthermore, Dionysius affirms ironically that the " 'perfect inadequacy' " of images in mysticism and consumable forms in the Eucharist emphasizes their vitality in the analogy of faith.[90] If they were fittingly proportionate to their signification, then we would have no incentive to negate them in favor of authentic divinity. Thus, trenchantly comments von Balthasar, Dionysius offers an argument against any demythologizing that would supersede the sensible media intrinsically containing the message.

Von Balthasar's retrieval of Dionysius decisively challenges much of the received interpretation. As a result, not surprisingly have his studies of Christian sources in *The Glory of the Lord* generated controversy. On the one hand, a critic finds von Balthasar's work " 'audaciously creative' ", " 'disconcerting' ", and " 'transgressive' of normal bounds of scholarship".[91] On the other hand, others note that his close textual work endeavors, not simply "to *replicate*" these thinkers, but "to *translate*" them into the contemporary conversation.[92] In so doing, he conducts "a dialogue with the tradition" that avoids a "narrow historicism, which constrains all interpretation to the meaning 'intended by the author' ".[93] In this sense, he shares a kinship with the hermeneutics of Rahner, who imports them from Heidegger, his seminar mentor in Freiburg. *Spirit in the World*, Rahner's creative exposition of Aquinas' metaphysics of knowledge, proceeds "meta-historically": it poses questions to the texts of Thomas generated by contemporary problems in the tradition from Kant to Heidegger.[94] Accordingly, both thinkers can be hailed as "exemplary *ressourcement*" theologians, because they

---

[90] *CH* II.2 (137D), quoted in ibid., 180.

[91] Dom Polycarp Sherwood, cited in Brian Daley, "Balthasar's Reading of the Church Fathers", in *The Cambridge Companion to Hans Urs von Balthasar*, ed. Edward T. Oakes, S.J., and David Moss (Cambridge: Cambridge University Press, 204), 187–206, at 202, quoted in Jones, "Dionysius", 753.

[92] Tamsin Jones, "Dionysius in Hans Urs von Balthasar and Jean-Luc Marion", *Modern Theology* 24 (October 2008): 743–54, at 746.

[93] Oleg V. Bychkov, *Aesthetic Revelation: Reading Ancient and Medieval Texts after Hans Urs von Balthasar* (Washington, D.C.: Catholic University of America Press, 2010), 99.

[94] Karl Rahner, *Spirit in the World*, trans. William V. Dych (New York: Herder and Herder, 19680), lii.

return to the ancient texts for guidance while maintaining a critical distance from outmoded teachings and methods.[95]

Wherever we stand in this debate, "Denys" does raise interpretative problems that it does not solve. A key set of issues centers on the relation between being, on the one hand, and the goodness, beauty, and eros in which being subsists, on the other. Because for Dionysius God "is 'of all forms' without himself possessing a form",[96] we are left wondering whether an equivocation between being and the predicates in which it subsists obtains in the divine essence. But if being and these predicates can, in some way, be explained as analogous, then we are still left wondering whether the utter simplicity of God is not significantly compromised; after all, this simplicity is necessary for solving the problem of the one and the many. This compromise is intensified by Dionysius' predicating eros of God. To be sure, Dionysius draws his warrant from the analogy of faith; but he also makes eros convertible with predicates warranted from the analogy of being, without, however, offering a philosophical warrant. The difficulty of providing such a warrant concerns the definition of eros as yearning and desire. It remains unclear how these acts, which entail achieving objects not possessed, can be affirmed of the infinitely self-sufficient absolute. I have attempted to resolve these issues elsewhere by placing Dionysius within a broader context that draws on other patristic and modern sources.[97]

In sum, under the unifying theme of analogy, our study thus far has brought into dialogue three of von Balthasar's discrete interpretations of the Platonic tradition. It has illustrated that, for philosophy and divine revelation to cohere, reason's conception of the One must be not merely replaced but enrichingly embraced by God manifested in Christ. This means that, even as philosophy defines reality's finite and infinite modes as analogous, so Christianity shows that its Infinite and Platonism's infinite are themselves analogous.[98] We will turn now to Karl Rahner's monograph *The Trinity*, which provides

[95] Edward T. Oakes, S.J., "Balthasar and *Ressourcement*", in *Ressourcement: A Movement for Renewal in Twentieth-Century Catholic Theology*, ed. Gabriel Flynn and Paul D. Murray (Oxford: Oxford University Press, 2012), 278–88, at 284–85.

[96] Dionysius, *DN* V.8 (821B), quoted in von Balthasar "Denys", 188.

[97] See Stephen M. Fields, *Analogies of Transcendence: An Essay on Nature, Grace and Modernity* (Washington, D.C.: Catholic University of America Press, 2016), chaps. 5–6.

[98] For more, see Hans Urs von Balthasar, *The Theology of Karl Barth: Exposition and Interpretation*, trans. Edward T. Oakes (San Francisco: Ignatius Press, 1992), 273–76.

us with additional resources for understanding the correlation of the analogies of being and faith.

Essence in the West

Rahner posits the distinction between the analogy of being's "ontic" use of expressions and the analogy of faith's "logical" use of them. Their ontic use explains a state of affairs according to a secular discipline, especially philosophy, based on natural reason apart from grace. Their logical use explains divine revelation and so formulates theology and its dogmas in some way detached from any ontic explanation with which the logical use may, nonetheless, be connected.[99] The relation and distinction between these uses can assist us in discerning how patristic Christianity absorbs philosophy when it accounts for the monotheistic unity of the Trinity. We will find that the Greek East accomplishes this absorption with notable success, because it uses the Trinity, precisely as a datum of faith, to open and expand ontic understandings of unity. Consistent with our study of Dionysius' relation to Plotinus, we might therefore say that, for the East, divinity becomes analogous when posited logically and ontically.[100]

The Trinity surveys a range of official documents of the Church to demonstrate that the West defines the Trinitarian unity by equating the expressions "essence", "substance", and "nature". Used logically, these terms denote "divinity" and "supreme reality" in the sense "that the Father is God; that the Son is God, and comes to meet us as such; and that the Holy Spirit is God and meets us as such; yet that in these three beings, who are God, only *one* God is given. To express *this* ... we are told that one and the same divinity (hence one 'essence,' one 'substance,' one 'nature') is given to us in the three 'persons.'"[101]

---

[99] Karl Rahner, *The Trinity*, trans. Joseph Donceel (New York: Seabury Press, 1974), 52–55.

[100] In the rest of this essay, the word "concept" refers to an ontic expression and the word "term" refers to a logical one. Both concepts and terms can be ontological, because they explain realities in the metaphysical order of being.

[101] Rahner, *Trinity*, 51–52. Rahner cites the documents from *Enchiridion Symbolorum: Definitionum et Declarationum de Rebus Fidei et Morum* (hereafter cited as DH), ed. Heinrich Denzinger and Peter Hünermann, Eng. ed., ed. Robert Fastiggi and Anne Englund Nash (San Francisco: Ignatius Press, 2012): 804, for substance, essence, nature; 501, for person, subsistence; many other citations are given for other non-officially defined uses of these terms.

Yet as J. N. D. Kelly observes, the West's starting point consists in the "profound conviction of the unity of God, the divine monarchy".[102] As a result, its understanding of the Trinity leans toward modalism, which "tended to blur the distinctions between Father, Son and Holy Spirit".[103] Although early Western and Antiochene Fathers regarded modalism as an error, they nonetheless considered it "a well-intentioned distortion".[104] One such distortion, represented in the third-century Paul of Samasota, develops "dynamic monarchianism". It builds a halfway house between strict monotheism and the classic modalism that, in Paul's contemporary Sabellius, posits the Father as the Godhead's essence and the Son and Spirit as his modes of expression. Paul's position, tantamount to unitarianism and adoptionism, claims that, although the Word dynamically inspires Christ, Christ is not the Word. Another distortion, represented in the second-century Noetus of Smyrna, formulates "indivisible monarchianism". It denies the independent subsistence of Father and Son and, on this basis, adheres to patripassianism (namely, that the Father suffers together with the incarnate Son).[105]

Tertullian bears the influence of this modalist trend, even as, ironically, he is the first Christian writer to use the term Trinity and is regarded as the founder of its occidental theology.[106] At the outset, we should note that Tertullian is keenly aware of the need to distinguish among the divine "Persons" while preserving monotheism. For instance, in explicating John 10:30, " 'I and the Father are one [note ἕν, not εἷς]' ", he draws the distinction between *unum* and *unus*, saying that the verse means: " '*we are one thing*' *Unum*, not 'one person' *Unus*.... He [Jesus] accordingly says *Unum*, a neuter term, which

[102] J. N. D. Kelly, *Early Christian Doctrines* (San Francisco: Harper and Row, 1978), 123. Throughout, Kelly quotes the sources "generally" from either J.-P. Migne, supra, or *Dei griechischen christlichen Schriftsteller der ersten Jarhunderte*, known as the Berlin Corpus of the Greek Fathers, begun by the Royal Prussian Academy of Sciences in 1891, and the *Corpus Scriptorum Ecclesiasticorum Latinorum*, known as the Vienna Corpus of the Latin Fathers, edited by the (Imperial) Austrian Academy of Sciences, 1864–2012. He does not further specify his source for each quotation.

[103] Kelly, *Early Christian Doctrines*, 115.

[104] Ibid., 123.

[105] Ibid., 117–19.

[106] See Tertullian, *Adversus Praxean* (hereafter cited as *AP*) 3, 11, 12; Kelly, *Early Christian Doctrines*, 113; Jürgen Moltmann, *The Trinity and the Kingdom: The Doctrine of God*, trans. Margaret Kohl (San Francisco: Harper and Row, 1981), 138.

does not imply singularity of number, but unity of essence, likeness, conjunction. . . . When he says, 'I and my Father are one' *in essence—Unum*—He shows that there are Two, whom He puts on an equality and unites in one."[107] When we delve farther into his thought, it becomes apparent that the distinction between *unus* (εἷς) and *unum* (ἕν) is intended to deny that the Persons possess an essence that is in any way different from the divine essence. But his understanding of essence stresses God's uniqueness, indivisibility, and eternal solitariness.[108] The Godhead is "indivisibly one", and the "threeness" of the Persons refers to the " 'manifestation' (*species*)", " 'grade' (*gradus* = Greek τάσις)", and " 'aspect' (*forma*)" "in which the Persons are present".[109] Accordingly, although the Word exists eternally as God, still God generates the Word as " 'a second in addition to Himself' " to accomplish the extroverted missions of creation and redemption.[110] Yet the Word cannot be said to participate in the divine essence, because sometimes Tertullian understands the Father as the whole essence and the Son as derived from it, although without division or severance.[111]

In a word, Tertullian effectively defines the unity of the Christian Godhead as what we might call "unicity". He stresses monotheism's simplicity of nature without adequately integrating the Trinitarian relations within it. This inadequacy is intensified when we recall that the Latin *persona* renders the Greek *prosopon*, which means the mask worn by actors to emphasize their dramatic role.[112] Consequently, the Trinity, properly speaking, appears to result from God's economic activity in the world. In their substantiality, Father and Son are not "separated" but "distributed", in the sense of " 'extended' ", not unlike matter.[113] Tertullian's use of these predicates shows the influence of the Stoics in whose ontic concepts he was steeped. As Kelly notes, for them, as for Tertullian, divinity, even as spirit, still

[107] Tertullian, *AP* 22.10–11. From the Vienna Corpus, trans. in *Latin Christianity: Its Founder, Tertullian*, vol. 3 of *The Ante-Nicene Fathers*, ed. Alexander Roberts and James Donaldson (Peabody, Mass.: Hendrickson, 1995), 618.

[108] Kelly, *Early Christian Doctrines*, 111.

[109] Tertullian, *AP* 9; quoted in Kelly, *Early Christian Doctrines*, 114–15.

[110] Tertullian, *AP* 5, 9; quoted in Kelly, *Early Christian Doctrines*, 111.

[111] Kelly, *Early Christian Doctrines*, 114.

[112] Ibid., 115.

[113] Tertullian, *AP* 8, *Apology* 21, 12; Kelly, *Early Christian Doctrines*, 113.

constitutes "a highly rarefied species of matter".[114] It therefore seems that, although Tertullian uses essence as a logical term to define the Scripture, still this use seems largely transferred from its ontic use.

In sum, we might conclude that, beginning with Tertullian and rippling through the West, a certain equivocation obtains in using essence to account for the Godhead's unity. Although appearing to be used logically, it is mainly used ontically as unicity. Resisting a full detachment from modalism, essence thus remains, at least in the West, a problematic Trinitarian term insufficient for the analogy of faith.

Ousia *in the East*

By contrast with the West's handling of essence, the East draws the concept *ousia* from its ontic use in the Nicene era and, over time, effectively adapts it as a logical term for the Godhead's unity. Broadly meaning being, it can also denote reality, essence, and substance. But the East incorporates *ousia* into the Nicene dogma without specific ontic use as, for instance, middle Platonism or Stoicism would coherently develop it in their systems. Nicaea, Kelly reminds us, primarily intends, not to proclaim a specific teaching about the divine unity, but to rule out the Arians' denial of the Son's co-eternality with the Father.[115] Nonetheless, *ousia*'s logical meaning cannot be totally divorced from the ontic context from which it is taken, even as, for the council, its theological use assumes priority. But precisely because this divorce is not possible, deciding the logical meaning of *ousia* becomes knotty. Kelly observes that the term *homoousios*, in both its pre-Nicene ontic and logical uses, conveys a " 'generic' " meaning as the commonality among individuals of a class.[116] Origen, for instance, uses it to signify that the Son is " 'of the same nature' " as the Father, not necessarily consubstantial with him, if by consubstantial we mean the single identity of the Father and the Son's substance.[117]

Nonetheless, it is widely assumed that Nicaea intends to convey this single substantial identity. But if Nicaea does intend this identity

[114] Kelly, *Early Christian Doctrines*, 114.

[115] Ibid., 236.

[116] Ibid., 234. For the pre-Nicene history of *ousia*'s logical and ontic uses, Kelly cites George L. Prestige, *God in Patristic Thought* (London: SPCK, 1959), chap. 10.

[117] Kelly, *Early Christian Doctrines*, 130, 234.

without further specification, then *ousia* would present little advantage over the West's notion of essence in accounting for the Godhead's unity, and the two terms should be rendered synonymously. Still, that Nicaea intended this identity is highly unlikely, contends Kelly, because otherwise the council's Eusebian majority, as disciples of Origen, would have decisively rejected it as modalist.[118] Kelly thus concludes that Nicaea's explicit use of *ousia* is more limited than "sometimes supposed". It affirms only "the Son's full divinity and equality with the Father".[119] Nonetheless, as he further says, "in the last resort", because "the divine nature is immaterial and indivisible, it follows that the Persons of the Godhead Who share it must have, or rather be, one identical substance."[120] Just how, therefore, as consubstantial, the Persons constitute a unity will occupy us next. But first let us first draw some conclusions.

If Kelly's solution to the problem of Nicaea's use of *ousia* is accepted, then the claim that Nicaea's logical meaning should be seen as entailing consubstantiality results from a subsequent development of the dogma. But to what extent this development is logical, to what extent ontic, is not altogether clear. Perhaps it ensued when Eastern and Western Trinitarianism came into post-Nicene contact. A synthesis between them could have carved out a middle position between Origen's non-consubstantial use of *ousia* and Tertullian's modalist-tinged use of essence. In any case, we can say that *homoousios*, as meaning consubstantial, is forged as a logical term expressly to define the unity of God as revealed by Christ. Yet it is consistent with its pre-Nicene ontic use as the commonality among individuals of a class. The logical term, in other words, embraces the ontic concept, even as it enriches it.

Perichoresis

If engagement between East and West leads to defining *homoousios* as consubstantial, still this triumph in the formulation of logical terms only intensifies the problem of the divine unity. It raises the question

[118] Ibid., 234, 236.
[119] Ibid., 236.
[120] Ibid., 234.

of how the Persons are related precisely in order to be consubstantial. The answer comes with the term *perichoresis*, rendered in Latin as *circumincessio*. It denotes the divine unity, not as a static substance, but as a reciprocal dynamism, in which the Persons move (*incedere*) around (*circum*) within each other. It thus posits that the unity of the Trinity is best framed as a "union" of distinct subsistences, even as a "communion".

Because the term originates in the East, it is not surprising that, within the immanent Godhead, it should account for distinctions among the Persons. Its first use occurs in Gregory Nazianzen's post-Nicene theology that applies it, not to the Trinity, but to the union of Christ's two natures.[121] John Damascene first predicates it of the Trinity in the eighth century,[122] although previous post-Nicene harbingers appear in both East and West. Cyril of Alexandria, for instance, speaks of the " 'reciprocal irruption' " among the Persons in their " 'unceasing circulation of life' ".[123] The eleventh Council of Toledo (675) asserts that the mutual relations binding the Persons and referring them to one another lie at the deepest roots of the doctrine of the Trinity.[124] Aquinas synthesizes the East's and West's understandings by explaining *perichoresis* as embracing both the unique substantiality of God and the origin in it of the Persons.[125] Catholic exegetes like K. Knabenbauer, A. Wilkenhauser, and J. Leal, together with Protestant ones like C. Barrett and W. Hendriksen, view John's Gospel as warranting "a mutual divine immanence between Father and Son" (cf. Jn 10:38, 14:11, 17:21). Nonetheless, explicit scriptural basis for the *perichoresis* of the Holy Spirit is lacking.[126]

The genesis and use of *perichoresis* show that it has no significant, if any, ontic association. Implied in the Scriptures, it denotes the reciprocal union of the Persons within their consubstantiality. Because it postdates Nicaea by half a millennium, and because its scriptural pedigree is incomplete, it does not seem endowed with the same

---

[121] Gregory Nazianzen, *Epistle* 101.

[122] John Damascene, *De Fide Orthodoxa* 1.8.

[123] Cyril of Alexandria, *Commentary on John* 1.5.

[124] DH 532.

[125] Thomas Aquinas, *Summa theologica*, I, q. 42, a. 5.

[126] A. M. Bermejo, "Circumincession", in *New Catholic Encyclopedia*, 17 vols. (New York: McGraw-Hill, 1967), 3:880. Quotations from the primary works that follow come from this source.

dogmatic status as *ousia*. Nonetheless, it is incorporated into (at least) quasi-official teaching (DH 112f., 115, 1331). Once the Council of Constantinople (381) defines the Holy Spirit's *homoousios*, attaching the Father and Son's *perichoresis* to the third Person becomes necessary. It is all the more necessary if, as Rahner argues, the economic Trinity, which in Christ reveals the *perichoresis*, *is* the immanent Trinity.[127]

Our overview of *perichoresis* shows that this expression develops the unity of the consubstantial Trinity by accounting for the reciprocal communion of the distinctly related Persons who constitute the Godhead. Furthermore, it shows that this development is logical; it results from expressly deepening the meaning of *homoousios* as a dogmatic term. Ontically, *perichoresis* is not entailed in *homoousios*. If ontically *homoousios* means the commonality among individuals of a class, that commonality is not, by definition, a circumincession of the individuals constituting it. Yet logically, circumincession is, by definition, entailed in *homoousios'* Nicene meaning. The council develops the Trinity's unity into union (or communion) as *ousia* is first subsumed from its ontic context into the Nicene dogma, where it develops into *homoousios* and consubstantiality, then into *perichoresis* (relational reciprocity). Moreover, in enriching *ousia*'s logical meaning, Nicaea also enriches its ontic meaning, expanding the very understanding of being's unity. Our final section will say more about this point. For the moment, we would note that, in the West, by contrast, the equivocation in essence between its ontic and logical uses mires Trinitarian unity in unicity. The West thus handicaps a robust analogy of faith in which grace can congenially incorporate philosophy's concepts of being. But as we shall now see, the Cappadocians, as heirs of the East's *ousia*, *homoousios*, and *perichoresis*, integrate into the analogy of faith the West's concern for the Godhead's essence as both unique and simple.

Cappadocian Synthesis

The Cappadocians develop their integrated analogy of faith by grounding their interpretation of Nicaea's dogma in an analogous understanding of unity. A precedent could be found in the previous

---

[127] Rahner, *Trinity*, throughout.

century's Clement of Alexandria, for whom God absolutely and ineffably transcends oneness. Yet, paradoxically, he abides as "'unity, but beyond unity'", because, as embracing all reality, he retains a direct ontological relation with the world that he creates and redeems.[128] Although the Son is subordinate to the Father, still because the Son is essentially one with the Father, the Son is the Father's equal in being. Within this unity, it is the Son who, properly speaking, embraces plurality.[129] But in virtue of his co-equality with the Father, the Father, it would seem, may also be said to embrace plurality, at least in an analogous sense.

For their part, the Cappadocians, in framing their analogy, lend a sympathetic ear to the West's use of essence as it denotes the Godhead's simplicity, lack of composition, and indivisibility. But crucially, they do not equate these predicates with an understanding of numerically identical oneness. As Kelly notes, they expansively apply to the Trinity "the old Aristotelian doctrine that only what is material is quantitatively divisible".[130] In Gregory of Nyssa, for instance, "number is indicative merely of the quantity of *things*, giving no clue as to their real nature."[131] Evagrius of Pontus, a Cappadocian disciple, affirms "'that we worship one God, not one in number but in nature'".[132] In defending this teaching against the charge of tritheism, Evagrius turns the tables on modalist-tinged views, saying: "'Whatever is described as one in a merely numerical sense *is not one really*, and is not simple in nature'".[133]

In a further development, Basil of Caesarea notes "that while each of the persons is designated one, They cannot be added together", because "the divine nature which They share is simple and indivisible."[134] Adumbrating the *perichoresis*, he views the divine simplicity as *koinonia*, a "continuous and uninterrupted" community.[135] In

---

[128] Clement of Alexandria, *Paedagogus* 1, 71, 1; *Stromateis* 2, 6, 1; Kelly, *Early Christian Doctrines*, 127.

[129] Kelly, *Early Christian Doctrines*, 127.

[130] Ibid., 268. Aristotle, *Metaphysics* 12.8, 1074a; 14.2, 1098b.

[131] Kelly, *Early Christian Doctrines*, 268; emphasis added.

[132] *Epistula Fidei* 2, often listed as *Epistula* 8 of Basil; Kelly, *Early Christian Doctrines*, 269.

[133] Ibid., emphasis added.

[134] Kelly, *Early Christian Doctrines*, 268.

[135] Basil of Caesarea, "Letter 38", in *The Letters*, trans. Roy J. DeFerrari, Loeb Classical Library 190 (Cambridge, Mass.: Harvard University Press, 1926), 1:197–226, at 209. Cited in the text.

it, "there is nothing which intrudes itself" among the distinctions, because "there is nothing which subsists that could really divide it from itself".[136] Presaging Dionysius, a paradox thus obtains in God, whose distinctions constitute a "united separation" and a "disunited connection".[137] In short, Trinitarian unity becomes analogous, because it frames *koinonia* as a logical term that incorporates the ontic concept of simplicity. When, therefore, we define consubstantial as the single identity of the Trinitarian Persons' substance, the term "single" does not entail the number one.

Moreover, the Cappadocians' analogy of unity between finite and infinite modes of reality works because it entails an apophatic moment. These Fathers could find precedent for it in both ontic and logical contexts. As to ontic context, in Neoplatonism, known to the Cappadocians either directly through Plotinus and/or through Origen, the One, as we will recall, rises transcendently above all realities that are emanated from it.[138] Hence, even as this flowing-forth establishes the ontological unity of the cosmos, it likewise entails successively descending negations as each level of archetype generates its subordinate image that nonetheless contains it.

As to logical context, Origen, a student like Plotinus of Ammonius Saccas, so emphasizes the Father's apophatic transcendence that subordination and emanation define the Godhead's unity. Hearkening to the Plotinian One, the Father transcends being-form-truth so that only he alone, strictly speaking, is God. Although only the Father is ungenerated, Origen avoids Arianism because he affirms the Son's eternal generation. Sometimes Origen considers the Son as one in nature with the Father, but he does draw the distinction among the Persons so decisively that he can claim, "We are not afraid to speak in one sense of two Gods, in another sense of one God."[139] The Trinity's unity, as grounded in love, volition, and action, is more moral than, as we have seen, consubstantial. The subordination of the Son and the Spirit to the Father's absolute transcendence accounts for Origen's doctrine of emanation. As a graded hierarchy, the Godhead mediates itself to the formally structured reality of the created

---

[136] Ibid., 209.

[137] Ibid., 213.

[138] Anthony Meredith, *The Cappadocians* (Crestwood, N.Y.: St. Vladimir's Seminary Press, 1995), 24.

[139] Origen, *Dialogue with Heraclites*, 2; Kelly, *Early Christian Doctrines*, 129.

order. The Father's action extends to all reality. The Son, hearkening to the Plotinian Nous, mediates between the Father and the Spirit whose ground is the Father. Accordingly, the Son's action extends the Father's to rational beings, whereas the Spirit's action extends the Father's through grace to sanctified rational beings.[140]

Against these ontic and logical contexts, the Cappadocians, adhering to Nicaea's doctrine, formulate a distinctively Christian understanding of the Godhead's transcendence. The council, for its part, affirms that creation ensues from God *ex nihilo sui et subjecti*. Consequently, no Platonic or Origenist grades of emanated mediation can account for creation; only divinity's loving freedom can.[141] God and the world are thus decisively divided, because no necessary ontological continuum establishes an affinity of nature between them. Within this transcendence, higher even than Plotinus', God, as absolutely omnipotent spirit, can negate the polarities required by time and space, the necessary conditions of the creation over which he is infinitely sovereign. In God, in other words, the plurality entailed in *koinonia* provides no obstacle, *a priori*, to the simplicity required of the divine nature. Yet this negation does not posit God and the world as equivocal; they are analogous, because the immanent Trinity is the source of all truth lodged in the finitude that the Godhead both fashions and redeems.

Crucially, because of this analogy, God is not removed from form, as the Plotinian analogy removes the One. Basil, for example, asserts that " 'the hypostasis [distinct subsistence] of the Son is, so to speak, the form and presentation by which the Father is known, and the Father's hypostasis is recognized in the form of the Son'."[142] Other thinkers, like Augustine, work out more explicitly the Nous-like function of the Logos in generating the sensible world. But by adumbrating the *perichoresis*, the Cappadocians give structure to divinity, even as they suggest that this structure contains, in the Logos through whom "all things came into being", the formal principles structuring creation (Jn 1:3). In short, the genius of these thinkers harnesses

---

[140] Kelly, *Early Christian Doctrines*, 128–32.

[141] Andrew Louth, *The Origins of the Christian Mystical Tradition from Plato to Denys* (Oxford: Oxford University Press, 1981), 75–77.

[142] Basil, *Letter* 38, 8; Kelly, *Early Christian Doctrines*, 264.

analogical apophasis to incorporate into *homoousios* and *perichoresis*, logical terms that entail form and structure, the simplicity of the divine essence. In so doing, they show the West how to remove from its understanding of essence the equivocation between its ontic and logical uses, which tinged its Trinitarianism with modalism. Most important, the Cappadocians interpret Nicaea in order to produce a divine transcendence worthy of God's loving freedom that, nonetheless, establishes the deepest intimacy with the finite world of form.

In sum, we have argued that Nicene theology fashions an analogous understanding of divinity when posited ontically and logically, even as von Balthasar shows Dionysius to fashion the same in relation to Platonism. Using von Balthasar's and Rahner's insights into the origins of Christianity's relation to the analogy of being has thus enabled us to see that these two thinkers, whose disciples are sometimes at odds even as they themselves were, can share common conclusions despite diverse methods.[143] It is true that explicitly articulating God as analogous in faith and philosophy is owing more to von Balthasar in his study of Karl Barth than to Rahner. Nonetheless, that we can here use Rahner's distinction between ontic and logic to explain von Balthasar's insight corroborates the overlay between them. Although von Balthasar accused Rahner's relation between faith and reason of equivocation, still a more sympathetic reading of Rahner could show his agreement with von Balthasar that reason's knowledge of God "is incorporated as an inserted moment in the ultimate" knowledge given by faith.[144]

Myth and Analogy's Future

If the patristic age reveals Christianity's debt to the ontic categories of the classical age, it is equally true that Christianity, by infusing those categories with its own content, has altered and enriched

---

[143] For a discussion of the dispute, see Stephen Fields, S.J., "Balthasar and Rahner on the Spiritual Senses", *Theological Studies* 57 (1996): 224–41, at 224–25.

[144] Hans Urs von Balthasar, *The Theology of Karl Bath: Exposition and Interpretation*, trans. Edward T. Oakes (San Francisco: Ignatius Press, 1992), 318. Admittedly, though, Rahner's relation between nature and grace presents its share of problems. For more on this issue in both thinkers, see Fields, *Analogies*, chaps. 2, 5.

reason. Can the ontic concept of unity, for instance, ever be the same after Nicaea's logic? That it cannot is evinced in Hegel, however we may assess his philosophy. According to it, only in and through reason's appropriation of the dogma of the Trinity does reason come to its own consummate understanding of reality as a dynamic unity-in-diversity.[145] Positive religion thus "quickens" reason's discovery of truths that nonetheless fall within its ambit.[146] Yet the method of correlation favored by liberal Christianity since Schleiermacher, despite Barth's critique, tends to keep the analogy of faith defensive in the face of reason. It gives reason the priority to ask the fundamental questions while placing on faith the onus of responding. Von Balthasar and Rahner give us resources to assert the prerogative of the analogy of faith to challenge reason more deeply to appropriate itself. They remind us, in a word, of the importance of myth that the analogy of faith implicitly carries.

Von Balthasar's study of Plato gives us a working definition of myth. It is a story that communicates the light of knowledge when philosophy reaches its limits. It both transcends theoria and nourishes it. In Rahner's words, myth is "filled with the soft music of infinity" and thus "evokes the blinding mystery of things".[147] Thus, myth is a symbol that, appealing to the imagination, uses poetic tropes like metaphor and allegory to communicate realities inexpressible by rational *logos*. As von Balthasar also observes, even though Plotinus endeavors to eliminate the myths of the Greek gods, his system does not obviate the irreducible sense of the mystery of the revelation of being as it devolves epiphanously from the One. If, as the Platonic tradition shows, philosophy's analogy needs myth, how much more must the analogy of faith require it. The absolute transcendence of God to creation that Nicaea dogmatically enshrines means that reason will always stretch beyond its limits to know anything more of the divine than, as Saint Thomas affirms, "that" it exists.[148] The gap between

---

[145] Georg W. F. Hegel, *Lectures on the Philosophy of Religion*, one-volume edition, *The Lectures of 1827*, ed. Peter C. Hodgson, trans. R. F. Brown et al. (Berkeley, Calif.: University of California, Press, 1988), part 3.

[146] Immanuel Kant, *Critique of Judgment*, trans. J. H. Bernard (New York: Hafner Press, 1951), 160.

[147] Karl Rahner, "Priest and Poet", in his *Theological Investigations*, vol. 3, trans. Karl-Heinz and Boniface Kruger, O.F.M. (London: Darton, Longman and Todd, 1974), 294–317, at 295.

[148] Thomas Aquinas, *ST* I, q. 12, a. 12.

this "that" and the divine "what" is breached by the symbolism of myth that, crucially, can only obtain by the divine initiative.

Yet even as the Christian narrative fulfills this function, it embodies a distinctive form of myth. Its starting point, Schelling reminds us, "is the particular, which must become the universal".[149] In other words, the Incarnation, which hypostatically joins God and mankind, means that the uniquely singular becomes the saving paradigm for all. Equally important, the Christian narrative claims "to rest on a historical basis", which "protects its message from being dispersed into the limitless interpretations" of other myths.[150] A magisterial institution like the Council of Nicaea exists precisely to give this protection. The council, no substitute for the divinely revealed narrative, serves only as its hermeneutical norm. But Nicaea's hermeneutics is possible only because the revealed myth itself expresses the divine mind and will. It thus mediates infinite intelligence to human intelligence, which uses metaphysics to explain it. Only this science, whose object is itself universal, can do justice to a message from the absolutely universal.[151] Using metaphysics, Nicaea effects a leap in meaning, as Lonergan avers, because it translates the Scripture's descriptive, culturally conditional imagery into explanatory, trans-cultural language.[152] This leap guarantees continuity of meaning, precisely because the metaphysics depends on the Scripture's mythic symbolism, even as it depends on the historic communications of the theandric person. Yet this leap, formulated in light of the Cappadocian apophasis that we have described, makes no claim exhaustively to reduce the imagery to reason, a claim that Hegel does make when explicating the Trinity.[153]

---

[149] Friedrich W. J. Schelling, *Sämmtliche Werke*, ed. Manfred Schröter (1927; Munich: C. H. Beck, 1965), 3:574, in Louis Dupré, *The Quest of the Absolute: Birth and Decline of European Romanticism* (Notre Dame, Ind.: University of Notre Dame Press, 2013), 321.

[150] Dupré, *Quest*, 327.

[151] Karl Rahner, "On the Relationship between Natural Science and Theology", in his *Theological Studies* 19, trans. Edward Quinn (New York: Crossroad, 1983), 16–23, at 19.

[152] See Bernard J. F. Lonergan, *The Way to Nicea: The Dialectic Development of Trinitarian Theology* (Philadelphia, Pa.: Westminster, 1976).

[153] Our notion of "the myth of God incarnate" presents a decided contrast with that put forth by the influential collection of essays bearing this title. Their notion of myth denies the binding truth of the Nicene dogma's interpretation of the historical Jesus given in Scripture and ecclesial tradition. In its place, it favors an adoptionism that, citing Acts 2:21, is reluctant to go beyond affirming Jesus as "'a man approved by God'" for a special role within the divine plan (*The Myth of God Incarnate*, ed. John Hick [Philadelphia, Pa.: Westminster Press, 1977], ix).

In sum, our study claims that: if the analogy of being requires myth, because reason, conditioned by time and space, cannot satisfactorily reduce history's origin and telos; and if the analogy of faith requires myth, because that origin and telos can only be divinely revealed in history; then it follows that both analogies are correlated by what we might call an "analogy of myth". The Christian myth, to use the famous term of Irenaeus of Lyon, "recapitulates" the myths of secular reason, fulfilling and perfecting them.[154] In concurring, Schelling observes that the mythic polytheism of Greece foreshadows the Trinity; both posit a plurality of divine interrelations.[155] Whereas the first offers nothing but anthropomorphisms, the second leaps from Scripture's narratives to consubstantial *perichoresis*. Insofar as Plato's myth-making remains forever a recognition of reason's finitude in the face of the Awesome, then Plato's legacy likewise remains a constitutive moment within the Nicene doctrine. Finally: if, as von Balthasar says, "the kenosis of God in Christ has an analogous structure in the metaphysical mystery of being", then faith's "logic", embodying the consummate myth, should shrug off all trepidation in boldly challenging "ontic" concepts that, continually stretched to their limits, struggle to frame their own myths.[156]

---

[154] Irenaeus of Lyons, *Against the Heresies*, in vol. 1 of *The Ante-Nicene Fathers*, trans. and ed. Alexander Roberts and W. H. Rimbaud (Peabody, Mass.: Hendrickson, 1996), 315–567, at 548, citing Ephesians 1:10.

[155] Dupré, *Quest*, 320.

[156] Von Balthasar, *Realm*, 38. For more on myth and metaphysics, see Stephen M. Fields, S.J., *Being as Symbol: On the Origins and Development of Karl Rahner's Metaphysics* (Washington, D.C.: Georgetown University Press, 2000), 98–104.

7

Reading the Mystery of God:
The Ignatian Roots of Henri de Lubac's
Understanding of Scripture

Joseph S. Flipper

The writings of Henri de Lubac on Scripture and its interpretation are expansive and not easily summarized. They span five decades and include *Histoire et Esprit: L'Intelligence de l'Écriture d'après Origène* (1950), the four-volume *Exégèse médiévale: les quatre sens de l'Écriture* (1959–1964), *L'Écriture dans la tradition* (1967), *La Révélation Divine* (1968), and the two-volume *La Postérité spirituelle de Joachim de Flore* (1979–1981). Despite de Lubac's extensive research on the history of interpretation of the Bible, the primary object of his work was not biblical hermeneutics. Although he sought to recover a patristic understanding of Scripture and had reservations concerning the adequacy of modern historical-critical methods of interpreting the Bible, he neither sought to supplant modern methods of biblical interpretation nor denied the advances made with a modern attention to historicity. While de Lubac had an influence on *Dei Verbum*, the Second Vatican Council's document on divine revelation, his theological contribution to biblical hermeneutics remains elusive. Many scholars have criticized de Lubac's lack of attention to historicity in his understanding of Scripture. But it is not exclusively through a hermeneutic lens that de Lubac's contribution should be understood but, instead, at the nexus of Scripture, spiritual practices, and historicity.

In this essay, I shall interpret de Lubac's recovery of the spiritual sense of Scripture in relationship to Ignatian spirituality. Unlike his contemporaries Gaston Fessard and Karl Rahner, de Lubac wrote no major work on Jesuit spirituality.[1] References to Saint Ignatius of Loyola in his writings are sparse and dispersed. This is perhaps why little attention has been given to interpreting de Lubac's theology in the light of Ignatian spirituality or his Jesuit vocation.[2] Despite the paucity of direct references to Ignatius, de Lubac's work is densely Ignatian, replete with distinctively Jesuit practices of spiritual reading and discernment. While de Lubac does not explicitly link his retrieval of spiritual interpretation to Ignatian spirituality, his characterization of spiritual interpretation bears the imprint of his Jesuit identity and formation. Philippe Geneste explains that though Henri de Lubac avoids systematization, "a kind of circularity emerges between the two thoughts; at certain points, it is even possible to detect a common method."[3] There is, he says, an "Ignatian filiation" in Henri de Lubac's thought. This is certainly the case with the spiritual senses of Scripture. For de Lubac, the spiritual interpretation of Scripture is less a theological method than it is a spiritual practice derived from his Jesuit formation and his reading of the history of scriptural exegesis.

1. Historicity and the Lubacian Scriptural Legacy

Despite making history a central theme within his work, Henri de Lubac has been accused of lacking a sufficient appreciation for

[1] See Karl Rahner, *Betrachtungen zum ignatianischen Exerzitienbuch* (Munich: Kösel, 1965); Gaston Fessard, *La Dialectique des Exercices spirituels de saint Ignace de Loyola: Tome 1: Liberté, temps, grâce* (Paris: Aubier, 1956); Gaston Fessard, *La Dialectique des Exercices spirituels de saint Ignace de Loyola*, vol. 2: *Fondement, péché, orthodoxie* (Paris: Aubier, 1966); Gaston Fessard, *La Dialectique des Exercices spirituels de saint Ignace de Loyola*: vol. 3: *Symbolisme et historicité* (Paris: Lethielleux, 1984).

[2] Andrew Prevot points out the lacuna in scholarship on de Lubac's mysticism more broadly. There are monographs examining Ignatian mysticism in the theology of Hans Urs von Balthasar and Karl Rahner, but none on that of de Lubac. "Henri de Lubac (1896–1991) and Contemporary Mysticism", in Robert Aleksander Maryks, ed., *A Companion to Jesuit Mysticism*, Brill's Companions to the Christian Tradition 78 (Leiden and Boston: Brill, 2017), 280. Narrowly focusing on the "soul", Lewis Ayres suggests a systematic relationship between de Lubac's spiritual theology and his theology of Scripture. See Lewis Ayres, "The Soul and the Reading of Scripture: A Note on Henri de Lubac", *Scottish Journal of Theology* 61, no. 2 (January 2008): 173–90.

[3] Philippe Geneste, *Humanisme et Lumière du Christ chez Henri de Lubac*, Études Lubaciennes 11 (Paris: Cerf, 2016), 58.

historicity. His broad appeals to the theological tradition, especially his *ressourcement* of the early Christian theology, can present
an image of unity that passes over profound theological divisions
with an ahistorical leap.[4] It is not only the fact of theological unity
but also the content of de Lubac's theological retrieval that is subject
to contention.

The question of de Lubac's inattention to history is made by scholars of Scripture who find fault with his retrieval of spiritual interpretation of Scripture. In addition to the literal-historical meaning of
the text—that is, the meaning intended by the author and conveyed
by the historical context—premodern Christian exegesis is characterized by interpreting additional spiritual senses. The allegorical sense
is the Christological meaning of the text. The tropological sense is its
meaning for Christian life. The anagogical sense relates to the eschatological meaning of the text. De Lubac's extensive studies on Scripture unveiled the patterns of thinking behind the premodern spiritual
senses of Scripture, that is, those meanings found beyond or beneath
the literal meaning of the text. De Lubac's historical recovery and
endorsement of the "spiritual sense" of Scripture in the early Church
could be interpreted as a depreciation of the historical meaning of
biblical texts in their authorial intention and original context.

Though appreciative of de Lubac's historical research, scholars of
Scripture have trouble reconciling de Lubac's retrieval of the spir-
itual sense of Scripture with critical and historicist hermeneutics.
Among de Lubac's contemporaries, John L. McKenzie, reviewing
Histoire et Esprit, questioned whether the spiritual exegesis of the
Fathers can be reconciled with "scientific exegesis" of Scripture:
"It would appear that the scientific study of the Bible (supposing
that such a study is possible) can contribute nothing to the spiritual understanding of the Bible, and that faith, led by the principles
of Origen, will find its way into the full spiritual understanding of
the inspired word.... It seems a perilous extreme to abandon the
science (for I believe de Lubac's opinions involve this) in favor of

[4] See Robin Darling Young, "An Imagined Unity: Henri de Lubac and the Ironies of
Ressourcement", *Commonweal* 139, no. 15 (September 14, 2012): 13–18, and Robin Darling
Young, "A Soldier in the Great War", in James L. Heft and John O'Malley, eds., *After Vatican
II: Trajectories and Hermeneutics* (Grand Rapids, Mich.: Eerdmans, 2012), 134–63.

the 'analogy of faith' as thus described."[5] As higher criticism was becoming accepted in Catholic circles of biblical scholarship in the mid-twentieth century, de Lubac appeared to defend the ahistorical approach of Origen of Alexandria.

Contemporary authors also question the value of de Lubac's *ressourcement* of the spiritual sense for contemporary study of the Bible. In *Receiving the Bible in Faith: Historical and Theological Exegesis*, David M. Williams explains that de Lubac's studies of patristic and medieval exegesis had two objectives, one historical and the other constructive. The historical objective was to correct a largely incorrect picture that historians held concerning premodern exegesis, particularly the meaning of allegory and the spiritual senses. Williams states that de Lubac was successful in this regard. However, Williams explains, his constructive goal was not attained: "He hoped that a substantive understanding of classical Christian exegesis would lead to a new and productive collaboration among systematicians, exegetes, and spiritual directors."[6] This constructive element of his project never materialized, at least, not in a way that broke down the methodological partitions that divided biblical scholars and theologians. Specifically, he explains, there were "doubts regarding the depth and reality of [de Lubac's] commitment to the role of history in biblical interpretation that are raised by aspects of his thought".[7] By placing an emphasis on the "overall biblical gestalt as the object of God's intention", the intention of the human authors of Scripture or the meaning of their historical context becomes a secondary consideration.[8] De Lubac's lack of engagement with historical-critical biblical interpretation is manifest. He was not concerned with providing a hermeneutic for relating the literal meaning to the spiritual meaning of the text.

For many biblical scholars, the recovery of patristic and medieval hermeneutics of Scripture appeared as an attempt to "repristinate"

[5] John L. McKenzie, "A Chapter in the History of Spiritual Exegesis: De Lubac's *Histoire et esprit*", *Theological Studies* 12, no. 3 (January 1951): 379.

[6] David M. Williams, *Receiving the Bible in Faith: Historical and Theological Exegesis* (Washington, D.C.: Catholic University of America Press, 2004), 131.

[7] Ibid., 170.

[8] Ibid., 171.

premodern exegesis.[9] De Lubac emphatically denied that this was his intent:

> I make bold nevertheless to hope that they will not hold it as a grievance against me that I am attached to so many ancient witnesses to our Catholic tradition, that I have loved them, and that I have tried to understand them and make them understood. I have not introduced, it must be reiterated, any sort of archaism, any sort of desire to arrest time or to stem its flow—although the very effort of reconstructing the past can sometimes give the appearance of being just such an enterprise. Nothing is more vain and fruitless than such attempts to return to one of these ancient stages of growth that history makes it possible for us to know, to settle down in it, to ensconce ourselves in it as in a dream.... If, then, I am loath to treat any of the twenty centuries of Christianity as a "prehistoric universe," I am no more inclined to envision any of them as a "paradise lost."[10]

De Lubac's study of patristic and medieval interpretation was clearly not mere disengaged historical scholarship. It had a theological aim. It was *ressourcement*, the recovery and utilization of something lost. It is his constructive proposals that have become the point of contention.

De Lubac's investigations into the history of exegesis and his understanding of theological tradition are closely related. The ancient hermeneutics of Scripture were, for him, something vital for the present. Among the chief aims of *la nouvelle théologie* was to recover an integral relationship between Scripture, theology, and the spiritual life. Catholic theology in the post-Reformation period is characterized by the methodological separation between positive theology and dogmatic theology, where Scripture provides the proof texts for dogmatic affirmations. Jean Daniélou's controversial essay "Les Orientations présentes de la pensée religieuse" (1946) addressed

---

[9] I borrow the term from Peter Casarella, who states "repristination" was neither the objective nor the effect of de Lubac's work. Peter Casarella, introduction to *Scripture in the Tradition*, by Henri de Lubac (New York: Crossroad, 2000), xiii.

[10] Henri de Lubac, *Medieval Exegesis: The Four Senses of Scripture*, trans. Mark Sebanc, vol. 1 (Grand Rapids, Mich.: Eerdmans, 1998), xx–xxi. Originally published as Henri de Lubac, *Exégèse médiévale*, vol. 1, *Les quatre sens de l'Écriture* (Paris: Éditions Montaigne, 1959).

the "rupture between theology and life".[11] Daniélou argued that the Scholastic model of theology as a science no longer had existential appeal to an age of historical consciousness. Daniélou pointed to a return to the Bible as a living tradition and to the early Church Fathers as a model for integrating theology and life. Similarly, de Lubac sought to bridge the divide between Scripture, theology, and mysticism, which had become largely independent specializations in the Catholic Church.[12]

De Lubac's studies on biblical exegesis are not primarily about *how* we should interpret the Scripture. Instead, they concern recovering an integrated theological whole that unites Scripture, theology, and mysticism. Introducing *Exégèse médiévale*, he wrote "this work, therefore, will have more affinities, on the whole, to a sociology of thought than to its history."[13] The object of his study was the world view made possible by a Christian synthesis in which life is read in conjunction with the Scriptures. He finds this world view present within early Christian exegesis:

> Now this "complete act" that is ancient Christian exegesis is a very great thing…. It sets up an often subtle dialectic of before and after. It defines the relationship between historical reality and spiritual reality, between society and the individual, between time and eternity. It contains, as one might say today, a whole theology of history, which is connected with a theology of Scripture…. In brief, this ancient form of Christian exegesis is something quite other than just an ancient form of exegesis. It forms "the thread" of Christian literature and Christian art. It constitutes, in one of its essential aspects, ancient Christian thought. It is the principal form that the Christian synthesis had for a

---

[11] Jean Daniélou, "Les Orientations présentes de la pensée religieuse", *Études* 249 (1946): 6. Translation from Hans Boersma, *Nouvelle Théologie and Sacramental Ontology: A Return to Mystery* (Oxford: Oxford University Press, 2009), 2.

[12] Following the marginalization of Neoscholasticism in the twentieth century, theology, exegesis, and pastoral life have grown farther apart, though many of the reasons for this are institutional rather than theological. Catholic theology no longer possesses the kind of methodological constraints that make theologians and exegetes talk to one other. In addition, in the last sixty years, the population of Catholic scholars has shifted from a majority clerical to a majority lay, and Catholic institutions of higher education have a greater independence from ecclesiastical institutions. The results are a further entrenchment of the division between pastoral practice and the scholarly disciplines.

[13] De Lubac, *Medieval Exegesis*, 1:xxii.

long time been shaped by. At the very least, it is the instrument that permitted the synthesis to be constructed, and today it is one of the devices by which a person can approach it most easily.[14]

De Lubac's scholarship on Scripture must not be understood as a recommendation to restore patristic exegesis. Instead, it is an examination of the integration of spirituality, Scripture, and theology in various contexts and a theological genealogy of the modern separation of exegesis from theology and theology from mysticism.[15]

If de Lubac's stated purpose was to rediscover an integrated whole of Scripture, mysticism, and theology, the form that it takes is a theological understanding of history. The mystery of salvation has a historical form. It constitutes the reality that binds Christians across generations as one body and constitutes the unity that binds together the Scriptures, making them witness to the same God. This is because history carries a surplus of meaning. As Peter Casarella states, "de Lubac asserted that history—precisely *qua* history—was already

---

[14] Ibid., xix.

[15] De Lubac's attempt to situate Scripture and its interpretation within a dynamic whole of Christian life resonates with those who find the exclusive use of historical-critical methods stifling and have turned to theological interpretation of Scripture. In *Everything Is Sacred: Spiritual Exegesis in the Political Theology of Henri de Lubac*, Bryan C. Hollon suggests that de Lubac provides a theological approach congruent with Postliberal concern to preserve the world-forming dimensions of the Bible. Hollon's treatment of Postliberalism and Radical Orthodoxy is an excellent summary of the theological and hermeneutical issues at stake. Bryan C. Hollon, *Everything Is Sacred: Spiritual Exegesis in the Political Theology of Henri de Lubac*, Theopolitical Visions 3 (Eugene, Ore.: Cascade, 2009). From a slightly different perspective, Kevin Storer's *Reading Scripture to Hear God* examines the relationship between Scripture and the interpreting community of faith. Storer seeks an ecumenical concurrence around how Scripture functions within God's redemptive action. Vanhoozer proposes a "covenantal ontology", which means that worldly realities are made to function in divine communication. In de Lubac's "sacramental ontology", Scripture, Eucharist, and Church become "incorporations" through which Christ is made present.

For both de Lubac and Vanhoozer, because Scripture constitutes a modality of God's redemptive action, there is always an ecclesial-sacramental dimension to its interpretation. Kevin Storer, *Reading Scripture to Hear God: Kevin Vanhoozer and Henri de Lubac on God's Use of Scripture in the Economy of Redemption* (Cambridge: James Clarke, 2014). Two works provide extensive examinations of de Lubac's theological-scriptural hermeneutics: Marcellino G. D'Ambrosio, "Henri de Lubac and the Recovery of the Traditional Hermeneutic" (Ph.D. dissertation, Catholic University of America, 1991); Eric J. Jenislawski, "A Comparative Study of the Hermeneutics of Henri de Lubac and Hans-Georg Gadamer concerning Tradition, Community and Faith in the Interpretation of Scripture" (Ph.D. dissertation, Catholic University of America, 2016).

pregnant with a spiritual force. The spiritual significance of history lies within history; it is not an ideological superstructure added to closed temporal realities."[16] The spiritual meaning present in history makes his understanding of history profoundly different from historicism or empiricist historiography. In other words, de Lubac assumes a purpose and continuity within history and a spiritual meaning present within historical events. Henri de Lubac is rightly associated with a recovery or retrieval of the spiritual sense. To be more specific, a great proportion of his publications were devoted to understanding the theological architecture of the spiritual interpretation of Scripture from ancient Christian sources until modernity. Furthermore, he associated spiritual interpretation with a spirituality and a way of seeing reality that, in part, he believed should be recovered. Both spirituality and exegesis are acts of discernment of the mystery of God active in history. Correctly reading Scripture is not just the result of an exegetical method, but it is also the discernment of God's presence in history and intention for it.[17]

To understand de Lubac's retrieval of the patristic-medieval "spiritual sense" of Scripture and its application, it is necessary to interpret this recovery as the recovery of a spiritual practice. Specifically, it is Jesuit spirituality that lies at the roots of de Lubac's recovery of Scripture. His recovery of the spiritual sense possesses a densely Ignatian framework, which can be found throughout much of his work.[18] By a framework, I do not mean a particularly Jesuit method of reading Scripture, though de Lubac sometimes exhibited methods of interpretation derived from Ignatius and his Jesuit formation. Principally, I mean de Lubac made themes within Ignatian spirituality—namely, spiritual warfare and discernment—integral to his understanding of Scripture. For him, authentic interpretation of Scripture is a spiritual practice characterized by warfare and discernment. While his understanding of warfare and discernment is derived from Ignatius of Loyola, de Lubac also discovered these Ignatian resonances

---

[16] Casarella, introduction to De Lubac, *Scripture in the Tradition*, xviii.

[17] I am indebted to conversations with Michael Spalione concerning exegesis and discernment in Evangelical theology.

[18] Christopher Ruddy uses the term "the Ignatian matrix" to describe de Lubac's writings. Christopher Ruddy, "The Ignatian Matrix of Henri de Lubac's Thought on Temptation, Ascesis, and the Homo Ecclesiasticus", *The Heythrop Journal* 56, no. 5 (2013): 789–805.

throughout the history of Christian interpretation of Scripture, particularly in the writings of Origen of Alexandria.

2. Scripture and Spiritual Warfare

Spiritual warfare is embedded in the way Jesuits understand their vocation and live out their spirituality. Although a form of spiritual militarism has been overly ascribed to the Jesuits, spiritual warfare resonates throughout the Jesuit formation. The "Meditation on the Two Standards" in the Spiritual Exercises of Ignatius is essentially a guided meditation on the fight between Christ and Satan on the battlefield of the world. The image of warfare is also inscribed in an early outline of the Jesuit Constitutions entitled "A First Sketch of the Institute of the Society of Jesus": "Whoever desires to serve as a soldier of God beneath the banner of the cross in our Society, which we desire to be designated by the name of Jesus, and in it to serve the Lord alone [and the Church, his spouse, under the Roman pontiff, the] ... vicar [of Christ] on earth, should, after a solemn vow of [perpetual] chastity, [poverty, and obedience,] keep what follows in mind."[19] Though the language is martial, the Jesuit notion of spiritual warfare is thoroughly Christological. Philippe Geneste explains, "on the one hand, the Christian affirms nothing human is foreign to Christ; on the other, the Christian aspires to be in the world without being of the world. Assuming this tension, the Jesuits affirm communally that only Christianity will save humanism from its warfare with idolatry in all its forms (Nation, State, Blood, the future human being, money, nature ...)."[20] For the Jesuits, spiritual warfare is first an antagonistic struggle against one's own selfish impulses. At its very foundations, Jesuit spirituality emphasizes the Christian life as spiritual struggle, the war of the new person in Christ against the old.

It is unsurprising, then, that de Lubac took up the theme of spiritual warfare. De Lubac's most extensive descriptions of spiritual warfare were written around the time of the Second World War, when the

---

[19] Ignatius of Loyola, *The Spiritual Exercises and Selected Works*, ed. George Ganss, Classics of Western Spirituality (Mahwah, N.J.: Paulist Press, 1991), 45.

[20] Geneste, *Humanisme et lumière*, 37.

dangers present were at the surface of his writings. In 1943, he wrote an article entitled "Spiritual Warfare", published in the journal *Cité nouvelle* (1943). In this piece, part of the *Témoignage chrétien*, a Christian witness against the violence of the Nazi and Vichy governments, de Lubac presented spiritual warfare as a struggle against heresy, which for him was a singular though multi-faceted reality. He explained that different periods of the Church had to contend with attacks against the "historical foundations of our beliefs", the denial of a "transcendent" dimension of reality or its knowableness, or opposition to the Church on a political plane. In the present moment, "What is in the fore-front, if not always in appearance at least in reality, is no longer a problem of the historical, metaphysical, political or social order. It is a *spiritual* problem. It is the total human problem."[21] The current opposition to Christianity, de Lubac explained, is an opposition to "the Christian concept of life, Christian spirituality, the inner attitude which, above any particular act or any external gesture, defines the Christian".[22] Neopaganism, "the great spiritual phenomenon of our time",[23] threatens to displace altogether a Christian spirituality. In contrast with a Nietzschean spirituality that idealizes the possession of power, de Lubac described the characteristics of the Christian:

> Gentleness and goodness, delicacy toward little ones, pity—yes, pity—toward those who suffer, the rejection of perverse means, the defense of the oppressed, humble devotion, resistance to lies, the courage to call evil by its name, the spirit of peace and concord, openness of heart, the thought of heaven ...: that is what Christian heroism will save. This whole "morality of slaves" will make it obvious that it is a morality of free men, that it alone makes man free.[24]

Spiritual warfare is the struggle in which Christians must engage in order to embody charity and to live in Christ. De Lubac's goal was to present clearly the spiritual options for humanity during a period in time when the existential battle between good and evil had a literal correlate in the resistance against the Nazis.

---

[21] Henri de Lubac, "Spiritual Warfare", in *Theology in History* (San Francisco: Ignatius Press, 1996), 488–89.
[22] Ibid., 489.
[23] Ibid., 493.
[24] Ibid., 500.

Yet, following the Second World War, the theme of spiritual warfare persisted in de Lubac's writings. Following the defeat of Germany and the Vichy government, de Lubac no longer spoke of spiritual warfare as a choice between neopaganism and Christianity. Instead, he emphasized spiritual warfare as a participation in God's historical redemption, a participation that is ecclesial, interior, and real. In his preface to Hugo Rahner's *Saint Ignace de Loyola et la genèse des Exercises* (1948), de Lubac's interpretation of Ignatius of Loyola and his understanding of spiritual warfare emerges:

> The authentic and complete Christian spirituality is, by all necessity, a spirituality of the man of the Church [l'homme de l'Église], and the man of the Church is authentically, not less necessarily, a spiritual person. In almost equivalent terms, we say, then, that spiritual combat must always be understood as having an apostolic meaning, as being a participation, "under the standard of the Cross", in the great redemptive Combat; and that the Church militant must always preserve, in each of her members, the living sentiment that the fight is a spiritual fight to be led "against the enemy of human nature" first in the depth of every heart. But, the genius of Saint Ignatius—his genius and, better, his grace—was to have reaffirmed powerfully, at the threshold of modern times, this link between the Church and the Spirit. Such is an abbreviation of the meaning of "Reign" and of the "Two Standards", which highlights one of the most important idea-forces of Christianity and that is at the center even of the *Exercises*. Such is then the meaning of the rules for the discernment of spirits, in their connection with the rules for feeling with the Church.[25]

In this *précis* of Ignatian spirituality, de Lubac describes spiritual warfare as the real participation in redemption. For our purposes, two characteristics of this description resonate with de Lubac's understanding of Scripture: spiritual warfare implies the human spiritual struggle within the history of redemption; second, it implies the central role of the Church in this history of redemption.

[25] Henri de Lubac, preface to *Saint Ignace de Loyola et la genèse des* Exercises", in *Paradoxe et Mystère de l'Église suivi de L'Église dans la crise actuelle*, vol. 9 of *Oeuvres complètes* (Paris: Cerf, 2010), 432. De Lubac locates the historical and spiritual importance of the Spiritual Exercises in the relationship between Church and Spirit. He explains that Rahner "transcends all the debates on methods of prayer, on the exterior forms of religious life, on the comparative merits of contemplation and of action. He is not bothered by quarrels between partisans of mysticism and proponents of pure asceticism or of communal piety" (ibid.).

First, de Lubac indicates that, for Ignatius of Loyola, spiritual warfare concerns our meaningful participation in redemptive history. The preface and brief sketch of Ignatius was published in 1948. Situated between de Lubac's book on atheist humanism and his book on Origen of Alexandria, it reflects de Lubac's thinking at the time concerning the spiritual situation of Christianity in modernity. De Lubac was concerned then with secularism, not as a cultural phenomenon (that is, the cultural dominance of non-religious groups or organizations), but as a spiritual phenomenon. The problem characteristic of modernity is that it has become increasingly difficult to recognize the interior relationship between human life and the historical mystery of salvation. This is the subject of his 1947 book *Surnaturel*, a study of the theological concept of "pure nature", the theological hypothesis of a natural order sufficient in itself without the supernatural. *Surnaturel* traced the theological roots of a modern ontology of a world that no longer requires God.[26] In the 1930s and 1940s, de Lubac also examined the existential correlate of this ontology in an understanding of history that interpreted the mystery of salvation as separate from and irrelevant to historical human existence. It is in his writings on Scripture that de Lubac pursued the interpretation of Scriptures

---

[26] In several places, Ignatian spiritual warfare frames de Lubac's theology of nature and grace. In his *Petite catéchèse sur nature et grâce* (Paris: Fayard, 1980) [translated by Richard Arnandez as *A Brief Catechesis on Nature and Grace* (San Francisco: Ignatius, 1984)], de Lubac frames spiritual warfare as the struggle between sinful human nature and grace. In this book, de Lubac relates the ontological categories (nature and supernatural) to biblical-patristic categories (sin and grace). Here, he places his theology of the supernatural in the framework of the history of redemption. He writes (p. 119), "Between sinful human nature and divine grace we have not only a dissimilarity, [but] a heterogeneity between two orders of being, an infinite distance that man alone cannot bridge. There is an antagonism, violent conflict ('*natura filii irae*' says St. Paul). Between grace and sin the struggle is irreconcilable. Consequently, the call of grace is no longer an invitation to a simple 'elevation', not even a 'transforming' one (to use the traditional words); in a more radical fashion it is a summons to a 'total upheaval', to a 'conversion' (of the 'heart', i.e., of all one's being)." The language here is important. He is no longer describing the transition between the natural and supernatural as an "elevation" of nature, as would be common with a Thomistic account of sanctifying grace. Instead, he uses Pauline language to describe a transition that can only occur through a death to self: "Before it can be 'transfigured' our sinful nature must first be 'turned inside out'" (120–21, quoting Pierre Teilhard de Chardin, *Le Milieu divin* [Paris: Seuil, 1957], 188). Although he uses the language of opposition, he later uses a language of union between nature and grace: "The union of nature and grace can be fully accomplished only through the mystery of the redemption" (122). There is certainly a tension, since de Lubac employs both a language of opposition and a language of union to describe the relationship between nature and grace.

in the early Church as a source for a theological understanding of history in which salvation was itself historical.[27] He argued that "spiritual interpretation" of Scripture in the early Church assumed that history is the milieu of salvation. It presented a theology of history in which God has entered history and saves mankind through history and in which human action is meaningful. According to de Lubac, Ignatius of Loyola was the beneficiary and interpreter of this theological understanding of history, and Ignatian spirituality presents a vision of human life bound up in the history of salvation. Thus, it is precisely the theological understanding of history preserved within Ignatian spiritual warfare that de Lubac pursues within his studies of patristic and medieval spiritual interpretation.

Second, speaking of spiritual warfare in his preface to Karl Rahner's book, de Lubac briefly mentioned the affirmation of the connection between the Church and the Spirit in the Spiritual Exercises. This is not a marginal theme within de Lubac's writings. In fact, the relationship between Church and Spirit—a theme that links spirituality and exegesis—forms a significant stream within de Lubac's writings on Scripture beginning in the 1950s. *Exégèse médiévale* examined the exegetical tradition launched by Joachim de Fiore (1135–1202).[28] His two-volume *La Postérité spirituelle de Joachim de Flore* (1979–1981) traced a dangerous trajectory in modern spirituality that he attributes to Joachim.[29] Joachim's interpretations of Scripture prophesied a new age of the Spirit that will follow and surpass the age of Christ, the present age of the Church. He awaited a "spiritual church" of the perfect that would take the place of the imperfect ecclesial body, and a "spiritual gospel" to replace the "corporeal gospel". De Lubac argued that Joachim's interpretation of Scripture had been stripped of its religious content and appropriated for modern secular ideologies. Modernity longs for a coming age of the spirit that surpasses the age

[27] This argument is developed extensively in Susan K. Wood, *Spiritual Exegesis and the Church in the Theology of Henri de Lubac* (Eugene, Ore.: Wipf and Stock, 2010), 31–35, and Joseph S. Flipper, *Between Apocalypse and Eschaton: History and Eternity in Henri de Lubac* (Minneapolis: Fortress, 2015), 91–128.

[28] Henri de Lubac, *Medieval Exegesis: The Four Senses of Scripture*, trans. E. M. Macierowski, vol. 3 (Grand Rapids, Mich.: Eerdmans, 2009), 327–419.

[29] Henri de Lubac, *La Postérité spirituelle de Joachim de Flore: de Joachim à Schelling*, vol. 1 (Paris: Éditions Lethielleux, 1979); Henri de Lubac, *La Postérité spirituelle de Joachim de Flore: de Saint-Simon à nos jours*, vol. 2 (Paris: Éditions Lethielleux, 1981).

of the Church, seeking salvation in political engineering and techno-logical advancement. According to de Lubac, the principal spiritual problem for modern humanity is recognizing the present Church's participation in the "age of the spirit". In de Lubac's interpretation, Ignatius of Loyola responded to dangerous spiritual trajectories by resisting the dissociation of Church and Spirit. For Ignatius, the struggle between the "two standards" revealed in Scripture is taking place now within human experience. These days are the last days. We live in the age of the Spirit. The spiritual warfare in Ignatius, like the traditions of spiritual interpretation de Lubac defended, seeks not to "transcend the Christ event" or move beyond the age of the Church. Instead, it seeks to interiorize the mystery of Christ. Spiri-tual warfare is, at its foundation, an interior struggle to live under the standard of Christ by embodying the virtues and actions of Christ. It is an interiorization of Christ.

Like Ignatian spirituality, the spiritual interpretation of Scripture that de Lubac explored assumes the Scriptures may be interiorized in the lives of the faithful. In his explication of mystical tropology, de Lubac elaborates the patristic-medieval theme that the events of Scrip-ture are fulfilled *quotidie* [daily] in the lives of the faithful. Paraphrasing Origen, he writes, "Each day, deep within ourselves, Israel departs from Egypt; each day, it is nourished with manna; each day it fulfills the Law; each day it must engage in combat ...; each day the promises that had been made to this people under a bodily form are realized spiritually in us."[30] Not only are the stories in Scripture applied to one's own life as examples, principles, or inspiration, but the Scrip-tures are fulfilled through their interiorization in the faithful. Ignatius made spiritual warfare elemental to the Jesuit spiritual life. Yet, this warfare is spiritualized and interiorized as the struggle of the soul.

Thus, de Lubac saw Ignatian spiritual warfare as preserving and transmitting a theological understanding of history and of the Church's place in salvation. But he also found antecedents in the early Church for understanding the spiritual interpretation of Scripture as an act of spiritual warfare. He explains: Origen's "description of the spiritual warfare that follows on Jesus, which is signified by the wars

---

[30] Henri de Lubac, *Medieval Exegesis: The Four Senses of Scripture*, trans. E. M. Macierowski, vol. 2 (Grand Rapids, Mich.: Eerdmans, 2000), 138. Paraphrasing Origen, *In Ex.* h. 5, n. 5.

of the Old Testament, has become one of the great commonplaces of the tradition: 'in all of divine history, exterior warfare signifies the interior warfare of the soul.'"[31] Origen "spiritualizes" warfare by interpreting it as interior warfare. But de Lubac also points out that Origen uses the metaphor of warfare to describe the appropriation and purification of the pagan philosophical and rhetorical disciplines by the Christian.[32] De Lubac saw Origen of Alexandria as the great systematizer of an intertwined Christian spirituality and exegesis that flows through the early Church and medieval periods. Summarizing a medieval understanding of the tropological sense of Scripture, de Lubac explains: "In everything, Scripture invites us to conversion of heart. All the wars that it recounts are wars of the Lord; all the migrations, all the travels it traces are the wanderings and travels of the soul: it is thus from one end to the other the book of spiritual combat at the same time as it is the book of departure and of mystical ascent."[33] The image of war has multiple valences. However, de Lubac finds in it a metaphor for the spiritual struggle to interiorize the Christ event narrated in the Scriptures.

In summary, the Ignatian theme of spiritual warfare constitutes the framework for de Lubac's recovery of the spiritual senses of Scripture. The notion of spiritual warfare recurs within de Lubac's writings. De Lubac did not relegate spiritual warfare to a particular sphere of Christian life but, instead, saw it as a broad vocation of the Church. Spiritual warfare, for de Lubac, assumes a real, human participation in the mystery of salvation insofar as Christians are enjoined to struggle against sin. He inherited this notion of spiritual warfare from Ignatius of Loyola and his Jesuit formation. Yet, de Lubac also recognized spiritual warfare as a theme within the early Church and medieval tradition associated with the interpretation of Scripture, specifically with the tropological sense. In this way, for de Lubac, spiritual interpretation is not merely a matter of a methodology but is wrapped up in a spiritual practice. As we will see, de Lubac also associated spiritual interpretation with Ignatian practices of discernment.

[31] Henri de Lubac, *Medieval Exegesis: The Four Senses of Scripture*, vol. 1, trans. Mark Sebanc (Grand Rapids, Mich.: Eerdmans, 1998), 170. Quoting Goscelin, *Lib. Confort.*, 2.
[32] Ibid., 1:213.
[33] De Lubac, *Medieval Exegesis*, 2:141.

3. Ignatian Discernment and the Spiritual Sense of Scripture

The thesis I have been advancing is that de Lubac thought of the spiritual interpretation (also, "spiritual understanding") of Scripture less as a method than as a spiritual practice. To interpret Scripture spiritually is to discover the spiritual sense beneath the literal-historical sense. In this way, the practices of Ignatian discernment closely align with the "spiritual senses of Scripture". Indeed, the spiritual interpretation of Scripture is a form of discernment of God's hidden intention for the world and God's action within it. For our purposes, I will limit myself to the main points of correlation between spiritual interpretation and Ignatian discernment. The fact of the Word of God acting within redemptive history forms the lynchpin for both spiritual interpretation and discernment. For de Lubac, the Word of God has acted definitively in time and history and continues to act as the leaven of history, drawing time to eternity. Discernment discovers the Word of God who is the same word acting in first-century Palestine and in the Church today. Both discernment and spiritual interpretation discover "final causes" within history, that is, God's ultimate intention for our world.

Central to the vision of de Lubac is the notion that the Word of God contains the same potency today as it did in the time of the historical Jesus. During his formation at Canterbury, in handwritten notes made for sermon preparations on the commandments, de Lubac expressed an understanding of the Word of God operating both in the historical Jesus and in the saints:

> "The word of God, repeated by a priest eleven centuries after the first time it fell from the lips of Jesus in a lost corner of Palestine, made arise, in an instant, one of the great marvels of the Church: the sanctity of Francis of Assisi and of his innumerable children." This same word of God is again "patient, it operates sometimes slowly, but it arrives infallibly at its end." It is thus what is impressed in the spirit of Francis Xavier, which Ignatius of Loyola repeats: "What does it serve a man to gain the universe and lose his soul?"[34]

---

[34] Georges Chantraine, *Henri de Lubac*, vol. 2, *Les Années de formation (1919–1929)*, Études Lubaciennes 7 (Paris: Cerf, 2009), 109.

Just as the Word entered into history to transform it, the Word continues to enter into time to transform our present. The Word of God has power to transform human life and to raise up saints. De Lubac's expression of the orality of the Word is striking. The words themselves have an efficacity capable of raising up saints. This is because the Word is one: God spoke in history, and this same Word continues to act in the world to draw history to its consummation.

In another sermon, de Lubac developed a principle that would become central to his subsequent studies on the spiritual interpretation of Scripture: the interior relationship between the historical events of salvation, their present fruition, and their eschatological fulfillment. To be specific, the Word of God in Jesus Christ is the same Word acting in our time, and it is the same Word to be fulfilled in the eschaton. De Lubac explains,

> Heaven, the Church, grace. All three compenetrate. This linkage and this reciprocal penetration of the most vast and most particular realities is one of the admirable aspects of our Religion. What is to happen at the end of time has its anticipation in what is happening before our eyes; the laws that govern the assembly of the body of Christ are reproduced in each of its members; and what happens to the Church happens to each Christian. The future society of the elect has at present its type in the society of Christians who combat on the earth; and the fights, the tests, the travails of the former find an echo in the heart of each of the faithful. Because there are in each of these things, grace, the Church, heaven, only diverse modalities of a unique principle and manifestations more or less developed, more or less blossomed, from the same life.[35]

One can recognize in this early sermon an anticipation of de Lubac's exposition on the spiritual senses of Scripture. There is an interior relationship between the Word of God in Jesus Christ (allegory), in the lives of the saints (tropology), and at the eschaton (anagogy). Thus, Christian spiritual life relates back to the historical Jesus and forward to the final fulfillment.

Despite the fact that the Word acts in history, discerning this Word remains an always difficult spiritual task. Yet, God's activity is

[35] Ibid., 112–13.

not simply available on the surface of history. Discovering the Word of God's activity and presence requires discernment, that is, peering beneath the surface to recognize its reality. In de Lubac's theology of the supernatural, the supernatural is present, yet hidden in human experience. He writes, "The supernatural good that the Church serves in this world is something that reaches its totality in the invisible order and finds its consummation in the eternal."[36] Because the supernatural is categorically different from the natural, it is not reducible to visible structures and practices. Even in the Church, the "sacrament of salvation", its effectiveness as the sacrament of salvation is not fully manifest in its visible reality. Salvation transcends all forms and institutions. With echoes of Blondel, de Lubac explains:

> The essential, which cannot remain as even a distant objective on our horizon if we do not find a place for it in the heart of our present activity, is not something that can be judged from a quantitative point of view. God brings about the saving of us according to laws that are hidden from us as far as their concrete application is concerned but that are imposed on our faith in principle.... But the question is whether our sight is clear enough and whether we have sufficient knowledge of where to look to discern among ourselves, in this order of sanctity, the effectiveness of the Church. Let us at least try to catch a glimpse of it.[37]

The fact that God acts in time and space makes possible the discovery of God's grace—as a different order of things—acting to bring history to its fruition. Yet, the project of salvation, though developing in time, remains ever incomplete within history. Salvation is not fully visible, though it is subject to discernment.

According to de Lubac, the spiritual understanding of Scripture, which traditionally draws on the profound symbolic linkages between the Old Testament and the New Testament, constitutes a form of discernment. Far from being an indiscriminate or subjective imposition of meaning on the text, for de Lubac, spiritual understanding requires a "principle of discernment" for interpreting the Scriptures. He explains, "This 'spiritual understanding' of Scripture can be the

[36] Henri de Lubac, *The Splendor of the Church*, trans. Michael Mason (San Francisco: Ignatius Press, 1999), 297. Originally published as *Meditation sur l'Église* (Paris: Montaigne, 1953).
[37] De Lubac, *Splendor of the Church*, 299.

exegetically arbitrary fruit of a reflection or a contemplation of a philosophical nature, or, to be sure, the fruit of a discernment whose principle is the Holy Spirit, the Spirit of Christ."[38] The spiritual understanding of Scripture is neither a mechanical process of deriving another layer of meaning from the surface of the biblical text nor an imposition of a foreign hermeneutic. Instead, it is a form of discernment, that is, the discovery of the inner relationships between the actions of God in history, our experience, and the end of time.

De Lubac drew his identification of spiritual understanding as discernment from Origen of Alexandria. Origen saw spiritual interpretation as a means by which one "discerns"—literally, "separates" [from the Latin *discernere*, "to separate"]—the literal meaning of Scripture from the spiritual meaning within it.[39] Origen used "spiritual explication" [*pnumatikē diēgēsis*], "discernment" [*dianoia*], "contemplation" [*theōria*] as synonyms that refer to passing from the letter to the spirit.[40] And in different terms, Origen described spiritual understanding of Scripture, not as accessing a hidden meaning latent in the text, but instead as the result of a new synthesis brought about by Christ. Origen described conversion of the Old Covenant with the New, or an assimilation of the Old by the New. De Lubac explains, "[Assimilation] is not the consequence of a simple discernment that is effected with prudence. But, as is indicated by the text from Deuteronomy and as Origen spoke of it, it can only be the result of a battle: 'For the Church's doctors marched out to do battle with their enemies, when, armed with the sword of the spirit, which is the word of God, they went forth to overthrow the dogmas of worldly wisdom' "[41] In Origen, the discernment that provides spiritual understanding is more than a profound reading. This discernment is part of a spiritual struggle, which de Lubac found symphonic with the Ignatian "spiritual battle".

Following Maurice Blondel's "History and Dogma", de Lubac explains that any explication of the meaning of historical events requires a principle beyond the brute facts of history. Only reference to

---

[38] De Lubac, *Medieval Exegesis*, 1:140. See also *Medieval Exegesis* 1:53.

[39] De Lubac, *Medieval Exegesis*, 2:27n1, referring to Origen of Alexandria, *In Lev.*, bk. 4, n. 8.

[40] De Lubac, *Medieval Exegesis*, 2:35nn20–21. Referring to *Sel in Thren.* (PG 14:609 A, 612–16, 616 C, 652 B), *Contra Celsum*, bk. 7, chap. 20 (2, 171), and *Sel. in Jer.* 1, 13 (PG 13:545 A).

[41] De Lubac, *Medieval Exegesis*, 1:220.

the final causes of facts can offer a complete understanding of them: "This is why, if any not merely partial and relative but total, comprehensive, and absolutely valid explication of history is truly possible, this explication can only be theological. Only faith anticipates the future with security. Only an explication founded upon faith can invoke a definitive principle and appeal to ultimate causes."[42] An ultimate or final cause is that for which something exists, a telos. De Lubac, thus, utilizes a Thomistic understanding of teleology to describe historical events. Especially when it concerns God's revelatory actions in history, those events have meaning in light of God's ultimate intentions. Susan Wood explains,

> A principle of discernment governs the explication of events, a principle which belongs to another sphere than that of the positivistic phenomena narrated and which transcends the mere recitation of phenomena. The principle refers events to final causes which the empirical events themselves cannot furnish and which illumine them. De Lubac concludes that such a total interpretation of history can only be theological since only faith can securely anticipate the future, provide a definitive principle of discernment, and refer discrete events to final causes.[43]

Thus, a principle of discernment is required to interpret historical realities in light of their finality. Finality is not just a chronological development, but a fulfillment.

As an extension of his understanding of history, de Lubac presents spiritual understanding a discernment of the final causes within the events recounted in Scripture. We find the meaning of Scripture, not only in the words of the text or the facts they convey, but also in light of God's plan of salvation. Spiritual understanding, he says, requires "a principle of discernment which can itself be inserted within the facts, but which, as such, pertains to a different sphere and overflows into the observation of the facts".[44] This principle of discernment, he says, is "the Mystery of Christ, the absolutely ultimate final cause", which constitutes the telos of previous historical

---

[42] Ibid., 2:71.

[43] Wood, *Spiritual Exegesis*, 35. See also Storer, *Reading Scripture*, 27.

[44] De Lubac, *Medieval Exegesis*, 2:71.

events.[45] The historical realities of the Old Testament take their ultimate meaning from their fulfillment in Christ. And spiritual meaning is the meaning the "Spirit gives to the Church".[46]

4. The Ignatian Imagination and the Spiritual Senses

Following Origen, de Lubac did not see discernment and spiritual interpretation as two separate activities. Both involve passing from the letter to the spirit. It is not surprising, then, that de Lubac deployed practices of discernment from Ignatius of Loyola within his own interpretation of Scripture. De Lubac's extant sermons and writings suggest that the Spiritual Exercises inform his own interpretation of Scripture and his understanding of the spiritual senses.

The Spiritual Exercises, a thirty-day contemplative retreat, is pivotal for the formation of the Jesuits. The retreat is taken prior to major steps in Jesuit life, such as final vows. The Exercises are thoroughly scriptural. In their substance, they are guided meditations organized around biblical narratives and the words of Christ in Scripture. The Exercises were not written to be read; rather, they are notes for retreat masters to guide those in formation. Like a sermon, they are meant to be heard. Furthermore, the Spiritual Exercises constitute a practice of spiritual interpretation. They contain a proposal for discerning the presence of God and the will of God through the imaginative interiorization of the Scriptures.

In the "Preludes" of the Spiritual Exercises, Ignatius repeatedly directs the retreatants to imagine a scriptural reality in its concrete and spatial dimensions. Ignatius calls this "la composición viendo el lugar", which translates as "composition made by imagining the place"[47] or "a mental representation of the place".[48] The "composition" is

---

[45] Ibid., 2:72. Bryan C. Hollon elaborates the ecclesial and spiritual implications of this scriptural finality in *Everything Is Sacred*, 190–94.

[46] Henri de Lubac, *Scripture in the Tradition*, Milestones of Catholic Theology (New York: Crossroad, 2001), 157. Quoting Origen, *In. Lev*, hom. 5, no. 5 (343).

[47] Ignatius of Loyola, *Spiritual Exercises and Selected Works*, 136.

[48] Ignatius of Loyola, *Spiritual Exercises of St. Ignatius*, trans. by Louis L. Puhl, S.J. (Chicago: Loyola University Press, 1951), 25. Puhl states that the original Spanish means something like "a representation of the place by seeing it in imagination" (171). *Composición*, he explains, is closer to its Latin root *con* + *pōnere*, "to put with" (170).

literally the product of the act of putting realities together by mentally reconstructing the place. The First Prelude of the First Exercise states that "the composition consists of seeing in imagination the physical place where that which I want to contemplate is taking place. By physical place I mean, for instance, a temple or a mountain where Jesus Christ or Our Lady happens to be, in accordance with the topic I desire to contemplate."[49] The Second Prelude on the Incarnation asks the retreatant to "see the great extent of the circuit of the world, with peoples so many and so diverse; and then to see in particular the house and rooms of Our Lady, in the city of Nazareth in the province of Galilee."[50] Making a mental representation is a process by which the story in the Scriptures takes on specificity and concreteness by being related to the world of the retreatant. The imagination of the place is a mise-en-scène for the mysteries of salvation, including a spiritual geography, and the initiation of an interiorization of the mysteries of salvation in Scripture.

The composition of concrete images is the entryway into the meditation on Scripture, through which the retreatant or hearer can arrive at the spiritual meaning. In the Spiritual Exercises, the *composición* is followed by the meditation on the passage of Scripture. The Ignatian method is characterized by an intentional engagement of the whole self—memory, understanding, and will—in the meditation.[51] In the Exercises, Ignatius had no hesitation in moving from the scriptural story to its implications for the individual's spiritual life. For example, he asks retreatants to begin from the meditation on the fall of the angels and first parents to the consideration of their own sin.[52] The Spiritual Exercises constitute a spiritual practice of meditation that begins in the literal sense and expands into consideration of the spiritual sense.

"La composición viendo el lugar" is present as a method in de Lubac's homilies and is suggested by his other writings. Geneste says that "de Lubac aims with this effort of the imagination to represent supernatural realities in a very concrete manner beginning

[49] Ignatius of Loyola, *Spiritual Exercises and Selected Works*, 136.
[50] Ibid., 148.
[51] See ibid., 137.
[52] Ibid.

from images or visualized scenes."[53] Geneste points to the example of de Lubac's 1937 article "Méditation sur le principe de la vie morale" (Meditation on the principle of the moral life). De Lubac uses images of being already "embarked upon the ocean of life" and "being rooted in the soil of being" to describe the dynamics of liberty and ontological necessity. Geneste says de Lubac deploys concrete images throughout his work: "He loves to utilize figures in the concern not only to aid the effort of imagination but also to create in the spirit of his readers the kinds of schemes, analogues to recollections, that everyone can lock up in the background in their memory."[54] In one homily, de Lubac asks the listeners to represent the place: "To allow this thought, the thought that it is Jesus himself who is speaking to us in the depth of our heart through the intermediary of these words that the evangelists have transmitted to us, to penetrate us more easily and so that this persuasion disposes us to receive his word better, we should begin by representing to ourselves the setting where, for the first time, before the astonished eyes of the Galilean crowd, the supernatural horizon and the radiance of a new world began to open."[55] For de Lubac, the composition is not merely a method of meditation. It is a preparation for the incarnate Word to penetrate the hearer and be interiorized by the hearer through the reading of the Scriptures.

De Lubac's sermons during his formation exhibit this Ignatian form of reading the Scriptures in which the spiritual meaning is discovered. In one sermon, after speaking about the Beatitudes in Matthew 5, de Lubac explores the meaning of the "salt and light" discourse. He writes, "We must stop for some time on this word of Jesus. Like most of the others, it hides a profound meaning under a familiar symbol: one must explain and make precise this symbolic meaning."[56] The "salt" has a literal meaning. But it also functions as a symbol. "Salt 'preserves' from corruption and 'gives flavor [saveur].' In contrast, what is decomposed is 'subject to disgust [dégoût].' "[57] De Lubac explains "[God] came in person to bring

[53] Geneste, *Humanisme et lumière*, 59.
[54] Ibid.
[55] Chantraine, *Henri de Lubac*, 2:109–10.
[56] Ibid., 2:110.
[57] Ibid.

them the remedy against corruption, the substance that preserves and gives flavor."[58] God's presence within us, grace, constitutes this substance that is salt of the earth. De Lubac's interpretation of the Scriptures, like that of Ignatius, is uninhibited in its application of the scriptural story to life through a movement from the literal to the spiritual meaning of the text.

De Lubac's interpretation of Scripture in early sermons reflects an Ignatian spirituality and method of reading Scripture. His later work would trace the sources of spiritual interpretation and would chart the relationship between exegesis and theology from the early Church to the modern period. One of his purposes was to understand and recover exegesis as a practice intertwined with theology and spirituality. It is in the Spiritual Exercises that de Lubac encountered this interconnected whole, a practice of discernment and spiritual warfare that is also a reading of Scripture.

5. Conclusion: Henri de Lubac's "Ignatian Filiation"

Far from presenting an account of the Ignatian roots or structure of de Lubac's theology, I have only sketched the Ignatian themes present in his writings on the history of exegesis. A broader historical and systematic account that examines de Lubac's religious epistemology, theology of the supernatural, and ecclesiology from the lens of spirituality is still needed. However, we can see that de Lubac's reading of Scripture is intimately tied to his spirituality. The Ignatian themes of spiritual warfare and discernment abound within de Lubac's writings and contribute to his understanding of the spiritual senses of Scripture. His formative years as a Jesuit provided a tradition that united the meditation on Scripture with the meditation on life. De Lubac believed Ignatius of Loyola was one of the modern figures who preserved and communicated anew a Christian sense of history, the spiritual warfare between good and evil, and the Christological orientation of human life. Furthermore, Ignatius modeled a unified spirituality, exegesis, and theology that de Lubac desired to retrieve in some form. Yet, his recovery of the spiritual senses took

[58] Ibid., 2:111.

the form of historical studies rather than a proposition for scholarly exegetical method. His overarching concern was not just a reconstitution of certain spiritual or exegetical practices, but a retrieval of a way of rediscovering the hidden presence of the supernatural and the Church as an agent in the historical unfolding of redemption.

8

Marriage as an Image of the Trinity

Matthew Levering

How should we understand Genesis' teaching that God created man "in his own image" (Gen 1:26–27)? Among contemporary biblical scholars, a consensus has formed that in its ancient Near-Eastern context, Genesis 1:26–27 originally meant—in the words of the eminent Old Testament scholar Walter Brueggemann—that "the image of God reflected in human persons is after the manner of a king who establishes statues of himself to assert his sovereign rule when the king himself cannot be present."[1] On this view, Genesis 1:26–27 teaches that not only the king but indeed *all* persons are in the image of God. This royal image of God, therefore, involves service to each other, not domination by one over all others. Brueggemann himself, however, goes farther and reasons that "humankind is a community, male and female. And none is the full image of God alone. Only in community of humankind is God reflected. God is ... not mirrored as an individual but as a community."[2]

This latter point suggests that the "image of God" already has something like the Trinity in view, since people can mirror God "as a community" only if God is in some mysterious sense a "community". Furthermore, if the community of mankind is preeminently understood as being "male and female" (Gen 1:27)—if the original man and woman are the paradigmatic community—then with the biblical scholar Francis Martin we can say that "Adam images God,

[1] Walter Brueggemann, *Genesis* (Louisville, Ky.: Westminster John Knox Press, 2010), 32.
[2] Ibid., 34.

that is, makes his power and authority present and interacts with God, in the relating of man and woman."[3] If so, then, arguably, the image of God in mankind is *primarily* found in marriage, which is the intimate "relating of man and woman" that we see already in the union of Adam and Eve.

In earlier writings on the image of God, I have defended the Augustinian-Thomistic view that the image of God (the Trinity) is in the soul and its powers of knowing and loving.[4] When properly oriented, the powers of knowing and loving relationally direct the person to God. I still consider the Augustinian-Thomistic perspective on the image of God to be true and salutary. But in the present essay, I argue that a loving and fruitful marriage (man, woman, and [potentially at least] child) is also an image of the Trinity. The Triune God, in creating humans "in his own image" and "male and female" (Gen 1:27), has bestowed upon the human race a marital image of himself, in accord with the fact that people are created for marriage with the Trinity.

In order to make this case, I draw especially upon the writings of Hans Urs von Balthasar. My first section explores his understanding of marriage as the best image of the Trinity, in light of his view of proposals made by Augustine, Richard of Saint Victor, Georg Friedrich Hegel, and Martin Buber. Second, because von Balthasar praises the view of the great nineteenth-century theologian Matthias Joseph Scheeben, I discuss Scheeben's position on this topic, along with the insights of Scheeben's sources, such as Gregory Nazianzen. Von Balthasar's position differs from Scheeben's in that von Balthasar is not attempting to show that we can find an image of the Trinitarian processions in Eve's coming forth from Adam's side and Seth from Adam and Eve. Instead, von Balthasar emphasizes that each married

---

[3] Francis Martin, "Male and Female He Created Them: A Summary of the Teaching of Genesis Chapter One", *Communio* 20 (1993): 240–65, at 259.

[4] I have treated this question most recently in my *Engaging the Doctrine of Creation: Cosmos, Creatures, and the Wise and Good Creator* (Grand Rapids, Mich.: Baker Academic, 2017), chap. 4. Since I interact with a number of biblical scholars and theologians in that chapter (and also briefly survey the fascinating patristic debates about this topic), I can refer readers to that chapter for background to the present chapter. See also my comparative analysis of Thomas Aquinas and David Novak on the image of God in my *Jewish-Christian Dialogue and the Life of Wisdom: Engagements with the Theology of David Novak* (New York: Continuum, 2010), chap. 3.

couple, in their self-surrendering and fruitful love, image the self-surrendering fruitfulness (difference-in-unity) of the Divine Persons. Von Balthasar's reflections on how the one-flesh bodily/spiritual act of marital intercourse, in its ordering to fruitful generativity, images the self-surrendering and fruitful love of the Triune Persons mean that in his view the human "image of God" fundamentally has to do with human self-surrender in spousal love (a spousal love that can be enacted by single persons, as Christ reveals).

Third, I engage other recent advocates of marriage as image of the Trinity, including Marc Ouellet, Paul Evdokimov, and Pope John Paul II, in order to clarify further why I think that von Balthasar's distinctive approach to marriage as an image of the Trinity is especially helpful. My conclusion is that although von Balthasar's understanding of marriage as image of the Trinity needs to be complemented by the Augustinian-Thomistic understanding of the image of God in each human soul, von Balthasar's focus on marriage as constituted by fruitful self-surrendering love not only helps us to understand the communion-in-unity of the Divine Persons revealed by Christ, but also calls married persons (and indeed all persons) to appreciate and strive to enact the radical self-surrendering love that alone fulfills human nature and perfects in us the image of God. This essay is dedicated to Father Joseph Fessio, S.J., a true defender of marital holiness and an inspiration to me and to Catholics worldwide.

1. Hans Urs von Balthasar on Marriage and the Trinity

Hans Urs von Balthasar considers sacramental marriage to be an image of the Trinity. In developing this argument, he begins by observing that because Jesus Christ is the truth—the supreme "image" and "likeness" (Gen 1:26) of the Trinity—this must mean that "the worldly realm must somehow image the trinitarian, and the self-expositing Logos can and must assume the way of this imaging in order to express himself."[5] How does the "worldly realm" image the Trinity? Exploring various possible ways, von Balthasar agrees with

---

[5] Hans Urs von Balthasar, *Theo-Logic: Theological Logical Theory*, vol. 2: *Truth of God*, trans. Adrian J. Walker (San Francisco: Ignatius Press, 2004), 35.

Maurice Blondel that the logical distinction between identity and difference requires a third element, namely, the stance from which one identifies difference, or, put another way, the relation between the differing parties. Along similar lines, he agrees with Paul Claudel that each thing exists in relation to a vast set of other things, and, together, this thing and the vast set of other things exist in relation to God. Thus, it is impossible truly to apprehend one thing without apprehending three realities at once.

Turning to the two classic analogies for the Trinity—those of Augustine and Richard of Saint Victor—von Balthasar suggests that both have value, but also weaknesses. He states, "The interpersonal model [that is, Richard's] cannot attain the substantial unity of God, whereas the intrapersonal model [that is, Augustine's] cannot give an adequate picture of the real and abiding face-to-face encounter of the hypostases."[6] For Augustine, the problem with the love shared by two friends (or by a man and a woman) is that, although it communicates a triad, it does not communicate absolute unity, and it also does not communicate the unchangeableness of God—since two friends can have a falling out. Augustine considers the triad of "being, knowing, willing" within the individual person, but, according to von Balthasar, Augustine thinks that this does not yet go deep enough. He wants to ground the unity of the image at the level of personal consciousness rather than at the level of being. For this reason, Augustine turns to the triad of *mens*, *notitia*, and *amor*. Von Balthasar points out that *notitia* here means active "self-knowing", the fruit of "its own self-knowing mind".[7] The love that flows from this self-knowing, then, is self-love. This poses a problem, because love of God, not self-love, has to be the highest human imaging of God.

Augustine then speaks of *memoria*, *intellectus*, and *voluntas*. These three are all states or functions of the one soul, but von Balthasar notes (citing Augustine's *Letter to Evodius*) that even Augustine admits that they are not strictly identical with the one soul. Drawing upon book XV of Augustine's *De Trinitate*, von Balthasar argues that in fact what Augustine has given us is "[t]he one 'I' with its three functions".[8]

[6] Ibid., 38.
[7] Ibid.
[8] Ibid., 40.

Von Balthasar also contests the connection that Augustine draws, in the analogy, between *intellectus* and the Son and between *voluntas* and the Spirit.[9]

Turning to Richard of Saint Victor's Trinitarian image of two self-less lovers who selflessly love a third person, von Balthasar finds this image to express "the full selflessness of Christian *caritas* and its per-fection in God".[10] In a number of ways, he considers this image to be a major advance over Augustine's proposal. He points out, too, that Richard avidly sought to preserve the divine unity in his proposal: four of the six books of Richard's *De Trinitate* are devoted to the unity of God. Von Balthasar is clearly in agreement with Richard's basic position, which he summarizes as follows: "For him [Richard] and his successors, the only relevant principle was the logic of *cari-tas*, which requires in God the presence of the 'other', that is, the beloved, and of the 'third', the common object of love."[11] But in von Balthasar's view, just as Augustine's image fails to convey adequately the threeness of the Divine Persons, Richard's image fails to convey adequately the divine unity. Besides, both images, at their best, offer only "the faintest glimmer of an elucidation of the superabundant triune life that indwells the divine unity".[12] Both images perform a service, but neither can suffice on its own, and even when taken together they offer a merest glimmer.

For von Balthasar, the key issue is what to think of otherness in God: Is it a threat to absolute unity, a "negation of the One or its 'reversal'"?[13] He argues that, in fact, divine difference (the difference of Persons) grounds human difference, and so difference is positive, not negative; difference in God does not negate the divine unity. Since God is "the God of love",[14] this requires for von Balthasar (as

---

[9] Von Balthasar asks, "If each of the Divine Persons possesses the whole Godhead, and if the Godhead itself knows and loves as a 'personality', how can knowledge and love be attributed to the Son and the Spirit except by way of appropriation?" (ibid.). I think that this question can be answered, and in fact is answered, by Aquinas. For discussion, see Gilles Emery, O.P., "Essentialism or Personalism in the Treatise on God in St. Thomas Aquinas?" trans. Matthew Levering, in *Trinity in Aquinas*, 2nd ed. (Naples, Fla.: Sapientia Press, 2006), 165–208. See also my *Engaging the Doctrine of the Holy Spirit: Love and Gift in the Trinity and the Church* (Grand Rapids, Mich.: Baker Academic, 2016).

[10] Von Balthasar, *Truth of God*, 41–42.

[11] Ibid., 42.

[12] Ibid.

[13] Ibid., 43.

[14] Ibid., 82.

for Richard of Saint Victor and Bonaventure) that there be positive personal difference in God. Positive divine difference, as true
intra-Personal divine love, requires that "in God receiving is just as
positive as giving."[15]

With respect to Trinitarian difference, von Balthasar proposes that
two methods for thinking about the image of the Trinity are possible: "dialectic" and "dialogic". He favors the "dialogic" because it
fully allows for the goodness of otherness; people image God precisely by handing themselves over to the other. To be a creature is
to imitate the Divine Persons in their self-surrendering love for each
other. Beginning with the Divine Persons, the "dialogic" approach
attempts to show that all creatures image the Trinity by self-surrender

---

[15] Ibid., 83. For von Balthasar, the key is "the unconditional self-surrender of each divine
hypostasis to the others" so that "none of the hypostases in God overwhelms any of the others with its personal property" (ibid.). I do not think that "unconditional self-surrender" is
the best way of describing the relations of the Divine Persons. It seems to me more precise
to begin with the biblically attested generation of the Word by the Father and the biblically
attested spiration of the Spirit from the Father (and—or through—the Son). The three Persons are not three "selves", nor is "surrender" sufficiently precise to describe the distinctive
notional acts to which Scripture attests, without undermining the unity and simplicity of
the Trinity. Yet, I appreciate what von Balthasar is getting at. Surely, even if theologians
should exercise maximal precision in speaking about so great a mystery as that of the Trinity, the Trinity is not less than self-surrendering love. Christ's Cross and the other mysteries
of Christ's life reveal that self-surrendering love is the form of the Word who is the image of
the Father. It follows that the Father, and the entire Trinity, is infinite, self-surrendering love.
Von Balthasar adds, "No one doubts that, as the New Testament tells us, the Father's act of
giving up the Son and the Spirit in the economy is pure love, as is the Son's and the Spirit's
act of freely letting themselves be given up. But how could this fundamental claim about the
economy of salvation have no foundation in any property of the essence of the triune God?
'The Father loves the Son and shows him everything that he does.... He has made over all
judgment to the Son so that all may honor the Son as they honor the Father' (Jn 5:20, 22f.);
these statements, and others like them, surely have an intratrinitarian resonance and presupposition" (ibid., 136; see also 140–41 for reflection on "the eternal gratuity of the Father's
love" and the "poverty of love"). This is correct, and yet "self" and "surrender" have to
be understood here in a manner befitting the mystery of divine unity and also befitting the
limitations of human speech. Otherwise, what we have here is simply three agents—three
gods—surrendering and allowing themselves to be surrendered. Moreover, for von Balthasar
the circumincession of the Persons is constitutive of the divine unity: "since the Persons are
all hypostases of the divine nature in its concrete unity, with which each of them is really
identical, their essential unity can also be described as their mutual indwelling, their circumincessio ..., through which they constitute together the one, free, 'personal' countenance of
God" (ibid., 137). I agree that the Persons' "essential unity" is at the same time their "mutual
indwelling", but one needs to be clear that it is not the mutual indwelling that constitutes the
unity. On this point, see chapter 7 of my Scripture and Metaphysics: Aquinas and the Renewal of
Trinitarian Theology (Oxford: Blackwell, 2004).

of various kinds. Dialectic proceeds from the opposite direction and seeks to move from creaturely difference to a Trinitarian difference in God.

Here von Balthasar has Hegelian dialectic in view. Specifically, in *Elements of the Philosophy of Right*, Hegel argues that love's essence consists in realizing that one is only who one is *when one gives oneself entirely to another person*. The person in love discovers the following: "I am not isolated on my own [*für mich*], but gain my self-consciousness only through the renunciation of my independent existence [*meines Fürsichseins*]."[16] In self-surrender, the person finds himself. Hegel goes on to speak of two "moments" in love. The first moment consists in no longer wishing to be independent, no longer wishing to be for oneself alone. The lover recognizes that such an existence would be "deficient and incomplete".[17] It is only through self-surrender that a person attains his own unity or complete self-consciousness. Thus, the second moment consists in finding oneself in another person and having the other person do the same in oneself. Hegel states: "I gain recognition in this person, who in turn gains recognition in me."[18] Clearly, this is moving close to an image of the Trinity, in which the relations (rooted in self-surrender) define the Persons without compromising the absolute unity of the Persons.

Hegel, however, considers the reality of love to be "the most immense contradiction".[19] It strikes him as beyond the realm of understanding, because he cannot see how self-consciousness can be established by surrendering one's own self-consciousness. He cannot see how the realization that one is radically incomplete without the other can be the basis for true completeness in oneself. For Hegel, there is an *opposition* between the negation of self-consciousness (in the lover's self-surrender) and the affirmation of self-consciousness (in the lover's self-surrender). He holds that love resolves this contradiction and establishes an "ethical unity".[20] In the family and the state, one learns that one is fulfilled by being a "member" rather

---

[16] G. W. F. Hegel, *Elements of the Philosophy of Right*, ed. Allen W. Wood, trans. H. B. Nisbet (Cambridge: Cambridge University Press, 1991), §158, p. 199.
[17] Ibid.
[18] Ibid.
[19] Ibid.
[20] Ibid.

than an independent person who lives for oneself.[21] The dialectical synthesis, then, is unity. The two persons mutually "consent to
constitute a single person and to give up their natural and individual
personalities within this union", in order to "attain their substantial
self-consciousness".[22]

Von Balthasar notes that although Hegel's position here could be
developed (as Hegel himself did) in terms of a dialectical logic of
"God's attainment of completion through his becoming world and
concrete spirit", it could also be developed along the dialogic lines
of Franz Rosenzweig, Martin Buber, and Ferdinand Ebner (among
others), who identify the "I–Thou relation as the primordial phenomenon", so that the "I" is "something that has always already
been addressed by, and addressed, a Thou"—a *"Logos Theou"*.[23]
Indeed, von Balthasar points out that we here find a triad, since in
this line of thought, "the condition of the possibility both of the I
and of the Thou is a having been addressed by the very ground of

---

[21] Ibid. Hegel defines marriage as follows: "Marriage is essentially an ethical relationship.
Formerly, especially under most systems of natural law, it was considered only in its physical
aspect or natural character. It was accordingly regarded only as a sexual relationship, and its
other determinations remained completely inaccessible. But it is equally crude to interpret
marriage merely as a civil contract, a notion ... which is still to be found even in Kant. On
this interpretation, marriage gives contractual form to the arbitrary relations between individuals, and is thus debased to a contract entitling the parties concerned to use one another. A
third and equally unacceptable notion is that which simply equates marriage with love; for
love, as a feeling ..., is open in all respects to contingency; and this is a shape which the ethical
may not assume. Marriage should therefore be defined more precisely as rightfully ethical ...
love, so that the transient, capricious, and purely subjective aspects of love are excluded from
it" (ibid., §161, p. 201). Hegel shortly afterward adds a note about indissolubility: "Marriage
differs from *concubinage* inasmuch as the latter is chiefly concerned with the satisfaction of the
natural drive, whereas this drive is made subordinate within marriage. This is why, within
marriage, one may speak unblushingly of natural functions which, in extra-marital relationships, would produce a feeling of shame. But this is also why marriage should be regarded
as indissoluble *in itself*; for the end of marriage is the ethical end [i.e., 'consciousness of this
union as a substantial end, and hence in love, trust, and the sharing of the whole of individual
existence'], which is so exalted that everything else appears powerless against it and subject
to its authority. Marriage should not be disrupted by passion, for the latter is subordinate to
it. But it is indissoluble only *in itself*, for as Christ says, divorce is permitted only 'because of
the hardness of their hearts'. Since marriage contains the moment of feeling ..., it is not absolute but unstable, and it has within it the possibility of dissolution. But all legislations must
make such dissolution as difficult as possible and uphold the right of ethics against caprice"
(§163, pp. 202–3).

[22] Ibid., §162, p. 201.

[23] Von Balthasar, *Truth of God*, 45.

the interpersonal dynamism itself."[24] In Martin Buber, whose work
he studied closely,[25] von Balthasar identifies a full-fledged (though
unconscious) image of the Trinity. He explains that for Buber, "spirit
reigns between the I and the Thou, who are pure relation to each
other, but each one, incommunicable in his core (as the Other),
nonetheless (and precisely for this reason) communicates all that he
has."[26] The self-communicating "I" and "Thou" share their "spirit"
with each other as their mutual bond.

Von Balthasar considers this dialogic emphasis on I-Thou-spirit to
be valuable but incomplete. In seeking an analogy for the Trinity, an
image that is the most adequate to the mystery of triunity, he suggests
that we should follow farther along the marital lines begun, but not
completed, by Hegel. Specifically, he urges that we think in terms of
the image of man, woman, and child. Augustine, of course, argued in
his De Trinitate against the viability of this image. Augustine observes,
"I do not find the opinion very convincing which supposes that the
trinity of the image of God, as far as human nature is concerned, can
be discovered in three persons; that is, that it may be composed of
the union of male and female and their offspring."[27] At first glance,
this triad lacks persuasiveness, in Augustine's view, because by placing the Holy Spirit in the female role, it makes the Holy Spirit into
a quasi-mother of the Son and a quasi-wife of the Father. But this
objection could be contested by arguing that we are here speaking
of spiritual relations, which bodily relations can signify. Augustine
grants the validity of this response, but he notes that his own concern
lies deeper: if the image of the Trinity is a man, woman, and child,
how could each individual human being be in the image of God, as
Genesis 1:26–27 implies? It would seem that, individually speaking,
a man at best could be the image of the Father, a woman the image
of the Spirit, and a child the image of the Son. The main point for
Augustine is that God in Genesis 1 makes clear that each human
being is fully the image of God. Besides, even if one insisted that

[24] Ibid., 49.

[25] See Hans Urs von Balthasar, Martin Buber and Christianity: A Dialogue between Israel and
the Church, trans. Alexander Dru (London: Harvill Press, 1961).

[26] Von Balthasar, Truth of God, 55.

[27] Augustine, The Trinity, trans. Edmund Hill, O.P. (Brooklyn, N.Y.: New City Press,
1991), XII.2.5, p. 324.

"male and female he created them" (Gen 1:27) means that the image of the Trinity is the man and the woman, there is here no mention (or existence) of a child. Augustine concludes, "We should not then understand man being made to the image of the supreme trinity, that is, to the image of God, as meaning that this image is to be understood in three human beings."[28] Each human being is made to the image of the Trinity.

Augustine therefore does more than argue, as von Balthasar reports, that the image of man, woman, and child is absurd. Like Augustine, Thomas Aquinas calls "absurd" the view that man, woman, and child collectively comprise the image, on the grounds that the man and woman (even prior to having a child) each fully possess the image of the Triune God.[29] Aquinas wishes to maintain as strongly as possible that the image of God is not the product of the conjunction of both sexes, but rather fully "belongs to both sexes, since it is in the mind, wherein there is no sexual differentiation."[30]

Given von Balthasar's critique of both Augustine's and Richard's understanding of the image of God, however, it makes sense that he pursues the "dialogic" I-Thou-spirit triad in the direction of the marriage relationship. Notably, in von Balthasar's view, it is not necessary to suppose that the image is found in actual childbearing, actual offspring. Rather, he highlights "fecundity" and "fruitfulness", not only bodily, but also spiritual.[31] He sees no need to institute a sharp divide between bodily and spiritual, since in actual marriage we find conjoined "the organic *and* personal fruitfulness of the two".[32] Here von Balthasar has recourse to the theology of Matthias Joseph Scheeben. Von Balthasar points out that in the begetting of a child, God is involved (not least because of the infusion of the spiritual soul). Even in non-sacramental marriage, God is involved due to marriage's natural role in the production of God's images. The marital act, which consummates the covenant of marriage, is not bereft of God; on the contrary, at its most fundamental level, it is done in God's name, as an

[28] Ibid., XII.2.9, p. 327.
[29] Aquinas, *Summa theologica*, I, q. 93, a. 6 ad 2, trans. Fathers of the English Dominican Province (Westminster, Md.: Christian Classics, 1981).
[30] Ibid.
[31] Von Balthasar, *Truth of God*, 60.
[32] Ibid., 60–61.

act of self-giving covenantal love. Marriage is never a mere contract, even when it is a natural rather than sacramental reality.

In the self-giving fruitfulness of the spouses, therefore, von Balthasar discerns the greatest possible creaturely analogue to the self-giving fruitfulness of the Divine Persons. Obviously, the Divine Persons do not engage in bodily actions, let alone in marriage; but their proper acts are supreme acts of self-giving fruitfulness, and, indeed, each Divine Person is infinite self-giving fruitfulness, and the one God-head is infinite self-giving fruitfulness in love. As von Balthasar states about marriage, "The relationship described here"—which builds upon the dialogic "I-Thou"—"remains, in spite of all the obvious dissimilarities, the most eloquent *imago Trinitatis* that we find woven into the fabric of the creature."[33] Von Balthasar then links the image in marital fruitfulness to the three models he has explored above: that of Augustine, Richard, and the dialogic I-Thou. He remarks that the image in marital fruitfulness "not only transcends Augustine's self-contained I, but also allows the '*condilectus* [co-beloved]' that Richard's model imports from the outside to spring from the intimacy of love itself—precisely as its fruitfulness—while avoiding the dangerous tendency of the dialogicians to allow interpersonal encounter to slide into a mere two-way monologue."[34] In the fruitfulness modeled by a married couple, von Balthasar finds a very simple "permanent proof of the triadic structure of creaturely logic".[35]

Again, the key here is fecundity, not the physical marital act per se. Von Balthasar argues that "supernatural fruitfulness"—as exemplified in vowed religious and clergy or, in a unique way, in the Blessed Virgin Mary—correlates with "the sacred character of matrimony" and is also foreshadowed by the way in which the I-Thou relationship in spiritual exchange finds fulfillment in "an objective third".[36]

---

[33] Ibid., 62.

[34] Ibid.

[35] Ibid. Von Balthasar cautions, "God's immanencing into the world in Jesus Christ can be neither constructed (Hegel) nor postulated (Baius) starting from the world" (ibid., 84). This was a mistake that, in von Balthasar's view, the "dialogicians" (Rosenzweig, Buber, Ebner, et al.) tended to make, since for them the I-Thou dimension could not function without "the immanent presence of the divine" (ibid.). Although grace remains sheer grace, however, the fulfillment by self-surrender that belongs to "the ontological language of creatureliness as such"—and that is present already in a high form in natural marriage—is "not foreign to the logic of God" (ibid.). It is not foreign because God has built it into his creatures.

[36] Ibid.

Nonetheless, it might seem that if marital fruitfulness is the greatest creaturely image of the Trinity, then Jesus Christ himself does not image God supremely. On the contrary: von Balthasar insists that Christ is "'image par excellence'", "the image that God himself finally places before us".[37] Christ is the one who "completes or retrieves the image-character that man has lost and darkened".[38] Von Balthasar supports this point from scriptural texts that present Christ as the true image to which we must be conformed: "we all, with unveiled face, beholding the glory of the Lord, are being changed into his likeness from one degree of glory to another" (2 Cor 3:18); "put on the new man, which is being renewed in knowledge after the image of his creator" (Col 3:10); "Just as we have borne the image of the man of dust, we shall also bear the image of the man of heaven" (1 Cor 15:49).[39] But if Christ is the true image, what has happened to the marital image that von Balthasar has praised so profusely?

Von Balthasar's answer is that Jesus did not need to use an image of the Trinity, whether the image of the soul and its intentional acts (Augustine), the mutual interchange of lovers (Richard), or the man, woman, and child (the marital image). Instead, Jesus, coming from above, could simply employ "worldly being as such, his everyday life".[40] The two elements that he employed were "shared existence with one's fellowmen" (or "love of neighbor") and "fruitfulness".[41] Jesus lived out this mode of life in order to image the fruitfulness of radical self-surrendering love, which gives positive value to difference and which is always for others. In this way, he stands out in his humanity as the supreme image of the Trinity.

Marital friendship and fecundity are not necessary, then, to image the Trinity. Spiritual or virginal friendship and fecundity can accomplish the same thing. But this does not take away the fact that marriage, with its especially intimate and profound friendship between the spouses, embodies a "shared existence with one's fellowmen" and

[37] Ibid., 72.
[38] Ibid., 73.
[39] See ibid. Von Balthasar also discuss Christ's parables. Parables show "the capacity of creaturely logic to sustain the full weight of divine logic", a capacity that comes from the fact that God "made the creature according to his own image and likeness, so that, by his grace, it might become inwardly capable of serving him as a loudspeaker through which to express himself and make himself understood" (ibid., 81).
[40] Ibid., 85.
[41] Ibid.

"love of neighbor" that has a particular intensity and whose fruitfulness is powerful in the world. Certainly, the imaging of God's fruitful self-surrendering love can be done virginally. Von Balthasar observes that "[t]he Christian correlative to the sacred character of matrimony is the bodily fruitfulness of the Virgin overshadowed by the Spirit, which is the basis of the (real-bodily) fruitfulness of Christian virginity."[42] Yet it remains the case that in the regular course of human life, the I–Thou bond of marriage (in which God is present), with its self-giving ordering toward fruitfulness, "remains, in spite of all the obvious dissimilarities, the most eloquent *imago Trinitatis* that we find woven into the fabric of the creature".[43]

2. Matthias Joseph Scheeben

In describing this "most eloquent *imago Trinitatis*" in *Truth of God*, von Balthasar repeatedly commends the theology of Matthias Joseph Scheeben. For Scheeben, the marriage of God and humanity is the heart of everything. As von Balthasar observes elsewhere, Scheeben rejoices in "God's central *conubium* with mankind (and, through it, with the whole world) in the Incarnation".[44] Scheeben argues that "the supernatural miracle of two natures constituting one person is 'natural' in the sense that in this union all nature's organic, moral, and matrimonial relationships find their highest form and fulfilment and indeed their ultimate ground."[45] Scheeben attends to the physical aspect of marital fruitfulness as much as to the marital friendship in order to underscore that body and soul are united in their imaging of the divine-human marriage that God has accomplished in and through Christ. According to von Balthasar, Scheeben's theology is "one great doctrine of *eros*", rooted in the Trinity as "an interior fruitfulness that pours itself out".[46]

---

[42] Ibid., 62.

[43] Ibid.

[44] Hans Urs von Balthasar, *The Glory of the Lord: A Theological Aesthetics*, vol. 1, *Seeing the Form*, trans. Erasmo Leiva-Merikakis, ed. Joseph Fessio, S.J., and John Riches, 2nd ed. (1982; San Francisco: Ignatius Press, 2009), 111.

[45] Ibid., 112.

[46] Ibid., 107.

In his *The Mysteries of Christianity*, Scheeben places Ephesians 5 at the center of his reflection on the Church: the husband and wife are an image of the self-surrendering, fruitful love of Christ and the Church. The Incarnation itself already is a marriage between God and mankind, but the union envisioned by God comes to full fruition only in the Church. Scheeben describes faith, baptism, and the Eucharist in marital imagery. The consummation of the marriage takes place in the Eucharist, which is a perfect communion between the (bridal) baptized and the Lord. For Scheeben, the justification of a sinner, by which the person is cleansed by the power of Christ's Cross, provides a "higher existence and life in the soul" that "is accomplished by a formal marriage of God with the soul".[47]

Scheeben amplifies the impact of this marital imagery by arguing that fruitful marriage itself is a sign not only of Christ and the Church, but also (in accord with Christ's manifestation of the Father and the Church's manifestation of Christ in the Spirit) of the Trinity. Most notably for my purposes, he proposes that the family—man, woman, child—images the unity of the Trinity. This is seen, he suggests, in the biblical narrative of Adam and Eve. He states, "In deriving Eve from the side of Adam, God wished to bring about the procession of human nature in the representatives of family unity (father, mother, and child) from one principle, just as the divine nature is transmitted from the Father to the Son, and from the Father and the Son to the Holy Spirit."[48] In the original family, Adam stands in the role of the Father; Eve in the role of the Son, since Eve comes forth solely from Adam; and their child (still not conceived prior to the Fall) in the role of the Holy Spirit, as "the fruit and crown of the union of man and woman".[49] This is the image of the unity of the Trinity because the original family exhibits such profound unity in its threeness: Eve comes forth from Adam alone, and their union bears fruit.

Furthermore, Scheeben thinks that the human family (man, woman, child) images not only the unity but also the Trinity of Persons. Scheeben explains that in humans, generation must be the work

---

[47] Matthias Joseph Scheeben, *The Mysteries of Christianity*, trans. Cyril Vollert, S.J. (New York: Crossroad, 2006), 633.

[48] Ibid., 182.

[49] Ibid.

of two persons (male and female), whereas in the infinitely perfect nature that is God, generation is the work of the Father alone. Even so, the relationship between Father and Son is mediated by the Spirit in a way that is analogous to the way the relationship between a human father and son is mediated by the mother. Scheeben comments, "As the mother is the bond of love between father and child, so in God the Holy Spirit is the bond of love between the Father and the Son; and as she brings forth the child in unity of nature with the father . . . so the Holy Spirit manifests the unity of nature between the Father and the Son."[50] The Holy Spirit does this as the bond of love between the Father and Son, or, more specifically, as "the fruit" of the "mutual unity and love" of the Father and Son.[51] The generation of Eve here parallels the spiration of the Spirit, according to Scheeben. He gives various reasons for this, among them the point that "as Eve was taken from the side of Adam, from his heart, the seat of love, seeing that the material of her body was taken and given out of love, so we must say of the Holy Spirit that He proceeds not from the bosom, but from the heart of the Father and the Son."[52]

The imaging of the Trinity by the generative love apparent in the original human family—with Adam imaging the Father, the child the Son, and Eve the Spirit—may seem, Scheeben recognizes, to be a *novum* of his own fertile imagination. For this reason, he cites various Fathers of the Church on the symbolism of Adam and Eve. He notes that according to Saint Methodius, Eve (formed of Adam's rib) symbolizes the Spirit, because the Spirit is the "divine vital principle which constitutes the Church the bride of Christ".[53] When Adam/ Christ stands in (death-like) selfless love, from his side comes forth the vital principle that enables his Church to be established. Surely the vital principle is the Holy Spirit, and just as surely, what comes forth from Adam's side is Eve. If Adam is here the Father, however, why is it that the New Adam is the incarnate Son? Scheeben replies that the generative principle is in fact the Father and the Son, God and the New Adam. Recall that God draws the vital principle (the rib, or,

---

[50] Ibid., 183.
[51] Ibid.
[52] Ibid., 184.
[53] Ibid.

in the New Adam, the blood) out of Adam's side. Thus the Spirit comes forth from the union in self-surrendering love of the Father and the Son.

Scheeben also cites Gregory Nazianzen's Fifth Theological Oration. Gregory links Adam to the Father, Seth to the Son, and Eve to the Holy Spirit. He states, "What was Adam? Something molded by God. What was Eve? A portion of that molded creation. Seth? He was the offspring of the pair."[54] The offspring, the son, was Seth, whereas Eve came directly from Adam without being an offspring. They all share the same nature (Adam's). In this way, Gregory attempts to show that the generation of the Son is not the same as the spiration of the Spirit, even though both derive from the Father. It is not exactly a family image of the Trinity, but it is an argument by which the derivation of Eve helps us to understand the difference between the generation of the Son and the spiration of the Spirit. Richard of Saint Victor and Bonaventure make a similar analogy, though with Eve in the role of the Son and Seth in the role of the Spirit.[55]

Scheeben goes on to argue that there is a connection between the Hebrew name "woman" (given to Eve) and the name of the Spirit. He explains that "as the Hebrew word for woman serves to show that the woman ... is joined to him most intimately as a companion and helpmate of like nature, so the name 'Spirit' in the case of the Third Person in God indicates that He proceeds from the other two persons as their most perfect companion", sharing in their nature.[56] Scheeben connects this argument to the argument from a perfect family. As in a family the bond between father and child (son) is the mother, who bears the child in her womb and thereby testifies to the fleshly unity between father and child (in a manner that the father cannot do), so also in the Trinity the bond between Father and Son is the Spirit, who "represent[s] the spirituality unity, the unity of spirit, of the spiritual nature between Father and Son; not indeed

---

[54] Gregory Nazianzen, Oration 31: On the Holy Spirit, trans. Lionel Wickham, in St. Gregory of Nazianzus, *On God and Christ: The Five Theological Orations and Two Letters to Cledonius* (Crestwood, N.Y.: St. Vladimir's Seminary Press, 2002), 117–47, at 124 (§11).

[55] For discussion, see Marc Cardinal Ouellet, *Divine Likeness: Toward a Trinitarian Anthropology of the Family*, trans. Philip Milligan and Linda M. Cicone (Grand Rapids, Mich.: Eerdmans, 2006), 25.

[56] Scheeben, *Mysteries of Christianity*, 186.

as its intermediary, but as its flower and culmination".[57] The family image gives the Spirit a place not merely as an intermediary between the Father and Son, but as a fullness of spiritual unity or spirituality, just as the mother manifests a fullness of fleshly unity between the father and child. With Mary in view, Scheeben adds that "generation in God is virginal; hence the Holy Spirit must be the bond of union between the Father and the Son in virginal fashion."[58]

For von Balthasar, Scheeben's view that the Holy Spirit is feminine in the Trinity ultimately is untenable.[59] But as we have seen, von Balthasar nonetheless supports Scheeben's emphasis on the family as an image of the Trinity, indeed as the greatest image of the Trinity. For von Balthasar, as we saw, the reason consists in the connection between marriage and fruitful self-surrendering love. Spiritual fruitfulness is not impeded when the marriage happens to be childless through no fault of the couple, but the fleshly dimension of fruitfulness must not be minimized.[60] Although Scheeben does not ground the family image upon self-surrendering love and fruitfulness, he does hold that the conception of a child is the conception of an image of God and, therefore, is always done (in marriage) in the service of God. The fruitfulness of the husband and wife is never on a merely this-worldly level; there is always a reference to the conception of an image of God. This is fertile ground for imaging the Trinity, since it involves the generation of God's image (as in the generation of the Son) and the bond of love (as in the spiration of the Spirit). Thus, Scheeben's approach differs from von Balthasar's but complements it.

In *The Christian State of Life*, von Balthasar urges once again that Genesis 1:26–28 presents human fruitfulness, in marriage, as the

[57] Ibid., 187.

[58] Ibid., 187–88.

[59] Von Balthasar comments with Scheeben's position in view: "because 'generation' is already exclusively reserved as an analogue for the Father-Son relationship, and because the Son, if anyone, would have to represent the feminine element therein, we cannot legitimately argue from the feminine form of the Hebrew words 'spirit' (*ruach*) and 'wisdom' (*kochma*) that the Spirit is the feminine in God" (*Truth of God*, 60; see also 60n97).

[60] See Scheeben, *Mysteries of Christianity*, 594. Von Balthasar emphasizes that the fruitfulness that pertains to Christian marriage does not require that there be an actual child; it simply requires that the couple be open to God's gift if it comes. The couple "awaits the fruitfulness bestowed by God from above whether as a child sent them by God or as a spiritual fruit if the physical one is denied them" (von Balthasar, *The Christian State of Life*, trans. Mary Frances McCarthy [San Francisco: Ignatius Press, 1983], 246).

fundamental image of the Trinity.[61] Yet, he also affirms Scheeben's intuition that the origination of Eve from the side of Adam constitutes "a direct physical image of the origin from the Father's substance of the eternal Son who shares his nature"[62]—even if von Balthasar applies this point to the Son rather than to the Spirit. Von Balthasar thinks that the formation of Eve from Adam's side gives the original pair a "spiritual oneness and fecundity" that establishes them from the outset as "the image of the concrete divine oneness of nature and fecundity within the Trinity".[63] One can see how this emphasis on Eve's origination from Adam fits with Scheeben's emphasis, even though von Balthasar directs it toward his own emphasis on the fruitfulness of Trinitarian difference-in-unity. After the Fall, the key is that marriage obeys the self-surrender of the Cross, through "which all desire, insofar as it is disordered and selfish, is vanquished by the self-lessness of Christian self-giving".[64] For von Balthasar, consecrated virgins and married Christian couples are following the same basic state of life, namely, that of Christ's fecundity in self-surrendering love.

3. Other Contemporary Approaches

We have seen that von Balthasar insists above all on the fact that marital fecundity follows a "trinitarian model".[65] Marriage is based on self-surrendering difference in love and fruitfulness, and marriage thereby images the Trinity. Even more than the acts of the mind (Augustine) or the workings of love (Richard), marriage serves for von Balthasar as the best image of Triune self-surrendering difference and fruitfulness. Obviously it is not a perfect image, but then again, neither are the others.

This way of grounding the family's image of the Trinity strikes me as quite helpful. It makes sense to affirm that the self-surrendering

---

[61] See von Balthasar, *Christian State of Life*, 226: "God's being in the Trinity is an infinite fecundity that reveals itself externally in creation; whatever is made in his image must, of its very nature, have a share in this fecundity."

[62] Ibid., 227.

[63] Ibid., 228.

[64] Ibid., 248.

[65] Ibid., 232.

Triune God, who is fruitful unity-in-difference, has an image in the fruitful difference and mutual self-surrendering love found in marriage. Scheeben's argument for an image based upon the origination of Eve from Adam strikes me as less helpful, but even so, I find that both theologians have demonstrated the usefulness of identifying the family as an image of the Trinity.

In his 1994 "Letter to Families", Pope John Paul II agreed with Scheeben's and von Balthasar's proposals—though without naming them personally—by remarking, "The primordial model of the family is to be sought in God himself, in the Trinitarian mystery of his life."[66] Yet, in *Divine Likeness: Toward a Trinitarian Anthropology of the Family*, Marc Ouellet has observed that "this theme of the family, image of the Trinity, is still far from being unanimously welcomed. It has yet to rally those who follow the long tradition founded upon the authority of Augustine of Hippo and Thomas Aquinas, who preferred the 'psychological' or 'intra-subjective' analogy as an approach to the Trinitarian mystery."[67]

Admittedly, I am not concerned by this lack of unanimity. If we conceive of the Trinity in terms of self-surrendering love and fruitfulness, then the image from marriage (man, woman, and child) shows its power. But if we conceive of the Trinity in terms of the relationship of unity and trinity and in terms of the Johannine teaching on the Father's generation of the Word, then a more precise image of the Trinity is the one offered by Augustine and refined by Aquinas. In other words, much depends upon the angle from which we approach the mystery of the Trinity. If our concerns are to achieve metaphysical precision in avoiding tritheism and accounting for the Son's unique name "Word", then Augustine and Aquinas have set forth the best path. If our concerns are to highlight the Trinity's fruitful selflessness, evident in the Father's generation of the Son and in the spiration of the Spirit, then the image drawn from marriage serves our purposes well.

Ouellet argues that "the meaning of the relationship between the Trinity and the family depends upon whether or not the man-woman

---

[66] Pope John Paul II, "Letter to Families", Gratissimam Sane (February 2, 1994), no. 6.

[67] Ouellet, *Divine Likeness*, 20. Drawing upon Lionel Gendron's *Mystère de la Trinité et Symbolique familiale* (Rome, 1975), Ouellet notes that in fact the Church's theological tradition has always possessed a family image of the Trinity, although not in a precise or uncontroverted manner. In the West, however, the influence of Augustine brought this image to an end.

relationship is included within the *imago Dei*. If man—man and woman—is the image of the Trinity, then the communion and participation of the family 'we' in the Trinitarian 'We' goes far deeper."[68] In my view, however, the inclusion of the man–woman relationship within the *imago* is not necessary. After all, if each human being is an image of the Trinity in the manner described by Augustine and Aquinas, then the communion of persons in marriage will also image the Trinity—precisely because two images of the Trinity (a man and a woman) are involved in an intimate relational bond. Even if the image is *strictly speaking* found solely in individual persons, a communion of such persons would also serve to image the Trinity.

When one looks at the Trinity in terms of fruitful self-surrender, marriage stands out as an image of the Trinity, since self-surrendering love and fecundity belong to the essence of Christian marriage. In this sense, Pope John Paul II's "Letter to Families" is correct that "the divine 'We' is the eternal pattern of the human 'we', especially of that 'we' formed by the man and the woman created in the divine image and likeness."[69] Ouellet's mistake, then, consists, not in promoting the marital image of the Trinity, but rather in exaggerating its serviceability. He comments that "Augustine's major objection to this analogy [of the family] is the impossibility of realizing a true unity, that is to say a substantial unity, within a human family; in the three human *hypostases* of man, woman, and child there exists such a disparity that any real unity is inconceivable."[70] Actually, however,

[68] Ouellet, *Divine Likeness*, 21. Ouellet later points out, "The common fecundity of the divine 'We' and the human 'we' must not be seen exclusively from the angle of fertility. It is no doubt its most creative moment but it also expands to the many relationships of education, sharing, and affection that make up the community life of persons committed one to another and one 'for' another in the family's framework" (ibid., 36). Ouellet is obviously well aware of the two points that von Balthasar singles out, namely, self-surrendering love (unity-in-difference, communion) and fruitfulness. Ouellet remarks, "On what precisely does it [the family analogy of the Trinity] hinge? On the correspondence between the persons or the communion of persons? A recurring expression in the writings of John Paul II guides us towards the second hypothesis: the *communio personarum* is the common meeting place of the deeper reality of the family and of the mystery of the Trinity.... This analogy is based fundamentally on the interpersonal love which, by means of gift and reception, engenders persons, maintains them in relation, and allows them to fulfill themselves as persons 'by a sincere gift of self'" (ibid., 34).

[69] Pope John Paul II, "Letter to Families", 6.

[70] Ouellet, *Divine Likeness*, 22.

the even more pressing problem is that if the best image of the Trinity is found in the married couple and their child, then unmarried individuals are not in the image of God—a point that is clearly wrong. As we have seen, von Balthasar gets around the problem by simply arguing that marriage exemplifies love of neighbor and fruitfulness but that consecrated virginity does so, too. It follows that even if von Balthasar calls the marital image the "greatest" image of the Trinity, he qualifies this by making clear that individuals who obey God's call to singleness (such as Jesus) also exemplify the image of the Trinity, and indeed do so with supreme perfection insofar as their self-surrendering love and fruitfulness are perfect (as in the case of Jesus).

As Ouellet notes, Augustine appreciated that the love of neighbor can produce "a common soul and a common heart among those who love one another", and this unity is a reflection of the unity of the Trinity.[71] This kind of unity-in-difference is what von Balthasar has in view when he highlights self-surrendering love of neighbor and fecundity as the two key elements of the image of the Trinity. The Orthodox theologian Paul Evdokimov has the same elements in view when, quoting John Chrysostom, he states, " 'When husband and wife are united in marriage, they are no longer seen as something earthly, but as the image of God Himself.' These words of St. John Chrysostom allow us to see in marriage a living icon, a 'theophany.' "[72] Somewhat like Gregory Nazianzen, too, Evdokimov emphasizes that just as the Divine Persons are of one nature (and thereby a single subject), so also the married couple, joined by God as the third, make up a single subject. Evdokimov states, "It is therefore nuptial man who is in the image of the Triune God, and the dogma of the Trinity is his divine archetype, the icon of the nuptial community."[73] This is because of the graced bond of love shared by the married couple. As Evdokimov remarks, "The human being, as a closed monad, would not be His image."[74] A "closed monad" would, of course, not be a human being, since all humans

---

[71] Ibid., 24. Ouellet draws attention here to Augustine's Tractate 39 on the Gospel of John.

[72] Paul Evdokimov, *The Sacrament of Love: The Nuptial Mystery in the Light of the Orthodox Tradition*, trans. Anthony P. Gythiel and Victoria Steadman (Crestwood, N.Y.: St. Vladimir's Seminary Press, 1985), 118.

[73] Ibid., 117.

[74] Ibid., 115.

are intrinsically relational vis-à-vis God and neighbor even if they do not realize this.

The logic that Evdokimov employs here justifies the consecrated virgin's stature in the image of the Trinity, insofar as the consecrated virgin (preeminently Christ) is filled with self-surrendering love of neighbor and is spiritually fruitful.[75] In *Mulieris dignitatem*, Pope John Paul II argues, along Evdokimov's lines, that "man and woman, created as a 'unity of the two' in their common humanity, are called to live in a communion of love and in this way to mirror in the world the communion of love that is in God, through which the three Persons love each other in the intimate mystery of the one divine life."[76] This point is best spelled out by von Balthasar's emphasis on triune self-surrendering love and fruitfulness.

4. Conclusion

I hope to have shown that it would be a mistake to fail to recognize that marriage is an important image of the Trinity. Yet in making this point, we must also affirm, as von Balthasar does, that "the sexual man/woman fruitfulness need be no longer the exclusive model of fruitfulness", since Christ's "suprasexual fruitfulness" brings the Church into being.[77] Von Balthasar appreciates that we can also see this image of the Trinity in the suprasexual fruitfulness of the Virgin Mary. Indeed, he observes in *New Elucidations* that ultimately "the concept of fruitfulness brings us into a sphere that affects every Christian, without distinction between the married and those who have consecrated their virginity to God."[78] Nonetheless,

---

[75] As Ouellet puts it, Christ is the one who fulfills God's covenant with Israel and who thereby consummates the marriage of God with his people. See Ouellet, *Divine Likeness*, 29.

[76] Pope John Paul II, *Mulieris dignitatem*, 7.

[77] Hans Urs von Balthasar, *Theo-Drama: Theological Dramatic Theory*, vol. 2: *The Dramatis Personae: Man in God*, trans. Graham Harrison (San Francisco: Ignatius Press, 1990), 413.

[78] Hans Urs von Balthasar, *New Elucidations*, trans. Mary Theresilde Skerry (San Francisco: Ignatius Press, 1986), 222. In this section of *New Elucidations*, von Balthasar has in view Pope Paul VI's 1968 encyclical *Humanae vitae*. As von Balthasar says of that encyclical's teaching, in light of scriptural revelation: "For sexuality as Christians understand it—sexuality that takes as its norm the relationship between Christ and his Church—Christ's words hold true: 'Let him grasp it who can.' But Christ is saying something more here than that very few men and

it is specifically Jesus Christ who, through his self-surrender on the Cross as received by Mary at the foot of the Cross (embodying the Marian Church), reveals the full meaning of marriage as an image of the Trinity. Von Balthasar states that "it is from the fruit-fulness of Christ and the Church that the model for the married state may be drawn. For the source of this fruitfulness lies in the fact that no limits whatsoever are imposed on self-surrender, either on Christ's part or on that of the Church."[79] Human marriage is a sign of this marriage of Christ and the Church, in which Christ images the Trinity—and Christ enables Mary and all his follow-ers to image the Trinity—through the fruitfulness of absolute self-surrender in love. In marriage, the couple's "physical fruitfulness" is conjoined with their "spiritual fruitfulness" or "total surrender to each other".[80] Christian marriage, then, introduces us to "a form of existence in which God's Agape ... becomes the all-inclusive total meaning of life".[81]

In a Thomistic vein, the 2009 Pastoral Letter of the United States Conference of Catholic Bishops, *Marriage: Love and Life in the Divine Plan*, comments upon marriage and the Trinity: "As we learn from the mystery of the Trinity, to be in the image and likeness of God is not simply to have intelligence and free will, but also to live in a communion of love. From all eternity the Father begets his Son in the love of the Spirit."[82] Put otherwise, while affirming that the Father's begetting does not depend upon the Spirit (so as not to over-throw the Father's sufficiency as the font of the Trinity or to under-mine the order of origin), we can say that in his eternal begetting, "the Father gives himself entirely over to the Son in the love of the Holy Spirit. The Son, having been begotten of the Father, perfectly

---

women will actually grasp his doctrine. He is issuing us a challenge to serious endeavor, the same challenge, essentially, that rings through the whole of the Gospel: take up your cross every day, sell all you possess, and do not cheat as did Ananias and Sapphira. Why should the sexual area alone offer no challenge to the Christian? Sexuality, even as *eros*, is to be an expres-sion of *agape*, and *agape* always involves an element of renunciation. And only by renunciation can the limits that we set on our own self-surrender be transcended" (ibid., 227–28).

[79] Ibid., 222.

[80] Ibid., 223.

[81] Von Balthasar, *Theo-Drama*, vol. 2: *The Dramatis Personae*, 414.

[82] United States Conference of Catholic Bishops, Pastoral Letter *Marriage: Love and Life in the Divine Plan* (Washington, D.C.: United States Conference of Catholic Bishops, 2009), 35.

returns that love by giving himself entirely over to the Father in the same Spirit of love."[83] On the basis of this Trinitarian theology, the bishops draw the conclusion that to be in the image of God—in the image of the *Triune* God—involves being in relational communion. Knowing and loving is never without real personal communion. There is no human "image of God" abstracted from the relational call of the God who made us to know and love him. Marriage, as a uniquely intimate communion of knowing and loving, is therefore a Trinitarian image.[84]

To my mind, von Balthasar captures the central element of this communion of persons (and Persons) when he emphasizes fruitful surrender and gift. Both in God and in marriage, such fruitful surrender is generative. Intelligence and love, in the Triune God and in human beings, are never intended to enclose a solitary person within himself. Thus, von Balthasar's recognition that marriage is an image of the Trinity because of the exemplary way in which marriage embodies fruitful self-surrendering love stands as a major contribution to the theology of the *imago* and to the theology of marriage as a real path (though certainly not the only path) of participating in the Trinity.

---

[83] Ibid., 35–36. On the importance of the Trinitarian order of origin, see the introduction to my *Engaging the Doctrine of the Holy Spirit*.

[84] The bishops quote the *Catechism of the Catholic Church*: "The Christian family is a communion of persons, a sign and image of the communion of the Father and the Son in the Holy Spirit" (*Catechism of the Catholic Church*, 2nd ed. [Vatican City: Libreria Editrice Vaticana, 1997; Washington, D.C.: United States Catholic Conference, 2000], no. 2205, cited in *Marriage: Love and Life in the Divine Plan*, 37). On the same page, the bishops also cite Thomas Aquinas' *Summa theologica*, I, q. 93, a. 3, trans. Fathers of the English Dominican Province (Westminster, Md.: Christian Classics, 1981), where Aquinas (in treating the image of God) describes "a certain imitation of God, consisting in the fact that man proceeds from man, as God from God."

9

What Does Hans Urs von Balthasar Mean by Drama?

Francesca Aran Murphy

One of Father Joseph Fessio's greatest achievements at Ignatius Press has been the translation and publication of most of Hans Urs von Balthasar's books. The publication in print of von Balthasar's trilogy and his minor books is one of the decisive events in Catholic theology over the past thirty-five years. If publishing them was heroic, then maintaining them in print is an epic achievement. Father Fessio must take a lion's share of the credit for it. When I was a young Ph.D. student and then a young professor, these books rolled off the presses and into my hands. Amongst the first writings I published were reviews of each of the volumes of the trilogy in the *Downside Review*, edited at that time by the Benedictine Blondel scholar Dom Iltyd Trethowan. The Jesuit and the Benedictine monk were responsible for the most formative experience in my intellectual life.

It is unfortunate that Ignatius Press had not yet begun to translate, collate, and publish von Balthasar's personal writings, such as his letters, while his original executor, Cornelia Capol, was still alive and representing his legacy. The decision of those who later came to control his papers to close the von Balthasar archive will render it impossible to clarify his motivations and intentions by reference to his own personal writings. They have overturned the express intentions of Cornelia Capol, and the damage to scholarly study of von Balthasar's writing is incalculable.

While von Balthasar was the rising star of the 1980s and 1990s, when his translated writings first appeared from Ignatius, there is now a great body of critical opposition to von Balthasar's theology. While the questions raised by von Balthasar's critics can only help us to clarify his intentions, the damage done by von Balthasar's current executors is irreparable. The criticism of his opponents will be fruitful in requiring von Balthasar's followers more carefully to examine and explain his project.

There are two kinds of criticism. On the one hand, there is criticism that objects, "why didn't you set out to achieve what *I*, and my tradition, would have done? Why didn't you write the book *I* would have written?" Such criticism can be wounding, if the author represents a commonly held perspective. But such external criticism is not likely to move anyone who recognizes that the author himself did not share the critics' aims. A much sharper kind of criticism is internal and shows that the work fails by its own criteria.

Ben Quash and, reiterating his case, Karen Kilby appear to propose such an internal critique of von Balthasar.[1] Von Balthasar's trilogy consists in a theological aesthetics, a theo-dramatics, and a theo-logic. Like that of Hegel, von Balthasar's notion of drama contrasts it with, on the one hand, all-seeing, super-objective epic and, on the other, introspective lyric. The objection of Quash and, in imitation, Kilby to von Balthasar is that he pretends to write "dramatically" about Christ and the Blessed Trinity while all the while making observations that could only be offered by an omniscient, epical observer. Von Balthasar purports to provide a "dramatic" vision of the Trinity while surreptitiously assuming an epical, all-seeing observation post.

Von Balthasar's lack of tentativeness renders itself offensive to these critics because it is not ordinary mortals or even walk-on characters like fauns or elves on which the author claims to give us an objective "lowdown" but the immanent Trinity itself. One feels that the Swiss theologian has been caught out red-handed: How could he know *at all* that the Father begets the Son in such a moment of wild abandon that it eternally creates the possibility of the Father "abandoning" the Son on the Cross, and "know" this while modestly claiming to a bit

---

[1] Ben Quash's *Theology and the Drama of History* (Cambridge: Cambridge University Press, 2005) antedated Kilby's work by nearly a decade and seems to contain it *in nuce*.

player in the divine *drama*?[2] The assumption is that, in order to take us behind the scenes into the eternal life of the immanent Trinity, von Balthasar could only be standing outside and above his characters, like Homer or Virgil in relation to their epical protagonists. It is felt to be gravely improper for the theologian, supposedly a mere drama critic, to teleport into the eternal interior life of the Trinity.

It could be countered that every renowned theologian has made what Quash and Kilby call "epical" observations about God and that it is impossible to write systematic theology without making objective generalizations about the eternal and transcendent Trinity. Such a repost, however, does not get at the criticism that the very effort to regard the eternal Trinity dramatically is undramatic. The Quash/ Kilby case is that von Balthasar claimed to offer us a "theo-dramatic" theology and then went on to pull back the curtain on the processions and the pathos of the Trinitarian mystery, seeming to know about God just as Homer knows all the backstory on Mount Olympus. Their objection is that von Balthasar assumes a 'God's-eye view" that he ought, as the proponent of theo-*dramatics*, to deny himself.[3] Who can summon sufficient world-weariness to imagine that these critics would prefer a deferential agnosticism about the Trinity to the impolite roaring of a rowdy Celtic poet? Few would dream of imagining that the internal objection belies external objections, such as much post-Kantian and transcendental Thomist thinking, like that of Karl Rahner, would make to von Balthasar's positive, enthusiastic use of colorfully "cataphatic" language about God and about the immanent Trinity.[4]

In von Balthasar's metaphor for theo-drama, God the Father is like the author of the "play" of world history, and in becoming man, God the Son sets out to incarnate and "perform" the intentions of the author. The Holy Spirit thus acts like a producer, inducing the incarnate Christ to say his lines, feeding the enfleshed Lord his cues and his directives. In von Balthasar's conception of drama, moreover, the

---

[2] Karen Kilby, *Balthasar: A (Very) Critical Introduction* (Grand Rapids, Mich.: Eerdmans, 2012), 99–102 and 111–14.

[3] Ibid., 13.

[4] D. C. Schindler rightly sees the central problem of Kilby's work as a misplaced demand for agnosticism: "A Very Critical Response to Karen Kilby: On Failing to See the Form", *Radical Orthodoxy: Theology, Philosophy, Politics*, vol. 3, no. 1 (September 2015), 68–87.

baptized Christian is both in the audience of the "theo-drama", the drama written and performed in history by God, and also, by virtue of baptism in Christ and the ensuing calling by Christ, a member of the cast.

One might ask why anyone would think that either the cast or the audience of a drama about God would be fairly much in the dark about the nature of God. Is it commonly the case that drama is a cloudier and more opaque medium than epic? Are we in the dark about what Euripides proposes about the nature of the gods in the *Bacchae* or what Aeschylus is telling us about divine justice, the Furies, and Athena in his trilogy about the house of Atreus? Are we more in the dark about what Euripides or Aeschylus say about the divine in these plays than we are about the gods in the *Iliad* or the *Odyssey*? Are the gods any less visible in these plays than in the great epics of antiquity? Or do they actually become enfleshed, on stage, before the audience, state their grave intentions with terrifying clarity, and then enact them? Is the soliloquizing of dramatic actors, that is, the long, self-interpreting speeches of Oedipus, Medea, Pentheus, or Dionysius (Denys) more ambiguous than the speeches of Zeus, Achilles, or Odysseus? Does drama, in distinction from epic, leave us in the dark about the play or its plot or its characters or its author's intentions? Why would the dramatic medium render these things, all of which are incarnated on stage, more and not less opaque to the audience or cast?

Drama critics, scholars, and specialists have expended rivers of ink in arguing about the meaning of both those plays and the ancient epics. Do they expend any more hot air over Aeschylus and Aristophanes than over Homer or Milton? Drama critics and scholars of the theatre argue over the meaning of *scripts*. For von Balthasar, the "theo-drama" is not a script. It is the actual history of salvation, as commencing with Adam and coming to a climax with the life, death, and Resurrection of Christ the Lord, incarnate God. A performed play, as opposed to a script, embodies and expresses the intentions of the author and producers.

Is it commonly the pleasure of theatregoers to undergo a "common feeling" or, in fancy language, a moment of "communion" as they collectively experience a single plot that crystallizes a single set of motivations, values, and ideas? Does the theatre audience share in witnessing the mystery of man embodied and made into a story on the stage? How could this moment of communion be possible if what was performed on stage were was not a mystery made flesh but, instead, something unspeakably ambivalent and mind-bogglingly indescribable?

There are a few cases of theorists who have proposed that drama is or ought to be unclear or that it would do well to leave its over-arching intention to the diverse guesswork of audiences. New Wave French cinema maintained that the *auteur* or director ought to leave the ending unresolved or "open", so that the cinema audience could "make of it as they will". Kilby is perhaps conditioned by European mid-twentieth-century art cinema when she praises von Balthasar for saying that we may *hope* that all will be saved but that such hope rules out *knowing* that they will all be saved from perdition.[5]

One can see why von Balthasar's contention that "we cannot know in advance what the stage will look like at the end of the play" would appeal to the canon of French New Wave cinema. But we have no reason to believe that von Balthasar's conception of drama was modeled on that canon. He never mentions François Truffaut or even Eric Rohmer. The unknowability of the final act, to which Jesus alludes when he says that no one except the Father knows when the "end" will be (Mt 24:36), is not only a matter of what the actors will make of themselves: it comes down to the too-generous abundance of "the great promise expressed by Isaiah, that God will create a new heaven and a new earth (65:17; 66:22; cf. Rev 21:1)".[6]

Kilby's notion of drama as the "ambiguous" genre is also reminiscent of the twentieth-century Russian literary critic Mikhail Bakhtin's claim that the novels of Dostoevsky are "dialogical", using their diverse characters continuously to present new perspectives and new ways of seeing the core of the drama.[7] The fact that all the characters in Dostoevsky, for example, express diverse opinions, and perhaps also the fact that this gave a bit of cover for studying Dostoevsky in Stalinist Russia, led Bakhtin to claim that truth in great literature is dialogical, ever varying, ever changing, and impossible to pin down.

---

[5] Kilby, *Balthasar*, 63–70.

[6] Hans Urs von Balthasar, *Theo-Drama: Theological Dramatic Theory*, vol. 2: *The Dramatis Personae: Man in God*, trans. Graham Harrison (San Francisco: Ignatius Press, 1990), 186.

[7] Mikhail Bakhtin, *Problems of Dostoevsky's Poetics*, trans. Caryl Emerson (Manchester: Manchester University Press, 1983), 17–18.

"Dialogical" sounds something like "dramatic", in that plays are constructed out of dialogue. There is a similarity between Bakhtin's claim that "Truth is not born nor is it to be found inside the head of an individual person, it is born *between people* collectively searching for truth, in the process of their dialogic interaction"[8] and von Balthasar's contextual, social, and ultimately ecclesial notion of truth. One problem, though, is that von Balthasar only mentions Bakhtin a few times, in passing, and gives no evidence of defining literature or drama in the way that is ascribed to the Russian theorist. There is no reason within his writings to think that he conceived of the "theo-drama" as a dialogical play of irreconcilable and incommensurable perspectives.

I am not sure how "postmodern" Bakhtin actually was; but in the heyday of postmodernism, the most cited lines in Bakhtin's Dostoevsky book describe truth as polyphonic, contrasting polyphony with a mere monologic "merger" of voices. So Bakhtin operates on two planes: either contrastive, distinct voices of polyphony or an impersonal "monologue":[9] he knows identity and equivocity. Von Balthasar, by contrast, speaks of a third possibility, which is analogy, or the symphonicity of truth. He compares the divine economy to a symphony of different instruments and applies the comparison (that is, analogy) to the Trinity itself: "In his revelation, God performs a symphony ... the [human] players ... are integrated. Not in unison, but what is far more beautiful—in sym-phony." It is God, the divine analogist, who integrates the symphony. "Even eternal Truth itself is symphonic."[10] For von Balthasar, drama is an epistemologically and metaphysically realistic "theo-genre", within which the truth about God and mankind are reflected.

Von Balthasar employs the term "drama" analogously. The term "drama" is normally used to categorize a type of literature. So it is a stretch, that is, a use of analogy, to speak of a human life or of human events, like the Battle of Britain, or of human history as a whole as a "drama". No one is *literally* on the stage, and no one literally plays a role before an audience. As used for non-theatrical circumstances,

[8] Ibid., 110.

[9] Ibid., 18 and 95.

[10] Hans Urs von Balthasar, *Truth Is Symphonic*, trans. Graham Harrison (San Francisco: Ignatius Press, 1987), 8–9 and 12.

drama is an analogous category. It is stretched even farther when one applies the term "drama" to God and to the divine economy, God's actions in history. That does not mean that when one speaks of drama "theologically", applying the term to God's salvific action, one is using the term "less literally" and more "spiritually". In a funny kind of way, one may be speaking both *less* literally (since "all the world" is actually not "a stage"), but also more literally. In "theo-drama", drama is not a literally literary genre, but, if one may be forgiven for speaking like this, a "theo-genre". Von Balthasar turns "drama" into an analogous "theo-genre" in order to use the analogue of drama to capture and reflect truth about God and humanity.

Von Balthasar sees the same problem that Bakhtin, living under Stalinist tyranny, acknowledges: the monologue that scythes everything in its pass into uniformity. For von Balthasar, such "mono-logics" are responsible for reducing everything, from stage plays to human life to God, to one single "mono-drama". What has gone wrong here is that the "difference between tragedy as play and the Christian Passion as seriousness is abolished: analogy, which is essential to a theory of theo-drama, is absorbed in identity."[11]

It is plausible to suggest that Bakhtin's notion of the "dialogical" is likewise intended to be analogical. Bakhtin most probably found the "dialogical" element in great nineteenth-century literature because he realized that human life itself increasingly involved a pluralistic and dialogical element.[12] With the emergence of a more introspective self-consciousness came the awareness of oneself as a historical being, living at one particular moment of history, played upon by one's ancestors and contemporaries. A greater historical consciousness, in turn, enabled people more deeply to acknowledge that fellows who lived in specific past eras of history had their own way of viewing life, which was not better or worse, but simply different from our own and characteristic of the era in question. Thus there arose an awareness of the "perspectival" quality of truth, that it can be seen from many different angles and positions, depending on when one lives, on one's status, one's sex, class, and so forth. When Bakhtin

---

[11] Hans Urs von Balthasar, *Theo-Drama: Theological Dramatic Theory*, vol. 1, *Prolegomena: Man*, trans. Graham Harrison (San Francisco: Ignatius Press, 1989), 67.

[12] On the self-consciousness of Dostoevsky's characters, see Bakhtin, *Poetics*, 47–49.

calls Dostoevsky's novels "dialogical", he is commending them for capturing the new awareness of human life itself as dialogical, perspectival, and contextualized.

This awareness of the multi-aspectual nature of our perception of truth belongs to the modern self. Moderns are more self-conscious and aware of their own subjectivity. This awareness is a *gain*, but it carries with it the danger of loss, that is, the danger of losing the recognition of truth as real and objective. Von Balthasar's notion of "drama" is partly intended to assimilate what is valuable and enduring in the "dialogical" without losing objectivity and truth. The theo-dramatic hermeneutic recognizes the perspectival quality of human knowledge and sees contextualization, not as a barrier to the recognition of truth and reality, but as our only means to reality and truth. Von Balthasar uses the "theo-genre" of "drama" as an analogical way of gathering together and perceiving truth about the divine economy, about humanity within that economy, and about the eternal Trinity as truly and authentically made known to us in and through the economy. For von Balthasar, the economy is a dramatic analogue of the theology, that is, a historical reflection of the eternal Trinity.

But does that compel him to write about the Trinity with such drunken, cataphatic abandon? Does it require him to propose that the Father and the Son experience "surprise" when they breathe the Holy Spirit,[13] like spouses are surprised to discover that their love has conceived a novel third party? Does it put him under marching orders to develop a whole line in gross, exaggerated metaphors of abandonment between Father and Son, from the begetting to the cry of forsakenness on the Cross? Appearing at a time when a dominant theology constantly returns to the act of apophasis within theological speech, von Balthasar's impolitely concrete language about God, his continuous linguistic projection of Chagallian wedding scenes into the immanent Trinity, was bound to be taken amiss. It is this childish, "Chagall-type", illustrative language about God that perhaps is the real sore point when von Balthasar is accused of espousing an epical, hyper-omniscient perspective from which he can view the nuptial

---

[13] Hans Urs von Balthasar, *Theo-Logic*, vol. 3, *The Spirit of Truth*, trans. Graham Harrison (San Francisco: Ignatius Press, 2005), 237 and 243.

dance of the blessed Trinity. *"Language!"*, as people say when someone refers to his bodily functions.

It is an important concern of many modern Catholic philosophers,
such as David Burrell, an admirer of Kilby's work on von Balthasar,
to require that what a writer "says about God" be apostrophized, or,
as we say in English, put into inverted commas. So as to ward off the
impression that when we speak about God we are intending a super-
massive entity within the range of human experience and cognition,
like the "sky-fairy" of neo-atheist mockery, such thinkers make it a
methodological rule that positive, affirmative language about God be
consistently negated. Because we cannot fully gauge the range of our
intentions when we speak about God, negation must be an elemental
moment of our language for God, taking away even what is offered
"negatively". It is not that all our language for God is negative, or
apophatic, but rather that it is a grammatical requirement or a "rule"
of a language for God that it be consistently undermined, under-
erasure, or negated. The "rule" that we must follow, in speaking of
God, is negation. This notion of a grammatical rule for speaking
about God is widespread. Kilby elsewhere applies it to the theology
of Karl Rahner and of Thomas Aquinas.

It is surprising, then, that one does not explore the possibility that,
just as much modernized, post-Kantian Thomism makes it a *grammatical*, formal rule to speak about God negatively or apophatically,
so, perhaps, von Balthasar, likewise, is making a cataphatical but no
less *grammatical* move in the theological game when he makes his
colorful assertions about the immanent Trinity and its begettings, sir-
ings, and breathings.[14] Perhaps the Swiss theologian is not so much
assuming an epical vantage point on the operations and processions
of the Trinity as making a grammatical, or at least *strategic*, point. Von
Balthasar is using cataphatic language strategically.

The strategic purpose (end) and principle (formal cause) of von
Balthasar's use of extreme cataphatic language is to bind together the
medium and the message of his theology. The point of his advertent
use of cataphatic language is to pick out the most robustly dramatic
way of speaking about God. It is startling to hear God spoken of in
this way, startling and unsettling. This use of overly concrete speech

---

[14] The suggestion that von Balthasar's use of positive language about God is grammatical
was put to me by University of Notre Dame graduate student Timothy Troutner.

about God dramatizes the first principle of von Balthasar's theology, that the Trinity makes its entrance and by so doing makes itself known to us. Apophatic language is politely and discreetly conscious that it is an ascendant, philosophical lingo for God, which only stretches so far. Cataphatic language is a "descendant" vernacular, made possible by the Word's coming down from the Father and dwelling among us. Von Balthasar's drastic use of concrete speech about the transcendent Trinity is a methodological means of indicating that the Triune God is known through his self-illumination and that the kenotic self-revelation of the Incarnation is abundant and generous, reckless in its self-abandonment.

Drama, or theatre, is the most "incarnational" of the artistic genres: one sees the characters and the story "take flesh" before one's eyes, as the actors tread the boards before us. A poetically cataphatic use of language about God is a means of making the medium of the "theo-genre" adequate to the message of theo-drama. In the theatre, neither actors nor audience have any "overview" of the play. But both actors and audience can quite literally see what is going on. We do not make a mental image of the proceedings, like the readers of an epic novel, or look at a sequence of photographs of the actors, like a cinema audience. Rather, we contemplate the performance itself. Von Balthasar's use of blunt, literal language is thus strategically dramatic.

We all know how "cultured" von Balthasar was, and it seems most plausible that his critics have erred by assuming his notion of "drama" has a much more sophisticated and less ordinary and populist basis than it actually does. In conclusion, I will compare von Balthasar's notion of drama with that offered by the philosopher Maurice Blondel, in his little book about the Oberammergau Passion Play. Performed every ten years since 1634, the Oberammergau Play is a living version of the medieval mystery plays. It is a group, amateur endeavor, put on by the inhabitants of one village in Upper Bavaria. Like the medieval mystery plays, it is a pious and simple attempt to stage the life of Christ. This devotional work brings us much closer to von Balthasar's own idea of drama than French New Wave cinema or the writings of Bakhtin. Blondel attended the performance in 1890 and again in 1900. His book about it appeared in 1910.

When he published the book, the modernist crisis had yet to run its course, and Blondel recognizes that the staging of this play has quite a lot to teach modern biblical critics about how Jesus Christ "would have" comported himself. So much of the modern urge to separate the Jesus of history from the Christ of faith is, as Blondel notes, predicated on guesswork about what the "real" Jesus "would have" done: but the highbrow "hypothesizers" seldom imagine his life in the concrete, scene by scene. But that is just what the Bavarian peasants at Oberammergau set out to accomplish. Blondel thus claims that "it is a form of metaphysical and psychological experimentation that is given to us at Oberammergau, in the vulgarizing lens of popular theatre."[15]

Von Balthasar refers to this booklet several times. But my use of the comparison is not intended to demonstrate the literary dependence of the Swiss author on this text. Although von Balthasar shows signs of a thorough study of Blondel, referring for instance to his letters to Laberthonnière, still, the weight of the evidence currently indicates that Blondel's phenomenological metaphysics was largely mediated to the Swiss author through his Jesuit mentor Henri de Lubac.

The comparison between Blondel's booklet on Oberammergau and von Balthasar's *Theo-Drama* seems apposite here because Blondel is answering similar objections to those laid by the critics at von Balthasar's door. For centuries, the peasant-actors at Oberammergau have been interrogated by clerics and by intellectuals about whether it is seemly or possible to represent the Passion of Christ on stage. How can the historical record of Christ be subjected to the rules of artistic taste without one or the other giving way?

The Oberammergau tradition began in 1633, when, threatened by approaching plague, the villages solemnly vowed to perform the Passion every ten years, if only they could be spared the killer disease. The tradition comes down to a solemn vow that dedicated the village to become an acting troupe that performed only one play, the Gospel. Blondel claims that,

> the fiction becomes a reality, since the actors seek to participate substantially in what they represent; since, obedient to a vow, they desire, in performing, to work as Christians; since, before they play and in order to play, they fall on their knees, they pray, they commune in Christ; since they literally want to manifest his permanent life and his real presence through the ages. According to the meaning one

---

[15] Maurice Blondel, *La Psychologie dramatique du mystère à Oberammergau* (Paris: Bloud, 1910), 6, my translation.

gives the word, they are thus more and less "actors" than anyone else; and they do so in order to serve us as mediators and interpreters, like a kind of priesthood. They grow up from childhood with a feeling for the "ministry" they must one day fulfill. Through a prolonged novitiate, through a constant meditation, through the legacy of a tradition that has accumulated all the experiences of the past, they are so intimately penetrated with the reality of the life they incarnate that it resurrects in them: to the point that they themselves no longer appear, that they are moved to manifest the sincerity of their personage; whence an excellent naturalness and spoken simplicity that no artifice can succeed in equaling. This brings about the invention of more little details so that one can find in each expression and in each attitude an unprompted charm and an original emotion.[16]

Blondel compares the Oberammergau actors to a priesthood, because their vocation as actors is, like the clerical vocation, bound up with representation. Von Balthasar speaks of a kind of competitive rivalry between the clerical and the acting professions:[17] this kind of rivalry is typical of groups that share, and fight over, the same territory.

Like a priest, an actor is a representative, that is, an analogue, because he mediates between the ideal, or some kind of transcendence, and the reality of this world, in which the audience is mired.[18] The actor is interesting, because his *acting* raises questions about the ultimate point of acting and of playing a role. Everyday life forces roles upon all of us; to be human is to play roles. The audience sees this reality self-consciously reenacted by the actor. All theatre is thus in part *about* role play and what the exigence of *acting* says about the inability of human lives to find fulfillment in any acting project they create for themselves. Acting is a human exigence, a requirement of being human, and it is fundamentally unsatisfying: but its unsatisfying quality orients it to transcendence, toward the ideal that it cannot attain on its own terms. One might imagine that this conception of human life and, analogically, of the stage could be regarded as methodologically self-reflexive.

Form is to art what the role is to acting. Both "form" and "role" are kinds of representation, or "analogues". The difficulty of human life is that one cannot simply "represent" oneself. One cannot give one's

[16] Ibid., 40–41.
[17] Von Balthasar, *Theo-Drama*, 1:93.
[18] Ibid., 261.

own life form, because one cannot stand outside oneself and "see" what would integrate this self-consciousness. The more deeply one is aware of one's self-consciousness, the less one knows oneself. And without knowing one's own truth, one cannot give one's life an aesthetic form or find one's right and fitting dramatic role. Von Balthasar asks whether "theatre [does not always] presuppose the dichotomy between a life that cannot satisfy itself and its own self-realization."[19] The actor in his role reminds us of the human condition, in which one is repeatedly *self*-commandeered into roles that do not fit. The sense of absence or dissatisfaction at the heart of human acting and role play points us, negatively, toward the "ideal" situation for an actor, where he is *given* his role and achieves his vocation and becomes the unique individual that he is precisely by acting under direction from another. The way Blondel, in *Action*, and von Balthasar, in the *Theo-Drama*, describe the experienced lack of the grace to be ourselves is not entirely at odds with what Rahnerians dub the supernatural existential, the existential orientation to the supernatural.

But again, reflexively, this absence only becomes clear to us when, through the analogy of the ritual "Christ-actor", we see what it could be like to be a person who actually fulfills his role. As Blondel puts it in his booklet on the Oberammergau Passion, "In this consists the unique beauty of such a role: a role, yes, Christ, without exceeding the human and without debasing the divine, is indeed here, in a more profound sense than the ancients meant it, *personae*."[20] The source of the "role" analogy is in God, that is, in God's creating a world analogous to himself and in God acting out, in the economy, an analogue to the eternal life of the Trinity.

One final way of explaining such terms as "analogue", "form", "role", "representation", or "mediation" is that of the "concrete universal". Blondel answers the objection that a real, artistic play cannot be made of the materials of the Passion by arguing to the contrary that every universal human destiny and the providential designs for one unique person are united in the Passion of Christ:

What is the ground of all drama? It is a destiny that decides itself, through the conflict of passions, in the grandeur of heroic or bloody

[19] Ibid., 79.
[20] Blondel, *Oberammergau*, 38.

events that are the occasion or effect of sentiments capable of filling the human heart to the breaking point. And isn't what we find here just the problem of an individual destiny—it is not a matter of either the lot of a people or a race. It is not some particular or passing passions that are at stake; it is all the passions that secretly coalesce or strike against one another in a mystery of hatred and of love. Love!... [I]f one allows oneself to borrow pagan language from Plato to recall that above earthly Love, whose ardor can only be conquered by death, there is the light of heavenly love that is generated for immortality, one cannot fail to see that the *Passion*, which has the power to germinate and give birth to the idea that humanity is regenerated at the price of divine blood, might prove more gripping to spirits than a novelistic adventure. Human passion is egoistic or, at least, singular; one can only interest oneself in the hypothesis through sympathy; the divine Passion is, by definition, so universal that it really penetrates each one of us, and the drama is completely directed to the heart of all.... Where would one find the more perfect art, more confirmed to its essential idea, more revelatory, more strengthening, than the representation of the Passion? Everywhere else, poetry and history do not coincide with each other and therefore do not coincide with us; whence the apparent opposition of drama and of reality; but here, we are suddenly face to face with the ultimate ground of humanity.... And from this point of view, it is our ordinary life, with its subjections and passions, that repairs to the distance of inferior regions, like something superficial and inconsistent. The Passion, which is at once the supreme Drama and our drama to us; it is entirely something of universal truth and something of ineffable intimacy and singularity. Understood at its root, art is thus the expression of the problem to which the religious life alone offers a solution; here because it is bound to cult, prepares the cult, follows the cult. And, at the extreme limit, the most sacred mystery of Christianity is, at the same time, the perfection of dramatic beauty. Thus, taken in itself by philosophy, the object that is presented to us in the spectacle of Oberammergau responds with an incomparable precision to the demands of art, without losing its supernatural character. The apparent conflict of aesthetic rules and of Christian propriety is only an artificial difficulty, born of an imperfect conception of art and of life, and it is necessary to repeat to fearful or dry souls, the Passion is truly a drama, the supreme Drama, the Act in which the demands of historical reality and esthetic ideals coincide with moral and religious truth.[21]

[21] Ibid., 25–27.

The conclusion to which we are drawn is twofold. On the one hand, the criticism of Kilby and Quash is not really "internal". Their complaint is that von Balthasar does not stay within a post-Kantian methodological self-limitation to his inquiry into what formal categories underpin theological speech. But he has never, by dint of using the "theo-genre" of drama, bound himself to restricting theology to an explanation of the possibility of its own conceptual tools. Instead, his project is founded on the notions of form, role, representation, mediation, that is, on analogizing. His project is founded on a four-fold analogy: God's self-analogizing in creation and in revelation and human analogizing in its re-creation of itself in everyday life and in its self-revelation in theatre. On the other hand, the self-reflection necessary to inquire into what categories underpin theological speech does not operate unless there is a sort of disproportionate analogy between what the human person is, in existential "reality", what the human person wants to be (that is, in Christ), and what Christ wants for the human person, that is, for the human person to share in his role and "persona". The methodological, self-reflexive project only works within the project of theo-dramatic analogy founded in Christ. Von Balthasar claims that

> the drama of Christ is bound to make a universal, catholic claim; and it does this by imparting something of its own catholic and concrete universality to the individual human destiny.... Within the drama of Christ, every human fate is deprivatized so that its personal range may extend to the whole universe, depending on how far it is prepared to cooperate in being inserted into the normative drama of Christ's life, death and Resurrection. Not only does this gather the unimaginable plurality of human destinies into a concrete, universal point of unity; it actually maintains their plurality within the unity, but as a function of this unity.[22]

Unless Christ is indeed "the living framework within which every human destiny is acted out",[23] then reflecting on the conditions of the possibility of our efforts to know and name God is an empty exercise.

[22] Von Balthasar, *Theo-Drama*, 2:50.
[23] Ibid., 87.

10

The Theological Mind and Method of Pope Benedict XVI as Revealed in His Catechetical Instructions

Matthew J. Ramage

Introduction: The Way of Beauty and the School of the Saints

Throughout his career and especially in his catecheses as pope, Joseph Ratzinger/Benedict XVI has time and again made it a point to recall that "the *via pulchritudinis*, the way of beauty, is a privileged and fascinating path on which to approach the Mystery of God."[1] The emeritus pontiff's catechetical reflections concern beauty as presented in all its modes. Particularly dear to Benedict's heart is that form of beauty experienced through *actuosa participatio* in the liturgy, fostered above all by the *ars celebrandi*, the proper celebration of the rite itself.[2]

---

[1] Benedict XVI, General Audience: The Cathedral from the Romanesque to the Gothic Architecture: The Theological Background (November 18, 2009). Other formulations of Ratzinger's leading apologetics principle are found in his General Audience on Art and Prayer (August 31, 2011); *The Feast of Faith: Approaches to a Theology of the Liturgy*, trans. Graham Harrison (San Francisco: Ignatius Press, 1986), 124; *The Ratzinger Report: An Exclusive Interview on the State of the Church*, with Vittorio Messori, trans. Salvator Attanasio and Graham Harrison (San Francisco: Ignatius Press, 1985), 129–30; *Principles of Catholic Theology: Building Stones for a Fundamental Theology*, trans. Sister Mary Frances McCarthy, S.N.D. (San Francisco: Ignatius Press, 1987), 373; *Truth and Tolerance: Christian Beliefs and World Religions*, trans. Henry Taylor (San Francisco: Ignatius Press, 2005), 226; Meeting with the clergy of the Diocese of Bolzano-Bressanone (August 6, 2008).

[2] Benedict XVI, Post-Synodal Apostolic Exhortation *Sacramentum caritatis* on the Eucharist as the Source and Summit of the Church's Life and Mission (February 22, 2007), 38. Although we will see below that Benedict touches upon liturgy in his catecheses, a fuller view of his thought on beauty in relation to the liturgy can be found in his *The Spirit of the Liturgy*, trans. John Saward (San Francisco: Ignatius Press, 2000) and *Feast of Faith*.

Moreover, the beauty of creation and the arts of painting, iconography, architecture, sculpture, music, film, and literature are all highways to God in Benedict's view. The reason for this perspective, he argues, is that beauty speaks a universal language that is uniquely capable of reaching individuals who initially may not be open to hearing the Gospel proclaimed directly. The arts play a critical role in fostering a "pedagogy of desire", for they teach believers and unbelievers alike to seek that which is above and "to ... rediscover the taste of the authentic joy of life". Further, they inoculate us from spiritual disease, "producing antibodies that can fight the trivialization and the dulling widespread today".[3]

Yet in the emeritus pontiff's view, it is another reality paired with beauty that ultimately proves the most compelling testimony to the truth of the Gospel: "I have often affirmed my conviction that the true apology of Christian faith, the most convincing demonstration of its truth ..., are the saints, and the beauty that the faith has generated."[4] He expands upon this assertion with respect to the saints: "[T]he beauty of Christian life is even more effective than art and imagery in the communication of the Gospel Message. In the end, love alone is worthy of faith and proves credible. The lives of the Saints and Martyrs demonstrate a singular beauty which fascinates and attracts, because a Christian life lived in fullness speaks without words."[5] It is precisely in light of the above conviction that we grasp the rationale of Pope Benedict's extensive, multi-year project of using his General Audiences to tell the story of the Catholic Church through the lives of her saints. Through his pontificate, Benedict made it his central concern to manifest the truth of Catholic faith in the context of today's world, and, in his view, there is no better way to achieve this than by sitting at the "school" of those who lived "the experiment of faith".[6]

---

[3] Benedict XVI, General Audience: The Desire for God (November 7, 2012).

[4] Joseph Ratzinger, Message to the Communion and Liberation Meeting at Rimini, "The Feeling of Things, the Contemplation of Beauty" (August 24, 2002).

[5] Benedict XVI, Address to Participants in the Plenary Assembly of the Pontifical Council for Culture (November 13, 2010).

[6] For the expression "school of the saints", see Benedict's catechetical addresses on June 23, 2010; March 23, 2011; April 6, 2011. The expression "experiment of faith" is taken from Joseph Ratzinger, "Why I Am Still in the Church", in Fundamental Speeches from Five Decades, ed. Florian Schuller, trans. Michael J. Miller et al. (San Francisco: Ignatius Press, 2012), 132–53, at 151.

Benedict XVI's General Audience addresses, published in seven volumes by Ignatius Press, unfortunately have received very little attention from academic theologians, yet I am convinced that they rival in importance the catecheses on marriage from his predecessor John Paul II.[7] Because these important texts risk being forgotten by the Church, and in honor of Father Joseph Fessio for bringing them into such easy availability in English, in this chapter I will reflect synthetically on Benedict's catechetical corpus, meditating upon his five volumes of catecheses on the saints as well as on those that concern the closely associated subjects of prayer and of faith, respectively. My aim is to bring into view as well as possible a certain vision of the whole: the purpose of the catecheses, some important theological themes that unfold throughout, and the distinct method Benedict characteristically employs to achieve his end. The constraints of writing only a chapter on this topic require that I focus on a limited number of themes. Accordingly, after a thorough perusal of Benedict's corpus of catecheses, the following have been selected because of their centrality to his thought: encountering and experiencing beauty in art, prayer, and the medieval cathedral; faith as a gift and the virtues needed to experience it; the humility needed to ask the tough questions and let ourselves be "called into question"; and, finally, Benedict's understanding of the "school of faith" in Christ as a progressive exodus, struggle, and "gamble". I will conclude the chapter by returning to its point of departure, adding an important nuance concerning what particular type of saint is in Benedict's view especially suited as an *apologia* for the truth of the Catholic faith.

An Overview of the Method and Scope of Benedict's Catechetical Series

Before diving in, a few more preliminary observations will help the reader to understand better the logic that undergirds Benedict's catecheses. First, I find it especially revealing that Benedict applies the

---

[7] For an excellent overview and analysis of Benedict's catecheses on the saints (and, as far as I can tell, the only other extended academic treatment of them in English to date), see Christopher Shannon and Christopher Blum, *The Past as Pilgrimage: Narrative, Tradition, and the Renewal of Catholic History* (Front Royal, Va.: Christendom Press, 2014), chap. 4.

same method in his catecheses that we have found him employing
time and again throughout his career in the domain of biblical exegesis: he always begins by grounding given authors, texts, or subjects
in their historical context; throughout his presentation he then seeks
to elucidate the kernel, the core truths that emerge from the historical enquiry; finally, he pauses at key moments throughout the
work—especially at the end—to ask how the topic in question is
relevant to the life of the Church today. By doing this in such a
consistent and systematic fashion over a span of several years, Benedict makes it clear that he wished to provide a model for Christians
in our approach to the Bible, to Church history, and to life in the
Spirit. This model method will emerge again and again throughout
the present essay, whose organizational principle will be thematic
as I attempt to tease out some of Benedict's overarching concerns
throughout his catechetical enterprise.[8]

Finally, with regard to the themes treated in Benedict's catecheses,
a few words regarding their scope may help the reader to ascertain
Benedict's catechetical points of emphasis throughout his pontificate.
Generally one to two thousand words in length, the Wednesday
addresses presented at the Vatican by the emeritus pontiff fall into
several series. After his election, from May 2005 to February 2006, he
simply continued the reflections on the Psalms and Vespers canticles
prepared by his predecessor.[9] Benedict's first series of original works
then began in March 2006 and continued to February 2007 for a total
of thirty-one lessons on the mystery of Christ and the Church reflected
in the experience of the apostles.[10] In March 2007, he immediately
transitioned from figures of the New Testament to the Apostolic
Fathers, the first and second generations of the Church subsequent
to the apostles. He continued to reflect upon the Church Fathers
through June 2008, temporarily interrupting his historical thread with
a cycle of twenty lectures on Saint Paul in commemoration of the

---

[8] For treatments of Benedict's model method such as he applies it in biblical exegesis, see
Matthew J. Ramage, *Dark Passages of the Bible: Engaging Scripture with Benedict XVI and Thomas
Aquinas* (Washington, D.C.: Catholic University of America Press, 2013), and, more recently,
Matthew J. Ramage: *Jesus, Interpreted: Benedict XVI, Bart Ehrman, and the Historical Truth of the
Gospels* (Washington, D.C.: Catholic University of America Press, 2017), especially chap. 3.

[9] Benedict XVI, General Audience (April 27, 2005).

[10] These audiences are collectively published by Ignatius in the volume entitled *Jesus, the
Apostles, and the Early Church* (San Francisco: Ignatius Press, 2007).

Pauline Year.[11] Resuming his series on the Fathers in February 2009, Benedict extended it to include notable teachers and women of the medieval period and beyond. After an additional seven audiences on exemplary priests in observance of the Year for Priests, by April 2011 Benedict had gifted the Church with another seventy-eight catecheses subsequently published by Ignatius.[12] In May 2011 Benedict departed from his chronological trajectory, focusing until October 2012 on a specific theme that had emerged throughout his reflections over the years: Christian prayer.[13] Finally, beginning in October 2012, Benedict developed a series of catecheses for the Year of Faith, only to interrupt his efforts by resigning in February 2013.[14]

Encountering and Experiencing Beauty: Art, Prayer, and the Medieval Cathedral

Given its central place in Benedict's thought as discussed in the introduction above, it is appropriate that we begin with the theme of encountering and experiencing beauty, which recurs throughout the emeritus pontiff's catechetical corpus. Two of Benedict's catechetical addresses in particular focus on the subject of the *via pulchritudinis*, or "way of beauty". The first is a 2009 reflection on the cathedral, described by Benedict as "the true glory of the Christian Middle Ages".[15] In characteristic fashion, the author begins by discussing the

[11] The first cycle of catecheses on the Fathers is published in Benedict XVI, *Church Fathers: From Clement of Rome to Augustine* (San Francisco: Ignatius Press, 2008). The Pauline Year texts are found in Benedict XVI, *St. Paul* (San Francisco: Ignatius Press, 2009).

[12] Excepting the seven catecheses for the Year of Priests, these audiences are contained in Benedict XVI, *Church Fathers and Teachers: From Saint Leo the Great to Peter Lombard* (San Francisco: Ignatius Press, 2010), and Benedict XVI, *Holy Men and Women of the Middle Ages and Beyond* (San Francisco: Ignatius Press, 2012).

[13] Benedict XVI, *A School of Prayer: The Saints Show Us How to Pray* (San Francisco: Ignatius Press, 2012).

[14] Benedict's final series of papal audiences, along with an appendix containing his final General Audience as pope, are collected in the volume *The Transforming Power of Faith* (San Francisco: Ignatius Press, 2013).

[15] Benedict XVI, General Audience: The Cathedral from the Romanesque to the Gothic Architecture: The Theological Background (November 18, 2009). As the author himself mentions in the catechesis, he delivered it just three days before his Meeting with Artists, which included an address that develops many of the same points. For a discussion of the Meeting with Artists and Benedict's understanding of beauty as a whole, see Matthew J. Ramage, "Pope Benedict XVI's Theology of Beauty and the New Evangelization", *Homiletic and Pastoral Review* (January 2015).

historical background to the medieval cathedral. He surveys various factors that contributed to the rebirth of religious architecture, concluding that it was "mainly thanks to the enthusiasm and spiritual zeal of monasticism ... that abbey churches were built in which the Liturgy might be celebrated with dignity and solemnity."[16] Romanesque cathedrals and churches came into being in this way, while in the twelfth and thirteenth centuries another kind of architecture spread from the north of France: the Gothic. Benedict here turns from his historical contextualization to the core message that he wants to convey by means of his meditation on the cathedral:

> [Gothic sacred architecture] had two new characteristics in comparison with the Romanesque, a soaring upward movement and luminosity. Gothic cathedrals show a synthesis of faith and art harmoniously expressed in the fascinating universal language of beauty which still elicits wonder today. By the introduction of vaults with pointed arches supported by robust pillars, it was possible to increase their height considerably. The upward thrust was intended as an invitation to prayer and at the same time was itself a prayer. Thus the Gothic cathedral intended to express in its architectural lines the soul's longing for God.[17]

The Gothic cathedral was no mere building, not even just a sacred building. It evinced a unique synthesis of faith and reason in the form of man's art, whose dialect is the universal language of beauty. The cathedral's very structure could almost be described as sacramental in the sense that its soaring upward movement and luminosity were intended to signify and elicit wonder, prayer, and longing for God. Indeed, Benedict says that the building's upward thrust is itself a prayer.

After discussing the soaring vaults, arches, and pillars characteristic of the medieval cathedral, Benedict next considers the equal significance of their stained-glass windows and sculptures. For its part, Gothic sculpture turned cathedrals into "stone Bibles", depicting Gospel episodes and making present the entire liturgical year in visible form. Moreover, by employing new technical solutions, Gothic

---

[16] Benedict XVI, General Audience: Cathedral from the Romanesque.
[17] Ibid.

architecture made it possible to create openings in the structure's outer walls and to embellish them with stained-glass windows. Scene by scene, they recounted biblical events, Gospel parables, and lives of saints. Citing the great artist Marc Chagall, Benedict reminds us that artists who produced such works "dipped their brushes into that colorful alphabet which is the Bible".[18] However, the end game of these artists and the Church who commissioned them was not just to recount history: "A cascade of light poured through the stained-glass upon the faithful to tell them the story of salvation *and to involve them in this story.*"[19]

Here we arrive at the third movement typical of Benedict's catechetical symphonies. The purpose of his catecheses is not just to teach history or even theology but, moreover, to move the soul to greater lived participation in the mystery of Christ. The faithful of centuries past—and we today no less—became involved in the story of salvation through an encounter with the cathedral's beauty. As he said above with respect to the upward thrust of its architecture, for Benedict, the cathedral is an invitation to prayer, to wonder, to union with God. But as the Holy Father explained on the occasion of his visit to New York City in 2008, the beauty of God's proposal to the soul can ultimately be grasped only from the inside of the building. Celebrating Mass in Saint Patrick's Cathedral, Benedict delivered a homily similar to the catechesis we are considering in which the pontiff reflected upon the cathedral as an allegory of faith and the search for truth. Like any Gothic cathedral, he explained, from the outside Saint Patrick's windows appear dark and heavy, even dreary. But upon entering the Church, these same windows suddenly come alive with the resplendent light that passes through their stained glass. The allegory is clear: "It is only from the inside, from the experience of faith and ecclesial life, that we see the Church as she truly is: flooded with grace, resplendent in beauty, adorned by the manifold gifts of the Spirit."[20]

A second catechesis that captures the theme of the *via pulchritudinis* and the power of beauty to convert is Benedict's 2011 address on art

---

[18] Ibid.
[19] Ibid. (emphasis added).
[20] Benedict XVI, Homily: Votive Mass for the Universal Church (April 19, 2008).

in relation to prayer. Reminiscent of his description of the Gothic cathedral's soaring upward structure, Benedict writes of aesthetic works broadly speaking: "Art is able to manifest and make visible the human need to surpass the visible, it expresses the thirst and the quest for the infinite. Indeed it resembles a door open on to the infinite, on to a beauty and a truth that go beyond the daily routine. And a work of art can open the eyes of the mind and of the heart, impelling us upward."[21] While art as such has the capacity to draw man out of himself and lift his eyes to the eternal, the emeritus pontiff quickly adds, "However some artistic expressions are real highways to God, the supreme Beauty; indeed, they help us to grow in our relationship with him, in prayer."[22] He recalls in this connection the Gothic cathedral and Romanesque church, while adding a deeply personal anecdote to illustrate the compelling role sacred music has played in his own faith life:

> I remember a concert of music by Johann Sebastian Bach in Munich, conducted by Leonard Bernstein. At the end of the last passage, one of the *Cantatas*, I felt, not by reasoning but in the depths of my heart, that what I had heard had communicated truth to me, the truth of the supreme composer, and impelled me to thank God. The Lutheran bishop of Munich was next to me and I said to him spontaneously: "In hearing this one understands: it is true; such strong faith is true, as well as the beauty that irresistibly expresses the presence of God's truth."[23]

I can think of no better illustration from Benedict's corpus of his persuasion that the greatest *apologia* for the Church is the beauty and saints she has produced. Through beauty, the Lord speaks to the soul in a most profound, intimate way that is by no means irrational yet nevertheless transcends logical explanation. In taking the time to pause and contemplate the reality expressed by the beautiful things of this world, we discover "moments of grace, incentives to strengthen our bond and our dialogue with the Lord". In this encounter, the

---

[21] Benedict XVI, General Audience: Art and Prayer.

[22] Ibid.

[23] Ibid. Then–Cardinal Ratzinger also recounted this experience in a particularly revealing lecture delivered to members of the Communion and Liberation movement. The address is entitled "The Feeling of Things, the Contemplation of Beauty" (August 24, 2002).

arrow of beauty "wounds" us, as it were, making us yearn for the transcendent and giving us wings that we might rise toward God.[24]

It is worth noting that we find this same theme of aesthetic experience as religious apology in Benedict's final interview book with Peter Seewald. Though not a catechetical work, it is telling that this "last testament" should reveal the line of thinking present even after the Lord called the emeritus pontiff to "scale the mountain" and await the Lord's coming in prayer and meditation.[25] Asked if there was ever a time in his life when he wondered whether or not everything we believe about God might turn out to be wrong, Benedict frankly replied: "The question 'is it really proven?' comes to one again and again. But then I've had so many concrete experiences of faith, experiences of the presence of God, that I am ready for these moments and they cannot crush me."[26] The emeritus pontiff does not mention here the specific experiences he has in mind, but in light of Benedict's whole corpus they doubtlessly include aesthetic experiences of beauty such as that of the Bach concert narrated above. In any event, it is fascinating that Benedict admits to never having had a crisis of faith but rather of having "always been held firm. Thanks be to God" precisely because of so many "experiences of faith".[27] The theologian par excellence of our day, Ratzinger/Benedict understood that a robust rational defense of the Catholic faith was necessary. At the same time, he also knew that the proof of the faith transcends any reasoned account of its veracity; it must be found elsewhere through living "the experiment of faith".[28]

---

[24] Benedict XVI, General Audience: Art and Prayer. The same language of "wounding" drawn from Plato is echoed in Ratzinger, "Feeling of Things".

[25] For a reflection on his retirement as "scaling the mountain", see Benedict XVI, Angelus (February 24, 2013).

[26] Benedict XVI and Peter Seewald, *Last Testament: In His Own Words*, trans. Jacob Phillips (London: Bloomsbury, 2016), 207.

[27] Ibid.

[28] Joseph Ratzinger, "Why I Am Still in the Church" in *Fundamental Speeches*, 132–53, at 151. While not reflected upon systematically as in the above two catecheses, we find Benedict's concern for beauty as an apologetic already in his first catechetical series as in his address on the apostle Matthew. Here Benedict weaves together seamlessly biblical, patristic, and modern exegetical approaches to the apostle, yet he also invites his audience to ponder the scene of Matthew's calling in light of Caravaggio's famous canvas found in Rome's San Luigi dei Francesi church. Relating the lesson learned by Matthew to Christian living today, the emeritus pontiff concludes, "The application to the present day is easy to see: it is not

Faith as a Gift and the Virtues Needed to Experience It

The emeritus pontiff's emphatic insistence upon the connection between a rational defense of the faith and the transforming experience of beauty discussed above provides a fitting segue into our next major theme: Benedict's repeated teaching on the centrality of seeing faith as a grace from the Lord whose experience requires specific inner dispositions. Preliminary to exploring how this theme unfolds in his catecheses, it is instructive once again to note its most recent articulation in *Last Testament*, his final interview book. Asked how one deals with problems of faith, Benedict replied:

> Primarily by the fact that I do not let go of the foundational certainty of faith, because I stand in it, so to speak, but also because I know if I do not understand something that doesn't mean that it is wrong, but that I am too small for it. With many things it has been like this: I gradually grew to see it this way. More and more it is a gift; you suddenly see something which was not perceptible before. You realize that you must be humble, you must wait when you can't enter into a passage of the Scriptures, until the Lord opens it up for you. *And does He open it up?* Not always. But the fact that such moments of realization happen signifies something great for me in itself.[29]

Humility, docility, and patience are three key virtues emphasized by Benedict in this passage and throughout his corpus. The need to have an accurate understanding of one's own goodness in proportion to God, to be open to the wisdom of others, and to endure trials well are hallmarks of the emeritus pontiff's teaching on the life of faith. If we do not understand a mystery, our first inclination should be to suppose that the problem lies in us, not in God or in the Church. This attitude is enshrined in Benedict's saying "I am too small for it" in the above text. Throughout his life, Benedict came to see faith more and more as a gift. Sometimes if we are patient, the Lord will clarify a problem we have been having or open up a heretofore

---

permissible today either to be attached to things that are incompatible with the following of Jesus, as is the case with riches dishonestly achieved." Benedict XVI, General Audience: Matthew (August 30, 2006).

[29] Benedict XVI and Seewald, *Last Testament*, 10.

troubling biblical text. While these moments of realization occur, at other times the Lord does not fulfill our expectations and calls us to persevere lovingly anyway.

Peter, the Fisherman

In his first series of catecheses, Benedict demonstrates how the apostles exemplified the above virtues and thus serve as a model for our life in the Church today. Emphasizing again the importance of Christian praxis for knowing the truth of the faith, Benedict tells us that through meditating on the apostles' lives, we come to understand "what it means to *experience the Church* and what it means to follow Jesus".[30] Following his own characteristic model outlined in the introduction, Benedict begins by contextualizing the first pope's life historically, discussing such matters as the Greek and Aramaic forms of his name, his Galilean accent, his marital status, and his character as suggested by the Gospels. He even brings to light ancient graffiti invocations to Peter unearthed in recent archaeological excavations in Capernaum in order to ground Peter further in first-century Palestine.

At this point, Benedict turns his attention from the historical to the theological and spiritual kernel to be gleaned by considering central events in Peter's life. "The Gospels", he writes, "enable us to follow Peter step by step on his spiritual journey."[31] The starting point here is Jesus' call of Peter, which "happened *on an ordinary day* while Peter was busy with his fisherman's tasks."[32] Asking permission to board Simon's boat and then to put out a little from the land, Jesus taught the crowds from the boat, thus turning the boat of Peter into the chair of Jesus. Though Peter was a skilled fisherman and Jesus a carpenter, the apostle had the humility to "put out into the deep" (Lk 5:4) and was rewarded abundantly by the Lord for this trust. Benedict highlights the truth that Peter's actions are able to be imitated by us: indeed, the miracle occurred because Peter was faithful to the Lord in the ordinary circumstances of his daily life and work.

---

[30] Benedict XVI, General Audience: Peter, the Fisherman (May 17, 2006). Emphasis added.
[31] Ibid.
[32] Ibid. (emphasis added). For the Gospel account to which Benedict refers, see Luke 5:1–11.

Another pivotal step of Peter's spiritual journey took place near Caesarea Philippi when Jesus asked the disciples the question, "Who do men say that I am?" (Mk 8:27; Mt 16:13). After confessing Jesus to be the Christ and being rewarded with a new name and office (Mt 16:18–19), Peter was quickly shocked by the Lord's announcement of his impending Passion and death. Benedict observes:

> Peter had not yet understood the profound content of Jesus' Messianic mission.... Peter wanted as Messiah a "divine man" who would fulfill the expectations of the people by imposing his power upon them all: we would also like the Lord to impose his power and transform the world instantly. Jesus presented himself as a "human God", the Servant of God, who turned the crowd's expectations upside-down by taking a path of humility and suffering.[33]

Though his reaction was immediately met with being called Satan by our Lord (Mk 8:33; Mt 16:23), Peter eventually learned to accept Christ's mission and his own vocation to share in his patient suffering. Benedict draws another lesson from this step of Peter's journey that is directly applicable to believers of every epoch: "This is the great alternative that we must learn over and over again: to give priority to our own expectations, rejecting Jesus, or to accept Jesus in the truth of his mission and set aside all too human expectations."[34]

James the Greater

Benedict's fondness for the evangelically inspired image of the boat as a way to talk about faith recurs in his catechesis on the apostle James the Greater.[35] As in the case of Peter, the Holy Father begins with a historical analysis of the saint. He examines the biblical evidence that differentiates this James from James "the Lesser". The titles, Benedict informs us, are not intended as a measure of holiness but, rather, indicate the relative importance of the two men in Jesus' earthly life as

---

[33] Ibid. On Peter's misplaced desire for the Lord to impose his power and transform the world instantly, see also Benedict XVI, *Jesus of Nazareth: From the Baptism in the Jordan to the Transfiguration*, trans. Adrian J. Walker (San Francisco: Ignatius Press, 2008), chap. 2, especially 42–43.

[34] Benedict XVI, General Audience: Peter, the Fisherman (May 17, 2006).

[35] Benedict XVI, General Audience: James, the Greater (June 21, 2006).

narrated in the Gospels. After discussing the apostle's name, *Iakobos*, itself a Hellenized form of the name of the patriarch Jacob, Benedict treats (because it was very hot that day in Saint Peter's Square, he tells his audience) just two episodes in James' life: his appearance with Jesus at his agony in the Garden of Gethsemane and his presence with Jesus at his Transfiguration.

Following his summary of the biblical data and as part of his effort to contextualize the saint historically, Benedict brings to light later traditions that give us a fuller picture of James' life. He recalls the tradition dating back at least to Isidore of Seville that speaks of a visit made by James to Spain to evangelize the far reaches of the Roman Empire. According to another tradition, meanwhile, it was rather his body that was taken to the city of Santiago de Compostela in Spain. In light of this city's eventual importance as a venerable pilgrimage site, the iconographical tradition represented Saint James with the pilgrim's staff and the scroll of the Gospel in hand, both "typical features of the traveling Apostle dedicated to the proclamation of the 'Good News' and characteristics of the pilgrimage of Christian life".[36] In addition to teaching Christians of all generations that life itself is a pilgrimage, Benedict identifies the specific virtues that we may acquire by imitating James: "Consequently, we can learn much from Saint James: promptness in accepting the Lord's call even when he asks us to leave the 'boat' of our human securities, enthusiasm in following him on the paths that he indicates to us over and above any deceptive presumption of our own, readiness to witness to him with courage, if necessary to the point of making the supreme sacrifice of life."[37] Like Peter and James, we must be ready to follow Christ even to the point of giving our very lives for him. And even if our faith never requires blood martyrdom, surely we all must have the readiness and docility to leave the "boat" of our human securities and presumptions whenever the Lord should call us.

Bartholomew

Time and again throughout his catecheses, Benedict drives home the above point about the docility needed to abandon our own

[36] Ibid.
[37] Ibid.

presumptions and expectations of how we think the Lord must act. We find this, for instance, in the Holy Father's meditation on the apostle Bartholomew. As in the case of the other apostles, Benedict contextualizes the saint in question historically. He observes that Bartholomew is traditionally identified with Nathaniel in the Gospels (cf. Jn 1:45–51) and treats these texts accordingly. He then discusses the apostle's subsequent apostolic activity as recorded by Eusebius while making mention of Bartholomew's relics venerated in the Roman church dedicated to him. Further, as in the case of Matthew and in keeping with his conviction of the importance of the artistic tradition, Benedict recalls Michelangelo's painting of Bartholomew in the Sistine Chapel, wherein the saint is holding his own skin (on which the artist depicted his own face) in his left hand. But the most important feature of this catechesis lies in Benedict's reflection upon Bartholomew-Nathaniel's character—in particular, his strong prejudice that nothing good could come out of Nazareth (Jn 1:46). Benedict writes, "Nathanael's protest highlights God's freedom, which baffles our expectations by causing him to be found in the very place where we least expect him."[38] Like Peter, we may not expect to find Jesus in the mundane events of our daily living, and like Nathaniel we may not think it possible for God to operate in certain unexpected ways, yet the apostles' experience—and our own—proves that God's ways are not always our ways.

The Humility to Ask the Tough Questions and Let Ourselves Be "Called into Question"

Andrew, the Protoclete

A particularly pointed instantiation of the virtues discussed above can be found in Benedict's frequent emphasis upon the need for the believer to cultivate the twofold humility of asking the Lord tough questions while being prepared to accept his challenging answers to them. The emeritus pontiff's early catechesis on the apostle Andrew offers one such instance of this teaching. As the reader will expect

---

[38] Benedict XVI, General Audience: Bartholomew (October 4, 2006).

by now, Benedict begins by commenting on the historical evidence we have for Andrew "in the measure that sources allow us".[39] After commenting on the biblical data and the reality that the apostle's name was not Hebrew but Greek, Benedict pauses to make his central point by way of reflecting upon John 1:40–41. In this text we learn that Andrew had initially been a disciple of John the Baptist and that he was thus "a man who was searching".[40] Indeed, it was Andrew who was the first of the disciples to follow Jesus. For this reason, Benedict tells us, the liturgy of the Byzantine Church honors him with the nickname *Protokletos* ("the first called"). Here we are presented with but one illustration of how Benedict draws on the full gamut of available tradition (biblical, patristic, apocryphal, artistic, secular, and so on) to paint his portraits of the apostles.

Another key event that figures into this catechesis centers on the biblical account of Jesus predicting that not one stone of the Temple's great walls would be left upon another (Mk 13:1–37). Together with Peter, James, and John, Andrew privately questioned Jesus: "Tell us, when will this be, and what will be the sign when these things are all to be accomplished?" (Mk 13:3–4). It was precisely this bold question that prompted Jesus to give his important discourse on the destruction of Jerusalem, the end of the world, and the need to be constantly watchful and wise in interpreting the signs of the times. Benedict draws a critical lesson from this episode: "From this event we can deduce that we should not be afraid to ask Jesus questions but at the same time that we must be ready to accept even the surprising and difficult teachings that he offers us."[41] When they shared with Jesus how much they admired the Temple's great architecture, presumably the disciples had not expected the reply that the physical focal point of their faith was soon to be destroyed! Moreover,

---

[39] Benedict XVI, General Audience: Andrew, the Protoclete (June 14, 2006).

[40] Ibid.

[41] Ibid. Benedict draws a related lesson in his catechesis on the apostle Philip. By serving as mediator for the Greeks asking him to bring them to see Jesus, the apostle serves as a model for us: "This teaches us always to be ready to accept questions and requests, wherever they come from, and to direct them to the Lord, the only one who can fully satisfy them. Indeed, it is important to know that the prayers of those who approach us are not ultimately addressed to us, but to the Lord: it is to him that we must direct anyone in need. So it is that each one of us must be an open road towards him!" Benedict XVI, General Audience: Philip, the Apostle (September 6, 2006).

in reading Jesus' discourse that ensued, we see it is likely that the disciples received more than they had bargained for in asking when and with what sign these events were to take place. The same dynamic occurs in our lives: we may pray for a sign or ask the Lord to intervene in a particular way, but then sometimes his response shatters our expectations. We must have the boldness to ask him for great things in the first place, but then we must also humbly receive whatever response he should give us.

A final lesson in the life of the apostle Andrew is gleaned by Benedict, not from Scripture, but from the later tradition to which he also characteristically attends. First he discusses ancient traditions that build on the biblical account of Andrew and Philip mediating and interpreting for a small group of Greeks who wished to meet Jesus (Jn 12:3–4). These traditions consider Andrew the apostle to the Greeks not only here in Scripture but also in the years subsequent to Pentecost. A later tradition tells of Andrew's crucifixion at Patras. Like his brother, Peter, he humbly asked to be nailed to a cross different from that of Jesus—thus the origin of the diagonal or X-shaped "Saint Andrew's cross". In a final illustration of Benedict doing his homework with respect to the tradition, he relates these words attributed to the apostle upon being martyred in the sixth-century *Passion of Andrew*: "Hail, O Cross, inaugurated by the Body of Christ and adorned with his limbs as though they were precious pearls. Before the Lord mounted you, you inspired an earthly fear. Now, instead, endowed with heavenly love, you are accepted as a gift." Benedict finds here "a very profound Christian spirituality". For, Andrew views his cross, not as a mere instrument of torture, but rather as "the incomparable means for perfect configuration to the Redeemer, to the grain of wheat that fell into the earth".[42] As with anything from the tradition, the lesson here is essentially evangelical. Yet for Benedict, the lives of the saints illustrate that Jesus' Cross-centered spirituality was not just for the incarnate Lord but for all of us who wish to be conformed to him.

Thomas the Twin

The life of the New Testament questioner par excellence, the apostle Thomas, serves to teach us a similar lesson to that which Benedict

---

[42] Benedict XVI, General Audience: Andrew, the Protoclete (June 14, 2006).

drew from Andrew above. After discussing the Hebrew root *ta'am* ("twin") of the apostle's name and that the reason for this biblical appellation for him is unclear, Benedict concentrates on select biblical texts in which Thomas makes an appearance. For instance, he notes that it was Thomas' question, "Lord, we do not know where you are going; how can we know the way?" (Jn 14:5), that provided Jesus the opportunity to make his famous revelation, "I am the Way, and the Truth, and the Life" (Jn 14:6). Benedict comments:

> Thus, it is primarily to Thomas that he makes this revelation, but it is valid for all of us and for every age. Every time we hear or read these words, we can stand beside Thomas in spirit and imagine that the Lord is also speaking to us, just as he spoke to him. At the same time, his question also confers upon us the right, so to speak, to ask Jesus for explanations. We often do not understand him. Let us be brave enough to say: "I do not understand you, Lord; listen to me, help me to understand." In such a way, with this frankness which is the true way of praying, of speaking to Jesus, we express our meagre capacity to understand and at the same time place ourselves in the trusting attitude of someone who expects light and strength from the One able to provide them.[43]

According to Benedict, Thomas' humility and courage in confronting the Lord with this challenging question serve as a model for us to do the same today. And not only that, it "confers upon us the right, so to speak, to ask Jesus for explanations".

Later, in the proverbial instance of questioning—this time seemingly posed without humility on Thomas' part—the apostle maintains that he will not believe Jesus has risen unless and until he is presented with direct evidence: "Unless I see in his hands the print of the nails, and place my finger in the mark of the nails, and place my hand in his side, I will not believe" (Jn 20:25). As we know, Jesus later did appear to Thomas and bid him to put his hand in his side (Jn 20:27), at which point Thomas confessed the risen Jesus to be his Lord and God (Jn 20:28). Even here positive lessons are to be drawn from Thomas' blunt skepticism, for once again it was Thomas' words that led Jesus to make a powerful revelation: "Have you believed because

---

[43] Benedict XVI, General Audience: Thomas the Twin (September 27, 2006).

you have seen me? Blessed are those who have not seen and yet believe" (Jn 20:29). According to Benedict, this sentence can equally be put into the present: Christians of all ages who have never seen Jesus in the flesh are "blessed" for not seeing and yet believing. What is more, Thomas' frank willingness to confront the Lord is put forward by Benedict as an example for us: "The Apostle Thomas' case is important to us for at least three reasons: first, because it comforts us in our insecurity; second, because it shows us that every doubt can lead to an outcome brighter than any uncertainty; and, lastly, because the words that Jesus addressed to him remind us of the true meaning of mature faith and encourage us to persevere, despite the difficulty, along our journey of adhesion to him."[44] Accordingly, for Benedict, doubt is not something unequivocally negative but, rather, a reality that if confronted sincerely and with humility can lead to a great good. In this way, Thomas' persevering questioning becomes a model for us on the path to mature faith in Christ.[45]

Mary, Mother of God

Perhaps an unexpected figure in this section dealing with Benedict's conviction of the necessity to confront the Lord with tough questions, it turns out that our Lady is a stalwart example of one who has done precisely this in the most faithful way. In an address from his final series of catecheses on the virtue of faith, Benedict proposes Mary's conversation with the angel Gabriel (Lk 1:26–38) as a model to be emulated by the faithful. Mary was initially troubled by the greeting of the angel. After Gabriel's announcement that she was to bear the Messiah, she responded, "How can this be, since I have no husband?" (Lk 1:34) Yet Mary's very question demonstrates that she did not remain locked in her initial troubled state. In seeking

[44] Ibid.

[45] While on the precise aspect of Thomas' life I am trying to emphasize here, it is revealing to observe that Benedict also considers Thomas in light of postbiblical tradition. He treats the apocryphal *Acts of Thomas* and *Gospel of Thomas* written in his name, recalling the ancient tradition that the apostle evangelized Syria, Persia, and India, where he was martyred. According to Benedict, these sources, while apocryphal, are "in any case important for the study of Christian origins". Moreover, considering them leads to yet another lesson: the need to put our faith "in missionary perspective, expressing the hope that Thomas' example will never fail to strengthen our faith in Jesus Christ, Our Lord and Our God" (ibid.).

to understand the meaning of the angel's greeting, she becomes an image of the Church considering the Word of God, trying to penetrate its meaning and guard it in her memory. Benedict raises his own question of this narrative:

> Confronting all this, we may ask ourselves: how was Mary able to journey on beside her Son with such a strong faith, even in darkness, without losing her full trust in the action of God? Mary assumes a fundamental approach in facing what happens in her life. At the Annunciation, on hearing the Angel's words she is distressed—it is the fear a person feels when moved by God's closeness—but it is not the attitude of someone who is afraid of what God might ask. Mary reflects, she ponders on the meaning of this greeting (cf. Lk 1:29). The Greek word used in the Gospel to define this "reflection", "*dielogizeto*", calls to mind the etymology of the word "dialogue". This means that Mary enters into a deep conversation with the Word of God that has been announced to her; she does not consider it superficially but meditates on it, lets it sink into her mind and her heart so as to understand what the Lord wants of her, the meaning of the announcement.[46]

Drawing a spiritual lesson from the Greek text of the Gospel, Benedict teaches that we in our own turn must learn to enter into "dialogue" with the Lord in prayer as Mary did. Like Mary, we ought not to refrain from asking the Lord the tough questions for fear of what he might ask in return.

The brief report of Mary's interior state described in the next chapter of Luke's Gospel (Lk 2:19) affords Benedict the opportunity to reflect upon the significance of another Greek word in the Gospel text:

> We find another hint of Mary's inner attitude to God's action—again in the Gospel according to St Luke—at the time of Jesus' birth, after the adoration of the shepherds. Luke affirms that Mary "kept all these things, pondering them in her heart" (Lk 2:19). In Greek the term is *symballon*, we could say that she "kept together", "pieced together" in

---

[46] Benedict XVI, General Audience: The Virgin Mary, Icon of Obedient Faith (December 19, 2012). For a robust synopsis of Mary's three-step response to the angel, see Benedict XVI, *Jesus of Nazareth: The Infancy Narratives*, trans. Philip J. Whitmore (New York. Image, 2012), 31–32.

her heart all the events that were happening to her; she placed every individual element, every word, every event, within the whole and confronted it, cherished it, recognizing that it all came from the will of God.[47]

In addition to association of the word *symballon* with the Profession of Faith (*symbolon tes pisteos*), its appearance here is significant because Benedict finds that it conveys the spiritual lesson that the individual elements, words, and events in our lives can only be understood properly within the whole of God's plan for us. A given moment in our life may make no sense when considered in isolation; it is only when looked at from a God's-eye perspective in light of the whole that we are able to make sense of our failures, desolations, and sufferings.

Finally, the Mother of God does not just ask tough questions. She exhibits a willingness to let herself be questioned with respect to the Lord. Writes Benedict:

Mary does not stop at a first superficial understanding of what is happening in her life, but can look in depth, she lets herself be called into question by events, digests them, discerns them, and attains the understanding that only faith can provide. It is the profound humility of the obedient faith of Mary, who welcomes within her even what she does not understand in God's action, leaving it to God to open her mind and heart. "Blessed is she who believed that there would be a fulfilment of what was spoken to her from the Lord" (Lk 1:45), her kinswoman Elizabeth exclaims. It is exactly because of this faith that all generations will call her blessed.[48]

In Mary, therefore, we learn that our freedom as men to ask questions of our Lord does not imply that the Lord has an obligation to answer us, or at least not to answer in the way we expect. Indeed, his reply sometimes takes the form of another unsettling question. In concluding this section, I think it appropriate to cite again from Benedict's final interview book, which casts further light on the reality that God is not an object capable of being circumscribed by our

[47] Benedict XVI, General Audience: Virgin Mary, Icon of Obedient Faith.
[48] Ibid.

created intellects. Asked how he came to choose his episcopal motto "co-worker of the truth", the emeritus pontiff replied:

> Like this: I had for a long time excluded the question of truth, because it seemed to be too great. The claim: "We have the truth!" is something which no one had the courage to say, so even in theology we had largely eliminated the concept of truth. In these years of struggle, the 1970s, it became clear to me: if we omit the truth, what do we do anything for? So truth must be involved.
>
> Indeed, we cannot say "I have the truth", but the truth has us, it touches us. And we try to let ourselves be guided by this touch. Then this phrase from John 3 crossed my mind, that we are "co-workers of the truth". One can work with the truth, because the truth is person. One can let truth in, try to provide the truth with value. That seemed to me finally to be the very definition of the profession of a theologian; that he, when he has been touched by this truth, when truth has caught sight of him, is now ready to let it take him into service, to work on it and for it.[49]

Here we find a theme that emerges throughout the career of Ratzinger/Benedict. Truth is a person, and Christianity is not merely a religion of the truth that can be found in a book but is a religion of the living and incarnate Word who is Truth. Thus, it is not so much that we are in pursuit of capturing this truth. On the contrary, it is first and foremost the Truth that pursues us, has us, and guides us. At the end of the day, the deep questions that Benedict encourages us to ask in imitation of the apostles and the Mother of God have as their end this dynamic relationship with truth and a consequent readiness to be taken into its service.

A School of Faith: Our Journey with Christ as Progressive Exodus, Struggle, and "Gamble"

If the truth is not something that we simply possess but rather a Divine Person who is constantly in search of us, it is only fitting that this relationship somehow be expressed diachronically, which

---

[49] Benedict XVI, *Last Testament*, 241.

is precisely how Benedict approaches it. For him, faith is not static. Indeed, in another reflection on the apostle Peter, the emeritus pontiff speaks of Peter being put through a "school of faith" by our Lord. This school "is not a triumphal march but a journey marked daily by suffering and love, trials and faithfulness".[50] Even the first pope's initial rash generosity with our Lord did not protect him from the risks connected with human weakness. From his naïve enthusiasm, the apostle had to pass through the sorrowful experience of denial and the weeping of conversion. Benedict argues there is a lesson in this for all of us: "Peter succeeded in entrusting himself to that Jesus who adapted himself to his poor capacity of love. And in this way he shows us the way, notwithstanding all of our weakness. We know that Jesus adapts himself to this weakness of ours."[51]

Benedict conveys the same message about the pilgrim nature of our faith in his other catecheses on the apostles. Of James the Greater, he writes that his journey of traveling to proclaim the gospel to the far reaches of the Roman Empire was "not only exterior but above all interior".[52] And of John the Theologian in particular but of the disciples collectively, Benedict affirms, "Their journey with Jesus was not only a physical journey from Galilee to Jerusalem, but an interior journey during which they learned faith in Jesus Christ, not without difficulty, for they were people like us."[53] More significantly still, in a catechesis from his series on the life of prayer, Benedict regards the patriarch Jacob's nocturnal struggle and encounter with God as emblematic of our own journey of faith.[54] While biblical

---

[50] Benedict XVI, General Audience: Peter, the Apostle. For other instances of Benedict's use of the term "school of faith", see his following audiences on September 17, 2008, and May 19, 2010.

[51] Benedict XVI, General Audience: Peter, the Apostle. In his catecheses on Saint Paul, the Holy Father also speaks eloquently of how the Lord accommodates himself to our weaknesses. Commenting on Paul having the grace sufficient to bear the "thorn" in his side (2 Cor 12:7), Benedict writes: "This also applies to us. The Lord does not free us from evils, but helps us to mature in sufferings, difficulties and persecutions. Faith, therefore, tells us that if we abide in God, 'though our outer nature is wasting away, our inner nature is being renewed every day', in trials (cf. [2 Cor 4:]16)." Benedict XVI, General Audience: Contemplation and the Power of Prayer (June 13, 2012).

[52] Benedict XVI, General Audience: James, the Greater (June 21, 2006).

[53] Benedict XVI, General Audience: John, the Theologian (August 9, 2006).

[54] Benedict XVI, General Audience: The Nocturnal Struggle and Encounter with God (May 25, 2011).

exegetes give a variety of interpretations to this passage, when looked upon canonically in light of the biblical narrative as a whole, the text opens up to broader dimensions. Benedict's profound commentary merits to be cited at some length:

> For the believer the episode of the struggle at the Jabbok thus becomes a paradigm in which the people of Israel speak of their own origins and outline the features of a particular relationship between God and humanity. Therefore, as is also affirmed in the *Catechism of the Catholic Church*, "from this account, the spiritual tradition of the Church has retained the symbol of prayer as a battle of faith and as the triumph of perseverance" (no. 2573). The Bible text speaks to us about a long night of seeking God, of the struggle to learn his name and see his face; it is the night of prayer that, with tenacity and perseverance, asks God for a blessing and a new name, a new reality that is the fruit of conversion and forgiveness.
>
> For the believer Jacob's night at the ford of the Jabbok thus becomes a reference point for understanding the relationship with God that finds in prayer its greatest expression. Prayer requires trust, nearness, almost a hand-to-hand contact that is symbolic not of a God who is an enemy, an adversary, but a Lord of blessing who always remains mysterious, who seems beyond reach. Therefore the author of the Sacred text uses the symbol of the struggle, which implies a strength of spirit, perseverance, tenacity in obtaining what is desired. And if the object of one's desire is a relationship with God, his blessing and love, then the struggle cannot fail but ends in that self-giving to God, in recognition of one's own weakness, which is overcome only by giving oneself over into God's merciful hands.[55]

I find the above text especially compelling because it echoes the theme of questioning discussed above and applies it to the most intimate dimension of our lives: our life of prayer, our ongoing inner dialogue with the Lord. Citing the *Catechism*, Benedict speaks of prayer as a "battle" that requires of us great perseverance and great nearness, to the point of "hand-to-hand combat" with the Lord. Like Jacob, we too have to pass through the long night of seeking God. But why does the Lord come to us in this and not some easier way? Benedict writes: "Dear brothers and sisters, our entire lives

[55] Ibid.

are like this long night of struggle and prayer, spent in desiring and asking for God's blessing, which cannot be grabbed or won through our own strength but must be received with humility from him as a gratuitous gift that ultimately allows us to recognize the Lord's face. And when this happens, our entire reality changes; we receive a new name and God's blessing."[56] Thus we return to a theme discussed further above: Benedict drives home again and again the point that God's blessing is not something we can attain through our own power. Faith itself is a gift to be received with the virtues of humility, docility, and patience. Yet if we are willing to accompany the Lord on the long night of his Passion, we will be rewarded with a new name and God's blessing.[57]

Several times throughout his catecheses Benedict describes the journey exemplified in the life of Jacob as a "school of prayer", echoing the language employed above in regard to faith. According to Benedict, the first school of prayer is the Word of God, Sacred Scripture. This explains why a large number of the emeritus pontiff's catecheses on prayer focus, not on the doctrine of the mystics, important as it is, but instead on biblical spirituality. One of the most illuminating dimensions of Benedict's thought here concerns his insight that what we find in the history of the Chosen People's journey with God mirrors how the Lord works in our lives as well: "Sacred Scripture is an ongoing dialogue between God and man, a progressive dialogue in which God shows himself ever closer, in which we can become ever better acquainted with his face, his voice, his being; and man learns to accept to know God and to talk to God. Therefore, in these weeks, in reading Sacred Scripture we have sought to learn from Scripture, from this ongoing dialogue, how we may enter into contact with

---

[56] Ibid.

[57] This reflection on faith as a "struggle" with God reflects Benedict's understanding not only of how God reveals himself to us but also of how he worked with the Chosen People. Benedict describes the Bible as the story of a twofold struggle: God's struggle to "make himself understandable to them over the course of time" and the People of God's struggle to "seize hold of God over the course of time". This familiarization between God and man was a journey of faith, and "only in the process of this journeying was the Bible's real way of declaring itself formed, step by step" (Benedict XVI, *In the Beginning: A Catholic Understanding of the Story of Creation and the Fall* [Grand Rapids, Mich.: Eerdmans, 1995], 9). Elsewhere in his catecheses, Benedict speaks similarly of the Bible's origins, describing divine revelation as developing gradually in stages as he struggled, as it were, to make himself known to his people. See Benedict XVI, General Audience: The Stages of the Revelation (December 12, 2012).

God."[58] In passages like these, Benedict weaves seamlessly between speaking of the God's people of ages past and his people today, since God revealed himself historically to the people of Israel progressively, just as he gradually reveals to us his full plan for our lives today. In the "school" of the divine pedagogue, pupils are met where they are, taking into account all their weaknesses, so that they may eventually be led by the Lord's hand to the fullness of truth and life.[59]

A number of times Benedict adds an additional biblical angle to the above account in speaking of our path toward the Lord as a gradual pilgrimage or, citing his own encyclical *Deus caritas est*, as "an ongoing exodus out of the closed inward-looking self towards its liberation through self-giving, and thus towards authentic self-discovery and indeed the discovery of God".[60] On another occasion, Benedict speaks in this way of believers' free acceptance of Christ: "Indeed, it involves them and uplifts them in a gamble for life (*scommessa di vita*) that is like an exodus, that is, a coming out of ourselves, from our own certainties, from our own mental framework, to entrust ourselves to the action of God who points out to us his way to achieve true freedom, our human identity, true joy of the heart, peace with everyone."[61] In keeping with the Holy Father's image in the above quote, we may say that the quest for union with the Lord demands that all our chips be on the table. We must be willing to endure a long night in this search. Moreover, the exodus out of ourselves may entail a certain "loss", but it is of such a kind so as to be counted as nothing because of the surpassing worth of what we thereby gain: knowledge of Christ Jesus our Lord (cf. Phil 3:7–8).

Conclusion

By way of drawing these remarks on Benedict's catecheses to a close, I would like to return to our point of departure and add an additional

---

[58] Benedict XVI, General Audience: The Liturgy, School of Prayer—The Lord Himself Teaches Us to Pray (September 26, 2012).

[59] For Benedict, the liturgy is another critical place or source wherein we learn to develop our life of prayer. Delving more deeply into this subject exceeds the constraints of the present chapter, but for more on this, see the above catechesis.

[60] Benedict XVI, General Audience: The Desire for God (November 7, 2012); Benedict XVI, Encyclical Letter *Deus caritas est* on Christian Love (December 25, 2005), 6.

[61] Benedict XVI, General Audience: What Is Faith? (October 24, 2012).

nuance to the discussion. If the beauty and the saints the Church has produced over the millennia stand as her greatest *apologia*, then it must also be recalled that for Benedict it is actually a particular sort of saint who most exudes that beauty which has the power to convert souls:

> Actually I must say that also for my personal faith many saints, not all, are true stars in the firmament of history. And I would like to add that for me not only a few great saints whom I love and whom I know well are "signposts", but precisely also the simple saints, that is, the good people I see in my life who will never be canonized. They are ordinary people, so to speak, without visible heroism but in their everyday goodness I see the truth of faith. This goodness, which they have developed in the faith of the Church, is for me the most reliable apology of Christianity and the sign of where the truth lies.[62]

Here at last we come to the heart of Benedict's conviction regarding how one comes to know the truth of the Catholic faith. To be sure, the canonized saints whose lives Benedict spent years recalling have a pivotal role to play in confirming and deepening our faith. However, it is above all the non-canonized saints—the "simple" or "ordinary" people we know—who for Benedict and for most of us are the truest sign of where the truth of the faith lies. This claim especially makes sense in light of Benedict's above emphasis on our need to have "first-hand experience" of the faith in order to see its truth.[63] For while some souls may be granted a profound spiritual encounter with a canonized saint of ages past, for most of us it is our direct and intimate experience with a living member of the communion of saints that proves life-changing. A true witness such as this is one whose very life bids us to become personally involved with Jesus and urges us as the apostle Philip urged Nathaniel, "Come and see!" (Jn 1:46).

---

[62] Benedict XVI, General Audience: Holiness (April 13, 2011).

[63] For this precise formulation, see Benedict XVI, General Audience: Bartholomew (October 4, 2006).

II

Taking Truth for Granted:
A Reflection on the Significance
of Tradition in Josef Pieper

D. C. Schindler

A story has been handed down that, when he had made the decision
to found Ignatius Press—in the first place to make available in English
the works of Ratzinger, von Balthasar, de Lubac, and von Speyr—
Father Joseph Fessio asked von Balthasar himself whether he could
recommend which authors it would be most important to publish.
Apparently, von Balthasar said, "First, you ought to publish anything
you can by Josef Pieper." Though Pieper's work has always been
easily accessible in German in inexpensive editions, von Balthasar
himself went on to publish several books by Pieper in his own Johan-
nesverlag and was around that time helping to compile an anthology
of texts by Pieper, for which he himself wrote the preface.[1] Von
Balthasar was recommending Pieper, not in the first place because
Pieper was an innovative thinker on the contemporary scene, but
because he opens up access to the great classical tradition in philosophy in an almost incomparable manner. Publishing a writer like
Pieper thus provides a vital foundation for a press that would aspire
to be both Catholic and catholic.

It is right to associate Pieper with the classical tradition, not only
because he carries the tradition forward like few other contemporary

[1] The title of the German edition is *Josef Pieper: Lesebuch* (Munich: Kösel Verlag, 1981),
which Fessio published in English as *Josef Pieper: An Anthology* (San Francisco: Ignatius Press,
1989).

figures, but also because he himself has reflected directly on tradition as a philosophical theme. Tradition first appears in his work as significant for philosophy in the 1947 essay "The Philosophical Act", which Pieper published jointly with what is no doubt his best known essay, "Leisure, the Basis of Culture".[2] In 1957, he delivered a lecture on the theme (which was then published in 1958, along with critical responses to it, as *Über den Begriff der Tradition* [Cologne: West deutscher Verlag, 1958]), which he took up again in a 1960 lecture, "Tradition in a Changing World".[3] His most sustained treatment of tradition is the book published in 1970 as *Tradition: Begriff und Anspruch* (*Tradition: Concept and Claim*),[4] which was based on the 1957 lecture, but elaborated some of the themes, especially in the light of criticisms. It is this book that we will be discussing in the following.

When Josef Pieper explores a philosophical theme, his typical practice is to begin by laying out what has already been said, and has generally found acceptance, on the matter. There is a certain irony in the fact that, when he sets himself to reflect specifically on the theme of *tradition*, he finds that virtually nothing has been handed down on this subject in the realm of philosophy. Surprisingly, there is no entry on "tradition" in the great German philosophical dictionaries, and the classic dictionaries in theological and classical literature provide entries of such narrow scope as to offer very little to the philosophical mind. Thus, when he takes up this particular theme in his 1970 book, *Tradition: Concept and Claim*, Pieper discovers he has to start more or less from scratch.[5]

It is ironic, but there is perhaps something fitting in the absence of an explicit philosophical theory or account of tradition. A tradition is something we inherit *uncritically*, without a demand for justification. We feel no need to certify the precise origin of tradition, and, indeed, details about the time and place a tradition was instituted tend to diminish its status as tradition, especially if the origin turns out to be recent and accessible in some way other than its transmission through

---

[2] Josef Pieper, *Leisure, the Basis of Culture*, trans. Gerald Malsbary (South Bend, Ind.: St. Augustine's Press, 1998), 117–20.

[3] Published in English as "Tradition in the Changing World" in the book *Tradition as Challenge*, trans. Daniel J. Farrelly (South Bend, Ind.: St. Augustine's Press, 2015), 1–19.

[4] Josef Pieper, *Tradition: Concept and Claim*, trans. E. Christian Kopff (Wilmington, Del.: ISI Books, 2008), henceforward: *Tradition*.

[5] Pieper, *Tradition*, 6–7.

others. The initiation of a tradition is most properly hidden in the mists of time. Rather than critically assessing it, we are meant to take a tradition *for granted*; a kind of spontaneous and unreflective acceptance seems to belong to its essence. In this respect, we might say of tradition something analogous to what Nietzsche said of all genuinely good things: "Honest things, like honest men, do not carry their reasons in their hands. . . . It is indecent to show all five fingers. What must first be proved is worth little."[6] To have to make an explicit case for it would be a kind of admission that it no longer exists as a tradition.[7] If this is true, the absence of an entry on "tradition" in the philosophical dictionary could very well be a sign of its living reality, whereas the fact that Pieper felt the need to reflect on it in the latter part of the twentieth century, and make arguments on its behalf, could be the symptom of a coming crisis.

This possibility is sobering in the current cultural climate, in which one hears the word "tradition" with increasing frequency and in somewhat peculiar contexts. The regular use of the word is particularly surprising, given that the form of the culture in which we live is hardly a traditional one. Indeed, one of the more adequate ways to characterize modernity is as the first age in history to understand itself as *not* receiving its basic view of the world and its governing values from ages past, but beginning itself anew.[8] It may be that the

---

[6] Friedrich Nietzsche, *Twilight of the Idols*, in *The Portable Nietzsche*, trans. Walter Kaufmann (New York: Penguin, 1976), 476.

[7] An anecdote in this regard: My wife and I once attended an academic event that was "emceed" by two faculty members, somewhat in the way television hosts accompany the Macy's Thanksgiving Day parade. In response to what the university no doubt rightly perceived to be a general cultural ignorance, the two faculty members narrated, in a conversational manner, every detail of the event as it transpired, explaining the symbolic meaning and recounting theories about its origin. However informative such an accompaniment may have been, the participants and spectators could not fail to have been struck by its inappropriateness. There was a decided "lack of transcendence" in the event, a transcendence that is usually evoked by the solemnity of the pageantry. It is not possible to *participate* in an event that is so staged; one can only appreciate it in detachment, like an episode of something or other on the History Channel.

[8] As Robert Spaemann has observed, while other historical periods are defined by a particular content that is definable in principle, modernity is unique in having a principally formal and empty character: "It defines itself essentially in opposition to all the history that preceded it. It is so to speak an open project that can never be completed, so that to say that it has ended and has been replaced by a new period would be to say that it has failed", "The End of Modernity?" in *A Robert Spaemann Reader: Philosophical Essays on Nature, God, and the Human Person*, trans. D. C. Schindler (Oxford: Oxford University Press, 2015), 211.

apparent freedom gained by such a breaking of the bond to the past is the flip side of a loss of something essential to human existence, and this loss is one of the reasons we are so frequently encouraged to recover our "family traditions" (or, if they are irretrievably lost, to create new ones), to bring back our native languages, or at least some of the basic words, which the people of our culture were pressured to forget during the past century. But there is another irony in all of this. Pieper ends his book on tradition by citing a contemporary figure who worries about the possibility that the moment may arrive in the future when tradition is simply forgotten and, with it, the only genuine form of human solidarity, since it is only tradition that can unify people.[9] This moment seems not only to have come, but also to have gone: tradition has been forgotten, but "traditions" have taken its place, and these are understood above all as things that make us unique, practices and values that distinguish us from others. The very fact that we can talk about the importance of celebrating our traditions without recognizing the fundamental challenge that tradition poses to the basic cultural form that defines modernity, setting the horizon, and so the most basic terms, within which any such celebration may take place, tells us that the word "tradition" has changed its meaning. It now refers, not to the core of existence (which, as we will see in the discussion below, is how Pieper understands it), but only to what we might call the external "trappings" of a culture— literally, the cut and color of the clothes one wears or the particular seasonings one adds to one's food. Hence the disconcerting irony that we are only just beginning to fathom: the first radically anti-traditional culture in history, liberalism, presents itself as the champion of tradition(s), insofar as it provides a protective framework that liberates the (private) spaces in which these differences, these unique practices that may belong to one group but not to another, may be cultivated in peace. One cannot help but suspect that the modern age calls up new cultural energies to be devoted to the promotion of such practices (appeals to family tradition, for example, are often

---

[9] See his mention of Viacheslav Ivanov in *Tradition*, 54 and 67 (see Pieper, "Tradition in the Changing World", 19). For an account of how the fragmenting of tradition that occurred in the Protestant Reformation has resulted in the disorder of a radical cultural pluralism, see Brad Gregory, *The Unintended Reformation: How a Religious Revolution Secularized Society* (Cambridge, Mass.: Harvard University Press, 2012).

at the base of ad campaigns) because they distract us from the loss of tradition that cannot but be imposed on us by the basic cultural form of liberalism.

Now, it may be the case that a certain absence of critical reflection is natural to tradition, but in an age in which a sense for tradition has all but gone missing, it becomes necessary to provide a defense, at the level of first principles, however untraditional such an endeavor might be. In this regard, we can be grateful to Josef Pieper, not only for having attempted to give a general account of what tradition is, but for penetrating to its essence and arguing for its fundamental importance in properly human existence. One of the striking aspects of Pieper's account is that, far from accepting the "uncritical" character of tradition as foreign to the philosophical spirit—as the modern mind tends to do (Adorno states bluntly, for example, that "Tradition stands in opposition to rationality")[10] he argues that philosophy cannot be uprooted from tradition without losing its inner life. In recalling philosophy's responsibility to and dependence on tradition, Pieper opened himself to the criticism of subordinating thought to what is ultimately irrational. A philosophical defense of tradition would appear, from this perspective, to be self-undermining. To defend it, thus, would seem to make inevitable a kind of "traditionalism" that can avoid cultural relativism only by being despotic. Pieper responds to such criticism in his book by insisting on the fundamental difference between philosophical reflection and the reception of tradition, but argues that the two subsist in a "contrapuntal" relationship:[11] even in its irreducible difference, philosophy needs tradition; the relative opposition creates a harmony more beautiful than the melodies of each alone. But we wish to propose, here, that his account offers resources for a more fundamental statement regarding the relationship between tradition and truth. In what follows, we will first present a general outline of Pieper's understanding, and then, on the basis of this understanding, we will carry out a further reflection on the place of tradition within the task of thinking.

[10] Theodor Adorno, *Theses on Tradition*, cited in Pieper, *Tradition*, 24. To be sure, as Kopff points out (xix–xx), Adorno does not mean simply to disparage tradition here in favor of modernity; he is a well-known critic, after all, of the instrumental form of rationality that is privileged by the Enlightenment.

[11] See Pieper, *Tradition*, 66.

I

As is well known, the English word "tradition" comes from the Latin *traditio*, which is an abstract noun formed from the past participle (*traditum*) of the verb *tradere*, "to surrender", "to hand over", "to hand down". According to its etymology, the verb comes from *trans* ("across") and *dare* ("to give"), implying the sense of giving, as it were, across a certain distance (cf. the corresponding Greek verb, παραδίδομαι, which conveys the same sense). According to Pieper, we can best get at the essence of tradition if we consider it as a particular kind of "giving", which is an activity transpiring between two parties. Let us first look at *traditio* itself, before we attend to the elements that constitute it, each of which receives an illuminating analysis in Pieper's study.

What distinguishes *traditio* from other kinds of giving (*dare*) is the "trans" aspect, which, Pieper explains, designates in this case the crossing of the distance that separates two generations. We tend to picture a tradition most simply as something that parents pass on to their children, but it is not the particular relationship between the individuals as such that is decisive. The individuals who give and receive a tradition stand, according to Pieper, as representatives of their generation: "The person who receives a *traditum* by listening receives it as a member or representative of the next generation. Even if by chance he were to be older in years than the transmitter, he is still the disciple [in German, *Jünger*] and heir to whom the tradition will be entrusted in the future. That is why Paul calls those who accept his message his 'sons' (1 Corinthians 4:14–15)".[12] Now, to say that *traditio* is a giving that crosses the distance that separates two generations is most immediately to highlight its "trans-temporal" character. A tradition is not something meant to belong to one age to the exclusion of others but is meant to be *shared* by them. While the temporal dimension of *traditio* is crucial, however, it is not the only significant dimension here. When we speak of a "generation", we mean something more than a quantity of people at a particular time (and place). The word also has a qualitative aspect: we give names to particular generations (the "Greatest Generation", the "Baby

[12] Ibid., 11.

Boomers", the "Millennials", and so forth) and attempt to distill the character that distinguishes this generation from others. A generation represents a distinctive way of seeing things and inhabiting the world, a distinct set of values and attitudes, and is typically interpreted as having "grown out" of the previous one, standing in some sense over against the generation that preceded it. In this respect, if *traditio* represents a bridging of the distance between two generations, it is the introduction of something that *relativizes* that which distinguishes the generations from each other. It does not allow the difference between generations to be absolute.

This initial reflection already serves to bring out what will be the decisive feature of what is passed on in tradition: if it bridges the distance between two generations, tradition cannot belong in an exclusive way to either one of the generations in its particularity; it can *belong* to both of them, which is to say, it can be actually handed down from one generation to the next, only if it transcends each. In other words, what is passed down specifically as tradition has to transcend any given historical period; it has to possess an essentially time-transcending character.[13] This is one of the reasons that the one who receives a tradition receives it specifically as a representative of his generation: insofar as the tradition transcends the particularity of space and time, it is not something he can take into his own personal possession as concerning himself alone. It is instead something in which he participates, something he is "brought into".

Now, Pieper highlights three elements in the core of tradition: there is the transmitter, the recipient, and the thing itself that is passed on, that is, the *traditum*. Let us consider the distinctive character of each, beginning with the last. Pieper explains, first of all, that he is going to focus his discussion, not on the customs or practices we typically identify with tradition, but specifically on the handing down of

---

[13] This is why Pieper's notion of tradition requires him immediately to face the question whether he takes the particularity of *history* seriously enough (the first chapter of his study is called "Is Tradition Anti-Historical?"). His 1957 lecture "Tradition in Changing Times", in fact, was intended in part to counterbalance the timelessness of tradition against the constant movement of history. It is interesting that Alasdair MacIntyre's emphasis on tradition, by contrast, forces him to deal with the charge that his concept of reasoning is *too* historical (see Christopher Lutz's thorough account of and response to this debate in *Tradition in the Ethics of Alasdair MacIntyre* (Lanham, Md.: Lexington Books, 2004). At issue in the difference here is a different understanding of the essence of tradition, as we will see below.

a "teaching", a certain understanding of the world.[14] We will come back to the relation between tradition as an idea and as a practice below, but the first thing worth pointing out here is that, even when the *traditum* is a doctrine, there is more to tradition than simply the communication of an idea. It may initially seem, given the "trans-temporal" character of tradition just highlighted, that the activity of *traditio* is simply the passing on of a timeless truth. But Pieper illumi-nates a decisive difference between the passing on of tradition and the teaching of a truth in two respects. On the one hand, while it is possi-ble to imagine someone *teaching* his own discoveries or contributions to a field of study, this cannot be the case with tradition: what one hands down in this particular sense can only be something one has oneself *received* from the generation before, and one hands it down *precisely as such*.[15] A passage from Augustine to which Pieper refers repeatedly sums this up succinctly: "Quod a patribus accepterunt, hoc filiis tradiderunt."[16] Second, "It is an essential part of the concept of tradition that no experience and no deductive reasoning can assim-ilate and surpass what is handed down."[17] It is not enough that the tradition be handed down as received from another; this quality must belong to its very essence, which is to say that there can be no other access to it outside of the mediation through others. One can teach addition and subtraction to a child, but when he learns it, it is some-thing he sees plainly for himself. He has, as it were, direct access to this truth; it is completely accidental that mathematics happens to be mediated to him through his parents. By contrast, mediation cannot be eliminated from tradition without it ceasing to have the character of tradition (if it *ever* actually had it in this case).

This point sets into relief another aspect of tradition on which Pieper does not explicitly dwell but which clearly informs his account. Though what is handed down by tradition transcends time in one respect, it is nevertheless bound to time in another respect. Receiving a tradition from others means receiving it from those who *come before*. We might say that tradition represents a transcen-dence that is both vertical and horizontal: tradition transcends the moment in which we live vertically in the sense that its content is in

---

[14] Pieper, *Tradition*, 9–10.

[15] Ibid., 14.

[16] Augustine, *Contra Julianum* 2.10.34 (PL 44:698).

[17] Pieper, *Tradition*, 19.

one respect "timeless", but at the same time it transcends the present moment horizontally in the sense that it has its source in some earlier time in history. Clearly, there is a certain paradox in the convergence of the timeless and the time-bound; it implies a sort of entry into time of what lies beyond time. Pieper uses the word "revelation" to describe the origin of tradition[18] and quotes Plato in this respect: "A gift from the gods was brought down by a certain (unknown) Prometheus in bright gleam of fire and the ancients, better than we and dwelling closer to the gods, handed down [παρέδοσαν] this saying to us."[19] The word indicates an event in history—even if it is difficult or perhaps even impossible in principle to "pinpoint" the moment, it is nevertheless a communication *to* history—but it is essentially the communication of something more than historical. As we saw above, tradition cannot originate in a human individual; instead, Pieper proposes, it has its origin in God. There is something like a "divine revelation" at the origin of every tradition. This no doubt controversial point will turn out to be the decisive one in Pieper's account, and we will return to it below.

We have been speaking, thus far, principally about that which is handed down in the activity of *traditio*; what we have laid out allows us to describe the other basic elements of tradition, namely, the recipient and the transmitter, the one who hands the *traditum* down. Of these two, it is the recipient that has primacy, since, as we indicated above, *traditio* occurs only where the giver passes on something he himself has received. Regarding the recipient, Pieper makes two observations. The first thing Pieper highlights is the fact that *traditio*, as a personal event, implies a dependence of the recipient on the giver: "This is reception in the strictest meaning of the term, hearing something and really taking it seriously. I accept what someone else offers me and presents to me. I allow him to give it to me. This means that I do not take it for myself. I do not procure it for myself out of my own ability."[20] This radical receptivity is natural given the characteristic of the *traditio* we saw above, namely, that it concerns something that one cannot simply verify for oneself. But this aspect stands in a certain tension with the second observation Pieper makes:

[18] Ibid., 30.
[19] Philebus 16c, cited in Pieper, *Tradition*, 27.
[20] Pieper, *Tradition*, 17.

"On the other hand, I do not accept the *traditum* 'because it is traditional,' but because I am convinced that it is true and valid."[21] To see why this point does not contradict the one just made will require a reflection on the *kind* of truth expressed in tradition, which is distinct from that of, say, a mathematical formula or a scientific "fact". We will attend to this in section 2 below. Here, we ought to see that the affirmation of the *truth* passed on entails a kind of reception *with assent*, beyond simple understanding. On this score, Pieper helpfully contrasts the recipient of a tradition from a historian, who perhaps has a thorough knowledge of the *tradita* but does not receive them with an inward assent; Pieper suggests that it may even be precisely the kind of knowledge he has that precludes such a "taking to be true".[22]

The giver of tradition presents the same two aspects as the recipient; he, too, gives the *traditum*, not as something arising from himself but in which he himself is a participant: he "takes what he is sharing not from himself, but 'from some other place'".[23] At the same time, he does not pass it on as something simply *separate* from him, like a cold, objective "fact". Pieper speaks of passing on the tradition as something "really alive",[24] though he does not elaborate what this means exactly. A hint as to its meaning nevertheless comes later on in the discussion, when in a different context he makes a decisively important observation that bears directly on the question:

> One can simply not expect people as personal beings to be obliged to say without the possibility of critical verification, "this is the way it is and no other way", unless what has to be believed concerns the center of the world and the core of their own existence. It is precisely this which gives to the claim its full weight. What the "wisdom of the ancients" talks about, however, are in fact precisely subjects that concern the core and center.[25]

If tradition concerns the core of existence, it cannot but concern me personally, so to speak. In other words, I cannot be indifferent

---

[21] Ibid.
[22] Ibid., 16.
[23] Ibid., 13.
[24] Ibid., 15.
[25] Ibid., 33.

toward it, but have to give myself over to it in order to grasp it at all. I take hold of it only by letting it take hold of me. In this respect, I cannot embrace tradition *except* as something "really alive". But this living quality implies that it does not come to a rest with me; my own taking hold of it implies an internal dynamic of handing it on further in love. The *traditum*, Pieper says, is by its very nature a *tradendum*, that which demands, of itself, to be passed on. I receive it only as giving myself to it, and in passing it on I also give myself along with it. This is what is meant by calling *traditio* something passed on by a "personal, voluntary act".[26] There is no doubt no better image of this passing on of tradition in love than Charles Péguy's woodsman, who ponders his children and the many things he hopes to hand down to them as he pours himself into his difficult work:

> With his tools certainly and his ancestry and his blood, his children
>   will inherit.
> What is above everything.
> God's blessing, which is on his house and on his ancestors.
> The grace of God, which is worth more than anything.
> He can be sure of this.
> Which is on the poor man and on the working man.
> And on him who raises his children well.
> He can be sure of this.
> Because God promised it.
> And because he is supremely faithful in his promises.[27]

Drawing on another of his poems, we might say of tradition what Péguy says of the soul: "You don't save your soul in the way you would save a treasure; you save it in the way that you lose a treasure, by spending it."[28] A tradition is something that can be preserved only through what *Gaudium et spes* has referred to as "a sincere gift of self".[29]

---

[26] This also illuminates the profound connection between *tradition* as a vision of the world and the *traditio*—the surrender—that Christ enacts on the Cross, a connection that Pieper seems to imply is accidental (see ibid., 76n8).

[27] Charles Péguy, *The Portal of the Mystery of Hope*, trans. David Louis Schindler, Jr. (Grand Rapids, Mich.: Eerdmans, 1996), 12–22, here: 15.

[28] Charles Péguy, *Le Mystère de la charité de Jeanne d'Arc*, in *Oeuvres poétiques complètes* (Paris: Gallimard, 1975), 392.

[29] Second Vatican Council, Pastoral Constitution on the Church in the Modern World *Gaudium et spes* (December 7, 1965), no. 24.

It is becoming evident that we can properly understand tradition only if we look, with but beyond its form, at its content. To get at the essential content of tradition in Pieper's understanding, it is helpful to return to discuss the point left open above, namely, that tradition always has its origin in divine revelation. This affirmation strikes us as implausible, no doubt, to the extent that we tend to identify tradition with such things as manner of dress and preparation of food. But to reduce the meaning of tradition in this way, as we have already pointed out, is to cash it out, so to speak, in modern currency. According to Pieper, the paradigm of tradition, which is to say the form of tradition that most fully expresses its essence and so presents a model, is *sacred* tradition.[30] It is important to recognize, however, that Pieper means by this expression more than simply the practice of the Christian faith, though that is obviously the first meaning. In two successive chapters of his book, he extends this meaning. First, he explains that any customs, beliefs, norms, and practices are "traditions" to the extent that they have been passed on from one generation to the next, "if not necessarily as authoritative, yet without explicitly questioning".[31] It is helpful, here, to introduce the term "analogy", though Pieper does not make use of it himself. Pieper's principal point is to draw a distinction: on the one hand, there are those practices that have no essential necessity and so can be neglected whenever conditions require. These "traditional practices" can change over time (his surprising example is the deliberate introduction of what we take to be the quintessential German expression *Aufwiedersehen* in 1914–1915 to replace the previously customary *Adieu*, borrowed from the French).[32] On the other hand, there is the explicitly sacred tradition, like the celebration of Easter, which has an absolute quality and which no circumstances—even being desperately at war—would permit a culture deliberately to fail to celebrate. If we recognize the importance of tradition in human existence, we will nevertheless tend to give the benefit of the doubt even to the non-essential practices and to admit change in their regard only gradually.[33] The notion of analogy is helpful here because it illuminates

---

[30] Pieper, *Tradition*, 23–35.
[31] Ibid., 37.
[32] Ibid., 38.
[33] Aquinas, *Summa theologica*, I-II, q. 97, a. 2.

a relation between the sacred and so-called secular traditions: in a healthy culture, the daily practices, manners, and customs are relative expressions of the sacred tradition, the core meaning of existence, diversely extended into the social order, which is to say, into an order that is "other" than the directly sacred.[34] There is, in principle, an infinity of possibilities at this level of existence, and, because this sphere is not directly sacred, any given practices will exhibit a certain contingence in the way Pieper describes. But recognizing an analogy reveals that these cultural phenomena, these various customs, beliefs, and norms, constitute a *way of life*, and not just a collection of individual peculiarities. They are elements of an organic whole, lying at varying distances from a center. Taken as a whole, they represent an interpretation of the sacred tradition in the particular time and place of a given people, or, to switch metaphors, the incarnation of a tradition in a particular flesh, which is not imposed from above but extends into a sphere beyond it while drawing on the native quality of that sphere.[35] We are proposing, here, an analogous extension of the notion of "inculturation", which is typically used in a theological context to describe a culture's ultimately unique way of practicing the faith; here, we mean to see that even the non-religious practices of a culture are an expression of sacred tradition, broadly conceived. We could call it a second-order expression of sacred tradition. One of the implications of this is that different sorts of customs will have different degrees of necessity and contingency depending on how "close" they are to the *central* meaning of tradition.

The second way Pieper extends the meaning of "sacred tradition" beyond the directly theological is by appealing to the clearly provocative notion of an "original revelation", which is distinct from the special revelation in Christ. He means by this phrase something more than the usual notion of "general revelation" that is often contrasted to "special revelation", namely, God's revelation of himself in creation, a revelation accessible to natural reason and so present

[34] This implies, not a "wall of separation" between the sacred and the secular, but rather a "relative autonomy" of the secular that arrives *precisely* by virtue of the priority of the sacred as revealed in Christianity. On this, see the chapter on culture in Rémi Brague's forthcoming *Curing Mad Truths* (University of Notre Dame Press).

[35] In the Incarnation, the Son of God takes on, not just flesh in general, or even flesh simply created for him from above by the Father, but specifically flesh given to him by his mother. Mary, moreover, raised Jesus in the tradition of the Jewish people.

in principle in any culture, no matter when and where it exists. In line with his argument above, Pieper speaks of this specifically as an "original revelation",[36] meaning that it was, in a manner analogous to "special revelation", inaugurated in history through God's initiative, a communication from God to the world. Exactly when and where this "original" revelation took place is, of course, necessarily obscure, and the notion of analogy allows one even to suspend any judgment regarding whether there would need to be some discrete historical event at the origin. Somewhat in the same spirit, John Henry Newman has observed, "There never was a time when God had not spoken to man, and told him to a certain extent his duty. . . . Accordingly, we are expressly told in the New Testament, that at no time He left Himself without witness in the world . . . so that revelation, properly speaking, is an universal, not a partial gift. . . . All men have had more or less the guidance of tradition."[37] However things may stand as to the manner of revelation in its more universal sense, Pieper points to the role that *mythology*, received stories about the gods and the origin of the world and man, has played in conveying tradition in premodern cultures.[38] The principal point is that the stories are received and that they operate, so to speak, in the mode of an authority.[39] In this sense, and by virtue of their content, they are indeed a *sacred* tradition, even if they are not immediately Christian. Perhaps we can refer to them as sacred in a "natural" sense. In any event, Pieper is quick to insist that even this "original" revelation arises from the Logos, who is incarnate in Christ—in other words, we are not dealing with a kind of "generic" religion, of which Christianity would

[36] Pieper, *Tradition* 30.

[37] Newman, *The Arians of the Fourth Century*, in *The Works of Cardinal Newman*, vol. 1 (New York: Longmans, Green, 1897), 80.

[38] This is a notion one finds, too, in Schelling, but it does not appear to be the case that Pieper is familiar with Schelling's positive philosophy. In any event, he does not make any reference to it. Schelling presents mythology as a form of revelation and posits a supra-individual authorship, the origin of which would be as mysterious as the origin of language, and indeed it seems as if the two origins may have some connection with each other. The supra-individual aspect may be the analogy with divine revelation; there is no particular human source. See Schelling's *Historical-critical Introduction to the Philosophy of Myth* (Albany, N.Y.: SUNY Press, 2007).

[39] Chapter 3 is called "Tradition and Authority" and begins with the observation that medieval thinkers took "authority" to be "the same for tradition" (Pieper, *Tradition*, 23).

simply be a particular instance.[40] It is not possible in the present context to enter into the profound and delicate question of Christianity
and what is called "religious pluralism"; but, recognizing the complexity of this question, especially today, we may nevertheless here
hold on to the importance of what Pieper calls "original" revelation,
which is in a certain respect presupposed by Christian revelation, as
preparing for that revelation in a manner essentially different from,
though of course analogous to, the Old Testament.

Interestingly—and in a certain continuity with the Fathers of
the Church—Pieper points to Plato as an eminent "witness" to the
"original revelation", not in the sense of his having "been there", but
in his acknowledging the importance of what has been said "by the
ancients" regarding matters at the limits, so to speak, of philosophical
reflection.[41] The fundamental importance of mythology in Plato has
often been recognized;[42] Pieper refers to the great Plato scholar Paul
Friedländer, who interpreted Plato as having gathered back together
the disparate fragments of an original "great myth".[43] We might add
to this that he integrated them and, more than that, received them
as having significant and intelligible content, rather than just repeating them or reducing them simply to otherwise senseless norms for

[40] Pieper notably critiques the sort of "Gnostic" interpretation one finds, for example, in
Leopold Ziegler (see Pieper, *Tradition*, 52). To found the point he makes in the tradition,
Pieper cites an illuminating text from Augustine's *Retractiones*: "The very thing which is now
called the 'Christian religion' existed among the ancients. Indeed it has never been absent
since the beginning of the human race, until Christ appeared in the flesh. That was when the
true religion, which already existed, began to be called the 'Christian religion'" (*Retractiones*,
I.12, quoted in Pieper, *Tradition*, 51).

[41] We might compare this to von Balthasar, who points to Virgil as in some sense summing
up pagan religion in preparation for Christianity: see *Glory of the Lord*, vol. 5, *The Realm of
Metaphysics in the Modern Age*, trans. Oliver Davies et al. (San Francisco: Ignatius Press, 1991),
630; cf. *The Glory of the Lord*, vol. 4, *The Realm of Metaphysics in Antiquity*, trans. Brian McNeil
et al. (San Francisco: Ignatius Press, 1989), 232–79. Each clearly seeks to highlight something
distinct: for Pieper, it is a *vision* of the world suffused by the good, while for von Balthasar,
the primary point seems to be *mission* in obedience to the gods.

[42] Among the many scholarly discussions, see Luc Brisson, *Plato the Myth Maker* (Chicago:
University of Chicago Press, 1998); J.F. Mattéi, "The Theatre of Myth in Plato", in Charles
Griswold, Jr., ed., *Platonic Writings, Platonic Readings* (University Park, Penn.: Penn State Univer-
sity Press, 1988), 66–83; Ludwig Edelstein, "The Function of the Myth in Plato's Philosophy",
in *Journal of the History of Ideas* 10:4 (1949): 463–81. Pieper himself has a book on the subject: *The
Platonic Myths*, trans. Daniel J. Farrelly (South Bend, Ind.: St. Augustine's Press, 2011).

[43] Paul Friedländer, *Platon I* (Berlin, 1954), 184 [*Plato: An Introduction* (New York: Pantheon Books, 1958), 173], cited in Pieper, *Tradition*, 53.

behavior.[44] It is significant that Plato typically refused to absolutize the "details" of any of the stories he recounted—they were not, for him, most basically empirical or historical in the positivistic sense— but instead pointed to the meaning they communicate, to an insight that we ought to draw from them.[45] That insight invariably concerns, in one way or another, the ultimate origin or end of things, the *archē* or the eschaton, the transcendent "sphere" that provides the horizon for our existence in time. It always refers, receptively, to a truth that lies at the farthest limits of philosophical reflection.

It is right here that we encounter the boldest and most provocative proposal that Pieper makes in his book, or at least what cannot but strike the contemporary reader as such. Up to this point, as is natural in philosophy, we have been discussing the meaning of tradition in more or less formal terms, though of course the notion of an "original revelation" already turns in a more concrete direction. Pieper makes this turn thematic and insists that tradition has a particular content.[46] Even more than that, he claims that there is, in the end, a single tradition that belongs to humanity as such, beyond any (liberal notions of the) diversity of tradition*s*, plural.[47] These two ultimately inseparable claims distinguish Pieper's vision sharply from the other, no doubt better known, defender of tradition in contemporary philosophy, Alasdair MacIntyre. While MacIntyre affirms that we can never get outside the particularity of a tradition to judge it on the basis of some "extra-traditional" criteria,[48] Pieper might

---

[44] Plato illustrates this point, for example, in the opening book of the *Republic*. Socrates questions Cephalus about the nature of justice that Cephalus had insisted was necessary to practice, but Cephalus is unable to answer. Before returning to practice his religious rites, he "hands down" (παραδίδωμι) his argument to Polemarchus, his son, who now has to deal with the challenge of providing a rational account (*Republic*, 331d).

[45] This is not meant to imply that the myth is simply an extrinsic vehicle communicating an abstract, universal meaning.

[46] Pieper, *Tradition*, 33.

[47] Ibid., see 54.

[48] See Kopff's discussion, xxii–xxiii. This does *not* necessarily imply relativism, though there have been some who criticize MacIntyre on that score. MacIntyre does indeed provide criteria for judging the superiority of one tradition over another, though it is important to note that his criteria remain strictly *formal*: see *Three Rival Versions of Moral Enquiry: Encyclopedia, Genealogy, and Tradition* (Notre Dame, Ind.: University of Notre Dame Press, 1990), 181. It might be argued that Pieper and MacIntyre are talking about two different things, not that they take up contrary positions. Though there is certainly some truth to this, we nevertheless need to recognize that Pieper is here *adding* something of decisive significance to MacIntyre's well-known account.

agree,[49] but would add that, as we saw above, tradition itself transcends historical particularity. This point becomes clearer once we recognize a content that belongs essentially to tradition, beyond the merely formal aspects of its mode of transmission. There is thus a *norm* by which traditions—in the plural—can be measured, a standard that can be regarded as "extra-traditional" only if we forget the "vertical transcendence" that belongs essentially to tradition (in this case, we ought to say "belongs essentially to *the* tradition"), as Pieper has argued.[50] Now, Pieper does not go into much detail regarding the essential content of the tradition; an attempt to specify it in an exhaustive sense would arguably betray its proper form. Instead, in his 1960 essay "Tradition in the Changing World", Pieper points to some of the principles that one discovers in Plato's work: "If we ask Plato what, in his opinion, is the quintessence of the 'wisdom of the ancients,' this is the answer we receive: that the world proceeded from the ungrudging goodness of God; that God holds in his hands the beginning, the middle, and the end of all things; that the soul of man survives death; that it is worse to do injustice than to suffer it; that, after death, judgment awaits us, along with punishment and reward, and so on."[51] Note that, though these principles clearly bear on conduct, and the way human beings ought to order their existence, this is not a list of moral norms. In this respect, these principles are different from what we find, for example, in C. S. Lewis' "Tao",

---

[49] He does present the philosophical act as transcending historical conditions, but this would mean it transcends one's tradition only if one identifies tradition and particularity.

[50] The standard objection that this presupposes a modern-rationalistic universal concept or abstract essence fails insofar as it allows only a modern-rationalistic understanding of universality. There are, however, *concrete* understandings of the universal in the ancient and medieval world (see the comments on this regard in Spaemann, "A Philosophical Autobiography", in *Spaemann Reader*, 12). For a profound meditation on a non-abstract sense of the universal, see William Desmond, *The Intimate Universal: The Hidden Porosity among Religion, Art, Philosophy, and Politics* (New York: Columbia University Press, 2016).

[51] Pieper, "Tradition in the Changing World", 14–15. One might take issue with some of the specific teachings mentioned: Plato clearly offers philosophical arguments for some of these points (like the preferability of suffering injustice [*Gorgias*, 469b ff.] and the immortality of the soul [*Phaedrus*, 245c-e]), but the eschatological *condition* of the soul and the goodness of the origin and end of all things seem to lie beyond such proof. For his part, Newman presents the following as belonging to the "universal revelation" handed down in tradition: "the doctrines of the power and presence of an invisible God, of His moral law and governance, of the obligation of duty, and the certainty of a just judgment, and of reward and punishment being dispensed in the end to individuals" (Newman, *Arians of the Fourth Century* [Aeterna Press, 2014], 46). There is evidently a significant overlap here.

which represents what Lewis takes to be a basic moral code found, it seems, in all cultures and representing part of the essential human patrimony.[52] Pieper is aiming, more basically, we might say, at the foundation of Lewis' "Tao". The list he draws from Plato concerns truth, a way of understanding, which would be the presupposed principles of moral norms. As we suggested a moment ago, the list can be simplified even further: it is a recognition, not just of goodness, but of absolute goodness, as the origin of all things. As such, it is that to which all things bear a relation and that to which all things return. Even more succinctly, God, as goodness, is the principle and end. Things therefore have come to be out of perfect generosity, by which they will ultimately be judged. This exitus-reditus "schema" is *the* tradition. More specifically, we ought to say that the content of the original revelation appears to be, not simply the formal structure of a schema, but also what is conveyed in and through this schema, namely, a goodness that *concerns* (and is in a certain sense *concerned with*) the world, a goodness that pronounces judgment and thereby *saves*.[53] Regarding the essentially obscure origins of ancient tradition, we may use the words Plato places in the mouth of Socrates: I won't insist on the particular details of any one account, but I will say with confidence: This story is true.

II

But can we know whether it is true? Is it even proper to call tradition true if it is unverifiable of its very nature? At this point, we

---

[52] C. S. Lewis, *The Abolition of Man* (New York: HarperCollins, 1974), 18ff.

[53] "In this connection, Plato used the word 'save.' The mythical story of the Judgment of the Dead and reward or punishment in the afterlife was in marvelous fashion 'saved.' He then astoundingly adds the wish that it 'can save us too, if we believe it' ", Pieper, *Tradition*, 47. Pieper is referring to the "myth of Er", recounted at the end of the *Republic* in 621c. There is no space in the present context, but it would be quite worthwhile to reflect on the subtle difference between what Pieper is here calling tradition and what the Church has recognized as the truths of "natural reason" accessible in principle to reason alone (*Dei Filius*). We might speak of a distinction here between form and content. Reason, considered abstractly, is able to grasp the *form* (first principle), while the tradition, which goes *beyond* abstract reason in the manner we have been discussing, conveys content (the first principle is *good*) and, indeed, reveals that this content *involves* man in his historical existence in some sense.

may reflect in a more general way on some of the implications of Pieper's account. Inside of a traditional culture, the question of truth does not seem to arise, not because it is forbidden by the powers-that-be, as the modern liberal mind might tend to think, but simply because such a question would appear strange or unnatural. On the other hand, in a culture uprooted from "sacred tradition", in the sense Pieper has given the term, the question cannot be avoided. The problem, however, is that the posing of the question in the modern context tends to *im*-pose modern assumptions concerning the nature of truth and the criteria for its assessment, which makes the problem insoluble (and this is quite different from showing tradition to be untrue or even simply non-rational). Pointing out in response that there is a contradiction in the uncritical absolutizing of critical reason tends only to deepen the despair. It makes a difference, a genuinely fundamental difference, whether one raises the question concerning truth from inside tradition or from an absolute point outside. One might object that this difference simply goes to show that, in the end, it is all arbitrary, since it makes truth finally depend on something other than reason, on nothing more than what one happens to take as one's starting point. But to raise such an objection is already to assume that one is approaching the problem as an abstract reasoner. It is unsurprising that people often find the question hopeless, but tragic that they simply resolve therefore to accept a certain arbitrariness about their fundamental identity as a result: I am an American Catholic living in the twenty-first century, but I could just as easily have been born a Buddhist in China five hundred years ago. (There is in fact no ground whatsoever for that possibility; to think that there is, is simply to concede the absoluteness of the current milieu, modern liberalism, which takes for granted an entirely unreal conception of the self.)[54]

Some other approach to the problem is needed. It would no doubt be possible to make some headway in showing the truth of tradition, as Pieper has presented it, by making a survey of various cultures, somewhat as Lewis does in his presentation of the universal moral

---

[54] For an excellent characterization of the liberal self along these lines, see the opening pages of John Milbank's essay "The Gift of Ruling: Secularization and Political Authority", *New Blackfriars* 85:996 (2004): 212–38.

code, the "Tao". But, even if the present context allowed for such an exploration, it remains the case that studies of this sort could not finally resolve the problem insofar as the claim Pieper makes about the tradition is not an empirical one in the first place, but a normative one. By saying that tradition is not just a form but also a content, Pieper opens up the possibility that certain ideas can be passed on from one age to the next without being genuinely traditional. What we propose to do here is not to try to *prove* the truth of tradition; instead, we will simply point to some things that may serve to illuminate why what Pieper says is inwardly compelling.

In a nominalistic and technological age, the point may be difficult to understand, but "rational" is not a univocal standard in the assessment of method or manner. A *rational* method is one in which the path (*hodos*) leads in truth to the object to which it is directed; in other words, a method has to be adequate to its object, which is to say that it is the *nature* of the object that determines the *nature* of the method. The object comes first. In his discussion of the good in the *Nichomachean Ethics*, Aristotle famously observes that one cannot demand the same necessity in the matter of ethics that is natural in mathematics.[55] With respect to tradition, we have seen that it is essential to tradition that its content lies beyond immediate apprehension or deductive reasoning. In this sense, tradition is not accessible to critical reason by its very nature. This does not mean that it fails when measured by the standard of critical reason, but simply that it cannot be so measured. To insist on critical reasoning, in this case, would be irrational. Indeed, it would show that one's understanding of rationality is itself arbitrary, since it amounts to a method that imposes conditions *a priori*, before considering any reasons that might bear on the method, and so without taking heed of reason's concrete object. In other words, it is a mindless use of reason. The first point we can make about the truth of tradition, thus, is that it is not a truth that can be reasonably subjected to critical reason. Again, this does not mean that it is *against* critical reason (as, for example, Adorno suggests: "Tradition is the opposite of reason"), but only that the truth proper to it is prior to the distinction between critical rationality and its opposite.

---

[55] Aristotle, *Nichomachean Ethics*, I.3.

Now, this is a fairly straightforward point, but it is important to understand that there is more at stake here than a merely technical issue. The different methods, or, more adequately put, the different conceptions of what a method *is*, give expression to something more basic. The "rationalistic" method, which would determine tradition to be arbitrary because one's acceptance of it does not come as the conclusion of a deductive process but precedes any such work of reasoning, is already "anti-traditional" from the outset. It takes for granted that the mind operates as a wholly autonomous power of reasoning, from an absolute perspective, which is to say, not as always already embedded within a context *from* which it receives its most basically determining horizon. This position is not itself arrived at as the conclusion of a reasoning process; indeed, it *cannot* be, because this would make it relative to the more basically given context as that *from* which the reasoning begins. And this is just what the position excludes. Critical reason's suspicion of tradition as arbitrary is *itself* arbitrary, and so its refusal of arbitrariness condemns itself to the very arbitrariness it refuses. The refusal of the givenness of the context from within which it thinks, or in other words its anti-traditional stance, is a *self*-refusal, or, to put the matter succinctly: this is a self-contradiction.

It is right at this point that we see the power of Pieper's proposal. One might conclude from the foregoing line of reasoning that even critical reasoning cannot help but be a kind of tradition; as MacIntyre has famously shown in a different, but profoundly related, context, liberalism, too, is a tradition, in spite of its self-understanding.[56] But Pieper's notion allows us to reach something more than the essentially negative conclusion that *some* kind of tradition is inevitable, so we do best by at least admitting that fact, which then puts us in the position of comparing traditions fairly. As we saw earlier, Pieper shows that there is ultimately just one tradition and that this tradition has a determinate content, which can be reduced more or less to the recognition of absolute goodness as the origin and end of all things. From this perspective, we can say not only that liberalism and absolutized critical reason, which is its epistemological counterpart,

<hr />

[56] Alasdair MacIntyre, *Whose Justice, Which Rationality?* (Notre Dame, Ind.: University of Notre Dame Press, 1989).

are also and inescapably "traditional" in their own way (and so not completely liberal or the product of critical reasoning). By virtue of the norm that Pieper provides, we can also say, more profoundly, that they are essentially *bad* traditions; they *fail* at being traditional in a decisive way. They are not traditions that touch the center of the world and the core of existence, in spite of the fact that they are passed on uncritically. We therefore have to qualify the claim a MacIntyrean thinker might make, namely, that these forms of thought are "no less" traditional than the traditions they intend to reject, a claim that reduces tradition to its formal features. As a matter of fact, liberalism and critical reason *are* less traditional, and it is for this very reason that they contradict themselves.

There is an extraordinary implication of all this that completely turns the tables on the critical reasoning that belongs to liberalism. We note the word "given" that appeared several times in the discussion above; it is inevitable in any discussion of reason, since one cannot begin reasoning except from within a context that precedes that activity and thus establishes its horizon from the outset. But according to Pieper's notion of tradition, *givenness is the very content of tradition!* In other words, absolute generosity at the origin of all things is not just one possible context for thinking among many, any one of which might be equally "given"; instead, it is the only "given" that is precisely confirmed *by* its being given. In this respect, to "posit" the good as the first principle is not in fact to *posit* anything at all, but simply to acknowledge *as* given what *is* given, or, in other words, to take *as* absolute what *is* absolute. It is interesting to note, in this context, that Plato refers to approaching the good specifically as one's "proceeding to the unhypothetical first principle of everything" (μέχρι τοῦ ἀνυποθέτου ἐπὶ τὴν τοῦ παντὸς ἀρχὴν ἰών):[57] it is "unhypothetical" because it is not something that reason hypothesizes on the basis of some more fundamental context—and thus in some sense "arbitrarily"—but is recognized *as* the *archē*, as the *first* principle. In this sense, not only is starting from tradition—*the* tradition, the *given* tradition—not arbitrary with respect to other possible given contexts, but the absolutzing of tradition is an absolutizing of the very structure that belongs to reason. *The total embrace of the claim of tradition*

[57] Plato, *Republic*, 611b.

is therefore the only way to avoid arbitrariness. Far from obfuscating or relativizing the role of reason, tradition liberates reason to be its most integral self.

But tradition does not mean only the establishment of a context from within which to carry out argumentation; indeed, it does not mean this principally. We tend to associate the word "tradition" with certain practices or, more adequately, as we suggested above, with a "way of life" rather than first of all with an idea or concept, and it is natural to do so. To be sure, as we noted at the outset, having acknowledged the kinds of practices we associate most immediately with tradition, Pieper specifies that, in his own discussion, "special attention will be directed to the tradition of *truth*, where the *traditum* (or *tradendum*) is a teaching, a statement about reality, an interpretation of reality, a proverb."[58] He goes on to make the crucial observation that theory and practice ought not to be separated from each other in a dualistic fashion: "[W]e have to acknowledge that a custom, a legal maxim and a holiday can contain a doctrine, explicitly or implicitly."[59] Let us strengthen this observation by saying not only *can* such practices contain some understanding of reality, some claim about the nature of things, but they inevitably *will* contain some doctrine at a certain level. And let us note, too, that the converse is also true as a general principle: a claim about the nature of things will inevitably imply, at a certain level, a particular way of acting. It seems clear that Pieper would accept both of these statements. The subtitle of his book, after all, is "Concept and Claim" (*Begriff und Anspruch*), which implies, as we have seen, a world view that can be understood in the proper sense only by being inhabited: the concept demands a response. In this regard, a tradition is not simply something that we recall (*anamnēsis*) but, at the same time, something we reenact, as it were. "The Hebrew word for appropriating what has been handed down", Pieper observes, "means the same as 'to repeat'."[60] The handing on of tradition implies, we might say, a synthesis of the Greek recollection and the Jewish repetition: "Do this in memory of me...."

[58] Pieper, *Tradition*, 9–10.
[59] Ibid., 10.
[60] Ibid., 21.

The unity of thought and action, however, manifests an even more profound self-confirmation when we think of tradition in the concrete terms Pieper has presented. In the beginning steps of his attempt to define tradition, to lay out what it is, Pieper says that "in every case we are dealing with something that can be received and handed down in a personal voluntary act."[61] As we have seen, he goes on to expound this act as a comprehensive giving and receiving, which is distinct from mere teaching and learning, both because its content is not simply "information" that can be conveyed in this manner and also because the communication is a kind of sharing that requires a personal involvement. On the one hand, there is a giving into which one pours oneself, and on the other side there is a receiving through which one entrusts oneself to another. All of this concerns, thus far, what we would call the formal elements of tradition. As for the material aspect, Pieper proposes, as we have seen, that the tradition has a particular content, namely, absolute goodness as the origin and end of all things. What is striking here, though Pieper himself does not seem to take note of it, is another astonishing convergence of form and content. It is fitting, *perfectly fitting*, that the truth that generosity is the most basic, and most ultimate, truth of all should be communicated in and through generosity, in and through free (personal and voluntary) acts of giving and receiving, uniting people through the ages and across generations by means of a truth that transcends time, remaining constant as time passes. The living of this truth is thus a demonstration of its content, and the intelligibility of the content makes itself manifest precisely in the giving and receiving. Here is a demonstration that is more than just a syllogistic inference. Though they remain distinct, of course, the theoretical and practical dimension of this most basic truth can never be separated from each other, and this inseparability shows itself both in the content and in the form.

It is therefore proper to speak in the case of tradition of an intrinsic intelligibility, an intelligibility that provides its own evidence—that is, is "*self*-evident"—and so is compelling essentially *of itself*. It is not compelling, therefore, in an extrinsic sense, in the form, that is, of coercion; nor is it compelling in the manner of deductive reasoning,

---

[61] Ibid., 10.

which, we might say, "forces" us to accept the conclusion once we admit the premises. Instead, it can be received, as we have seen repeatedly, *only* through an act of freedom, though at the same time, as we have been arguing, this freedom is anything but arbitrary: it is, instead, an entry into a comprehensive necessity, which governs both the receiving and the passing on. There is nothing more important than receiving the truth that gives sense to the whole of existence, and this *traditum* is by its very nature a *tradendum*: what we have been freely given, we must freely pass on. Our passing it on, our being generous in the very form of our existence, is the only genuine expression of our having properly received it.

By reflecting on the way tradition happens, we come to the realization of the essence of tradition, and the meaning of the manner gets deepened beyond expectation. What flashes forth here is the splendor of truth. More precisely, it is the light in which all truths show themselves as true. In other words, what is passed on in tradition is not just some truth, but the ground of all truth *tout court*. As Pieper put it, the *tradendum* is the center of the world and the core of existence. If truth does indeed have a ground, it is not surprising that this should be communicated in a mode that is fundamentally different from (even as it includes) teaching, which is the mode proper to the conveying of one truth or another. In the end, both the form and content of tradition are love.

Toward the end of his 1960 essay on tradition, Pieper affirms that "the ultimate, and, when it comes down to it, the sole sufficient reason" to preserve a tradition as true is because it has its origin in a " 'Divine' utterance—however this may have been heard".[62] While this is of course the final word to be said on the matter, it is important to see that this is not the *only* word to be said. One might otherwise have the impression that the only thing there is that finally serves to verify a tradition is an essentially unverifiable fact, which we accept on a trust that cannot ultimately be anything but blind. Here we would have only an extrinsic criterion, which means our acceptance of tradition would be nothing but an assent of the will that is purely spontaneous, since there is no given reason to which it responds. This is trust in a purely fideistic form. Such an interpretation would send

[62] Pieper, "Tradition in the Changing World", 18.

us back to the notion of "tradition as arbitrary" that we have been criticizing. To the contrary, we have seen that the proper notion of tradition offers more than the possibility of an extrinsic criterion for its verification. There is *also* an intrinsic criterion, namely, its inherent goodness. This criterion does not supplant the transcendent criterion, namely, that the tradition has its origin in a divine word, that is, in God's self-communication, because the intrinsic criterion depends on this, or, even more adequately put, it gives proper expression to this truth. But for that very reason, it shows that the transcendent criterion cannot be *isolated* as a criterion without its being thereby distorted. A generosity without generosity is an empty word, a show of truth without the reality. The trust required in the transmission of truth, in relation to this intrinsic criterion with a transcendent ground, can *never* be simply blind; a wholly blind trust would be a trust in something *other* than the communication of goodness. When Pieper criticizes the justification he once witnessed during a visit to India, in which a father responded to his son's question why the family kept a certain practice with nothing more than the vague assertion that this is what has always been done, it is not because Pieper thought some argument ought to have been made.[63] Instead, he insisted that one has to give a *living witness* to the truth of tradition.[64] Such a witness, we might say, is *part* of the argument, one of its deepest forms. What, after all, *is* a living witness? One offers a living witness when one enacts the practices of a tradition while recollecting their meaning, which is to say, their *ground* (*Grund*). If beauty is, as Hans Urs von Balthasar has suggested, the "appearance of the ground",[65] we can say that a living witness exhibits a certain beauty in his existence, taken as a whole. The beauty, the compellingness of the intrinsic truth, lies in the goodness that, as the ground of all things, gets refracted in each particular gesture.

On this score, Pieper's account of tradition should also make us wary of going to the other extreme, namely, saying that it ultimately makes no difference whether something is traditional or not; the

---

[63] As should be clear from the foregoing, this is not to imply that argument is simply *pointless*, but just that the essential matter is displaying the *ground*.

[64] Pieper, *Tradition*, 15.

[65] Hans Urs von Balthasar, *Theo-Logic*, vol. 1, *Truth of the World*, trans. Adrian J. Walker (San Francisco: Ignatius Press, 2000), 221–25.

ultimate question is simply whether it is *true*.[66] One sometimes hears
the justification of an education founded on classic texts—a Great
Books program, for instance—in terms like the following: We ought
to read the classic texts, not because they are old, but because they
represent some of the best responses given to perennial human questions, the quality of which is attested to by the fact that the books
have withstood the test of time. (Taken to an extreme, this justification amounts to the circular argument that we read these books
because we read these books.) As Pieper has suggested, if we understand tradition in the concrete sense, which means as a timeless truth
communicated in time, and add the point drawn out in our reflection
on his account, namely, that this is not just "a" truth, but the founding truth insofar as it concerns the goodness that is the ultimate origin
and end of things, then it follows that a reverence for the ancients
is not arbitrary or irrational. It does not in principle compromise a
devotion to the truth as such. Instead, being closer to the origin in
this respect is, in a certain sense, a proximity to the source of truth
(though of course this cannot be reduced simply to the formal aspect).
As Pieper puts it, "The essential element in this concept is closeness
to the origin, the beginning, the early, the dawn, the start."[67] The
origin is not something one invents, but something one receives, and
thus *being handed down* is its proper form. To put the matter somewhat provocatively, we might say that the more *genuinely* traditional
a notion is, the truer it is. Truth and tradition reveal themselves to be
correlative concepts.

Josef Pieper is himself an exemplary transmitter of tradition, first
in the love he invariably displays in his work for the "wisdom of the
ancients", but also in the theoretical account he has given of tradition,
an account that is philosophical without being in the least rationalistic. He explains tradition without "demythologizing" it. In line with
what emerged in our reflections, we might say that his explanation
lies not only in the specific claims he makes but in the mode of being
that comes to expression in and through his writing, the "spirit" of

[66] Pieper refers to Pascal on this score, who says, "No matter what weight we assign to
antiquity, truth must always be the prime consideration, however recently it may have been
discovered" (Pieper, *Tradition*, 6). While this is essentially true, we have seen that the claim
requires some qualification.

[67] Pieper, *Tradition*, 25.

his thought. If one were to choose a word to characterize Pieper's thinking, a good candidate would be "joy" or, perhaps even more precisely, "celebration". It is a spirit that corresponds beautifully to the reception, through the tradition, of the good, a reception that is always at the same time a further communication. His love for the tradition gives his thinking a childlike energy, and one suspects that the ineradicable "naïveté" that this stance necessarily implies is one of the reasons he has often been dismissed as a "popular philosopher" and has rarely been taken seriously inside the academy. But a whole army of "professional academics" will do little to help us, as a culture, to recollect the "love at the heart of things".[68] Indeed, with their all-too-heavy boots, they are more likely to stamp it out once and for all. If this love is, as we have suggested, the *ground* of truth upon which genuine thinking takes its stand, then the academy itself depends on the living tradition that Pieper conveys and calls us to keep alive.

In this respect, we can be especially grateful to Father Fessio, who has helped to make available to the English-speaking world, not just Josef Pieper, but an entire array of "living witnesses", who will continue to be "untimely" because they take their bearings from a reference that lies beyond the passing preoccupations of any particular age. As von Balthasar has remarked, it is just this that makes them indispensable to every culture.[69] By gathering these witnesses together through Ignatius Press, Father Fessio has been a "preserver of the preservers of tradition".

---

[68] Stephan Oster has an essay on the philosophy of Ferdinand Ulrich (who is himself an admirer of Josef Pieper), which is entitled "Thinking Love at the Heart of Things: The Metaphysics of Being as Love in the Thought of Ferdinand Ulrich", *Communio* (Winter 2010): 660–700. This is a phrase that Pieper would have affirmed with enthusiasm.

[69] Von Balthasar describes Pieper as "one of the Untimely Inopportunes, that group which as a rule is also the most necessary to a society": *Josef Pieper: An Anthology*, xi.

12

Theological Aesthetics as Method

Anne M. Carpenter

Introduction

My goal in this essay is relatively simple: to pay tribute to Father
Fessio by highlighting an essential and still only occasionally explored
element in the thought of Hans Urs von Balthasar, a theologian
whose works Fessio helped bring into English. I argue that, despite
von Balthasar's reticence toward "systems", he does have a keen
interest in theological method and employs several methods himself.
What is more—and here is the essential point—von Balthasar's theological aesthetics is also a method, one that is meant to contribute
to theology in new, substantive ways. Against a loose interpretation
of von Balthasar that would associate his interest in "beauty" with
beautiful paintings and lovely music, or one that might be satisfied
with a comparison between theology and the arts, we will see that
von Balthasar offers a method that borrows from the arts in order
to achieve something *theological* rather than something "artistic". For
von Balthasar, beauty is necessary to theology because our response to
it so starkly foreshadows our response to grace. Metaphysically speaking, the nature of beauty as a transcendental helps to assure the coherent unity and convertability of the other transcendentals and thus their
unity in theological reflection. In what follows, I review elements of
von Balthasar's theological "method" in general, including scholarly
approaches to it thus far; then I look more narrowly at *Glory of the Lord*
and what its particular "theological aesthetics" method might be. As

we examine its features, we will also uncover elements of what beauty enables for von Balthasar that other methods either do not or would struggle to mimic. That is to say, beauty allows for unique integrative moments in theology; it opens the door to questions, possibilities, and reconciliations otherwise obscured to us.

1. Hans Urs von Balthasar and Method

Von Balthasar is against what he calls "system", as more than one interpreter has noted,[1] and with this he seems to be resisting a type of theology that presents itself as a series of steps that result in an inevitable, logical slide to a conclusion—a system that masks rationalism: "It is not as if one could, by means of rational inquiry and argument, recognize [Christ] to be a (perfect? religious? inspired?) man and then, following the pointers provided by this rational knowledge, move to the conclusion that he is God's Son and himself God."[2] This is not a move against rationality so much as it is a move against what D. C. Schindler calls a "knowledge complete within itself", which Schindler associates with the likes of Descartes.[3] We might well add Hegel to the "systems" von Balthasar has in mind and, indeed, Neo-scholasticism. Against such a rationalist or completionist systemizing impulse, von Balthasar re-conceives faith and reason. Faith is supra-rational, and the subject of theology is the infinite God, so there can be no pretending that our understanding is anything like mastery or that it is comprehensive, univocal. So, if we are to speak of von Balthasar's "method"—particularly as his works might intend one or several of such—"method" cannot mean anything like *this* type of "system".

Yet von Balthasar is not against every organizing principle, and he is at pains not to be against reason. "Without philosophy," he

---

[1] Todd Walatka, *Von Balthasar and the Option for the Poor: Theodramatics in the Light of Liberation Theology* (Washington, D.C.: Catholic University of America Press, 2017), 31–38; D. C. Schindler, *Hans Urs von Balthasar and the Dramatic Structure of Truth: A Philosophical Investigation* (New York: Fordham University Press, 2004), 155–61, esp. 157–58; Karen Kilby, "Chapter 4: Central Images 2: Fulfillment and the Circle", in *A (Very) Critical Introduction to Hans Urs von Balthasar* (Grand Rapids, Mich.: Eerdmans, 2012), 71–93; among others.

[2] Hans Urs von Balthasar, *Glory of the Lord: A Theological Aesthetics*, vol. 1, *Seeing the Form*, 2nd ed. [= GL 1], trans. Erasmo Leiva-Merikakis (San Francisco: Ignatius Press, 2009), 148.

[3] Schindler, *Balthasar and the Dramatic Structure of Truth*, 157–58.

says in his introduction to *Theo-Logic*, "there can be no theology."[4] Nor, indeed, is von Balthasar totally against the word or logic of "system" itself; he describes his method in *Theo-Drama* as "a system of dramatic categories".[5] The act of systematizing without creating a closed synthesis is complex. Von Balthasar's tactics of organization can vary a great deal, just as his modes of argumentation do. Scholars have highlighted essential figures like Irenaeus[6] or offered a handful of conceptual "keys"[7] or suggested themes like the spiritual senses or the saints as modes of essential organization.[8] All of them *work* in their varying ways, throwing great light on von Balthasar's insights. All the same, we would be foolish to absolutize any single "style"[9] of von Balthasar's when he himself was against such absolutization. That these various styles or angles all work legitimately to interpret von Balthasar *and* that they resist absolutization have everything to do with von Balthasar's "method".

There is an important section in the *Prolegomena* of *Theo-Drama* where von Balthasar explains both why the *Prolegomena* exists and what he intends to do with the information presented in it. The *Prolegomena* itself is an extended study of (mostly) Western plays, from the Greeks to the moderns, with attention paid to the plays themselves and to the history of drama. He occasionally reaches outward from this geographical-historical world into Chinese and Japanese drama, among other cultures. Of particular interest to von Balthasar throughout the book is the troubled, complicated relationship between the Church and the theatre. Early in the *Prolegomena*, von Balthasar explains why such a vast and detailed examination must

---

[4] Hans Urs von Balthasar, *Theo-Logic: Theological Logical Theory*, vol. 1: *The Truth of the World* [= *TL* 1], trans. Adrian J. Walker (San Francisco: Ignatius Press, 2000), 7.

[5] Hans Urs von Balthasar, *Theo-Drama: Theodramatic Theory* [= *TD*], vol. 1: *Prolegomena* (San Francisco: Ignatius Press, 1988), 128.

[6] Kevin Mongrain, *The Systematic Thought of Hans Urs von Balthasar: An Irenaean Retrieval* (New Haven, Conn.: Yale University Press, 1991).

[7] Aidan Nichols, *A Key to Balthasar: Hans Urs von Balthasar on Beauty, Goodness, and Truth* (New York: Baker Academic, 2011).

[8] Mark McInroy, *Balthasar on the Spiritual Senses: Perceiving Splendor* (United Kingdom: Oxford University Press, 2014); Matthew A. Rohaus Moser, *Love Itself Is Understanding: Hans Urs von Balthasar's Theology of the Saints* (New York: Fortress Press, 2016).

[9] Angelo Scola, *Hans Urs von Balthasar: A Theological Style* (Grand Rapids, Mich.: Eerdmans, 1991).

exist, and it is not only in order to address controversy. An extended portion of his explanation bears repeating:

> Thus arises our task, which is to draw an *instrumentarium*, a range of resources, from the drama of existence which can then be of service to a Christian theory of theo-drama in which the "natural" drama of existence (between the Absolute and the relative) is consummated in the "supernatural" drama between the God of Jesus Christ and mankind.
>
> Initially, this *instrumentarium* can use the already-existing interpretation of the world as a "theatre", establishing the categories implied in it. But it will become clear that the "theatre of the world" theme ultimately reaches a level of reflection calling for special examination of the dramatic categories themselves. . . .
>
> The present work will enable us, in volume two, to embark upon Christian theo-drama and attempt to erect that framework for which, as we have indicated, the current trends in theology are calling.[10]

We need to note a couple of features of von Balthasar's dramatic "method" already. The first is von Balthasar's habit of gathering a range of resources (*instrumentarium*) all at once in order to understand a theological problem. Elsewhere, von Balthasar compares theological thinking to a constellation, which is a helpful image: several points of light come together in order to make a whole.[11] "*Systēma*", von Balthasar writes, "means a standing together: think of the shining points, separated by swatches of darkness, that form a constellation in the night sky. And yet, since every point can refer to thousands of others, it also gives us the freedom for endless combinations."[12] At least when he is *constellating*, von Balthasar wants to draw a litany of sources together, and he wants those sources to have contact with one another variously rather than, say, with a single conclusion or point to make. This, we might say, is the "system" von Balthasar prefers over any other. It also hints at what he wants from a method: a wholeness (form) perceivable through fragments and the freedom of plurality (though not of pluralism).[13]

---

[10] Balthasar, *TD* 1:130.

[11] A Balthasarian mode discussed in an extended fashion in James Fodor, *Theological Aesthetics after Von Balthasar* (New York: Routledge Press, 2008).

[12] Hans Urs von Balthasar, "The Plurality of Theology", in *Explorations in Theology*, vol. 5, *Man Is Created*, trans. Adrian Walker (San Francisco: Ignatius Press, 2014), 386.

[13] Ibid., 386–87.

A second insight we might draw from the *Theo-Drama* quote above is von Balthasar's employment of various anthropological categories—especially from the arts—in order to try to organize his sources and engage them with one another. This is delicate work, and it involves allowing his resources to inform his understanding and allowing for theology—which is never identical with the natural sources it borrows—to inform his transposition of these categories into the supernatural. As we will see later in this essay, much of this delicate balance is exemplified in his theological aesthetic.

To review, then: von Balthasar's understanding of "method" bears at least three characteristics so far: an articulation of wholeness within fragments, the use of plurality, and the acknowledgment of the relationship between the natural and the supernatural. These three features present us with a general frame of sorts for von Balthasar's various theological considerations. It is not quite a method, formally, but it begins to take the shape of one. Von Balthasar's favored strategy has much to do with his unique interests and background as a scholar. To help us better understand the direction of von Balthasar's thought, I want to highlight the work of three scholars and then triangulate them together.

The first and perhaps most important contribution appears in Cyril O'Regan's oeuvre, especially in the first of the *Anatomy of Misremembering* series.[14] For O'Regan, von Balthasar is engaged in a complex dialogue with modern philosophers like Hegel, one where von Balthasar at once recalls their philosophy in order to address it and re-remembers the Christian tradition that these modern philosophers elide by deliberately misremembering. This is one motive for von Balthasar's constellations, and it helps to explain why the points of light need to be *patterned*, need to express form, as much as to be *present*. "Tradition is not simply a cornucopia of memories held by the church to be faithful to the primal mystery", O'Regan explains, "but a memory of memories that critically sifts through individual memories for their aptness, their particular qualities, their relation to other perspectives, and their relevance for the moment."[15] Von Balthasar's remembering-again is both a counter and a dialogue, and

---

[14] Cyril O'Regan, *Anatomy of Misremembering: Von Balthasar's Response to Philosophical Modernity*, vol. 1, *Hegel* (New York: Crossroad Publishing, 2014).

[15] Ibid., 8.

it is one that bears in it the freedom of patterned multiplicity. For von Balthasar, tradition "is both plural and highly differentiated; the tradition is genuinely multivoiced and polyphonic."[16]

Jennifer Newsome Martin provides an account—an "excavation"— that allows further insight into the decisions von Balthasar makes; that is, into the reasoning that underlies how he patterns his constellations.[17] Martin's work highlights specific desiderata that shape von Balthasar's thinking. Some of the most important include a commitment to the *analogia entis*,[18] the affirmation of finitude,[19] and "the preservation of robust Trinitarian claims to equidivinity".[20] This is not an exhaustive review of Martin's presentation, but it serves to show that von Balthasar has key stances that he will not surrender at any cost. So, it is not polyphony itself that von Balthasar desires, but rather the illumination of a specific form through polyphony. The possible arrangements of memories, to borrow from O'Regan, are infinite—but not infinite in every direction. In Martin's words, von Balthasar "indulges but does not always readily sanction a plurality of voices".[21] There are limits as well as infinites. This makes von Balthasar's approach to theology profoundly creative.[22]

The final scholar of mention requires lengthier discussion because of his topic, which has been barely touched in Anglophone von Balthasar scholarship: this is Jonathan King's work on von Balthasar's early thought, including his literary training.[23] While my own work has described the inextricable link between the *how* of von Balthasar's expressions and *what* he means by them, King delves into von Balthasar's education in *Germanistik*, for which he received his

[16] Ibid., 31.

[17] Jennifer Newsome Martin, *Hans Urs von Balthasar and the Critical Appropriation of Russian Religious Thought* (Notre Dame, Ind.: University of Notre Dame Press, 2015), 1.

[18] Ibid., 62–63. "A fundamental Balthasarian *desideratum* for the success of a theological aesthetics of glory, however, is a commitment to the *analogia entis* ..., in language that both reflects his Ignatian principle of *Deus semper maior* and borrows from the fourth Lateran Council of 1215: 'the ever great dissimilarity to God no matter how great the similarity to Him'".

[19] Ibid., 75.

[20] Ibid., 183.

[21] Ibid., 201.

[22] Ibid., 204.

[23] Jonathan S. King, "Theology under Another Form: Hans Urs von Balthasar's Formation and Writings as a Germanist" (Ph.D. dissertation, Saint Louis University, 2016).

only Ph.D.[24] To the end of his life, von Balthasar considered him-self a Germanist.[25] As King points out, this results in something of a paradox in von Balthasar, since, "On the one hand, von Balthasar's approach to Germanistics was from the beginning guided by basic theological concerns; on the other hand, his mature approach to the-ology was equally shaped by his prior formation in Germanistics."[26] So, understanding what Germanistics meant to von Balthasar helps us considerably in understanding why he takes up his somewhat unusual, constellating approach to the theological task.

The field of Germanistics, which is devoted to studying the myths and literature of the Germanic peoples, emerged at first with a heavy focus on philology. It experienced a transformation a couple of gen-erations before von Balthasar. These *Neugermanisten* saw themselves as *Geistesgeschichtler*, or intellectual historians.[27] Under this banner, the New Germanists pushed for a more holistic understanding of philol-ogy and of the task of Germanistics. Wilhelm Dilthey, a key figure in the movement, argued that the field ought to focus on an individual's experiences (*Erlebnisse*), and this is because the various experiences of an individual build into a cohesive perspective, not apart from, but within the context of history, culture, and society, so that one can gain a meaningful understanding of an epoch or individual. "[N]ot a mere aggregate [of experience]", King says, "but the unity of life, which is teleological and means something".[28]

Rudolf Unger was a student of Dilthey's and a teacher of von Balthasar's. In a logic that closely follows Dilthey's, he describes the teleological and spiritual elements of Germanistics:

> *Geistesgeschichte* is not a particular domain to be objectively delimited, but rather a specific mode of consideration of spiritual things which directs itself toward the ideational superstructure of cultural synthesis, and which understands a given individual intellectual domain as an outcome of the total spirit of the culture as a whole at a given time,

---

[24] Anne M. Carpenter, *Theo-Poetics: Hans Urs von Balthasar and the Risk of Art and Being* (Notre Dame, Ind.: University of Notre Dame Press, 2015).

[25] See King's discussion of Balthasar's self-understanding of the matter in his introduction, in "Theology under Another Form", 1–2.

[26] Ibid., 8.

[27] Ibid., 44.

[28] Ibid., 47.

thus in its organic connections with the other ideational domains of culture, philosophy and theology.[29]

So Germanistics is a field that, in trying to understand intellectual history, moves to study every aspect of what makes "the total spirit of the culture", a spirit that—especially for von Balthasar—includes religion and theology. This helps to explain von Balthasar's constant fascination with highlighting specific individuals and reviewing their major contributions to a particular theme, since by the logic of Germanistics such a study is an irreplaceable window into a time and into the spirit of a human being before God. It also at least partially explains von Balthasar's willingness to search for theological meaning in a life or in works that are not readily theological, since for him such artifacts do contain theological meaning.

Von Balthasar's method—the light by which he sails—can be summarized according to the following characteristics: multiplicity or polyphony that reveals a unified form, the freedom of several kinds of engagements at once, commitment to certain non-negotiable positions like the analogy of being, and re-remembering as an act of dialogue and of response—all shaped by the foundational logic of his studies with the New Germanists. Broadly speaking, we might say that von Balthasar's method always returns to a habit of marking out constellations. His tactics nevertheless vary, sometimes rather significantly, depending on his present task or the mode in which he desires to articulate a conclusion—often varying within the same single work. From this broad perspective, then, we must turn to look at von Balthasar's theological aesthetics in particular.

2. The Place of Theological Aesthetics

Aside from perhaps the dramatics, von Balthasar's aesthetics has received the most intensive and frequent commentary in English-language scholarship. Such engagement ranges from interpretive summaries to critical attempts to unite it to other sections of the trilogy or non-Balthasarian writings, though the field is dominated

---

[29] Rudolf Unger, as quoted in ibid., 54.

for now by mainly hermeneutic gestures. Contemporary theology has experienced rapid growth in writings on imagination, poetry, literature, music, and the visual arts both alongside von Balthasar and apart from him, always gravitating back toward him and pushing away from his work as one of first serious theological engagements with the arts in the twentieth century.

Many of these works are primarily comparative. They move back and forth between theology and the art or arts under question, noting when they arrive at resonant (primarily theological) conclusions.[30] Others are more ambitiously synthetic, employing theology and the arts together in order to reach a moment of theological insight. This can resemble the highly experimental *theopoetics* movement, which has its roots in Mennonite faith and shares no direct connections to a project like von Balthasar's.[31] Or it can take the form of considerations like Jeremy Begbie's more traditional explorations, which, while operating something like *comparative* work with its long excurses on music theory, nevertheless move into moments of pause for the sake of straightforward theological reflection.[32] There is also work like Dan Quash's *Found Theology*, which attempts to resolve a theological problem by borrowing from a phenomenon in art; or one like Natalie Carnes' *Beauty*, which examines Gregory of Nyssa quite apart from von Balthasar, but with just as much of an aim toward a theological understanding of beauty.[33] Works like these last two in particular begin to resemble something like the project von Balthasar undertakes in his theological aesthetics, though they themselves do

[30] See, for example, David C. Mahan, *An Unexpected Light: Theology and Witness in the Poetry and Thought of Charles Williams, Micheal O'Siadhail, and Geoffrey Hill* (New York: Wipf & Stock, 2009); Sander Van Maas, *The Reinvention of Religious Music: Oliver Messiaen's Breakthrough toward the Beyond* (New York: Fordham University Press, 2009); W. David O. Taylor and Taylor Worely, *Contemporary Art and the Church: A Conversation between Two Worlds* (New York: IVP Press, 2017); Ruth Illman and W. Alan Smith, *Theology and the Arts: Engaging Faith* (New York, Routledge, 2015).

[31] See L. Callid Keefe-Perry, *Way to Water: A Theopoetics Primer* (New York: Cascade Books, 2014).

[32] Jeremy Begbie, *Music, Theology and Time* (New York: Cambridge University Press, 2000). Cecilia González-Andrieu, *Bridge to Wonder: Art as a Gospel of Beauty* (Waco, Tex.: Baylor University Press, 2012).

[33] Ben Quash, *Found Theology: History, Imagination and the Holy Spirit* (New York: T&T Clark, 2013); Natalie Carnes, *Beauty: A Theological Engagement with Gregory of Nyssa* (New York: Cascade Books, 2014).

not rely heavily on von Balthasar to do so. The point, for now, is to grasp the variety of directions aesthetics in theology has taken.

What, then, does *von Balthasar* want to do with beauty, and what does he think it does for theology? This is a slightly different question from what he means by *beauty*, especially beauty as form, which has been somewhat exhaustively rehearsed in secondary literature.[34] According to his introduction to *Glory of the Lord*, von Balthasar means for beauty to address specific ills in modern theology and in modern religion, since without beauty religion is "denuded" and its face disfigured.[35] Even matter becomes bare facticity, "an indigestible symbol of fear and anguish", and being itself is rendered untrustworthy.[36] How beauty addresses such problems is not yet clear at this point in the book. He narrates a general story about the loss of beauty in Western Christianity, with both Protestant and Catholic versions. We do receive some hints, though: beauty helps to "bring the truth of the whole again into view", the truth of all the transcendentals of being,[37] standing at the crossway between ethics and metaphysics (and truth).[38]

Von Balthasar's chief task is, however, to write a theology; in this first part of his triptych, von Balthasar aims both to recover beauty for theology and to push it forward via beauty. Most of all, though, his task is to write a theology that functions as a *theology*. "Theology" in the strictest sense for von Balthasar is God's perfect self-knowledge and self-utterance, and as a human field it is occupied with questions about God and salvation history, and it is shaped by revelation (rather than shaping revelation).[39] Other areas of inquiry are conceivably "theology" as well, though in a secondary sense, relying as they do on the "first" theologies for their sense. We might say more precisely

---

[34] Works particularly devoted to the question include Veronica Donnelly, *Saving Beauty: Form as the Key to Balthasar's Christology* (Bern: Peter Lang, 2007); Michael Maria Waldstein, *Expression and Form: Principles of a Philosophical Aesthetics according to Hans Urs von Balthasar* (Paris: Éditions du Cerf, 1998); Ulrich Simon, "Balthasar on Goethe", in *The Analogy of Beauty: The Theology of Hans Urs von Balthasar*, ed. John Riches (Edinburgh: T&T Clark, 1986), 60–76.

[35] Von Balthasar, *GL* 1:18.

[36] Ibid., 1:19.

[37] Ibid., 1:18.

[38] Ibid., 1:34.

[39] Ibid., 1:116–24.

that in the trilogy von Balthasar offers us the *structure of a theology*. He presents us with its shape, its bones, its frame. At no point does von Balthasar claim that the trilogy is a complete systematic theology, and it is helpful not to treat it as such.

The importance of this deliberate "lack" of a complete system ought not be underestimated. Von Balthasar, as we saw above, does not trust systems that present themselves as self-sufficient. His trilogy often functions as a structure—or a work of art, we might say—that strives to turn our eyes toward the "primal form" in Christ and to the tradition that guards and cherishes the memory of that form.[40] Von Balthasar's work of art does not ask every possible, or even every traditional, question about the primal form. Most urgently, von Balthasar does not wish to replace the phenomenon.[41] On this view, von Balthasar's constellations serve not only to illuminate the form of Christ but also to indicate sources beyond von Balthasar himself to read. Much as he explicitly attempted to defer himself and his work to that of Adrienne von Speyr, so also we should read his studies of other theological lights as acts of deference. If we remained with von Balthasar alone, we would be unable to address the "feedback loop"[42] that develops between von Balthasar and his vast interpretations of saints and epochs. Breaking out into those he reads (and even beyond) is, or could be, as much a part of Balthasarian method as attending to the *Gestalt* of his work. There we would mimic the author as well as interpret the schema.

Such a perspective on the trilogy would also place its missing pieces into context. If it is intended as the outline of a shape—or, to be more precise, intended to impress a form—rather than to offer a complete series of reflections on every locus in theology, then it was written in a vein quite different from that of either Karl Rahner or Thomas Aquinas. Von Balthasar tends to gesture toward, presume, or simply not address what he has not placed directly in his sights. Thomas in particular is a figure more presumed than explained, particularly in places like *Theo-Logic I*, without whom von Balthasar's theology of nature and grace makes little sense.[43]

---

[40] Ibid., 1:25.

[41] Ibid., 1:114–27.

[42] See King, "Theology under Another Form", 56–57.

[43] Cf. Carpenter, *Theo-Poetics*, chap. 3.

The frame-quality of von Balthasar's triptych also helps to address the way each "panel" speaks to the others, not only because they imitate the convertibility of the transcendentals but also because they mutually interpret one another. They both reinforce the form meant to be impressed upon a reader and provide further cartographical points to follow. Thus the *Epilogue* is a recapitulation more than a summary, *Theo-Drama* continues to employ aesthetic categories despite shifting firmly to matters of freedom, and elements of *Theo-Logic* make sense of ambiguities in *Glory of the Lord*.

3. Form and Method

Now that we have examined the structure of the trilogy in general, and something of the *Glory of the Lord*'s place within it, it is left to us to consider what it is that the aesthetics contributes to theology in particular. We begin with a quotation: "The beautiful form presents itself to us, it 'attests' itself, its character exhibits grace, favor [*Huld*]. In a twofold sense: it is grace on the part of Being that it can produce and sustain such a form, and this grace also attaches to the individual being itself."[44] Thus von Balthasar summarizes the previous section of his triptych, *Glory of the Lord*, in *Theo-Drama*. It is a gnomic set of phrases that deserve careful examining. "The form", he says, "presents itself." That is to say, beautiful objects and people "shine forth" or call out to us.[45] When he says that the beautiful "attests to itself", he means that the beautiful is in some way objective, which is not to say that it is far away from me or "out there", but rather that the beautiful is not under my control.[46] It is beautiful to me because it gives itself to me as beautiful; I acknowledge its beauty through gratitude or reverence. For example, we would not want to say that a woman is beautiful because of what we predetermine, though we often do speak like this, and feminists

---

[44] Hans Urs von Balthasar, *Theo-Drama: A Theological Dramatic Theory*, vol. 2: *Dramatis Personae: Man in God*, trans. Graham Harrison (San Francisco: Ignatius Press, 1990), 23.

[45] Von Balthasar, *GL* 1:19–20, 147.

[46] See for example ibid., 1:148, 422. "[I]f this form really is the crowning recapitulation of everything in heaven and on earth, then it also is the form of all forms and the measure of all measures, just as for this reason it is the glory of all glories of creation as well" (ibid., 1:422).

are right to call it objectifying. We would instead want to say that something about her has turned our eyes toward her beauty, and for von Balthasar that "something" would be the splendor of her beauty. Anything else is a game of power.

Because beauty in some way offers itself to me so that I might acknowledge it, which does not make it beautiful but which does enliven the beautiful (and me) in some way, von Balthasar uses the language of gift, grace, and dialogue/response. We have thus moved quickly through beauty's essential elements in von Balthasar's thought: the splendid form shining forth, acknowledged through the gratitude of the one who beholds it. But these are also, for von Balthasar, the essential elements of faith. The splendid God shines forth as beautiful, as Beauty itself, beheld by the one who looks on in gratitude. So for von Balthasar "the beautiful" provides a skeletal structure for theological categories. It is not a comparative venture, and this is because he is setting out to build theological scaffolding using categories of beauty transmogrified by theology—much as we saw him explicitly outlining in the *Prolegomena* to *Theo-Drama*—and his first volume in *Glory of the Lord* spends much of its time indicating where some of these categories would fit in a theology of faith and revelation. As von Balthasar himself says, "The quality of 'being in itself' which belongs to the beautiful, the demand the beautiful itself makes to be allowed to be what it is, the demand, therefore, that we renounce our attempt to control and manipulate it, in order truly to be able to be happy by enjoying it: all of this is, in the natural realm, the foundation and foreshadowing of what in the realm of revelation and grace will be the attitude of faith."[47]

Von Balthasar constantly moves between allowing the human experience of the beautiful to inform his theology and allowing the radically supernatural experience of faith to govern it, and the difference is often but a thin blade. He is quite clear: revelation, and the experience thereof, must win out—but not in such a way that erases nature or that veils how nature mirrors the supernatural that it is not, of itself, capable of engaging.[48] This is why he acknowledges the (modern) need to begin with the subjective experience of faith,

[47] Ibid., 1:148.
[48] Ibid., 430–36.

and indeed he does so—it is the longest section of the first volume—and yet everything subjective points to the object of faith "by way of anticipation".[49] There are two ways such an anticipation is made possible: one is through the obediential potency of human nature, and thus occurring at the level of nature; the other is through the supernatural object of faith (Christ) informing the subjective human experience of faith, an impress of form upon a person in a way that resembles natural experience and yet is qualitatively different because it is supernatural.[50] In *Love Alone Is Credible*, this dual anticipation appears as distinguishable yet simultaneous, as man recognizes the love of Christ *as love* through a kind of anticipation (*Vorverständnis*) and yet recognizes that he does not possess this love, and indeed could not recognize such love, even through anticipation, without conversion.[51] Ultimately what is natural can only be an analogy for the supernatural.

Notice for a moment how the beautiful does not lack a certain intelligibility and the involvement with truth and the judgment thereof that makes it possible. If what appears as beautiful fails this test, then it is imperfectly beautiful, an illusory reality, or the work of an aesthetic theology. That is to say, von Balthasar's theological aesthetic "has teeth". He is interested in how beauty can really be known, even rigorously so, while also distinctively from truth.

In other words, the beautiful bears the qualities of objectivity, since it is able to stop us short and pull our attention with the splendor that is its own; it also bears the qualities of subjectivity, since that same splendor causes the inner world of the subject to rise up in resonant greeting. This makes the beautiful particularly useful in von Balthasar's current theological task in *Glory of the Lord*, which so intricately twines the subjective and the objective in a theology of faith and revelation (of vision and rapture).[52] So it is that the beautiful is supposed to aid the theological task, and in this it is not intended as an extra flourish or an unnecessary option, even if there are also other ways to arrive validly at similar insights.

[49] Ibid., 1:419.

[50] Ibid., 1:143–47.

[51] Hans Urs von Balthasar, *Love Alone Is Credible*, trans. D.C. Schindler (San Francisco: Ignatius Press, 2005), 61.

[52] Von Balthasar, *GL* 1:122.

One of beauty's central features, both metaphysically and theo-logically, is the way it binds together truth and goodness. As John Dadosky explains, beauty is "the glue that holds the other transcen-dentals together".[53] Beauty is "the splendor of the transcendentals together", a view we can find not only in von Balthasar, but also in the likes of Jacques Maritain and Bonaventure.[54] In this context, we better grasp von Balthasar's radical statements in the introduction that describe the loss of beauty as the loss of goodness and truth as well, "in an act of mysterious vengeance".[55] Yet the idea also recol-lects von Balthasar's famous call for a "kneeling theology",[56] one that is capable of both contemplation and action together, since a deep recovery of the beautiful is at one and the same time a recovery of contemplative mystery and a recovery of the divine call to the person to enter into the theological drama of Christ.[57]

Beauty is a transcendental in a manner different from the others, since it always gives way to truth and to goodness—indeed, the an-cient and medieval worlds struggled to distinguish beauty from goodness—and since a fundamental element of its status is precisely this ability to reinforce the convertibility of the transcendentals.[58] Yet von Balthasar leads with this unusual transcendental for these same reasons, so that the hopelessly fragmented elements of faith, frag-ments whose unicity was once so easily presumed, can shine again with the wholeness they each, and together, contain.

This tactic or perspective appears in *Glory of the Lord* in a number of ways. In the latter half of the first volume, we glimpse more than one Christological implication of beauty's relationship to wholeness. The form of Christ is at once "the appearance of an infinitely deter-mined super-form" and "a unique, hypostatic union between arche-type and image".[59] Here again we get that double movement: Christ

[53] John Dadosky, *The Eclipse and Recovery of Beauty: A Lonergan Approach* (Toronto: Univer-sity of Toronto Press, 2014), 12.

[54] Ibid., 51.

[55] Von Balthasar, *GL* 1:18.

[56] Hans Urs von Balthasar, "Theology and Sanctity", in *Explorations in Theology*, vol. 1, *The Word Made Flesh* (San Francisco: Ignatius Press, 1989), 181–210.

[57] Hans Urs von Balthasar, "Contemplation and Action", in *Explorations in Theology*, 1:227–40.

[58] Cf. Dadosky, *Eclipse and Recovery*, 33–38, esp. 36.

[59] Von Balthasar, *GL* 1:422.

supernaturally standing *above* creation and yet also recapitulating it as a member of it. Or again, "This revelation ... does not have its place *alongside* the revelation in the creation, as if it competed with it, but *within* it", despite not being identical with creation, at least from our point of view.[60] This twofold vision, this stereoscopic perspective that permeates so much of von Balthasar's methodology, bears a strong aesthetic imprint both within the Incarnation and with respect to the relations of all else to it.

In Christ, von Balthasar explains, "The mandated task is divine, its execution human, and the proportion of perfect 'attunement' prevailing between them is both human and divine."[61] Here the aesthetic categories of *proportion* and *attunement* appear in order to stress the theanthropic unity of Christ while yet maintaining a careful distinction between the natures. Proportion presumes "parts", and a string must be tuned to a certain pitch, and yet both are only sensible when considered together with what they are tuned to or proportionate to, rather than when they are separated out into an individual instance. Christ's uniqueness as the God-man stands out in the way he is his own unrepeatable measure, and yet an aspect of this uniqueness is the harmony and unity of his humanity and divinity in the hypostatic union. The Incarnation is beautiful, both in the accord between the natures and in the radical difference between them.

For von Balthasar, such harmonic attunement in the Incarnation also refers to the "concordance" "between [Christ's] mission and his existence".[62] He is identical with his mission; the whole of *who* he is and *how* he is as Incarnate One is the expression of his purpose, not only because he is God, but also because he is wholly given over as man. "He himself is this concordance", von Balthasar stresses.[63] These claims strongly foreshadow those that appear in *Theo-Drama*, when von Balthasar identifies Christ's person and mission.[64] Here, the categories are aesthetic rather than "dramatic" (that is, focused on freedom and action), and so by the same inner principle that works

---

[60] Ibid., 1:447.

[61] Ibid., 1:457.

[62] Ibid., 1:456.

[63] Ibid., 1:460.

[64] Cf. Hans Urs von Balthasar, *Theo-Dramatics: A Theological Dramatic Theory*, vol. 3, *Dramatis Personae: Persons in Christ*, trans. Graham Harrison (San Francisco: Ignatius Press, 1992).

itself out in *Theo-Drama*, but here in a different mode, von Balthasar seeks to work out how image, archetype, proportion, expression, and so forth, fold together in Christ. He writes,

> The interior attunement, proportion, and harmony between God and man in Christ-form raises it to the level of an archetype, not only of all religious and ethical, contemplative and active behaviour, but equally of the beautiful, regardless whether this is agreeable or not to the person with a creative aesthetic sensibility and regardless of all the questions that may be raised concerning the 'aesthetic imitation' involved in following such an archetype. For this beautiful object *is* revelation: it is the beauty of God that appears in man and the beauty of man which is to be found in God and in God alone.[65]

Notice how von Balthasar manages to stress the unity of the Incarnation, indeed, the total identification of Christ with his mission, without thereby collapsing the two natures into one another. Form, after all, is wholeness expressed through fragments or parts.[66] Here, the form under question would not be the divinity "behind" the humanity of Christ—God cannot really be said to have form in the first place, since God has no parts—but rather the form is the Incarnation itself. Nor indeed is this a moral union of the sort suggested in the fifth-century Christological controversies. The *form* of revelation is, at its heart and its height, the Incarnation. In the above quote, von Balthasar is considering the accord between the two natures of Christ as a particular *quality* of the form (rather than the totality of the form).

Establishing this allows von Balthasar to treat the aesthetic aspect of the Incarnation from a new angle, which is the relationship between the beautiful form of Christ and those who "see" it. Von Balthasar does so at length from both a subjective and an objective standpoint, and we might say that much of its fullest development appears in his theology of the saints. To explain: as the objective form of revelation, Christ is the "center" and "measure" of all else. These sorts of

---

[65] Von Balthasar, *GL* 1:465.

[66] Cf. Hans Urs von Balthasar, "Transcendentality and *Gestalt*", *Communio* 11, no. 1 (Spring 1984): 5: "It signifies a coherent, limited totality of parts and elements perceived as such, yet which demands for its existence not only 'a' context, but 'the' context of being in its totality."

metaphors emerge from the arts. A painting, for example, has its harmony of proportions measured not only according to how the trees and river in a landscape relate to one another (between each other), but also according to the painting as an entire work. In Christ, we see both proportion-between *and* the entire work. What von Balthasar imagines with respect to revelation is intensified not only because it involves the supernatural expressing itself through the natural, but also because the "measure" itself—the Incarnation—is entirely unique.

One further example suffices to complete the logic. We have seen that Jesus is the archetype against which all else is measured. But, von Balthasar insists, we must remember that the archetype "is the indivisible God-man: man, in so far as God radiates from him; God, in so far as he appears in the man Jesus."[67] Thus von Balthasar's wariness of examining the Incarnation in terms of final causes, since this kind of analysis harms the delicate (aesthetic) balance between the united natures. "[I]n this event, the humanity of Christ is no longer the 'expression', but rather becomes the 'instrument'... by means of which 'someone else' strives for and attains to 'something else'."[68] The harmony between the two natures is expressive—and aesthetic—in a specific way, with the humanity revealing the divinity to which it is indissolubly united. It is not so much that causality subordinates Jesus' humanity as it is that, in von Balthasar's opinion at least, causality implies that I can move beyond this foundational harmony of expression. For von Balthasar, it is this harmony that reaches out, as the incarnate glory of God, to man. It is this harmony that the saints imitate in endless variety.

With this kind of framework in place, von Balthasar is able stress the bodiliness of the Incarnation and indeed of the creaturely response to revelation, precisely because the "harmonics" of the expression involve the flesh as much as faith in God. After his wary caution about the limits of causality, von Balthasar turns to the eschatological vision of Augustine at the end of *City of God*. "Augustine", he says, "attained a wonderful balance between the vision of God in the heart and the vision of his glory in the transfigured cosmos with the transfigured bodily senses."[69] At the end of all things, according

[67] Von Balthasar, *GL* 1:426.
[68] Ibid.
[69] Ibid., 1:428.

to Augustine, we will not only see the glory of God in our hearts, but also see it with "dazzling clarity" in the transfigured world with our transfigured eyes. In this, we arrive at the fullest imitation of Christological harmonics.

More than any of the other transcendentals, beauty is involved with matter and the body. Beauty is a visceral, "incarnate" experience. Western thinkers reflected on this as early as Plato's *Symposium*. It was one of the aspects of beauty that threw its status as a transcendental into doubt, alongside its resemblance to the good. Yet for von Balthasar, who looks upon the transcendentals of being under the light of the Incarnation, beauty's intense relationship with materiality is to its advantage. That is to say, beauty not only helps to bind together the true and the good as a reminder of their unity, but also helps to bind the theologian to the material world as a reminder, against all Gnostic impulses, that it, too, expresses the glory of God in its earthly beauty. To forget this aspect of beauty would be to forget not only what it helps to secure in the Christian tradition, but also to forget what *von Balthasar* is interested in securing in the Christian tradition.

We have thus far studied von Balthasar's method in theological aesthetics "properly" speaking; that is, we have examined major aspects of what it is he thinks that theological aesthetics helps to achieve in theology. With the analogy of being always operating under the surface, von Balthasar proceeds in two major directions: an articulation of form as wholeness, as integrative specificity; and a description of the relationship between the Christ-form and the rest of creation. Beauty's advantage in these paths of inquiry are several. Von Balthasar is able to describe "form" in a way that highlights the unicity of the Incarnation and that allows that unicity to serve as the foundation of the creaturely imitation of Christ. He is able to emphasize Christ's embodiment without conflating it with his divinity. Finally, he is able to harmonize varying kinds of proportion (within the Incarnation, between the Incarnation and faith, between the Word and the world) without forcing them to overlap. By borrowing categories from the arts—expression, harmony, form, proportion, and so on— von Balthasar can describe the complex realities of revelation in a way that allows them to stand together without confusion, much as many voices can be heard in a polyphonic chorus.

As a final examination of von Balthasar's "method" in theological aesthetics, we will now briefly examine his understanding of Blaise

Pascal. This is a somewhat unusual tactic, but a helpful one in the ways it will review von Balthasar's theological aesthetics by looking at one of the points of light in its constellation (that is, Pascal). It is also helpful because the topic has not been touched in any great depth in von Balthasar scholarship. With a fresh face to examine, as it were, we will be able to see the countenance of von Balthasar's aesthetics anew.

4. A Study in Theological Style: Blaise Pascal

"Pascal wrote no aesthetics", says von Balthasar near the end of his study on Pascal. "On the other hand, a concern with beauty and harmony is found in his whole work."[70] So the figure of Pascal—or, rather, von Balthasar's understanding thereof—is informative both because von Balthasar has to suss out just what Pascal's theological aesthetics is despite the fact that it exists only indirectly and because von Balthasar is not in total agreement with Pascal. What von Balthasar identifies as *aesthetics* serves as evidence of what he imagines the aesthetics to be and do in theology, and where he shows interest in correction further fills out that understanding. Our goal here is not so much to uncover how von Balthasar has or has not formed Pascal after his own image but, rather, to reveal how von Balthasar's methodological commitments function in his judgments as he collects a repertoire of aesthetic options through a lengthy examination of thinkers in the Christian tradition. Pascal himself will also speak to us, primarily through the *Pensées*.[71]

Of Pascal's hidden yet pervasive aesthetics specifically, von Balthasar focuses on Pascal's interest in how one can come to believe.

---

[70] Hans Urs von Balthasar, *Glory of the Lord: A Theological Aesthetics*, vol. 3, *Studies in Theological Style: Lay Styles* [= GL 3], trans. Andrew Louth, John Saward, Martin Simon, and Rowan Williams (San Francisco: Ignatius Press, 1986), 233–34.

[71] H. F. Stewart, *Pascal's Pensées with an English Translation, Brief Notes and Introduction* [= Stewart, *Pascal's Pensées*] (New York: Pantheon Books, 1950). The text contains a complete version of the French manuscript as well as a translation. To make references easier, I will add the enumeration from a critical copy of the French available through the University of Freiburg. It is digitally available here: https://www.ub.uni-freiburg.de/fileadmin/ub /referate/04/pascal/pensees.pdf.

I have at certain points retranslated the French, which I will indicate with [translation mine].

This points to one immediate source of interest for von Balthasar, since his aesthetics is shaped around revelation and its reception. Faith is no easy path for Pascal, whose religious fervor and association with Jansenism rendered him profoundly suspicious of any attempt intellect might make to brave the leap into the divine unknown. Yet, in von Balthasar's estimation, Pascal is too Catholic and too much a man of science to surrender intellect and judgment entirely. Pascal—a rhetorical and mathematical genius—seeks, in von Balthasar's words, to teach us something about "the *justesse* of the expression, not only of the literary but of existential expression too" of Christian faith.[72] That is, Pascal tries to describe the *justesse* of a faith ultimately too boundless for the bonds of mere intellect and will while these are also all that human beings have to give. There has to be something fitting, a rightness in Christianity that the person of faith sees or knows, even if a fundamental element of this very same *justesse* is the fact that Christianity outstrips the human beings for which it exists. As von Balthasar says, for Pascal, "one must come not only to a conviction that [Christianity] could not have been discovered by men, but also to a conviction in its inner measuredness and its outward fitness."[73]

This deserves a bit of attention from Pascal himself. When we look at *Pénsees*, we can see that *justesse* is really von Balthasar's word for a larger interest of Pascal's. It summarizes Pascal's fascination with the relation (or lack thereof) between orders of knowledge, between contraries, and between elements of salvation history. For these, Pascal will use words like proportion and disproportion[74] or contrast opposites as in *infini* (infinity) and *néant* (nothing).[75] In a typical passage, Pascal writes, "The unit joined to infinity does not increase it by anything, not any more than a foot to an infinite measure; the finite is annihilated in the presence of the infinite and becomes a pure nothingness (*pur néant*). So also our spirit before God, so also our justice before divine justice."[76] Pascal's attention, in other

---

[72] Von Balthasar, *GL* 3:234.

[73] Ibid., 3:235.

[74] See, for example, "Man's disproportion" in Stewart, *Pascal's Pensées*, 43–52. Cf. Pascal, *Pensées (français)*, 199–72 H.

[75] Stewart, *Pascal's Pensées*, 48. Cf. Pascal, *Pensées (français)*, 199–72 H.

[76] Stewart, *Pascal's Pensées*, 418–233. [L'unité jointe à l'infini ne l'augmente de rien, non plus que un pied à une mesure infinie; le fini s'anéantit en présence de l'infini et devient un pur néant. Ainsi notre esprit devant Dieu, ainsi notre justice devant la justice divine.]

words, is always on the acknowledgment of and the reconciliation of opposites, of differences, without destroying them. Indeed, these differences appear so radically as to suggest the impossibility of their reconciliation. Other words that von Balthasar also notes appear in this same puzzle: figure, cypher, *rapport, correspondance*.[77] When von Balthasar reads Pascal, then, he is trying to triangulate Pascal's various modes of thought, trying to discover a centralizing idea, a form, that allows us to perceive the whole. This is *justesse*. Von Balthasar himself acknowledges that "the teaching about *justesse* remains a bare idea that floats before Pascal."[78] Yet for von Balthasar, it is also key for understanding Pascal's aesthetics.

Pascal himself struggles between the extremes of the basic dialectic that men find themselves in—including the other dialectics that pull across it, like wires in tension stretching outward at difficult angles—and the equally as dramatic beauty and order of the world. "The way of God," he writes, "who arranges (*disposer*) all things gently, is to put religion in the mind by reason and in the heart (*coeur*) by grace."[79] And yet: "[Christianity] thus teaches human beings these two truths together: that there is a God, one they are able to find, and that there is a corruption in their nature that makes them unworthy (*indignes*) of God. It is important for human beings to know both of these points; it is equally as dangerous for human beings to know God without knowing their own misery (*misère*) as it is to know their misery without knowing the Redeemer who can heal it."[80] The universe is well-ordered, even gently so; at the same time, men hang in suspension (*suspension perpétuelle*), at least on earth, between the glory of heaven and the frustration of sin.

What is more, men resist the truth. They do not really desire it in their deepest selves; it frightens them. "Thus man", says Pascal, "is only a disguise, a lie and a hypocrisy, in himself and toward

[77] Von Balthasar, *GL* 3:193–202, 226–28.

[78] Ibid., 234.

[79] Pascal, *Pensées (français)*, 172–85. [La conduite de Dieu, qui dispose toutes choses avec douceur, est de mettre la religion dans l'esprit par les raisons et dans le coeur par la grâce.]

[80] Pascal, *Pensées (français)*, 499–556. [Elle enseigne donc ensemble aux hommes ces deux vérités: et qu'il y a un Dieu, dont les hommes sont capables, et qu'il y a une corruption dans la nature, qui les en rend indignes. Il importe également aux hommes de connaître l'un et l'autre de ces points; et il est également dangereux à l'homme de connaître Dieu sans connaître sa misère, et de connaître sa misère sans connaître le Rédempteur qui l'en peut guérir.]

others."[81] The situation of man is a tragic puzzlement and pain, and for Pascal—as von Balthasar stresses—even this shipwrecked aspect of human existence leads beyond itself to God. This separates Pascal rather firmly from the nihilism of later philosophers and from the starkly negative pronouncements on human nature in certain versions of Protestantism. Von Balthasar writes, "If Pascal calls man *monstre, chimère, chaos, prodige, contradiction,* he does so not to emphasise man's dreadfulness or depravity, but the indecipherability as a whole of his figure."[82] So, von Balthasar argues, we might see Pascal's concomitant interests in proportion, figure, infinity, cypher, and so on, as an attempt to arrange or read the world aesthetically, discovering a kind of reason or reasonableness where traditional logic finds contradictions.

Von Balthasar's emphasis on *justesse* in Pascal mirrors his own interest in the rightness (*Richtig*) of the form of Christ. This theme appears in von Balthasar's discussion of the measure, form, and quality of revelation, and it refers to von Balthasar's efforts to lay out how it is that the absolutely unique Incarnation is nevertheless recognizable to the eyes of faith. For von Balthasar, this measure or form is revelation itself. He writes, "What, as the grace of faith, illumines the subject that approaches the phenomenon has to be the objective light that indwells it—its objective and radiant rightness."[83] That is to say, it is the Christ-form itself, the whole event-phenomenon of the Incarnation, which includes the action of the Spirit, that makes itself recognizable. The subject, the person of faith, recognizes via supernatural participation. This is neither a violence to the human person[84] nor a denial of human nature, since the Incarnation both exalts and is the form of the relationship between God and creature.[85]

Pascal appears in just this section of the first volume of the aesthetics, a light to guide the way. Von Balthasar borrows another of Pascal's contraries, this time the tension between God as hidden yet knowable. For Pascal, God is not hidden because of sin only, though

[81] Pascal, *Pensées* (*français*), 978–100. [L'homme n'est donc que déguisement, que mensonge et hypocrisie, et en soi-même et à l'égard des autres.]

[82] Von Balthasar, *GL* 3:210.

[83] Ibid., 1:469.

[84] Ibid., 1:470.

[85] Ibid., 1:468.

that is so, too; God is hidden by choice, as a form of divine wisdom. That is, God is real but not obvious—a conviction that Pascal shares with Thomas Aquinas no less—and God is hidden especially in the redemption wrought in Jesus Christ. God is revealed *as mystery* within the redemptive mystery. This denies reason a ladder to climb immediately to Christ, but it is nevertheless a revelation, an unveiling of what is true and recognizable as such. "Pascal strikes a balance midway between Augustine and Luther", von Balthasar explains. "He lays aside the remnants of a Platonic *theoria* characteristic of the early Augustine but does not abandon authentic Christian *theoria* in favour of mere *latere sub contrario*. He recognises a form of evidence which corresponds exactly to the law governing the object that becomes evident: this law is the manifestation of God's hiddenness in Jesus Christ."[86] Pascal strives to arrive at the sort of whole yet fragmentary perspective that von Balthasar is so keen to address, and these strivings (like von Balthasar) do not intend to violate the mystery of God so much as recognize it. Thus von Balthasar adopts Pascal's position as one like his own.

To return to the study of Pascal: one of Pascal's major achievements is to assemble a unity between the aesthetic and the ethical, or what in von Balthasar's terms would be the aesthetic and the dramatic. In Pascal, von Balthasar says, "[t]he 'heart' is the organ of the aesthetic and the ethical alike, because it is at every level the organ of love."[87] This unity, because it is both ethical and aesthetic, makes possible "the most demanding asceticism", since in it the heart attempts "the human imitation of that archetypal and inimitable consuming of the heart of God in the death of love and in Christ's eternal transfiguration of love".[88]

Interestingly, von Balthasar dismisses the charge of Jansenism in Pascal rather easily, taking Pascal at his word[89] and exhibiting calm sanguinity over Pascal's severe opposition to the Jesuits.[90] This does not make Pascal perfect. Von Balthasar complains that Pascal

---

[86] Ibid., 1:472.

[87] Ibid., 3:237.

[88] Ibid., 3:238.

[89] Ibid., 3:173. "*Je suis seul*", writes Pascal in his letters, which Balthasar quotes.

[90] Ibid., 3:174.

does not have any interest in the metaphysics that might have helped him think through the dizzying climb of contradictions in his writings; but still, as if by purity of ardent faith or sheer grace, Pascal in von Balthasar's eyes pushes through the narrow rigors of both *Port Royale* and his father's philosophy into the heart of Augustine and the heart of faith.[91] Such a critique is significant in the context of a review of Pascal that is otherwise positive or, at times, lacking in explicit commentary. Metaphysics is, as we have seen, an essential element of theology for von Balthasar. "The Incarnation", von Balthasar insists, "uses created Being at a new depth as a language and a means of expression for the divine Being and essence."[92] Such a lack on Pascal's part is not enough for von Balthasar to dismiss him, as important as metaphysics is to von Balthasar. This tells us that von Balthasar is entirely willing to discover theological-aesthetic meaning in imperfect figures, which tells us as well that not all lights in the constellation shine in the same manner or with equal degrees of perfection.

As a final point in von Balthasar's interest in Pascal, though much more could be said, we ought to note that von Balthasar's studies extend into Pascal's mathematics, which von Balthasar understands to be integral to Pascal. Von Balthasar's interest in aesthetics is not always restricted to the arts as typically understood. Of particular fascination to von Balthasar is Pascal's insight that mathematical theories and formulae need to be imaged by positing infinity mathematically and then proceeding forward. This was not only a new mathematical principle, but also, for Pascal, testimony to a fundamental way of being. Von Balthasar explains, "The condition of everything finite (including therefore man) can in an exemplary manner, be read off the geometrically infinite."[93] In other words, as geometry can posit infinity in order to calculate the angles of a cone, as Pascal did, so also understanding the place of man in the world requires positing infinity. Here Pascal resembles not only the aesthetics, but also—in his contrast between the finite and the infinite—*Theo-Drama*.

[91] Ibid., 3:175–79, 185–88.
[92] Ibid., 1:29.
[93] Ibid., 3:193.

Conclusion

Pascal is an example of an essential part of von Balthasar's theological method, which is to seek out lights in the Christian tradition by which we might be guided. In this case, Pascal is that light. This aspect of the method is one of many ways to recollect Christianity in the midst of modern *grandeur et misère*, as Pascal himself might say. It is even an incarnate method of recollection, since von Balthasar seeks to remember not only ideas as if they were frozen in time, but rather the lives that lived and thus expressed the truth of Christ, in writing or in example, just as Christ's entire existence is the expression of the truth of God. Pascal's continual circling around the various fragments of human existence—its legibility and illegibility; the gift of grace and resistance to grace, and so on—in an attempt to reconcile them, without overcoming them in some kind of Hegelian synthesis or tragic conflation, resembles von Balthasar's own efforts and interests. For von Balthasar, the beautiful appears time and again as that which brings together without extinguishing difference. So too in Pascal. At least, in *von Balthasar's* Pascal, whom we did manage to see in Pascal's own *Pensées*. Another part of the method would be to keep reading Pascal without von Balthasar, in *Pensées* and beyond, to discover his theological aesthetics for ourselves.

As we have seen, von Balthasar's theological method stresses memory, wholeness through and in parts, and creativity out of freedom. Beauty, especially as form, is for von Balthasar particularly suited to the second of these three emphases. Yet beauty is not the solution to all things, and indeed von Balthasar's trilogy is not intended as such. The trilogy presumes or gestures toward what it does not address. (This is not to say that it does not also have lacunae.) What is perhaps most important to notice is how von Balthasar expects the aesthetic to do theological *work* in his "theological aesthetics". He expects it to reshape theological ideas or lead to new insights, as in his painstaking exploration of what our experience of the "object" of revelation might be or as in the example we observed: the harmony between divinity and humanity uniquely achieved in the hypostatic union. Perhaps the most challenging and least explored element of von Balthasar's theological aesthetics is this conviction that it is meant to encourage and enable further theologizing rather than further interpretations of von Balthasar's theologizing, that his aesthetics not only points to sources to read, but wishes to be a tool the theologian uses. Von Balthasar opens an exciting yet intimidating door for us. It is not only that theology and the arts can be reconciled; it is much more that aesthetic categories, transformed by theology, heal theology and lead to new theology.

13

Henri de Lubac on the Development of Doctrine

Nicholas J. Healy, Jr.

"Dear Master and Friend", wrote Hans Urs von Balthasar on the occasion of Henri de Lubac's ninetieth birthday: "It remains only for me to say that I learned from you from my years of study in Lyon until today: something about the Holy Spirit. The Spirit, you taught us, can unite much more than we are accustomed to think."[1]

Father Joseph Fessio, who also spent some years studying in Lyon under de Lubac, learned the same lesson. He also learned from his teachers de Lubac, von Balthasar, and Joseph Ratzinger that the Holy Spirit's surprising capacity to unite flows from, and leads back to, the sacramental mystery of Christ's flesh and blood.[2] The writings of Henri de Lubac, made available in English by Ignatius Press, are an enduring testimony to the unity of the threefold gift of spirit, water, and blood (cf. 1 Jn 5:8) as the abiding source of the Church.

In his own letter of dedication on the occasion of de Lubac's nine- tieth birthday, Father Fessio noted that de Lubac "is above all else a man of the Church, *homo ecclesiasticus*.... He has received all from the

---

[1] Hans Urs von Balthasar, *Il Padre de Lubac* (Milan: Jaca Book, 1986), 1–2.

[2] Cf. Hans Urs von Balthasar, "Spirit and Institution", in *Explorations in Theology*, vol. 4, trans. Edward T. Oakes, S.J. (San Francisco: Ignatius Press, 1995), 237–38: "There can be nothing of the Spirit in the Church that does not also coincide with Christ's reality, christo- logically, that does not let itself be translated into the language of the Eucharist—the surren- der of Christ's own flesh and blood, the streaming outward from Christ's self up to the very point of his heart being pierced and his side flowing with water and blood."

Church. He has returned all to the Church."[3] For de Lubac, the task of thinking with the Church called for a style of theology devoted to exploring and defending the deep and permanent unity of the Church's faith across the centuries:

> Without claiming to open up new avenues of thought, I have sought rather, without any antiquarianism, to make known some of the great common areas of Catholic tradition. I wanted to make it loved, to show its ever-present fruitfulness. Such a task called more for a reading across the centuries than for a critical application to specific points; it excluded any overly preferential attachment to one school, system, or definite age; it demanded more attention to the deep and permanent unity of the Faith, to the mysterious relationship (which escapes so many specialized scholars) of all those who invoke the name of Christ.[4]

The vocation to make the Catholic tradition better known and loved in light of the "the deep and permanent unity of the Faith" also called for thinking about the idea of the development of doctrine.

In 1948, amidst the growing controversy provoked by the publication of *Surnaturel, Études historiques* (1946), de Lubac published an important essay titled "The Problem of the Development of Dogma".[5] He later described the article as a survey of "the current principal theories concerning the *development of doctrine*" that "took Newman's principles as [its] basis".[6] One of the principal targets of the essay, Charles Boyer, S.J., had written a sharply critical review of *Surnaturel*.[7] De Lubac's article on the development of doctrine

---

[3] Joseph Fessio, dedication, in Henri de Lubac, *Splendor of the Church*, trans. Michael Mason (San Francisco: Ignatius Press, 1986).

[4] Henri de Lubac, *At the Service of the Church*, trans. Anne Elizabeth Englund (San Francisco: Ignatius Press, 1993), 143–44.

[5] Henri de Lubac, "The Problem of the Development of Dogma", in *Theology in History*, trans. Anne Englund Nash (San Francisco: Ignatius Press, 1996), 274 ["Le problème du développement du dogme", *Recherches de science religieuse* 35 (1948): 130–60].

[6] De Lubac, *At the Service of the Church*, 64.

[7] Charles Boyer, "Nature pure et surnatural dans le Surnaturel du P. de Lubac", *Gregorianium* 28 (1947): 379–95. In a footnote at the end of his article on the development of doctrine (*Theology of History*, 278n69), de Lubac writes: "These pages had already been drafted when another article by Father Boyer (*Gregorianum*, 1947) reached us, an article devoted to our *Surnaturel*, in which several of the problems raised here were indirectly touched upon. We hope

provided an opportunity to reply indirectly to the accusation that he was fostering a "new theology" that tended toward Modernism. The Jesuit from Lyon turned the tables on Boyer, showing how the latter's rationalistic theory of doctrinal development represented a misreading of Thomas Aquinas and a departure from the Catholic tradition. At a deeper level, de Lubac's reflection on the development of doctrine refocused the Church's attention on the mystery of Jesus Christ as the source and fullness of divine revelation. Presupposing Newman's brilliant account of development, de Lubac brings to light the concrete and personal form of the *depostium fidei*, which is summed up in the Person of Christ, whom de Lubac describes as "the Whole of Dogma".[8]

My aim in what follows is to show how de Lubac's Christocentric understanding of the form and content of divine revelation sheds light on the idea of the development of doctrine. As noted above, de Lubac takes Newman's theory of development as the basis of his own reflections. Accordingly, I briefly present Newman's theory of development before turning to the contribution of de Lubac. The final part of my essay considers the nature and limits of doctrinal development in light of the current debate surrounding the interpretation of Pope Francis' Post-Synodal Apostolic Exhortation *Amoris laetitia*.

1. John Henry Newman on the Development of Christian Doctrine

In 1834, while still an Anglican, John Henry Newman wrote as follows:

> Considering the high gifts, and the strong claims of the Church of Rome ... on our admiration, reverence, love, and gratitude, how could we withstand her, as we do; how could we refrain from being melted into tenderness, and rushing into communion with her, but for the words of Truth, which bid us prefer Itself to the whole world? 'He that loveth father or mother more than Me, is not worthy of Me.'

---

to be able to return to this later." At the request of the Father General of the Jesuits, de Lubac refrained from a public response to criticism of *Surnaturel*. Some years later, in his memoirs [*At the Service of the Church*, 63], de Lubac published a personal letter to Father Joseph Huby that Boyer's 1947 article had elicited.

[8] De Lubac, "Development of Dogma", 274.

How could we learn to be severe, and execute judgment, but for the warning of Moses against even a divinely-gifted teacher who should preach new gods, and the anathema of St. Paul even against Angels and Apostles who should bring in a new doctrine.[9]

As Newman saw it at the time, then, the Catholic Church had compromised the integrity of the gospel by adding new doctrines such as Transubstantiation and the Immaculate Conception. Some ten years later, after an intensive study of the Trinitarian and Christological controversies in the early Church, Newman changed his position. He began to see the importance of an organic development of the Church's devotion, faith, and doctrine. While still an Anglican, he wrote his masterpiece *An Essay on the Development of Christian Doctrine*.[10] Before the book was printed, he entered the Catholic Church.

The central thesis of Newman's book is that "the Christianity of the second, fourth, seventh, twelfth, sixteenth, and intermediate centuries is in its substance the very religion which Christ and His Apostles taught in the first."[11] He acknowledges, of course, that there have been significant developments in the Church's understanding and teaching, even "apparent inconsistencies and alterations in its doctrine and its worship".[12] However, Newman shows that these apparent variations are best understood as an organic unfolding and growth of the original gift of revelation. As a good teacher, God is mindful of our historical nature and of our limited capacity to receive the fullness of revelation. "The highest and most wonderful truths," he writes, "though communicated to the world once and for all by inspired teachers, could not be comprehended all at once by the recipients, but, as being received and transmitted by minds not inspired and through media which were human, have required only

---

[9] John Henry Newman, *Records of the Church*, xxiv, p. 7, in *An Essay on the Development of Christian Doctrine* (Notre Dame, Ind.: University of Notre Dame Press, 1989), ix.

[10] For the publication history of Newman's *Essay*, including a comparison between the 1845 and revised 1878 editions, see Nicholas Lash, *Newman on Development: The Search for an Explanation in History* (Shepherdstown, W. Va.: Patmos Press, 1975). See also, Ian Ker, "Newman's Theory: Development of Continuing Revelation?" in *Newman and Gladstone: Centennial Essays* (Dublin: Veritas Publications, 1978).

[11] Newman, *Development of Christian Doctrine*, 5.

[12] Ibid., 9.

the longer time and deeper thought for their full elucidation."[13] The gift of divine revelation requires time to be received and to unfold. New historical circumstances and new controversies will cause the same truth to be expressed in different terms or an implicit idea to be explicated and unfolded.

Throughout his *Essay on Development*, Newman emphasizes the original fullness or completeness of God's revelation to the apostles. The development of doctrine cannot be understood as continuing revelation or as the addition of new content to the original deposit of faith. As Newman writes: "the Church [today] does not know more than the Apostles knew."[14] Having received the gift of revelation in its integral completeness, the apostles had "implicit" knowledge of the fullness of faith. Newman's point, then, is that it is this implicit knowledge that has unfolded and developed in the subsequent life of the Church: "The Apostles had the fullness of revealed knowledge, a fullness which they could as little realize to themselves, as the human mind, as such, can have all its thoughts present before it at once. They are elicited according to the occasion. A man of genius cannot go about with his genius in his hand: in an Apostle's mind great part of his knowledge is from the nature of the case latent or implicit."[15]

According to Newman, the development of doctrine implies and requires a Church that possesses an infallible charism of discrimination between true and false developments. "A revelation is not given", he writes, "if there be no authority to decide what it is that is given."[16] Note the connection between infallibility and discernment. Infallible teaching comes into play in the context of discerning which developments do and do not unfold the implications of the original deposit of faith. What are the criteria of this discernment? Reviewing the historical record, Newman identifies seven "notes" that characterize the Church's discernment of authentic doctrinal developments. The "notes" are preservation of type, continuity of

[13] Ibid., 29–30.

[14] John Henry Newman, "Letter to R. F. Hutton", October 20, 1871, in *Letters and Diaries*, vol. 25, ed. Charles Stephen Dessain and Thomas Gornall (Oxford: Clarendon Press, 1973), 418.

[15] John Henry Newman, unpublished manuscript (1868); cited in Ian Ker, foreword, *Development of Christian Doctrine*, xxiv.

[16] Newman, *Development of Christian Doctrine*, 40.

principle, power of assimilation, logical sequence, anticipation of its future, conservative action upon its past, and chronic vigor. As Matthew Levering observes, "these 'notes' have to do with the coherence of the whole body of doctrine, not with establishing an easily traceable path for any particular doctrine."[17] Taken together, the seven notes bear witness to the essential unity of the Church's faith that develops over time in response to new situations in fidelity to the original fullness of God's revelation in Christ.

As his emphasis on organic continuity suggests, Newman's understanding of the development of doctrine precludes any break or rupture with what the Church has taught in the past. In the words of Paul Misner, "Newman regarded every development, once received by the Church, as a 'definitive and irreversible acquisition which could not be abandoned.'"[18] For Newman, the deepest source of the substantial unity of the Church's faith and the development of her doctrine is the one mystery of Christ as presented in the Gospels: "What Catholics, what Church doctors, as well as Apostles, have ever lived on, is not any number of theological canons or decrees, but, we repeat, the Christ Himself, as He is represented in concrete existence in the Gospels."[19] This fundamental claim that dogma is Christ himself leads us into the heart of de Lubac's account of doctrinal development, to which we now turn.

2. Henri de Lubac on the Mystery of Christ as Source and Fullness of Christian Doctrine

De Lubac's 1948 essay "The Problem of the Development of Dogma" begins with a survey of then recent literature on the concept of doctrinal development by authors such as Ambroise Gardeil, Léonce de Grandmaison, and Marin Sola. The initial focus of the essay is the theory advanced by the Louvain Dominican Marcolinus Tuyaerts in

[17] Matthew Levering, *Engaging the Doctrine of Revelation: The Mediation of the Gospel through Church and Scriptures* (Grand Rapids, Mich.: Baker Academic, 2014), 183.

[18] Paul Misner, *Papacy and Development: Newman and the Primacy of the Pope* (Leiden: Brill Academic, 1976), 68.

[19] John Henry Newman, *Discussions and Arguments on Various Subjects* (London: Longmans, 1907), 388.

1919 and rehabilitated by the Roman Jesuit Charles Boyer in a 1940 essay "Qu'est-ce que la théologie? Réflexions sur une controverse".[20] According to this theory, the development of doctrine is essentially a matter of rational or logical deduction from explicit premises within the deposit of faith. Boyer writes:

> I do not see that one can deny the logical connection, which not only exists in itself but which can be traced by our means of investigation, between the progressive precision of dogma and the greatest indefiniteness of origins. The development of a truth can only follow a logic, and this path, at least at the point of arrival, must be perceptible.... The Church, assisted by the Holy Spirit, places her authority on the side of true logic. If it were otherwise, it would not be of development that we would have to speak, when a dogma is defined, but of radical innovation and creation. How could we say that revelation was closed at the death of the last of the apostles if a subsequent belief were not connected to it by a truly rational and logical bond.[21]

Conceived in response to the errors of Modernism, this "logicist" theory of development secures the homogeneity of Catholic doctrine. Nevertheless, de Lubac detected in it what he saw as a fatal disregard of the supernatural and mysterious character of divine revelation and the *sensus fidei* of the whole Church. De Lubac concurs with the judgment of Ambroise Gardeil:

> [Tuyaerts' account of development] is too narrow, too inclined to measure the divine word (which has been given us, after all, to lead us to heaven) according to the sole demands of a reasoning that is given us to instruct us about the earth, too generous with regard to logic and not enough with regard to the freedom of divine initiatives and the unknown ways and means of men that divine Providence employs.[22]

---

[20] Cf. Marcolinus Maria Tuyaerts, *L'Évolution du dogme: Étude théologique* (Louvain, 1919); Charles Boyer, "Qu'est-ce que la théologie? Réflexions sur une controverse", *Gregorianum* 21 (1940).

[21] Boyer, "Qu'est-ce que la théologie?", 264–65; cited in de Lubac, "Development of Dogma", 255.

[22] Ambroise Gardeil, "Bulletin d'introduction à la théologie", *Revue des sciences philosophiques et théologiques* 9 (1920): 658; cited in de Lubac, "Development of Dogma", 249.

De Lubac illustrated this critique with the case of the dogma of Mary's Immaculate Conception. It is simply not true, he argues, that this teaching was declared on the basis of a logical demonstration from explicit premises of faith. Or that in pronouncing this doctrine, "the Magisterium ... has, so to speak, only guaranteed by its authority the value of a logical operation."[23] In this context, de Lubac cites his teacher, Léonce de Grandmaison, who in his view offers a more historically accurate and theologically nuanced account of the grounds for the proclamation of this dogma in 1854:

> There were texts, theological reasons, expediencies in particular, and a profound instinct of the Christian people *for*, [and] texts and theological reasons apparently *against* the dogma; humanly, the solution was undetermined, or only probable, let us say, infinitely probable, in the affirmative sense. But the Church knows, better than the beloved disciple, how to recognize her Lord, she has the power to discern the voice of her Bridegroom there where the human ear perceives only a weak or indistinct echo.[24]

> This authority to go beyond in certain cases ... the natural scope of the historical and logical "discourse" that prepares the definition; this superior gift of intuition that makes the Church clearly aware of truths that no demonstrative argument has shown obviously present in the deposit of revelation; this kind of prophetic instinct that gradually inclines the ecclesiastical Magisterium in the direction of an analogy, of an agreement of faith, of a warm propensity of the Christian people, and then makes it find the necessary distinctions and triumphant responses—this is the work of the Holy Spirit ... the driving force of dogmatic development.[25]

Commenting on these texts of Grandmaison, de Lubac writes:

> Without doubt, theologians have a role to play, and a very important one. The Church is served by them; she is attentive to their opinions; but she is never content simply to record these opinions. While

---

[23] De Lubac, "Development of Dogma", 262.

[24] Léonce de Grandmaison, *Le Dogma chrétien: Sa nature, ses formules, son développement* (Paris: Beauchesne, 1928), 259–60; cited in de Lubac, "Development of Dogma", 262.

[25] De Lubac, "Development of Dogma", 251.

consulting theologians, she examines them, she judges them. She is
not bound by the reasons they bring to her. In whatever direction she
decides, she does not mean, moreover, to make a pronouncement on
the value of these reasons. *What she seeks to find is not if such a proposition
is or is not correctly deduced but if such an assertion is or is not contained in
her faith.*[26]

For Grandmaison and de Lubac, the driving force of doctrinal
development is not logical analysis or demonstration, although both
affirm the indispensable role of theological arguments. When, in
response to a crisis or a new historical situation, the Church articu-
lates her faith anew, she enters more deeply into the original fullness
of revelation.

After showing the limitations of the "logicist" theory of doctrinal
development, de Lubac considers a basic objection raised by Tuyaerts and Boyer: "How could one say that revelation was closed at
the death of the last apostles if a later believer were not connected
to it by a truly rational and logical bond?"[27] De Lubac notes that this
objection is based on a legitimate concern. Together with Newman,
de Lubac firmly upholds the completeness of divine revelation. The
development of doctrine is not a new revelation: "All truth", he
writes, "has been given us by Christ and in Christ, and revelation,
according to the traditional formula recalled by a proposition of the
decree *Lamentabili*, was closed at the death of the last apostles."[28]
How, then, is it possible to hold together the completeness of revelation and the genuine novelty entailed by doctrinal development?

In order to answer this question, it is first necessary to have an
adequate understanding of the nature of divine revelation. Too often,
de Lubac notes, accounts of the idea of the development of doctrine
presuppose an abstract and misleading idea of Christian revelation.
For example, Tuyaerts "declared that his study rested entirely 'on the
definition of dogma, which is nothing else but a truth revealed by
God and defined by the Church'; and, from the fact this dogma 'is a
logical reality adapted to our human intelligence', he concluded ...
that 'it could evolve only with the aid of a logical process, the only

[26] Ibid., 262; my italics.
[27] Ibid., 267.
[28] Ibid.

thing our mind can use.' "[29] The mistake here, de Lubac notes, is to neglect the original source and content of God's self-communication in Christ. It is here that de Lubac displays his kinship with Newman's account of doctrinal development.

Before its articulation into distinct propositions or articles or dogmas, de Lubac says, the gift of revelation is summed up and concretized in the figure of Jesus of Nazareth. The formulation and teaching of doctrine begins already with the apostles. "The apostles", he writes, "were already catechists, and our 'New Testament' contains several passages that are true formularies of faith." But it is important to note, de Lubac continues, "that if the apostles were already catechists, they were, more fundamentally, witnesses."[30] It is a mistake to think of the content of revelation as a "series of propositions detached from that unique mystery and thereby separated from each other, like 'major premises', wholly ready for our future reasoning".[31] At this point in the article, de Lubac introduces the seminal idea that will inform the Second Vatican Council's teaching on divine revelation.[32] He writes:

> In reality, concretely, what is first and that from which one must start without ever leaving—what is first and last—is the redemptive Action; it is the gift that God makes us of himself in his Son; it is the definitive accomplishment of that great design hidden in himself since the beginning and now revealed: "Our gratuitous vocation to eternal life through Christ and in Christ, or, in other words, Christ, the fullness of God's gift and the unique source for men of eternal salvation." And it is at the same time the revelation of all that. For it is all that which, in Jesus Christ, is revealed to us. It is all that which, at first undivided, forms the total Object, the incredibly rich Object of revelation. We can call it, to use an equivalent expression, "the Whole of Dogma". And this "Whole of Dogma" is, as its name indicates, not susceptible to any increase. It, too, like the Whole of the redemptive Action, is at once first and last. It is unsurpassable....

[29] Ibid., 272.

[30] Ibid., 273.

[31] Ibid.

[32] Cf. Second Vatican Council, Dogmatic Constitution on Divine Revelation *Dei Verbum* (November 18, 1965), 2: "Intima autem per hanc revelationem tam de Deo quam de hominis salute veritas nobis in Christo illucescit, qui mediator simul et plenitudo totius revelationis exsistit." (By this revelation then, the deepest truth about God and the salvation of man shines out for our sake in Christ, who is both the mediator and the fullness of all revelation.)

It is [an] abstraction to separate from this total revelation or this "Whole of Dogma" certain particular truths, enunciated in separate propositions, which will concern respectively the Trinity, the incarnate Word, baptism, grace, and so on. Legitimate and necessary abstractions, we repeat—for the mind can only preserve the total truth by actively exercising itself on it and according to its own laws—but on condition that we be aware of it and that we not fail to understand the concrete "Whole" whose contents we will never exhaust.[33]

Let me briefly note four consequences that follow from de Lubac's understanding of the mystery of Jesus Christ as the source and fullness of Christian doctrine.

(1) The first point concerns the completeness of Christian revelation. This revelation is primarily the very life of the Son of God made man. This gift is a perfect, complete, and inexhaustible self-disclosure of God and his purposes. As John of the Cross says, in giving us his incarnate Word, God "spoke everything to us at once in this sole Word—and He has no more to say."[34] Given this fact, it follows that the growth or development of doctrine cannot consist in the addition of new content, nor is it the case (as might be implied from the analogy to organic growth) of a seed growing into maturity. "The case of revealed Truth", writes de Lubac, "is unique."[35] There is a perfection and inexhaustible fullness at the beginning.

---

[33] De Lubac, "Development of Dogma", 274–75. As Aidan Nichols notes in *From Newman to Congar: The Idea of Doctrinal Development from the Victorians to the Second Vatican Council* (Edinburgh: T&T Clark, 1990), a key source for de Lubac's Christocentric understanding of Christian doctrine was an unpublished manuscript of Pierre Rousselot titled "Petite théorie du développement du dogme". De Lubac edited and published this text on the fiftieth anniversary of Rousselot's death in *Recherches de science religieuse* 53 (1965): 355–90. In words that anticipate de Lubac, Rousselot writes: "The whole dogmatics of the Church, even in its most abstract concepts and judgments, is nothing other than the explication of the concrete personal knowledge that the apostles had of the man Jesus and that they transmitted, as they were able, to their disciples. . . . The whole of tradition issues in a catechesis about Jesus Christ, because all the saving truths were in Jesus Christ. His person is not an object of doctrine. His person is the source, goal, reality, truth, of all doctrine."

See also, Henri de Lubac, "Commentaire du préambule et du Chapitre 1 de la Constitution dogmatique Dei Verbum", in *La Révélation divine* (Paris: Cerf, 1968), 159–302.

[34] Cf. St. John of the Cross, *The Ascent of Mount Carmel*, 2, 22, 3–5, in *The Collected Works of St. John of the Cross*, trans. Kieran Kavanaugh, O.C.D., and Otilio Rodriguez, O.C.D. (Washington D.C.: Institute of Carmelite Studies, 1979), 179–80.

[35] De Lubac, "Development of Dogma", 273.

(2) The Church's reception of Christian revelation must be in a certain sense complete and perfect from the beginning. Nevertheless, there is also a sense in which the Church expresses and enacts her perfect reception of the deposit of faith in time. Accordingly, her reception of the *depositum* involves a temporal unfolding that finds expression in the development of doctrine. It is important to stress that for both Newman and de Lubac, this unfolding includes a propositional aspect, since part of explicating the original gift is to express it in words, indeed, in binding propositions. Indeed, the propositional aspect also corresponds to the form of revelation itself, inasmuch as Christ is the Word made flesh: God's own eternal, personal self-utterance stepping forth to declare itself once and for all in space and time.

The mystery of God's descent into the flesh, then, includes the humility of human words and dogmatic formulae. The precise formulation of doctrine—*homoousios* instead of *homoiousios*—safeguards and mediates the gift of divine love. The organic coherence and continuity of such propositions over time will be an expression and criterion of fidelity to the task of receiving and transmitting the gift of faith. The purpose of development is to conserve and faithfully transmit what the Church has always believed. Authentic development can never contradict or depart from a doctrine that has been proclaimed by the Church.

(3) For de Lubac, then, the weakness of the "logicist" theory of development is not its valorization of propositions or of logic, but its tendency to reduce doctrinal development to logical deduction from a *depositum fidei* conceived primarily (or even simply) as an ensemble of contextless propositions. De Lubac's own alternative to logicism, however, is not a "modernist" disjunction between religious experience and dogmatic formulation. On the contrary, the burden of his position was to restore dogma to the original form of revelation itself—not, however, by reducing revelation to propositions, but by reinserting propositions within the properly Christian conception of truth. Before dogma is something the Church formulates, dogma is something Christ himself *is*; dogma is first and foremost Christ himself as incarnate Word and enfleshed truth.

In its most original meaning, then, dogma is Truth-made-flesh in the Person of Jesus himself. Jesus, in his turn, is the "standard of teaching" (Rom 6:17) into which Christians are baptized and that is expressed in the Church's confession of faith. This confession, in its turn, is inseparable from the visible life of the Church, which, it goes without saying, includes dogma in the narrower sense. Yet it is no accident that this dogmatic formulation is bound up with the lives of the martyrs (and other saints) who proclaim it in an inseparable unity of word and deed—to the point of becoming living canonical exhibitions of the truth of Catholic doctrine.

(4) A fourth point is that the key to reconciling the completeness of the deposit of faith and the newness involved in development of doctrine lies in the mystery of Christ's Eucharist. Consider the mystery of Transubstantiation, which makes present Jesus' own *traditio*, his handing himself over to death for the life of the world. To be sure, Transubstantiation presupposes the completeness of Jesus' "traditioning", which happened once and for all in the Paschal Mystery. But it does something else, too: it reenacts or re-actualizes the Lord's traditioning in its original performance ("On the night he was betrayed, he took bread …"). Put another way, Transubstantiation re-actualizes Jesus' traditioning, not only *in facto esse*, but also *in fieri*, thus reconciling completeness and newness in one simple form.

Now, the *depositum fidei* is most of all the fruit of Jesus' "traditioning". Consequently, what Transubstantiation does for the latter, it does for the former as well. It makes the deposit present in its completeness once and for all, to be sure, but it also discloses the deposit's event-like freshness for all times. This disclosure, moreover, is not simply a matter of exhortation. Rather, it is most essentially an act of the Holy Spirit, who leads the Eucharistic Bride into all (enfleshed) truth. In the Eucharist, the Spirit draws the Bride into Jesus' "traditioning" so as to involve her, not only in receiving its completed fruit—the deposit of faith in *facto esse*—but also in receptively co-generating the fruit, which is to say: in bringing forth the deposit *in fieri*. Put another way, the mystery of the Eucharist assures the synthesis of completeness and newness in the Church's reception of the deposit of faith, thus providing the source, measure, and end of her development of doctrine, which, it bears stressing, is marked by the same form of enfleshed truth characterizing the *depositum* as the fruit of Jesus' primordial "traditioning" in flesh and blood.

3. The Idea of Doctrinal Development and the Interpretation of Amoris Laetitia

In order to appreciate better the common teaching of Newman and de Lubac, it is helpful to consider a concrete case of doctrinal development. During the 2014 and 2015 synods on the family, the question of pastoral care for civilly divorced and remarried Catholics emerged as an important, though contentious, theological and pastoral question. In terms of the development of doctrine, the relevant issue concerned the significance and further unfolding of John Paul II's teaching in *Familiaris consortio*—a teaching that was confirmed in the *Catechism of the Catholic Church* and further developed in Benedict XVI's *Sacramentum caritatis*. In response to the tragic situation of civil divorce and remarriage, John Paul II called for a "careful discernment of situations" and an effort on the part of the whole community of the faithful "to make sure that [civilly remarried Catholics] do not consider themselves as separated from the Church, for as baptized persons they can, and indeed must, share in her life.... Let the Church pray for them, encourage them and show herself a merciful mother."[36] At the same time, John Paul II recalled and reaffirmed the practice of the Church, "which is based upon Sacred Scripture, of not admitting to Eucharistic Communion divorced persons who have remarried."[37]

The question raised during the two synods on the family is whether a development in the Church's teaching and pastoral care might warrant a change in this sacramental discipline. Since the publication of Pope Francis' Post-Synodal Apostolic Exhortation *Amoris laetitia*, the question has become more acute: Has *Amoris laetitia* "changed" or developed the teaching set forth in *Familiaris consortio*? Theologians such as Christoph Cardinal Schönborn and Rocco Buttiglione argue that there has indeed been a change in sacramental discipline, and they argue that this change represents an organic development of John Paul II's teaching. Other theologians such as Gerhard Cardinal Müller appeal to the unity of the Church's faith and the nature

[36] John Paul II, Apostolic Exhortation *Familiaris consortio* on the Role of the Christian Family in the Modern World (November 22, 1981), no. 84.
[37] Ibid.

of authentic doctrinal development to argue that *Amoris laetitia* has not changed the sacramental discipline of the Church. I will briefly present these respective arguments before considering the underlying question of doctrinal development.

During the official press conference for the presentation of *Amoris laetitia* on April 8, 2016, Cardinal Schönborn was asked about the relationship between *Amoris laetitia* and section 84 of *Familiaris consortio*. He answered as follows: "Certainly there is a development, just as Pope John Paul developed doctrine.... John Henry Newman explained to us how the organic development of doctrine works. Pope Francis is developing things in this way.... There is continuity in teaching here, but there is also something really new. There's a real development, not a rupture." In an interview with Antonio Spadaro, S.J., published in *La Civiltà Cattolica* in July of 2016, Schönborn returned to the idea of *Amoris laetitia* as a development of doctrine:

> "The Joy of Love" is an act of the magisterium that makes the teaching of the Church present and relevant today. Just as we read the Council of Nicaea in the light of the Council of Constantinople, and Vatican I in the light of Vatican II, so now we must read the previous statements of the magisterium about the family in the light of the contribution made by "The Joy of Love." We are led in a living manner to draw a distinction between the continuity of the doctrinal principles and the discontinuity of perspectives or of historically conditioned expressions. This is the function that belongs to the living magisterium: to interpret authentically the word of God, whether written or handed down.[38]

Later in the interview, Schönborn explains in more detail how *Amoris laetitia* is an organic unfolding or development of *Familiaris consortio*:

> St. John Paul II did indeed distinguish a variety of situations. He saw a difference between those who had tried sincerely to salvage their first marriage and were abandoned unjustly and those who had destroyed a canonically valid marriage through their grave fault. He then spoke

---

[38] An English translation of the interview with Antonio Spadaro, S.J., "Cardinal Schönborn on 'The Joy of Love': The Full Conversion", was published in *America Magazine* [https://www.americamagazine.org/issue/richness-love].

of those who have entered a second marital union for the sake of bringing up their children and who sometimes are subjectively certain in their consciences that the first marriage, now irreparably destroyed, was never valid. Each one of these cases thus constitutes the object of a differentiated moral evaluation.

There are very many different starting points in an ever-deeper sharing in the life of the church, to which everyone is called. St. John Paul II already presupposes implicitly that one cannot simply say that every situation of a divorced and remarried person is the equivalent of a life in mortal sin, separated from the communion of love between Christ and the church. Accordingly, he was opening the door to a broader understanding by means of the discernment of the various situations that are not objectively identical.[39]

In an important lecture to seminarians in Oviedo, Spain, on May 4, 2016, "Was dürfen wir von der Familie erwarten?", Gerhard Cardinal Müller offered a different interpretation of the relationship between *Amoris laetitia* and *Familiaris consortio*.[40] For Müller, the organic development of the Church's doctrine precludes an interpretation of *Amoris laetitia* that authorizes a change in the Church's deeply rooted sacramental discipline. Müller's text is worth citing at length:

The key for the path of accompaniment is the harmony between the celebration of the sacraments and Christian life. Herein lie the reasons for the discipline with regard to the Eucharist, as it has always been preserved by the Church. Thanks to it, the Church can be a community that accompanies the sinner and welcomes him, without thereby approving the sin. Thus, she offers the foundation for a possible path of discernment and of integration. John Paul II has confirmed this discipline in *Familiaris consortio* 84 and *Reconciliatio et poenitentia* 34. The Congregation for the Doctrine of the Faith has also confirmed it in its document of 1994; Benedict XVI has deepened it in *Sacramentum caritatis* 29. We are dealing here with the consolidated teaching of the Magisterium, which is based upon Holy Scripture as well as upon

---

[39] Ibid.

[40] The full German text of Cardinal Müller's address "Was dürfen wir von der Familie erwarten?" was published in *Die Tagespost* on May 6, 2016. The text is also available online at http://www.collationes.org/component/k2/item/2310-was-duerfen-wir-von-der-familie -erwarten.

the Church's teaching: namely, the harmony of the sacraments necessary for the salvation of souls, the heart of the "culture of the bond"
as it is lived by the Church. There have been different claims that
Amoris laetitia has rescinded this discipline, because it allows, at least
in certain cases, the reception of the Eucharist by remarried divorcees
without requiring that they change their way of life in accord with
Familiaris consortio 84 (namely, by giving up their new bond or by living as brothers and sisters). The following has to be said in this regard:
If *Amoris laetitia* had intended to rescind such a deeply rooted and such
a weighty discipline, it would have expressed itself in a clear manner
and it would have given the reasons for it. However, such a statement
with such a meaning is not to be found in it. Nowhere does the pope
put into question the arguments of his predecessors. They are not
based upon the subjective guilt of these our brothers and sisters, but,
rather, upon the visible, objective way of life that is in opposition to
the words of Christ.[41]

Müller goes on to consider the counterargument based on a reading
of footnote 351 in section 305 of *Amoris laetitia*:

> Without entering into this question in a deeper way, it is sufficient to
> point out that this footnote refers in a general way to objective situa-
> tions of sin, and not to the specific cases of the civilly remarried divor-
> cees. Because this latter situation has its own distinctive characteristics
> that differentiate it from other situations.... Footnote 351 does not
> touch upon the earlier discipline. The norms of FC 84 and SC 29 and
> their application in all cases continue to remain valid. The principle
> is that no one can really want to receive a sacrament—the Eucharist—
> without at the same time having the will to live according to all the
> other sacraments, among them the Sacrament of Marriage. Whoever
> lives in a way that contradicts the marital bond opposes the visible sign
> of the Sacrament of Marriage. With regard to his bodily existence, he
> turns himself into a "counter-sign" of the indissolubility, even if he is
> not subjectively guilty. Exactly because his carnal life is in opposition to
> the sign, he cannot be part of the higher Eucharistic sign—in which the
> incarnate Love of Christ is manifest—by thus receiving Holy Commu-
> nion. If the Church were to admit such a person to Holy Communion,
> she would be then committing that act which Thomas Aquinas calls

[41] Ibid.

"a falseness in the sacred sacramental signs". This is not an exaggerated conclusion drawn from the teaching, but, rather, the foundation itself of the sacramental constitution of the Church, which we have compared to the architecture of Noah's Ark. The Church cannot change this architecture because it stems from Jesus himself and because the Church was created in it and is supported by it in order to swim upon the waters of the deluge. To change the discipline in this specific point and to admit a contradiction between the Eucharist and the Sacrament of Marriage would necessarily mean to change the Profession of Faith of the Church. The blood of the martyrs has been shed for faith in the indissolubility of marriage—not as a distant ideal, but as a concrete way of conduct.[42]

Müller's argument, in short, is that the unity of the Church's faith and the authentic development of doctrine require that we interpret *Amoris laetitia* in continuity with *Familiaris consortio* in the sense that what the Church has received from Christ regarding the indissolubility of marriage, and the sacramental discipline that is based on this teaching, must be fully preserved.

Let me return to Schönborn's double claim that (1) *Amoris laetitia* has changed the sacramental discipline of the Church; and (2) this change is an authentic development of John Paul II's teaching in *Familiaris consortio*. There are two issues or questions that call for further elaboration and qualification. First, according to Schönborn, "Just as we read the Council of Nicaea in the light of the Council of Constantinople, and Vatican I in the light of Vatican II, so now we must read the previous statements of the magisterium about the family in the light of the contribution made by *Amoris laetitia*." This statement is one-sided. While it is true that we read previous statements of the Magisterium in light of more recent pronouncements, the converse is also true. It is necessary to interpret current magisterial teaching in light of the living tradition of the Church. Given the organic nature of development, the prior tradition has a certain priority. The aim of development is to preserve and hand on the gift of faith. This principle can be demonstrated both theologically and historically. For example, the Fathers at Constantinople demonstrated a profound reverence for, and deference to, the Council of Nicaea's

[42] Ibid.

confession of faith. Unless further qualified, Schönborn's account of reading prior teaching in light of more recent statements is one-sided and misleading.

Secondly, Schönborn claims that *Amoris laetitia* extends and unfolds the principle set forth by John Paul II that pastors "are obliged to exercise careful discernment of situations. There is in fact a difference between those who have sincerely tried to save their first marriage and have been unjustly abandoned, and those who through their own grave fault have destroyed a canonically valid marriage." Developing this idea of a case by case discernment and highlighting the factors that mitigate subjective culpability, *Amoris laetitia*—Schönborn argues— opens a door for the discernment that some remarried Catholics can approach the Eucharist without the commitment to live as brother and sister. This line of argument seems to overlook or obfuscate an essential point: John Paul II's exhortation to pastors to exercise discernment regarding different marital situations does not allow for exceptions in terms of receiving the sacrament of the Eucharist. The simple reason, as John Paul II explains, is that the Church's discipline is based on the objective situation of living *more coniugale* with one who is not one's spouse. Varying degrees of subjective culpability do not change the objective countersign, or what Cardinal Müller, citing Aquinas, describes as "a falseness in the sacred sacramental signs".

In this sense, Müller's interpretation of *Amoris laetitia* is more in keeping with the Church's understanding of doctrinal development as understood by Newman and de Lubac. Perhaps the most important difference between these two representative interpretations of *Amoris laetitia* is that whereas Schönborn seems to overlook the pastoral significance of the perduring bond of marriage, Müller conceives the indissoluble bond as a sure guide and light for the faithful because it is the fruit and sign of Christ's undying faithfulness to the Church.

In conclusion, it is important to stress once again that Müller's interpretation of *Amoris laetitia* expresses neither a legalistic understanding of morality nor a denigration of the goodness of sex. As Müller himself makes clear, if civilly divorced and remarried persons not living as brother and sister cannot receive the Eucharist, it is precisely because their first marriage remains intact—as a covenant whose indissolubility objectively signifies, and communicates, the indissoluble bond uniting Christ and his Church. Clearly, such persons cannot receive the Eucharist without violating the truth, but the truth in question is primarily that truth which is synonymous (in English at least) with fidelity: the lifelong fidelity of man and woman, but also the everlasting fidelity of Christ and the Church. This kind of truth, that is, truth as fidelity, is not opposed to, or even in tension with, Christ's liberating love. On the contrary, it is a central expression of that love—an expression, moreover, that reaches all the way down into the sphere of sexual intimacy between husband and wife. What Cardinal Müller is trying to protect, then, is not some abstract "norm" unable to do justice to the complexity of concrete situations, but the capacity of the sexual embrace to image forth, and share in, Christ's loving self-gift, which is the substance both of the Church's Eucharist and of her faith. The point is simply that, in order to be faithful to the spousal covenant that it is innately called to symbolize, sex has to be an expressive enactment of an indissoluble marriage— which, absent a declaration of nullity, still binds civilly divorced and remarried people with the spouses to whom they first said "Yes" at the altar. Looked at from this point of view, John Paul II's and Benedict XVI's teaching about the conditions for the reception of Communion is not some external yoke foisted on struggling couples. No, it is a faithful articulation of that indissoluble fidelity which turns the existential realization of their mutual love into an act of ecclesial faith, indeed, into a developmental unfolding of faith's contents in the concreteness of their very flesh and blood.

It is significant that the current debate about Communion for the civilly divorced and remarried should raise questions about both doctrinal development and the relationship between the Eucharist and the indissolubility of marriage. For, as we saw at the end of the previous section, these realities are intimately interconnected. It is in the Eucharist that the Bride receives a share in the Lord's "traditioning", whose unity of completeness and newness, in turn, enables development of doctrine while distinguishing it from willful innovation. If the common teaching of Newman and de Lubac traced here is a promising resource in our post-*Amoris laetitia* context, this is because it reminds us of what is most deeply at stake in the current discussion: the Church's fidelity to the form of truth embodied by her divine Spouse, the form of truth exhibited in the "traditioning" of his own flesh and blood in the Holy Spirit.

ABOUT THE CONTRIBUTORS

Anne M. Carpenter is Assistant Professor of Catholic Theology at Saint Mary's College of California.

Peter Casarella is Associate Professor of Theology at the University of Notre Dame.

Michael Dauphinais is Professor of Theology at Ave Maria University.

Stephen M. Fields, S.J., is Professor of Theology at Georgetown University.

Joseph S. Flipper is Associate Professor of Theology and Assistant Director of the Ethics and Social Justice Center at Bellarmine University.

Nicholas J. Healy, Jr., is Associate Professor of Philosophy and Culture at the Pontifical John Paul II Institute for Studies on Marriage and Family at the Catholic University of America.

David Vincent Meconi, S.J., is Associate Professor of Patristics and Director of the Catholic Studies Centre at Saint Louis University.

Matthew Levering holds the James N. and Mary D. Perry, Jr., Chair of Theology at Mundelein Seminary.

Francesca Aran Murphy is Professor of Theology at the University of Notre Dame.

Matthew J. Ramage is Associate Professor of Theology at Benedictine College.

Aaron Riches is Associate Professor of Theology at Benedictine College.

D. C. Schindler is Associate Professor of Metaphysics and Anthropology at the Pontifical John Paul II Institute for Studies on Marriage and Family at the Catholic University of America.

David L. Schindler is the Edouard Cardinal Gagnon Professor of Fundamental Theology at the Pontifical John Paul II Institute for Studies on Marriage and Family at the Catholic University of America.

SUBJECT INDEX

Ad gentes (VII decree), 19
ad orientem, 82, 85, 90–91, 99
agape, 248
Amoris laetitia (Francis)
  de Lubac and, 15, 364–65
  Familiaris consortio (John Paul II) and, 359–64
  Newman and, 15, 348, 364–65
  Thomas Aquinas and, 362–63
analogia entis (analogy of being), 64n28, 164–65, 167, 197
apologetics, 115–16, 115n7, 116n9, 138
Apostles' Creed, 112, 128, 130, 137–38

beauty
  as an apologetic, 273n28
  in art, prayer, and medieval cathedrals, 269–73
  Benedict XVI on, 265–67, 290
  the Cross and, 106–10
  Plato on, 172–73
  redemptive beauty, 108–9
  redemptive beauty of Christ, 108–9
  transcendental meaning of, 107
  via pulchritudinis, 265, 269
  von Balthasar on, 316
Beauty (Carnes), 327
A Brief Catechesis on Nature and Grace (de Lubac), 212n26
Byzantine Rite, 85

canons (anaphoras), 85, 87, 89
Cappadocians, 193–97, 199–200
catechetical instruction of Benedict XVI
  on beauty in art, prayer, and medieval cathedrals, 269–73

on faith as a gift, 274–78
  General Audiences on saints, 265–67
  journeys of faith, 285–89
  method and scope of, 267–69
Catechism of the Catholic Church (CCC), 28, 287–88, 359
Catholic World Report (periodical), 18–19
Catholicisme (de Lubac), 154
The Christian State of Life (von Balthasar), 242–43
Christological meaning of the liturgy
  de Lubac on, 356n33
  divine unity, 104
  Pius XII on, 101–2
  Rahner and Ratzinger on, 105n169
  Ratzinger on, 99–100, 105, 105n169
Christus totus concept, 28
Church (Schillebeeckx), 10
The Church of God (Bouyer), 45–49
City of God (Augustine of Hippo), 336
College of Cardinals, 111
Communio (periodical), 11, 18–22, 44, 50, 111n192
communio sanctorum, 94–99
conceptio christiana, 61, 66, 71, 78, 102–3
Concilium (periodical), 68, 72, 111n192
Congregation for the Doctrine of the Faith, 112, 138
De la Connaissance de Dieu (de Lubac), 38
"Consumer Materialism and Christian Hope" (Ratzinger), 118n20
Corpus Mysticum (de Lubac), 38
Cosmic Liturgy (Daley), 144
Cratylus (Plato), 174
creatio ex nihilo, 117n14

369

INDEX OF NAMES